D1617412

JUST RIGHT

A Life in Pursuit of Liberty

LEE EDWARDS

ISI
BOOKS

Wilmington, DE

Copyright © 2017 by Lee Edwards

All rights reserved. No part of this publication may be reproduced or transmitted in any form or by any means, electronic or mechanical, including photocopy, or any information storage and retrieval system now known or to be invented, without permission in writing from the publisher, except by a reviewer who wishes to quote brief passages in connection with a review written for inclusion in a magazine, newspaper, broadcast, or digital publication.

Cataloging-in-Publication Data is on file with the Library of Congress.
ISBN: 978-1-61017-145-8

Chapter 36 first appeared, in slightly different form, as "Can Conservatism Rise Again?" in the Winter 2017 issue of *National Affairs*.

Published in the United States by

ISI Books
Intercollegiate Studies Institute
3901 Centerville Road
Wilmington, Delaware 19807-1938
www.isibooks.org

Manufactured in the United States of America

To the Heritage interns whom I have mentored, to the young people whom I have taught at the Catholic University of America, and to the youth organizations like the Intercollegiate Studies Institute, Young America's Foundation, the Leadership Institute, and the Fund for American Studies that seek to better the education of the rising generation

The future is theirs

Contents

Prologue

DEDICATION

I t was already hot and the air was close inside the tent that June morning as we waited for the forty-third president of the United States, who would, on behalf of the American people, dedicate the world's first memorial to the more than 100 million victims of communism.

I said a silent prayer of thanksgiving for my departed comrade-in-arms Lev Dobriansky; for the 103rd Congress, which unanimously authorized our memorial; for John Parsons of the National Park Service, who urged us to keep our design simple; for the academic troika of Robert Conquest, Richard Pipes, and Zbigniew Brzezinski, who endorsed us early on; for the unflappable architect Mary Kay Lanzillotta, who guided us through the Washington memorial maze; for the gifted artist Thomas Marsh, who waived his six-figure fee to sculpt the bronze replica of the Goddess of Democracy; for the lovers of liberty, especially ethnic Americans, who sent us their donations, large and small, early and late; and for George W. Bush, who agreed to be our honorary chairman, a rare act for a sitting president.

"POTUS has left the White House and will be here in ten minutes," a Secret Service agent said.

The long, black steel-plated limousine pulled in smoothly under the tent, and a smiling president bounded out of the back seat and strode toward us. He warmly embraced Congressman Tom Lantos, a liberal Democrat and the only Holocaust survivor to serve in the House. He glanced at Congressman Dana Rohrabacher, one of the original sponsors of the 1993 legislation authorizing the memorial, and remarked, "Dana, you're losing your hair." Then the president turned to me and shook my hand. "Congratulations, Lee." He looked at his watch. "Okay, let's go."

I kept my introduction short:

> Twenty years ago, President Reagan stood before the Brandenburg Gate in Berlin and said, "Mr. Gorbachev, tear down this wall!"
>
> Cynics scoffed at President Reagan's words, but two years later, the Berlin Wall came tumbling down, and soon after that, the "Evil Empire" was no more.
>
> A little over two years ago, standing on the steps of the U.S. Capitol, President Bush declared, "The best hope for peace in our world is the expansion of freedom in all the world."
>
> Once again, the naysayers scoffed, but the forces of freedom and democracy are in motion around the world, demonstrating that, in the president's words, "Freedom is the permanent hope of mankind."

As President Bush walked to the podium, I looked out at the thousand people, many in their native dress, who had suffered under communism, had fought against communism, and had come to Capitol Hill to honor the victims of communism. How remarkable, and how disturbing, I thought, that such a gathering for such an occasion had never before occurred in Washington.

"Good intro," the president whispered to me before opening his binder and beginning to speak. He noted that we could have chosen for our memorial an image of repression—"a replica of the wall that once divided Berlin, or the frozen barracks of the Gulag, or a killing field littered with skulls." Instead, we chose "an image of hope," a statue of a woman holding a lamp of liberty. "She reminds us of the victims of communism, and also of the power that overcame communism."

President Bush spoke of the millions who perished under communism: "innocent Ukrainians starved to death in Stalin's Great Famine; or Russians killed in Stalin's purges; Lithuanians and Latvians and Estonians loaded onto cattle cars and deported to Arctic death camps of Soviet communism; Chinese killed in the Great Leap Forward and the Cultural Revolution; Cambodians slain in Pol Pot's killing fields; East Germans shot attempting to scale the Berlin Wall in order to make it to freedom; Poles massacred in the Katyn Forest; and Ethiopians slaughtered in the 'Red Terror'; Miskito Indians murdered by Nicaragua's Sandinista dictatorship; and Cuban *balseros* who drowned escaping tyranny."

"We'll never know the names of all who perished," the president said, but "at this sacred place communism's unknown victims will be consecrated to history and remembered forever."

As President Bush stepped down from the platform and walked the line, shaking the hands of those who had once been captive and were now free, I reflected that the ceremony, condemned by the Chinese Communist Foreign Ministry and the Russian Communist Party, was a monumental victory in the war against communism I had joined as a graduate student in Paris almost fifty years earlier.

I offer a disclaimer: I didn't suffer under communism. I never waited for a knock on the door in the middle of the night by the secret police. I was never sent to a slave labor camp in Siberia as an "enemy of the people." I was born and raised in America and not a captive nation.

But I was so outraged by communist tyranny that as a young man in the 1950s I resolved that for the rest of my life I would do whatever I could to resist communism and fight for freedom. Sometimes I played a key role in the struggle for freedom. I was a founder of Young Americans for Freedom, which provided the ground troops for the Barry Goldwater and Ronald Reagan presidential campaigns. I was the director of information for the Goldwater for President Committee, which secured the 1964 presidential nomination for Senator Goldwater and changed the course of conservative (and American) history. I wrote the first political biography of Reagan. I was the founding editor of *Conservative Digest*, which had at one time the greatest circulation of any conservative journal. I organized the largest Washington rally for the Vietnam War and our troops. I was denounced as a "son of a Birch" by a nationally syndicated columnist and described by the *New York Times* as "The 'Voice' of the Silent Majority."

After decades as an activist, I decided to apply my passion for freedom in new ways: in my early fifties I went to graduate school to earn my PhD and became a writer, teacher, and lecturer on modern American conservatism. Over the next few decades, I wrote more than twenty books, which resulted in my being described as a "leading historian" of the conservative movement. So much for there being no second acts in American lives.

Sharing the platform with the president of the United States that morning in June 2007 was the pinnacle of my life, a life committed to freedom and opposed to every form of tyranny over the mind of man (to

borrow from Thomas Jefferson). The conservative activist and fundraising guru Richard Viguerie likes to remind me that, with the passing
of Phyllis Schlafly, I have been active in the conservative movement at
the national level longer than anyone else. Over the past six decades, I
have been present at nearly every major event of the modern conservative movement, and have known and worked with giants like Ronald
Reagan, Barry Goldwater, William F. Buckley Jr., Russell Kirk, and
Milton Friedman.

Mine has been a life in pursuit of liberty. And what a life it has been.

*"The pinnacle of my life": President George W. Bush acknowledging the author
at the dedication of the Victims of Communism Memorial, June 2007*

1

CRADLE CONSERVATIVE

I was born under the sign of FDR, on December 1, 1932, on the South Side of Chicago. I was the only child of Willard Ambrose Edwards, an award-winning, hard-drinking reporter for the *Chicago Tribune*, and Leila Mae Sullivan, the older daughter of the only Republican in the Irish American enclave of Bridgeport, within walking distance of Comiskey Park and the White Sox.

My father was a favorite of Colonel Robert R. McCormick, the imperious, mustached publisher and owner of the *Tribune*. In 1925, Dad's first year at the *Trib*, the Colonel once visited the newsroom, leaving a nervous hush in his wake, and brushed by Dad seemingly without a glance. An assistant to the managing editor later imparted good news: "Your career is made! The Colonel asked who you were and remarked, 'Nice-looking boy.'"

But it was my father's way with words, not his Irish good looks, that secured his place in the paper. Confirmation of his status came in January 1935, when he was assigned to cover the most sensational story of the year and perhaps the decade—the Lindbergh baby murder trial. After the trial ended, my father was assigned to the *Tribune*'s Washington bureau. I was almost three when we rented a yellow stucco house in Silver Spring, Maryland, a sleepy suburb of seven thousand just across the D.C. line.

Beginning in the mid-'30s, Dad covered presidents from Franklin D. Roosevelt to Richard Nixon; presidential campaigns including Truman

My father, Chicago Tribune *reporter Willard Edwards (left), on the
campaign trail with "Mr. Republican," Senator Robert A. Taft of Ohio*

versus Dewey and the media-driven Kennedy-Nixon contest of 1960;
every national convention, Democratic as well as Republican; and major
congressional hearings, often scooping the Washington press corps,
particularly in the early 1950s, when he was a confidant of Senator Joe
McCarthy, a frequent guest in our home.

I did not attend public school until the second grade, a reflection of
my mother's skepticism about the progressive education of Montgomery
County. I was bright but easily bored, with a temper I rarely bothered to
control. At Montgomery Hills Junior High School, to which I bicycled
every day, I learned some Latin and how to write an essay, was knocked
out in my first football game and never played again, pitched softball
tolerably well, and had a crush on our pretty young English teacher, who
encouraged my writing and approved my appointment, at fourteen, as
editor of the *MoHiJuHi News,* my first editorial post.

There were books in every room of our house—in the living room, in
the dining room, in the bedrooms, in the bathrooms, everywhere. Dad
preferred murder mysteries by Erle Stanley Garner and Rex Stout. Mom
liked historical novels and could recite the kings and queens of England

as easily as Dad could the chairmen of key congressional committees. They let me read whatever I wanted, and I soldiered through Kenneth Roberts's tales of the American Revolution, cheering on the *Rabble in Arms*. I remember evenings when we would all be in the living room, each of us in a chair reading a book.

Mom practiced as well as talked politics. Appointed to the Montgomery County School Board—she had been a substitute English teacher during World War II—she ran for a full term on a "Back to Basics" platform. She would have won, I am sure, but the muckraker columnist Drew Pearson, who lived in the county, wrote a half dozen columns for a local newspaper about Leila Edwards, the "radical right" candidate and wife of Willard Edwards, reporter for the "ultra-conservative" *Chicago Tribune* and adviser to the "infamous" Senator Joseph McCarthy. It was the fall of 1954, and liberals had so traumatized the public about McCarthyism that Mom narrowly lost, the ironic victim of guilt by association, which liberals accused McCarthy of practicing. She never again sought public office.

Her bitter experience influenced my decision never to be a political candidate—my skin was not thick enough for electoral politics. My resolution was later hardened by my wife, Anne, who said, "I will divorce you if you run for office." I told myself that Anne, a good Catholic, was bluffing, but I never tested her.

I enrolled at the all-male Bullis Prep School at the insistence of my mother, who would not let me go to Montgomery Blair High School, well known for its easy academics. I was poorly prepared for Bullis's academic rigor—my first report card was all Cs and Ds. But the school taught me to think critically. I studied hard and by the end of the year was second in my class. I went on to edit the school newspaper, organize and lead Bullis's first golf team, and score in the 98th percentile on the college entrance exams. In my senior year I won an award for all-around excellence. My years at Bullis strengthened my already evident self-confidence.

In my senior year, I applied to Amherst College in Massachusetts for the best of reasons: Bill Bonneville, my closest Bullis friend, was going there. I did not apply to any other school; in those days you did not send applications to a dozen colleges. To my shock, Amherst put me on its waiting list because, I surmised, of a poor grade in trigonometry—the rest of my grades were well above average. I decided I wanted nothing to do with the Ivy League and headed south to Duke University in North Carolina for the best of reasons: Duke had a winning golf team, and two of my golfing buddies had been accepted there. I learned later that Duke was a good university with exceptional teachers and a core curriculum.

I had won a four-year scholarship from the *Chicago Tribune* because of my scores on a college entrance exam administered by the University of Chicago. The scholarship provided $750 annually, which now sounds ridiculously low but covered most of tuition, room, and board at Duke in 1950–51. The total estimated cost, including books and laundry, was a low of $977 and a high of $1,185. That "high" would not cover the cost of one week at Duke today.

I had done so well on the ACE exam, scoring in the 98th percentile, that the University of Chicago said it would be happy to have me as one of its students. But it had no golf team, and my folks had long talked about the frigid winds coming off Lake Michigan and the snow almost as high as your waist. I declined the invitation. Among the professors under whom I might have studied were Richard Weaver, Milton Friedman, and F. A. Hayek. My high scores were not a true reflection of my intelligence—my IQ was under 130—but the product of the monthly ACE drills at Bullis.

JOURNALISM AND ANTICOMMUNISM

At Duke I joined the campus paper, the *Duke Chronicle*. I spent every Thursday evening, and then Tuesday evening when the paper became a biweekly, working my way up the editorial ladder. In my junior year I was one of two candidates for editor but lost to my prime rival, Bill Duke, no relation to the founder of the university. Bill was a better editor but I was the better writer.

In my senior year I became the founding editor of the *Duke Peer*, a new feature magazine. We attracted little campus attention until we profiled Senator Joe McCarthy with the title "Nice Guy or Demagogue?" It was early 1954, and according to liberals America was in the middle of a Reign of Terror engineered by Senator McCarthy.

I assigned the article to our associate editor, Connie Mueller, asking only that she write what she learned from her own research and draw her own conclusions. Without any coaching from me, Connie concluded that McCarthy was not a reckless demagogue but rather a patriot who would brook no compromise in "his main purpose of fighting 'the Red Menace.'" Studying the record and especially the press coverage of the senator, Connie wrote, "Clearly, Joseph Raymond McCarthy...has been the subject of vigorous character distortion by an opinionated press."

McCarthy had been front-page news since February 1950, when he made his famous Wheeling, West Virginia, speech ("I have here in my hand…"). Since then, my father had had almost unrestricted access to the senator and his top aides and investigators. It was the biggest running story of his career.

My first impression of Joe—he encouraged you to call him by his first name—was that of a shoulder-squeezing, joke-telling politician who drank but not any more than the average Irishman. He was serious about one thing—communism. When challenged about something he said about the communist menace, he would fix you with his dark Gaelic eyes and say in his deep rumbling voice, "You're either with me or against me. You're either with me or the communists. Which is it?" He was spontaneous, incapable of leading a conspiracy, because that would have required detailed planning and constant scrutiny.

His unbridled passion to expose the communists in our government inspired people by the millions. My mother, who was a volunteer in his office, wrote me that "never have I seen such devotion. The stenographers, the secretaries, the investigators, all of them working 16 hours a day." But don't expect any thank-you or recognition of your sacrifice from Joe, she said. "He eats, sleeps, and lives his crusade. His whole conversation is what to do next to further 'cleaning out the subversives.'"

Joe could be mischievous. One day, he and Dad were scheduled to have lunch in the Senate dining room. As they stood in the reception room of his office, Joe said, "Wait a minute," and walked into an adjacent room in which a half dozen volunteers were seated around a long worktable, opening and sorting the hundreds of letters he received every day. Many contained rosaries, prayer cards, coins and bills, even a Social Security check. Joe picked out a $20 bill and said, smiling, "That ought to cover our lunch."

In the spring of 1954, along with millions of Americans, I watched the televised Army-McCarthy hearings and despaired as Joe tried to turn back the phalanx of the Establishment. Public support plummeted. In December he was condemned by the U.S. Senate, with all Democrats voting for censure and Republicans evenly splitting. Barry Goldwater, one of McCarthy's strongest defenders in the Senate debate, voted no.

McCarthy's censure was a pivotal event in the early history of the conservative movement. Liberals invariably described it as a crushing defeat for conservatism. But in fact it hardened William F. Buckley Jr.'s resolve to launch *National Review* the following year, and it inspired the formation in 1958 of the John Birch Society, a major if controversial player in the movement. Conservatives did not abandon anticommunism but resolved to prove wrong Nikita Khrushchev's boast that "your grand-children will live under communism."

Five decades later, McCarthy's claims about the number of subversives in our government were conclusively shown to be not inflated but under-stated. In *Blacklisted by History: The Untold Story of Senator Joe McCarthy and His Fight Against America's Enemies* (2006), Stan Evans documented hundreds of communists and other security risks in official Washington during the 1930s and 1940s—double or perhaps triple McCarthy's esti-mates. Stan provided thirty-one pages of endnotes and a lengthy appendix plus dozens of FBI and other government documents obtained through the Freedom of Information Act. He concluded that "the Red network reached into virtually every important aspect of the U.S. government, up to very high levels, the State Department notably included."

MY OWN PATH

I enjoyed meeting power men like Joe McCarthy and Richard Nixon, who was a guest in our home, and I felt the pull of Washington, the most powerful city in the most powerful country in the world. But in my senior year at Duke, I decided that political writing was not for me. I determined to enter the Army as an enlisted man and then to live in Europe, probably in Paris, and write the Great American Novel. There was another reason for my eschewing political writing: I did not want to be compared with my father, knowing I would always come in second. Living 3,828 miles away from him seemed about right.

Private Lee Edwards, U.S. Army, 1954

2

PARIS HOLIDAY

In the fall of 1956, I was living on the Left Bank of Paris, attending classes at the Sorbonne now and again, trying to write a novel, and becoming a habitué at Le Select and other Montparnasse hangouts. I was two months removed from my honorable discharge from the U.S. Army after a year and a half of soft duty in Heidelberg in the Signal Corps and sixty days of temporary duty entertaining the troops in EM and USO clubs in France and Germany. I was pursuing as hedonistic a life as is possible on a monthly stipend of $125 from the GI Bill. I grew a Vandyke, smoked Gauloises, drank Algerian red, read Ernest Hemingway and Henry Miller, and was admitted without ceremony into the American expatriate community. I paid little attention to politics.

My agreeable little world exploded on October 23 when the students of Budapest—young men and women in their early twenties like me—ignited a revolution against the Hungarian People's Republic and its Soviet protectors. The streets filled with thousands of demonstrators demanding the dissolution of the communist government and free elections. They defiantly sang the Hungarian national anthem—"This we swear, this we swear, that we will no longer be slaves."

A thirty-two-foot-high bronze statue of Stalin was toppled. The hammer and sickle was cut out of the middle of the Hungarian flag, and the Flag with a Hole became a symbol of the revolution. In the face of the militant uprising, Soviet troops pulled out of Budapest, retreating into the countryside, and a new people's government was formed.

I was ecstatic. The French newspapers carried banner headlines like "Hongrie Libre." The radio resonated with the triumphant voices of the young revolutionaries who were sending packing the most powerful army in the world. Communism seemed to be toppling.

My dormant anticommunism came alive. All that I had learned from my reporter-father, who had covered congressional hearings about communism, came flooding back. I remembered reading his stories about show trials, firing squads, and Siberian exile, of those who had survived the KGB and the Gulag, of Americans who had willingly betrayed their country for a greater revolution, the Bolshevik Revolution.

Ex-communists like Freda Utley and Ben Mandel had explained to me the base treachery of the August 1939 Hitler-Stalin pact that started World War II. Alger Hiss, the golden boy of the liberal establishment, had been a Soviet spy in the 1930s and during World War II. Senator Joe McCarthy was right—there had been dozens of communists in our government, and at the highest levels. Now, caught up in the sights and sounds of a jubilant Budapest celebrating its freedom, I thought: How the Politburo in Moscow must be shaking in their Stalinist boots.

I put aside Baudelaire and Colette and devoured *Le Monde* and *Le Figaro* for the latest news. The new Hungarian government, headed by the reformer Imre Nagy, promised fundamental political change and said that Hungary would withdraw from the Warsaw Pact. My God, I remember thinking, we could be watching the unraveling of the Soviet Empire.

That Moscow was thinking the same thing became clear on November 4, when seventeen Soviet tank divisions invaded Hungary and, along with the five divisions that had remained, headed for Budapest. The young freedom fighters, with their World War II rifles and pistols and Molotov cocktails, were slaughtered by merciless Soviet troops and tanks.

I listened to the desperate cries over the Paris radio—"Help, America! We need your help now!" I waited for my government to answer their call. The only response was words, a pro forma White House statement, a meaningless United Nations resolution vetoed by the Soviet Union.

I was furious at my government—the leader of the free world—for not responding. Especially since Radio Free Europe, funded by us, had encouraged Hungarians to rise up. As the number of fallen freedom fighters passed two thousand and tens of thousands of Hungarians fled their once-again-communist country, I took an oath. I resolved that for the rest of my life, wherever I was, whatever I was, I would help those who resisted communism however I could. In the years to come, my anticommunism, inherited from my father, would be reinforced by my political mentors, Dr. Walter Judd and William F. Buckley Jr., and my political heroes, Barry Goldwater and Ronald Reagan, who shared a strategy about how to end the Cold War—"We win, and they lose."

GOING HOME

On May 2, 1957, six months later, Joe McCarthy died at the Bethesda Naval Hospital of cirrhosis of the liver, compounded by isolation and ignominy. In the Senate, Goldwater spoke for the millions who had idolized him: "Do not mourn Joe McCarthy. Be thankful that he lived, at the right time, and according to the talents vested in him by his Maker. Be grateful, too, that when it came his time to die, he passed on with the full assurance that, because he lived, America is a brighter, safer, more vigilant land today." I learned later that his eulogy was written by L. Brent Bozell, whose life and mine would intersect more than once.

I wondered what *National Review* and *Human Events* were saying about Joe's passing. First Robert Taft, dead of cancer, now Joe. Who would take their place as leader of the conservatives? Goldwater? He was a first-term senator from a small western state. Was he the right man? Things were happening at home. A conservative anticommunist movement seemed to be emerging. And I was nearly four thousand miles away writing a very predictable novel no one wanted to publish.

What was I doing in Paris? Was I a writer or a poseur? How many rejection notes did I have to receive before accepting I was not the next Hemingway? My biggest triumph was not literary but a one-line bit part in Bob Hope's film *Paris Holiday*.

I took and passed the final exam at the Sorbonne, receiving a Certificat de Français Usuel, degree *moyen*—that is, a C in practical French. I will always remember trying to recite from memory the famous Ronsard poem that begins, "Quand vous serez bien vieille, au soir, à la chandelle" and freezing after saying the first line. *Moyen* indeed.

I had only a few hundred dollars in my bank account, not nearly enough to pay bills until my next GI check in December. I tried to get a job, talking to the *Tribune*'s Paris correspondent, but my *Duke Chronicle* clips did not impress him. I asked Dad for a loan, but he said no, shocking me, his beloved only son. I took my disappointment to Le Select, where one evening I drank twelve bottles of Guinness. I was not trying to break Dylan Thomas's record but drowning my resentment.

The next day, nursing the mother of all hangovers on the terrace of Le Select, I suddenly said to myself, "I'm going home." I did not want to be one more expat who left family, country, and language to live in a strange land. I booked passage on the SS *Ryndam*, and during the ten-day voyage I found myself, of all things, thinking about God, whom I had abandoned as a freshman at Duke, assisted by a Methodist preacher teacher who had said, "Well, if you don't believe in the Resurrection, there's little reason to be a Christian." Looking back at the decade since, I admitted the futility of trying to center my life on me because there wasn't enough of me. I was not brilliant, only clever; not bold but rash; not creative, only imitative; not independent but selfish. I needed something, someone, besides and beyond myself to live by.

3

THE MOVEMENT

I found spiritual direction in the Catholic Church, led by the Holy Spirit, and political direction in the conservative movement, through M. Stanton Evans, then the managing editor of *Human Events*. Stan was one of our wittiest, capable of bon mots like "The trouble with conservatives is that too many of them come to Washington thinking they are going to drain the swamp, only to discover that Washington is a hot tub."

He invited me to join the D.C. Young Republicans, explaining that he was seeking votes for an upcoming election in which he was running for first vice president of the club. I signed up when Stan added that "lots of very pretty girls" were in the YRs. He was right about the pretty girls—I married one several years later—but wrong in thinking he had a chance against a popular young lady who easily defeated him.

Through Stan, I met young conservatives and anticommunists like Harvardite Tom Winter and Californian Allan Ryskind, son of the Hollywood writer Morrie Ryskind, who wrote several of the Marx Brothers movies and won a Pulitzer Prize for the Gershwin musical drama *Of Thee I Sing*. Tom and Allan took over *Human Events* after the deaths of founders Frank Hanighen and James Wick and made the weekly tabloid essential reading for Barry Goldwater and Ronald Reagan. When he was president, Reagan arranged for *Human Events* to be delivered to him in an unmarked envelope to evade the White House pragmatists who screened the president's mail and considered the weekly to be too conservative.

I heard through the conservative grapevine that Senator John Marshall Butler, Maryland Republican, was looking for a press secretary and I applied for the position. I showed Ed Hood, the senator's administrative assistant, my articles in *National Review* and *Human Events*. I spoke knowledgeably about the newspapers and television and radio stations in Baltimore, Frederick, and Hagerstown. I outlined a communications program ranging from a weekly newspaper column to TV clips, innovations for the senator.

"What salary would you require?" Hood asked.

"$7,500 a year," I replied. That was nearly one-half more than I was making as a reporter at the trade journal *Broadcasting*, for which I had been working for about a year.

"When can you start?"

It was my first experience with the cavalier attitude people in government have about spending money that is not their own.

Working for a respected Republican senator with a Republican president was near bliss. A Republican majority in the Senate and the House would have been paradise, but such confluence was impossible. Or so everyone thought for thirty-five years before the coming of Newt Gingrich and the Contract with America.

If you wanted the facts about a potential defense contract or the latest education figures, you called the Congressional Research Service (CRS), knowing you would get a quick answer. If you wanted to introduce a bill, you talked it over with aides to Majority Leader Lyndon Johnson, the most accommodating of leaders as long as you accommodated him. If you wanted a free dinner or drinks after work at the Carroll Arms Hotel across the street, there was always an obliging lobbyist—and no bothersome rules about gifts.

In those pre-9/11 days, you did not walk through a metal detector to enter the New Senate Office Building (now the Dirksen SOB), where our office was, and it was easy to visit the Senate floor. I saw the fabled ones up close: Jack Kennedy, Ivy League in dress, ironic in speech, never still, always jiggling a foot or tapping a pencil, plainly wishing he were somewhere else, like the campaign trail; Lyndon Johnson, heavyset and Texas tall, moving majestically around the floor, flattering, cajoling, threatening his colleagues, trading for the votes he needed to pass a bill; Barry Goldwater, with his silver hair and square jaw, bluntly criticizing liberal Democrats and modern Republicans for promising too much and spending too much, quoting Edmund Burke that "we can't make heaven on earth"—Barry Goldwater, my hero.

Master of all he surveyed, LBJ operated openly without fear or embarrassment. I saw him give my boss, Senator Butler, the full "Johnson Treatment," wrapping his arm around him and drawing him close, whispering ardently in his ear, causing my boss, the distinguished senior senator from Maryland and the senior partner of Baltimore's most prestigious law firm, to blush like a teenage boy. Whatever Johnson wanted, he got.

Like most young conservatives, I looked to *National Review* (and Bill Buckley) for guidance on all things, foreign and domestic. I noted *NR*'s scathing criticism of President Eisenhower for inviting the Soviet leader, Nikita Khrushchev, who had implemented the infamous forced famine of Ukraine in the early 1930s, to visit the United States. Buckley was so outraged that, with the help of the conservative impresario Marvin Liebman, he formed the Committee Against Summit Entanglements (CASE). He threatened to dye the Hudson River red so that when the Soviet dictator entered New York to visit the United Nations, it would be on a "river of blood."

MISSIONARY FOR FREEDOM

I was present at the 1960 Republican National Convention in Chicago as editor of the Young Republican National Federation's official publication, the *YRNF News*. Working around the clock from a small pizza-littered hotel suite to put out our daily newspaper, I saw Congressman Walter Judd of Minnesota nearly stampede the convention into nominating him for vice president. His keynote address was titled "We Must Develop a Strategy for Victory—To Save Freedom—Freedom Everywhere."

Dr. Judd, who had been a medical missionary in China in the 1920s and the 1930s, listed what the Republican Party under President Eisenhower had done to preserve freedom around the world: end the fighting in Korea and prevent threats from developing into war in Iran, Guatemala, Formosa (Taiwan), Suez, Lebanon, Quemoy, and West Berlin. This had been accomplished, he said, "not by sacrificing our principles to secret deals under the table but by steady patient firmness and strength in support of principles"; by "keeping our word" and through "steadfast support of friends and allies"; and by "wholehearted support of the United Nations." He stressed the importance of military strength to back up those principles, and he repudiated the Democratic charge of a "missile gap"—a gap that Kennedy after he was elected admitted did not exist.

Dr. Judd seized the offensive and asked ten questions about the Cold

War, pausing each time for a response from the delegates. Each time, the delegates grew louder until the amphitheater fairly rocked.

"Was it Republicans who recognized the Soviet Union in 1933 and gave it acceptance into our country and world society as if it were a respectable and dependable member thereof?" A muted "No."

"Was it Republicans who agreed to the Communist takeover of a people in Eastern Europe who are not Russian?" A shouted "No!"

"Was it a Republican administration that divided Korea and gave control of North Korea to the Communists?" "NO!" thundered the delegates.

When Dr. Judd asked the next question, he was drowned out by the delegates, who would have shouted "NO!" if he had asked them whether they wanted an income tax cut. He concluded that in the face of the communist challenge, America had no alternative but to "win the Cold War," not by military might but by "our strongest weapons, the values and virtues of [our] system of government.... We must let loose in the world the dynamic forces of freedom in our day as our forefathers did in theirs, causing people everywhere to look toward the American dream."

I was caught up in the rhetoric, as were hundreds of delegates who began waving huge photos of Judd and chanting "Judd for Vice President!" Wouldn't it be fantastic, I thought, to work with an inspiring, victory-seeking anticommunist like Dr. Judd? Before the end of the decade, I would be.

But the Judd boom did not sway the one man who had to be swayed, Richard Nixon, who stuck to his original choice of Henry Cabot Lodge, U.S. ambassador to the United Nations, former U.S. senator from Massachusetts, and Boston Brahmin. Dr. Judd later told me that "the greatest political mistake" of his life was that he had not given "the green light to certain people at the convention" to secure his nomination for vice president. For the rest of his life, he believed that Nixon-Judd would have defeated Kennedy-Johnson.

Is this a classic example of "if only," or is it a valid argument? Consider: If only 4,500 voters in Illinois and 28,000 voters in Texas—both states that Judd had often visited over the years—had changed their vote, those 32,500 votes would have moved Illinois and Texas with their fifty-one electoral votes into the Nixon column, giving him a slim electoral majority of two. A Nixon-Judd ticket might well have been a winning ticket.

Nixon agreed. Three years later, when both had left public office, Nixon admitted to Dr. Judd, "Walter, if I had chosen you instead of Cabot, we would both still be in Washington."

"LET'S GROW UP!"

The high drama of the 1960 Republican National Convention did not end with the Judd for Vice President effort. Many conservative delegates were less than enthusiastic about the pragmatic Nixon, preferring the unabashed conservative senator from Arizona, Barry Goldwater, who aroused the convention Monday night with his description of the "true Republican philosophy" founded on freedom, creative opportunity, and limited government. Echoing a major theme of his book *The Conscience of a Conservative*, which had been sent to every delegate, Goldwater said that Republicans must provide "the American voter with a real choice between the two philosophies competing in our world, the philosophy of the *stomach* or the philosophy of the *whole man*." First Judd, now Goldwater on the first evening of the convention. Were conservatives taking over the Republican Party? I asked myself.

The Nixon forces, who controlled the convention, allowed Goldwater to be nominated as a favorite son of Arizona. They were startled by the fervent demonstration that erupted. I watched as the banners of Arizona, Arkansas, Louisiana, North Carolina, South Carolina, Texas, Mississippi, Georgia, Nevada, Wyoming, Utah, and Idaho proclaimed Goldwater to be the favorite of the South and the West, sending shivers down the spines of eastern liberals. Many of those waving the banners were my age.

Standing at the podium, Goldwater signaled for quiet and asked, over shouted protests, that his name be withdrawn and that the delegates pledged to him shift their support to Richard Nixon. As shouts of "No!" echoed in the great hall, he spoke directly to the true believers: "This country, and its majesty, is too great for any man, be he conservative or liberal, to stay home and not work just because he doesn't agree. Let's grow up, conservatives! We want to take this party back, and I think some day we can. Let's get to work!"

With these words, Barry Goldwater became the leader of the conservative movement, the receptacle of the hopes and dreams of conservatives of both political parties. I said to the other young conservatives in our newspaper-cluttered hotel room, "Yes! Let's get to work, starting right now!" Two months later, one hundred young men and women gathered at the Buckley family estate in Sharon, Connecticut, to found the most consequential youth group of the '60s.

4

—

REBELS WITH A CAUSE

That September morning I walked across the broad green lawn of the Buckley estate to meet Doug Caddy and David Franke, the student leaders who had invited me to attend a meeting of young conservatives to form a national youth organization.

Most of the others had arrived the night before and were seated or reclining around a gigantic elm tree, discussing membership. Present, along with Doug and Dave, were Stan Evans, by then editor of the *Indianapolis News* (the youngest editor of a daily newspaper in America); brilliant, irreverent Robert Schuchman, studying law at Yale; Carol Dawson of Trinity College; Midwest YR leader Robert Croll; the Kolbe brothers, John and Jim, of Arizona; George McDonnell of Michigan; Howard (Howie) Phillips, the president at nineteen of the Harvard student body; Carl McIntire, son of the fundamentalist radio preacher; Herb Kohler, son of the Wisconsin manufacturer; and raven-haired Annette Courtemanche of Long Island. We were almost evenly divided between traditional conservatives and libertarians, but all of us were anticommunist.

As I approached the group, I heard someone say, "This organization must be a youth organization. I therefore move that the maximum age be set at twenty-seven." At the time a popular campus saying was "Don't trust anyone over thirty." I looked at my companion, Vic Milione, the president of the Intercollegiate Society of Individualists (ISI), and said,

"Well, Vic, I guess we might as well leave right now, because I'm going to be twenty-eight in December and I know you're older than I am."

The motion for a maximum age of twenty-seven was defeated after several people pointed out that such a limit would exclude many young conservatives on the way up, including congressmen. The maximum age was raised to thirty-five and then, as I recall, to thirty-nine, which seemed to me to be stretching it.

We moved on to more fundamental questions: What was the purpose of the organization? What would be its name? All day Saturday, we debated purpose and principle, agreeing on one major point: we would be a conservative action organization with ties to neither major political party, especially the Republicans. After dinner with Bill Buckley and a few older conservatives like Frank Meyer, Brent Bozell, William Rusher, and Marvin Liebman, we broke up into groups to draft a constitution and bylaws while Stan Evans, Carol Dawson, and a few others went off to write what became the Sharon Statement. Stan had written a first draft on the plane from Indianapolis—on a yellow legal pad, not the back of an envelope. His draft was short, only 369 words.

The next morning, after church, we met and approved the statement. The only serious objection came from hard-core libertarians over the phrase "God-given free will." Did God belong in our statement? they asked. The discussion included several references to Ayn Rand, a militant atheist, and John Galt, the atheist hero of *Atlas Shrugged*. In the end, with the prayers we had said earlier that morning perhaps having been heard, God won.

The statement represented the major strains of conservatism in 1960:

- *Traditional conservative:* "That foremost among the transcendent values is the individual's use of his God-given free will, whence derives his right to be free from the restrictions of arbitrary force."
- *Libertarian:* "That the market economy, allocating resources by the free play of supply and demand, is the single economic system compatible with the requirements of personal freedom and constitutional government, and that it is at the same time the most productive supplier of human needs."
- *Anticommunist:* "That the forces of international communism are, at present, the greatest single threat to these liberties" and "That the United States should stress victory over, rather than coexistence with, this menace."

I was tempted to cry, "Yes!" at the last words, but I was content that they concluded the Sharon Statement. The three pillars of my conservatism were my Catholicism, my anticommunism, and my individualism, but my anticommunism came first.

The ideas of the Sharon Statement would serve as the philosophical base of modern American conservatism for the next three decades, until the fall of the Berlin Wall in November 1989. As the historian George Nash has written, anticommunism was the superglue that bound conservatives and libertarians together. When the Soviet Union dissolved in 1991, American conservatism developed cracks that were later repaired but not permanently fixed with the 1994 Contract with America, the 2010 rise of the Tea Party, and the 2012 Republican tsunami. (Donald Trump's surprising 2016 victory presented problems and opportunities for conservatives, which I address in the final chapter.) Some conservatives have argued that big government can be the clear and present danger by which to unite all the various strains of the conservative movement. Perhaps, but the neoconservative and reform-conservative notion of "limited" government is far from the limited-government stance of conservatives like me.

The most spirited debate at Sharon revolved around the organization's name. The choice narrowed down to Young Conservatives of America or Young Americans for Freedom. The purists wanted to proclaim our conservatism to the nation and the world. The pragmatists like Dave Franke and me argued that the word *conservative* was exclusionary and would lose us anticommunists and libertarians. Dave argued, effectively, that conservatives should retain title to the word *freedom* and not let the left capture it as it had *democracy*. I noted how often the words *free* and *freedom* appeared in the Sharon Statement—nine times—more than any other concept. The vote was close: by a margin of forty-four to forty, as I recall, the nation's newest and most ambitious youth group became known as Young Americans for Freedom (YAF).

Marvin Liebman, the Oscar Wilde of our movement in more ways than one, mused whether the name made him and every other senior conservative an "OAF"—an Old American for Freedom. At the end of the day, we chose Bob Schuchman to be our first president and Doug Caddy our executive director. I was elected to the national board.

Who were we? We were more traditional than libertarian in our philosophy, political activists and not academics. We were public university, not Ivy League; believers, not agnostics; midwestern, not East Coast; middle-class, not rich; young men (and women) in a hurry to change the world and confident we would.

Audacious from the beginning, we decided to hold a public rally in New York City's Manhattan Center in March 1961, just six months after our founding. Even with our seemingly unlimited energy and unbounded confidence, we would not have attempted such an event—the center's capacity was 3,500—except that we could call on the organizing experience of Marvin Liebman, in whose Madison Avenue offices we were temporarily located. Marvin had been filling halls for years, first as a dedicated communist and now as an even more dedicated anticommunist. Marvin explained to me one day, "I got tired of their lies. They lied about everything."

We publicized the evening as our First Annual Awards Rally and ensured a good turnout by honoring William F. Buckley Jr., Russell Kirk, and Senator Barry Goldwater, the three men who had shaped the modern conservative movement. Kirk was the philosopher, the thinker; Buckley was the popularizer, the journalist; Goldwater was the politician, the man of political action. It was Goldwater's first major speech outside Arizona since John F. Kennedy's narrow win over Richard Nixon the previous November.

Six thousand conservatives showed up, only half of whom could get in, the others denied entry by a line of adamant fire marshals. It was a triumphant evening, a coming-out celebration for YAF. Goldwater, the catalyst for YAF's astounding growth in its first years, called us "the nation's young leaders of tomorrow," adding, "They are concerned with their future, and they don't want it mortgaged by political persuasions with which they are not in sympathy."

Just how concerned we were is reflected in the lead editorial of the first issue of the *New Guard*, our monthly magazine, which was distributed at the Manhattan Center rally. I had argued heatedly at the December board meeting that YAF *had* to have its own publication. "*Iskra* (The Spark) was essential to the early success of Lenin and the Bolsheviks," I said. Ever the anticommunist, I used the example of Lenin, the Russian revolutionary, rather than Sam Adams, the American revolutionary, who organized the Committees of Correspondence as a means of communication between the colonies. My passionate presentation carried the day, and my offer to serve without compensation won me the editorship. In the lead editorial of the first issue, I tried to capture YAF's radical spirit:

> Ten years ago, this magazine would not have been possible. Twenty years ago, it would not have been dreamed of. Thirty-five years ago, it would not have been necessary. Today, *The New Guard* is possible,

it is a reality, and it is needed by the youth of America to proclaim loudly and clearly: We are sick unto death of collectivism, socialism, statism, and the other utopianisms which have poisoned the minds, weakened the wills and smothered the spirit of Americans for three decades and more.

After tracing the political success of the New Deal and liberalism's dominance on the campus, I turned to the emergence of a counter-revolution led by groups like ISI and YAF and publications like *National Review* and *Modern Age*. Quoting the Sharon Statement, I stressed that YAF would be an "action" organization, because "action is imperative for [America's] preservation and that of the world." YAF was "conservative," I wrote, not reactionary, desiring to preserve and "extend those [first] principles responsible for the greatness of this Republic."

Pulling out as many stops as I could reach, I concluded:

> The tide of conservatism is rising all over the United States, and we will rise with it leaving behind those unfortunates still chained to the rotting posts of "liberalism," collectivism, and statism.... We offer them the pincers of liberty, individualism, and initiative to free themselves of chains as rusty as the shibboleths which undoubtedly our opponents will attempt to wrap around us....
>
> We extend to every young American an invitation to help build an Ark which will carry America to the highest peak of all.

The *New York Times* put us on page one. Television networks carried clips of our rally the following day. Hundreds of newspaper articles were generated. In one night, YAF became a national phenomenon because (a) no other political youth group existed (Students for a Democratic Society, or SDS, was not organized until the following year), (b) adults, whatever their political philosophy, are interested in what young people are saying and doing, and (c) YAF tied itself tightly to Barry Goldwater, who would blaze across the political sky for the next three years. I made certain that the *New Guard* charted his fiery course, filling our pages with articles about Goldwater rallies and demonstrations, Goldwater editorials, Goldwater endorsements, and Goldwater ads. YAF members enlisted as the ground troops of what we called the Goldwater Revolution. Our membership doubled and doubled again, reaching twenty-five thousand in our second year, sprouting up on dozens of campuses and in cities large and small. Our largest chapter was in New York City, the mecca of liberalism. We loved to wave the conservative flag in the faces of Governor Nelson Rockefeller, Senator Jacob Javits, mayor-to-be John Lindsay, and all the other leading progressive Republicans.

In the July 1962 issue of the *New Guard*, I proposed a platform for the "New Conservatives," borrowing freely from Goldwater, Buckley, and other OAFs as well as Stan Evans and other young conservatives. I included support of state right-to-work laws, a sharp reduction in farm subsidies, workfare rather than welfare (based on the successful New-burgh, New York, experience), a continuation of nuclear testing, opposition to federal aid to education, a balanced budget and reduction in the national debt, reduced personal income taxes, a realistic Alliance for Progress in Latin America, free access to West Berlin, and a strong anti-communist stand in Vietnam and the Far East, particularly in support of the Republic of China on Taiwan.

I was specific because many liberals accused conservatives of being too vague—all that "endless" talk about liberty and freedom. And I was specific about our goals because I was tired of being linked to the John Birch Society, the Minutemen, and every other extremist right-wing group in America. In his syndicated column, John Roche, a deputy chairman of the Democratic National Committee, referred to YAF members as "sons of Birch" who believed that highways and post offices were "communistic." I immediately telephoned Roche. To his credit, he apologized for the cheap shot. I then sent him an information packet, which led him to promise he would avoid mischaracterizations about us in the future. If all liberals were as fair-minded as Roche, our politics might not be so polarized.

I concluded the *New Guard* article (titled "The New Right: Its Face and Future") by saying that conservatives were engaged in a political struggle "for the next 20 years until the Conservative Establishment, the one certain vehicle to sustain a firm foreign policy and a competitive enterprise economy, has truly been established in this nation." My use of the term "New Right" came a decade before Richard Viguerie, Paul Weyrich, and other Washington conservatives formed what came to be known as the New Right. My prediction of how long we would need to become a major political force was nearly right—it took us eighteen years to build a Conservative Establishment and elect a conservative president.

My reference to "a firm foreign policy" reflected an article of faith for me and every young conservative I knew. In my *New Guard* column, I called repeatedly for a military second to none and for the United States to encourage the nations and peoples behind the Iron Curtain to challenge their captors directly and indirectly. In September 1961 I wrote a special report about my visit to East Berlin just one month after the Wall went up. I instructed Carol Dawson and the other editors to be prepared to mount an international "Free Lee" campaign if I was arrested and put in a communist jail. I was joking, sort of.

I knew that East Berlin would be depressing, but I was not prepared for near desolation.

BEHIND THE WALL

It was just after noon when I boarded a streetcar. As the car trundled along at about five miles an hour (any faster and I think it would have fallen apart), I examined my fellow passengers. No one said a word. Their faces were blank. Resignation was etched in every line of their bodies.

In 1953, after Stalin's death, the people of East Berlin had fought with little more than their bare hands against Soviet soldiers and East German police in a display of heroism surpassed only by that of the Hungarians in their 1956 revolution. But in August 1961, when the border between East and West Berlin was closed and the construction of the Wall began, East Berliners raised little public protest. It seemed that the East German communist government had broken the will of the people. Most of the VOPOs (*volkspolizei*) along the Wall were young men, many still in their teens. Without hesitation, they shot countrymen trying to flee; they fired at West Berliners trying to help escapees to safety. From childhood, they had been conditioned to think of themselves as communists and not as Germans.

I got off the streetcar and walked deeper and deeper into East Berlin. There were still many empty bombed-out buildings, unlike West Berlin, where workers were constantly, compulsively rebuilding. Even on the grand Stalinallee, with its high-rise apartment buildings and stores, tiles had fallen from the walls and had not been replaced. Weeds grew between the feet of a giant Stalin statue. The city was a gray, dusty ghost town out of the Old West.

I walked farther into the city. The few people on the streets were dressed in black and gray and walked quickly with their heads down. I came into view of the Wall, all concrete and barbed wire, patrolled by soldiers and dogs. Small groups looked west at freedom. Some whispered to one another, but most were silent, pale wraiths in the fading sunlight. When a small boy approached the Wall, guards ordered him back roughly.

Tired from walking, I stepped into the Restaurant Bukarest near Alexanderplatz. I seated myself among a clientele almost exclusively female and middle-aged. There were two empty seats at my table, and within minutes they were occupied by two young women—both dressed in the green uniform of the *volkspolizei* and both, I soon learned, dedicated communists.

In my *gasthaus* Deutsch, I explained that I was an American and not a communist. Rather, I said, "Ich bin kapitalist." They said they directed the traffic (*Why did they bother?* I thought) and launched into a description of the many entertainments in East Berlin—the opera, the symphony, the theater, the movies, and on and on. They shrugged when I asked them about the Wall. They said they had no relatives in West Berlin—I wondered whether that had been a condition for their getting a government job.

"The people of West Berlin are well-off," I said.

"So are the people of East Berlin," the older girl quickly replied, taking a large bite of her chocolate cake and ice cream.

You, perhaps, I thought, but not most East Berliners, like those I had seen standing silently at the Wall and looking West.

My day in sad, gray East Berlin intensified my determination to raise the banner of anticommunism whenever I could. I did so earlier that year at YAF's demonstration in support of the House Committee on Un-American Activities (HCUA) at Lafayette Park opposite the White House. Several hundred YAFers, including busloads from New York, picketed the White House. It was the first time pro-HCUA pickets had outnumbered anti-HCUA pickets, who were amazed to see so many conservatives in action. When a small group from the American Nazi Party, headed by George Lincoln Rockwell, tried to join us, we turned them away.

I was familiar with HCUA's record through my father, who covered every major congressional hearing about communism from the late 1930s through the early 1970s. He was there in August 1947 when Whittaker Chambers and Alger Hiss publicly confronted each other: Chambers stated that he and Hiss had belonged to the same underground communist cell in the 1930s, a charge that Hiss vehemently denied. Dad was initially impressed by Hiss's calm but firm demeanor and not convinced by Chambers's almost inaudible accusation. But when Richard Nixon privately shared his skepticism about Hiss—"His answers are too calculating. He's hiding something"—Dad studied Hiss more closely and decided that Nixon was right. He was guided to that conclusion by Robert Stripling, the committee's chief investigator, a primary source for my father.

On the fortieth anniversary of the Hiss-Chambers congressional hearings, Dad wrote a special report emphasizing their importance in American politics. He said that "if Hiss was guilty so was an entire generation in the Roosevelt-Truman era." After two lengthy trials in New York City, Hiss was convicted of perjury—the statute of limitations for espionage having lapsed—and was sentenced to forty-four months in jail. Despite evidence subsequently uncovered in Soviet archives that Hiss was indeed a communist spy, some ultra-liberals insist to this day that Hiss was innocent. Whenever I grew tired or discouraged in my battle against communism, I would remind myself of the Hiss case. On those occasions when I thought about giving up, I would read the first chapter of Chambers's *Witness*, "A Letter to My Children." If he could keep going, confronted as he was by the liberal establishment and with his heart and other health problems, so could I.

From the late 1940s through the mid-'50s, my father was deeply immersed in the anticommunist crusade. He spent so much time with ex-communists, who were his best sources on and off Capitol Hill, that at one party he looked around and said to Mom, "Do you realize we are the only people here who have never been members of the Communist Party?" My parents often took me along, and I met Isaac Don Levine, who wrote the first English-language biography of Joseph Stalin, and Freda Utley, who wrote the classic *The China Story*, as well as Ben Mandel, a Communist Party member for twenty years and now director of research for HCUA.

Levine and Utley welcomed the opportunity to instruct youngsters like me about the crimes and victims of communism. Don took a liking to me and later gave me a complete set of his journal, *Plain Talk*, which in the late '40s published for the first time in the West a map of the Gulag, the Soviet system of forced labor camps later made famous by the Russian dissident and Nobel laureate Aleksandr Solzhenitsyn.

At one party, I met and bonded with Jon Utley, Freda's teenage son, who had been born in Moscow. His father, Arcadi Berdichevsky, had been arrested during the Stalin purges of the 1930s and sent to the dreaded Vorkuta camp in Siberia, where he was executed. In the documentary film *Return to the Gulag*, Jon tells the moving story of his decades-long search for his father. Jon and I have remained close friends, although he has joined the ranks of the paleoconservatives as publisher of their lively monthly the *American Conservative*, and I have remained a conservative given to libertarian impulses. We are joined by our love of liberty and our unwavering hostility to communism.

5

RELUCTANT CHAMPION

YAF was so new to major-league politics we did not know what couldn't be done, like holding a rally in New York City's Madison Square Garden with its eighteen thousand seats.

The theme of our March 1962 rally was "Victory Over Communism," and liberals smugly predicted an embarrassing turnout and a significant setback for the conservative movement. But eager conservatives filled the huge arena to hear Senator Strom Thurmond of South Carolina, still a Democrat; Senator John Tower of Texas, who the year before had won Lyndon Johnson's Senate seat in a special election; and our hero, Barry Goldwater. An estimated ten thousand people were turned away. Brent Bozell warmed up the crowd by issuing an order, anticipating Ronald Reagan by a quarter of a century: "To the [U.S.] commander in Berlin: Tear down the Wall!"

By the time Goldwater was introduced by William Schulz (who would become the number-two editor at *Reader's Digest*), it was past 11 P.M. Every half hour or so, one of us sitting on the stage had snuck back to the waiting room and told an increasingly impatient senator that it would not be much longer. On the last visit, a grim-faced Goldwater promised that if he did not go on in another ten minutes, he was heading back to his hotel.

When he was at last introduced as "the next president of the United States," the Garden exploded. Conservatives had been waiting since

Robert Taft had been denied the presidential nomination, since Joe
McCarthy had been censured by the Senate, since John Kennedy had
"stolen" the election from Richard Nixon. They had endured the slurs and
the smears, been called "extreme right," "radical right," "ultra right," "far
right," and now they beat their hands together and raised their voices,
creating a cataract of sound that lasted five, ten, fifteen minutes.

Goldwater stood at the podium patiently, then impatiently, then puzzled, finally resigned. The crowd was transported into a state of ecstasy
common to true believers. They chanted over and over, "We want Barry!"
"We want Barry!" "We want Barry!" They shifted to a verbal game in
which one half of the Garden shouted, "Viva!" and the other responded,
"Olé!" This was no ordinary political rally but a revival meeting. At last,
Goldwater brought them back to earth by leaning into the microphone
and saying—his voice cutting through the lingering cries of "We want
Barry!"—"Well, if you shut up, you'll get him!" They laughed and cheered
their hero once more and at last fell silent.

Goldwater told the rapt audience: "Conservatism is the wave of the
future. It has come of age at a time of great national need." No wonder, he said, "that the proponents of the Welfare State are becoming
alarmed.... They are beginning to read the handwriting on the wall and
it spells the twilight of radical liberalism...in this country." They roared.

Addressing the central theme of the rally, "Victory Over Communism," he declared solemnly that "we must—for the sake of survival—
recognize communism for the enemy it is and dedicate ourselves once and
for all to a policy of victory."

It was an unconditional call for action against the barbarians who
were at the gates of Berlin and Saigon and a dozen other outposts of freedom around the world. Later that year, Goldwater formulated a strategy
for the Cold War in his little book *Why Not Victory?* that conservatives,
including me, constantly quoted.

Regarding Cuba, Goldwater wrote, "We must take whatever action
is needed to dislodge communism from its foothold in the Western
Hemisphere."

Regarding the U-2 spy plane: "We should all be proud that American
ingenuity and industry produced an aircraft capable of penetrating Russia's vaunted defenses." I later learned that Goldwater had test-flown the
U-2, one of approximately 180 aircraft he piloted in his life.

Regarding his policy of "Freedom Through Strength": "We are
ashamed of our strength and hesitate to use it at a time when only by
the vigorous use of that strength can we hope to avert war"; "We should

I believe announce in no uncertain terms that we are *against* disarmament. We are against it because we *need* our armaments—all of those we presently have, and more. We need weapons for both the limited and the unlimited war."

Regarding the UN: "The government of the United States should declare that if the United Nations votes to admit Red China, our government will, from that moment until the action is revoked, suspend its political and financial support of the United Nations."

Regarding the communist threat: "Whether we like it or not, we are engaged in a death struggle with an enemy which is waging a new kind of total war and which has declared its intention to bury us"; "Victory in the Communist War means…the opposite of defeat; it means freedom instead of slavery; it means the right of every man to worship God; of nations to determine their own destiny free of force and coercion.… It means peace with honor for men who prize liberty and do not fear death."

I read and reread *Why Not Victory?* Yes, I thought, we must recognize the enemy for what he is, proclaim victory as our goal, and use our strength to oppose communism wherever it exists. That was a crusade worthy of joining.

THE CONSCIENCE OF A CONSERVATIVE

I was familiar with the arguments in *Why Not Victory?* because I had already encountered them in Goldwater's bestselling manifesto *The Conscience of a Conservative,* the last third of which deals with "The Soviet Menace." We are losing the Cold War, he wrote, because our enemies have understood the nature of the conflict and we have not. "They are determined to win the conflict, and we are not."

And so he set forth a strategy that included superior military strength; keeping America economically strong; effective alliances like NATO; limiting foreign aid to countries that "are committed to a common goal of defeating world Communism"; no more summits with the Soviets, who have no intention of abiding by the agreements made; continuing nuclear testing; revisiting our membership in the United Nations; stopping all aid to communist governments; encouraging the captive nations "to revolt against their Communist rulers"; being prepared to undertake "military operations against vulnerable Communist regimes"; and above all declaring that "our goal in the Cold War must be victory."

Here was a call to arms to which there was only one possible response.

YAF decided to challenge our government and its big-business allies with a campaign against the Firestone Tire and Rubber Company, which had announced it would build a synthetic rubber plant in Communist Romania.

Our Philadelphia chapter, under the direction of John LaMothe, initiated a national protest against trading with the enemy. Soon there were picket lines, demonstrations, a letter-writing campaign, and boycotts against Firestone dealers. Apparently believing that YAF had thrown its best punch, an undeterred Firestone proceeded with its construction plans.

Until YAF announced it was going to hand out thousands of anti-Firestone leaflets at the Indianapolis 500 on Memorial Day, which attracted a half million car-racing enthusiasts every year. We also said we planned to hire an airplane with a banner reading "Firestone: Stop Trading with the Enemy" to fly back and forth over the racetrack. The threat was enough. Firestone abruptly canceled the synthetic rubber plant project, and YAF was cited as the main reason for the cancellation in dozens of articles and editorials.

ENTER ANNE

As memorable as it was, the Madison Square Garden rally in March was not the highlight of 1962 for me. The most important and life-changing event of the year came in September at YAF's annual convention in New York City, when I first saw Anne Libby Costanzo Stevens.

I was at a reception in the Commodore Hotel when I glanced across the room and noticed a group of young conservatives laughing hard at something one of them, a young woman, had said. Intrigued, I walked across the room, noticing as I came closer that she had dark brown, almost black hair, a classic oval face, and a shapely Italianate figure. Her eyes sparkled as she said something that elicited another round of laughter. She raised a tiny ivory pipe to her mouth and took a puff from a cigarette standing upright in the bowl of the pipe. I had never seen anyone, male or female, smoke that way, and with such assurance.

I would learn that the beautiful, animated young woman was Anne Stevens, the president of the New York Young Women's Republican Club, whose membership of 1,200 made her one of the most sought-after political activists in the city. She could deliver a hundred workers for a campaign with a few telephone calls. At twenty-three, Anne was the youngest president in the club's history by more than a decade and a possible candidate for the state legislature and even the U.S. Congress. I stepped forward to introduce myself, but someone announced that the convention was reconvening and Anne headed back into the meeting. We would not connect until the following year, but I never forgot my first look at the woman who would become my wife, my partner, my colleague, my editor, my senior counselor, the true love of my life.

When she arrived in New York City, Anne had not read *The Road to Serfdom* or *The Conservative Mind*, but she knew she was not like the liberals in her office or the Republican Party, who seemed so sure that the best answer for almost every economic or social problem could be found in government. After hearing what Bill Buckley had said at the Manhattan Center YAF rally, she realized she was a conservative, opposed to big government, in favor of the little platoons of society Bill mentioned, and willing to enlist in the Movement.

As the editor of the club newsletter, she wrote an editorial praising Buckley's remarks. A few days later, she was in her third-floor walk-up on the Upper East Side when the telephone rang.

"Miss Stevens?" the voice drawled. "This is Bill Buckley and I want to tell you how much I enjoyed your editorial in the young women's newsletter and to invite you to attend the next editorial meeting of *National Review*."

"Oh, Schuchy," Anne responded, thinking it was Bob Schuchman doing one of his spot-on imitations, "stop bothering me. I had a long day." She hung up.

A minute later, the telephone rang again and the same drawling voice said, "But, Miss Stevens, I assure you this *is* Bill Buckley, and we would like you to join us next Tuesday. Can you come?"

An embarrassed Miss Stevens apologized profusely and said she would be honored to come although she was not sure what she could contribute. Midway through the editorial meeting, a smiling Buckley leaned forward and asked Anne for her opinion of the latest violence in Katanga—in the news because of a forthright anticommunist named Moise Tshombe. The senior editors—James Burnham and Frank Meyer—as well as publisher William Rusher turned their heads toward her. Taking a breath, Anne murmured the need to support Tshombe, whose name she had heard from Schuchy. By the end of the meeting, she had relaxed enough to perceive that Burnham was the intellectual superior of everyone in the room and that Buckley deferred to him on nearly every topic, including U.S. politics.

Anne had already met the other Bill—Bill Rusher—who served as an informal senior adviser to the Young Republicans and YAF. Whenever Rusher needed Anne's support for his Machiavellian moves, he would invite her to dine at an expensive restaurant with starched tablecloths and whispering waiters. Amid a learned discourse on the relative merits of this Bordeaux or that Burgundy, Rusher would explain why it was necessary to replace Don with Doug or Karl with George or Nancy with Rita for the good of the Movement. Usually, although not always, Anne followed Rusher's suggestion, appreciative of his political acumen and his taste in wines.

Once, when Rusher asked her where she wanted to eat, Anne named a popular Greek restaurant near the Village that featured belly dancing along with baklava. One of her fondest recollections is of a zaftig dancer wrapping a scarf around Rusher's neck and drawing him, Brooks Brothers suit and all, onto the dance floor and undulating before him.

THE DRAFT COMMITTEE

In 1962 Senator John Marshall Butler decided not to seek reelection, requiring me to look for another job. I wound up in early 1963 as a vice president at Sorin-Hall, a small Washington public relations firm founded by Republican activist J. R. (Pat) Gorman. Weighing more than 250 pounds with a booming voice and matching personality, Pat had worked hard for Richard Nixon in his 1960 presidential campaign. His signal contribution was a handheld device he would click while saying, "Click for Dick." He passed out hundreds and perhaps thousands of the clickers during the campaign, the clicks driving Democrats and some Republicans crazy. Sorin-Hall had one major client, International Telephone and Telegraph (ITT), for which I was the account executive.

I spent most of my time arranging luncheons for ITT vice president William Merriam with media people like the syndicated columnist William White at the Metropolitan Club, the city's most exclusive private club. It was not onerous work, allowing me to monitor the narrowing polling gap between President Kennedy and Senator Goldwater. I knew from friends about the remarkably effective efforts of political strategist F. Clifton White to line up convention delegates for Goldwater, who kept insisting he was not interested in running. In one interview, the senator volunteered he was not sure he had the brains to be president. But I noted with the passing weeks that his protestations became more and more pro forma. His candidacy was all that young conservatives like me discussed. I was prepared in an instant to join any Draft Goldwater effort.

So when Peter O'Donnell, the millionaire Republican state chairman of Texas, and Clif White, the New York professional politician, formally launched the National Draft Goldwater Committee on April 8, 1963, at a packed press conference at the Mayflower Hotel, I was there, handing out news releases as a volunteer. O'Donnell and White were strikingly different in background but in agreement on one thing: the Republican Party was ripe for a conservative takeover. Formal in his dress and speech, Peter was a cool, calculating mathematics major who made many millions as a securities investor and gave much of it to the University of Texas and other institutions of higher learning in his home state. Known for his bow ties and his encyclopedic knowledge of politics, Clif had won the Distinguished Flying Cross during World War II and taught politics at Cornell University before becoming a full-time political operative. Peter and Clif found a common cause in the nomination of Goldwater for president.

I made it a point to drop by the Draft Goldwater offices on Connecticut Avenue almost every day. I wrote news releases, drafted statements for Peter, and produced an organizational brochure. In July I served as technical director of an Independence Day rally at the National Guard Armory and wrote remarks for Efrem Zimbalist Jr., the star of the popular TV adventure series *The FBI*.

"I know something about law and order," said Zimbalist, "and I am confident that if he is elected president, Barry Goldwater will enforce the law and protect the public order. No longer will those who break the law be given greater consideration than those who enforce the law." Zimbalist got some of the loudest applause at the rally and maybe in his professional life. Seven years later, I flew to Los Angeles to ask Zimbalist to head up a pro-FBI citizens' group I was organizing. He remembered the rally and the speech and said yes.

To the astonishment of the media and many political professionals, seven thousand conservatives traveled by car, bus, train, and plane to fill the old, creaky, un-air-conditioned armory, even though Goldwater was not present but riding down Phoenix's main street on his favorite palomino. The armory crowd chanted his name and filled baskets with bills of all denominations and made the front pages of the newspapers. Peter O'Donnell's cool exterior concealed the gambling instincts of an oil wildcatter. His gamble to schedule a rally on the Fourth of July and without the candidate paid off. The media now took the National Draft Goldwater Committee seriously.

MARCH ON WASHINGTON

Another rally in Washington the following month would have lasting consequences for conservatives and for America. Throughout the year, race dominated the national dialogue, highlighted by Dr. Martin Luther King Jr.'s nonviolent campaign in Birmingham and police chief Eugene (Bull) Connor's violent reaction, complete with fire hoses, nightsticks, and dogs. Millions of Americans saw the shocking image of a snarling dog lunging at a terrified woman. In response, President Kennedy asked Congress to enact a civil rights law committed to the premise "that race has no place in American life or law." It was an eloquent plea but did not seem to satisfy blacks and others who carried out 759 civil rights demonstrations in 75 cities, resulting in 13,786 arrests. Nor did it move the group of segregationist southern senators who promised to filibuster any such "unneeded" and unconstitutional legislation.

One demonstration was faithful to Dr. King's theme of Gandhian nonviolence—the March on Washington in late August. More than 200,000 people, with perhaps one-third of them white, marched peacefully down Constitution Avenue and assembled on the National Mall in front of the Lincoln Memorial to hear civil rights leaders A. Philip Randolph, Roy Wilkins, and Floyd McKissick and the United Auto Workers' Walter Reuther. I was there as an observer and yet more than that, because I was uneasy with the adamant states' rights editorials and articles in *National Review*. Normally I looked to *NR* for guidance, but its editors seemed unmoved by the ugly images of Birmingham and the telling contrast between Dr. King and Chief Connor.

Civil rights was never a priority issue for YAF—Jay Parker was our only black national board member for years—but in the November 1962 issue of the *New Guard*, I wrote a signed editorial about James Meredith's enrollment at the University of Mississippi, condemning the segregationist actions of Governor Ross Barnett and former major general Edwin A. Walker, and concluding:

> As conservatives, we understand and support the theory of states' rights but as conservatives concerned about freedom and respectful of order, we cannot endorse lawlessness, insurrection or racism. If Meredith is a "tool" of the NAACP he is a charlatan of the worst shape. But if he is a young man with a family interested in the best possible education, we wish him well as he pursues his course of studies.

In the summer of 1963, I walked, along with 200,000 others, to the Lincoln Memorial to hear Dr. King's "I Have a Dream" speech. I was moved, caught up in his words and the palpable yearning of the black Americans around me. Could there be a day, I wondered, when people of all colors, creeds, and political persuasions joined hands? I was no student of black history in America, but I had seen enforced segregation, first as a child in Washington, D.C., and then as a Duke student in Durham. You did not have to be a civil rights activist to insist that Jim Crow had to go and without further delay.

Dr. King's theme of freedom—"Free at last! Free at last! Thank God almighty, we are free at last!"—was consistent with Barry Goldwater's political and personal philosophy. The senator revealed his sympathy with black frustration when he said to visiting students three months before the march, "If I were a Negro, I don't think I would be very patient." He refused to join white southern senators, most of them drinking buddies and all of them Democrats, in opposition to the march. "Anybody has the right to come to Washington and visit his congressman," he said. "I'll be in my office to receive people from my state."

I was familiar with Goldwater's consistent support of civil rights in Arizona, starting with the desegregation of the Arizona Air National Guard after World War II, before President Truman desegregated the armed forces. I knew that he had personally desegregated the Senate cafeteria in January 1953, insisting that his black legislative assistant, Katherine Maxwell, be served along with every other Senate employee. Maxwell was denied service her first day on the job by black servers. One blistering telephone call by Goldwater swept away the Senate's long-standing Jim Crow policy. He generously supported the Arizona branches of the NAACP and the Urban League.

But all of this would count for little when the Senate took up the Civil Rights Act of 1964 and Goldwater had to cast the most difficult vote of his life.

FIRST DATE

One of the Goldwaterites who traveled to Washington for the July 4 rally at the National Guard Armory was Anne Stevens, who afterward went to Carol Dawson Bauman's home. My name came up, and Anne took a never-mailed letter out of her purse and showed it to Carol. It was in the form of a letter to the editor of the *New Guard* in which Anne congratulated me for finally putting out a good magazine filled with news and photos about YAF and its political activities and not pretentious columns and articles by young conservatives not yet ready for prime time—that is, *National Review*. Carol laughed and put the letter in her purse, promising to give it to me at the next editorial meeting of the *New Guard* (she was managing editor). Anne protested that she never meant to mail it, but Carol would not give it back.

My initial reaction to Anne's letter was incredulity. What did she mean "finally"? The *New Guard* had been brilliant from the beginning under my editorship. Our editorials were clever, our book reviews insightful, our analyses about Cuba, the National Student Association, the House Committee on Un-American Activities, hard-hitting.

I was also intrigued. Who was this girl who did not recognize my many talents? I did what any young cock of the walk would do—I telephoned her and after some preliminary bantering asked for a date. She replied she was quite busy at present. I was stunned—I had not been turned down by a girl since high school.

A week later, I asked her out again and got the same cool response. I was now determined. The volleying went on for another month until late August, when I wrote Miss Stevens that I would be traveling in Europe with my mother for the next two weeks. When I returned, I said, I would call on her and we would begin a weekend together with dinner at a very good French restaurant.

It was mid-September, I recall, when I walked up the three flights to her railroad flat on the Upper East Side and knocked on the door. I had read that on a first date the boy would make a good impression if he presented flowers and candy to the girl and made her laugh. Anne opened the door. She was wearing a white molded dress that set off her dark hair and olive skin. She was more beautiful than I remembered. It was almost a year since I had seen her for the first and only time at the YAF convention.

I handed her a single red rose and then a Hershey chocolate bar, which brought a smile. Encouraged, I pulled out of my pocket a New Year's Eve horn and blew vigorously, the rude noise echoing in the hallway. The smile disappeared. Well, I thought, two out of three isn't bad. I did not learn until later that when she went to get her coat, she said to her roommate, Joan Lawton, "It's going to be a long evening."

In fact, we had a wonderful evening over steak au poivre and a Caesar salad and Châteauneuf-du-Pape at Le Chambord, followed by a Saturday afternoon visit to the Metropolitan Museum of Art, a leisurely dinner at the Gay Vienna in Yorkville, Sunday Mass at Saint Patrick's Cathedral and a lighted candle at Our Lady's Chapel, and coffee, cake, and violins in the Palm Court of the Plaza (where we would spend our wedding night a year and a half later). It was the beginning of a fifty-year marriage and partnership filled with two daughters, eleven grandchildren, honors foreign and domestic, gambles and mistakes, embezzlement, and hard-gained financial security, the deaths of good friends and loving relatives, collaborations with Dr. Judd, Bill Buckley, Barry Goldwater, Russell Kirk, Ed Feulner, Jay Parker (we were the first racially integrated public affairs firm serving the right), Lev Dobriansky, David Jones, all bound up in our mutual commitment to freedom and opposition to all forms of tyranny.

"BREATHLESSLY CLOSE"

By early October 1963, it was clear that Barry Goldwater would be a presidential candidate—he had directed his old friend and family lawyer Denison Kitchel to open a Washington office. The political news got better for Goldwater and worse for Governor Nelson Rockefeller of New York, the senator's principal opponent for the Republican nomination. When Governor Rockefeller and his new wife, Happy, visited a Republican picnic in Illinois, they were greeted with a sea of Goldwater buttons and balloons. One columnist wrote of their visit, "It was like observing a political corpse who did not realize he was dead." Republicans preferred their leaders to be above moral reproach. Rocky had sorely disappointed them by divorcing his wife of three decades and marrying a much younger and just divorced woman who had been his private secretary and who relinquished custody of her four children to obtain her divorce.

In contrast, nearly fifty thousand enthusiasts jammed Dodger Stadium in Los Angeles to hear Goldwater deliver an address written by Karl Hess, a new speechwriter whom the senator nicknamed "Shakespeare." He was interrupted by cheers and applause forty-seven times. Clif White kept lining up delegates in the wake of Goldwater's appearances. Our cup overflowed when *Time* published a state-by-state survey that showed Goldwater giving President Kennedy "a breathlessly close race," especially in the South.

In early November, Peter O'Donnell hired me as news director of the National Draft Goldwater Committee. I was given no assurance I would be retained when the Draft Committee was folded into the forthcoming

Goldwater for President Committee, but I was confident they would find something for me to do. It was worth the gamble to be part of a campaign and a crusade to put a conservative in the White House.

In the fall of 1963, the idea of a President Goldwater was not a chimera. This was pre-Camelot, and though President Kennedy's approval ratings were good in the North, they were weak in the South, where Goldwater was strong. The news media were intrigued by the possibility of a Kennedy-Goldwater contest with its clear philosophical choice between left and right.

The two men were looking forward to the campaign. They had talked about participating in a series of great debates, like Lincoln and Douglas in 1858, traveling from city to city on the same plane. Although they differed mightily on issues, except for communism, they liked and respected each other. Kennedy was a moderate liberal who looked to government to solve the most difficult economic problems. Goldwater was a libertarian conservative who had never met a government program he didn't want to cut or repeal—with the exception of the Pentagon budget.

Joining the Draft Goldwater team was like being called up from Class AA Harrisburg to play for the Washington Nationals. I was sure I could make the cut. The senator knew me from YAF, as did his veteran press secretary, Tony Smith, who looked on me as something of a protégé. My first official day with the National Draft Goldwater Committee was set for Monday, November 25. I could hardly wait. I didn't have to.

6

THE DAY KENNEDY DIED

I was having a mai tai in Trader Vic's in the Statler Hilton Hotel with an old friend when a waiter came running through the restaurant crying, "The president's been shot! The president's been shot! In Dallas!"

I looked at my watch: it was 1:40 P.M. I was up the stairs and out of the hotel in less than a minute. I hurried along K Street. All around me, people were walking fast, almost running, as if they did not want to be caught out in the open. I turned right at Farragut Square, headed up Connecticut Avenue, and turned in at 1025. Across the small lobby and alongside the curtained French doors was a small brass plaque that read, "National Draft Goldwater Committee."

I entered a large workroom with faded yellow walls, a scuffed wooden floor, a half dozen secondhand metal desks, and unforgiving fluorescent light. Along the walls were piles of pamphlets and stacks of paperbacks— mostly *The Conscience of a Conservative* and *You Can Trust the Communists (to Be Communists)* by Dr. Fred Schwarz. A dented coffee urn with a dripping spigot stood on a small metal table in the corner.

This is what I wrote in my campaign diary (the only diary I ever kept):

> The Goldwater Committee was bedlam—phones ringing, girls walking back and forth, people huddled around the radio. Peter O'Donnell was somewhere on his way back to Dallas. Clif White and Tom Van Sickle were in St. Louis for a meeting of the Midwest

GOP state committees. No one was in charge. The press release about my appointment had gone out that day and I had 12 calls already. "No comment" was all I could say until I talked to Peter or Clif.

We "kids," as Clif White called us, had been left to answer the phones and take messages on what should have been a lazy fall day. The traffic was light and the lunches were long as they always were when the president was out of town. Most congressmen had already left for the weekend, aides were thinking about the happy hour at the Carroll Arms Hotel across from the New Senate Office Building, and the press galleries in the House and the Senate were deserted except for a few hearts players.

But the city was jolted into a frenzy by the bulletin from Dallas—"Kennedy Shot!"—and we were drawn into the vortex. Nearly everyone, including me, thought that someone on our side, a Bircher, a Minuteman, a follower of General Edwin Walker, had pulled the trigger.

I walked into Clif's small, windowless office and turned on his twelve-inch black-and-white TV to get the latest news. As the minutes passed, the faces of Walter Cronkite and the other network anchors became fixed as though they knew something they did not want to report.

At 2:33 P.M. ET, an out-of-breath Malcolm Kilduff, an assistant to White House press secretary Pierre Salinger, stepped before an impatient pack of reporters at Dallas's Parkland Memorial Hospital. Slowly, reluctantly, he said, "President John F. Kennedy died at approximately one o'clock Central Standard Time today here in Dallas." The AP and UPI reporters ran from the room to find a telephone. "He died of a gunshot wound in the brain. I have no other details regarding the assassination of the president. Mrs. Kennedy was not hit. Governor [John] Connally was hit. The vice president was not hit."

Judy Lewis and the other Goldwater girls began crying. I murmured three Hail Marys for the repose of the president's soul. I couldn't help thinking: were we dead, too?

Someone pounded on our door so hard the windowpanes rattled and the shades shook as if in a strong wind. "Murderers!" someone cried. I walked over and locked the doors.

Judy picked up a phone and turned white. "He says there's a bomb."

We called 911. Two police officers arrived and cleared the lobby. There was no sign of a bomb. They looked behind the pamphlets and books and under a few desks. They looked at us, pale and dazed, and suggested we go home.

"They were just blowing off steam," one officer said. "You can't blame them. Everyone's upset with the president being murdered."

"But we had nothing to do with it," Judy said in her soft southern accent. The black policeman looked at her. "We didn't," Judy insisted, her voice suddenly more southern.

None of us wanted to go home and sit alone waiting to learn who had killed the president. So we stood before the small TV in the dim light of an old brass desk lamp and watched the networks try to bury Barry Goldwater and his campaign.

"President Kennedy was in Dallas, the heart of Goldwaterland," NBC's Chet Huntley said, "seeking to repair political fences."

"The ultra-right John Birch Society has become increasingly active in Dallas," one network reported. "Last month they made it clear they did not want UN ambassador Adlai Stevenson in their city." The screen showed angry middle-aged white men and women crowding and jostling Stevenson.

The anti-Goldwater rhetoric crested when Walter Cronkite said, "Senator Goldwater is giving a political speech in Indiana and is not expected to attend President Kennedy's wake and funeral."

I was furious. Anyone covering Goldwater, and that included CBS, knew he was in Muncie, Indiana, with Mrs. Goldwater for her mother's funeral and burial. And every political reporter in Washington was aware that Goldwater and Kennedy were good friends despite being philosophically as different as Hayek and Keynes. I called the Washington bureau of CBS News, but all the lines were busy.

The next two hours moved as slowly as a Senate debate. I sat drinking coffee in Clif's office, waiting for the word that Kennedy's assassin was one of ours. It was reported that the Dallas police were conducting a massive manhunt for a gunman who had shot a Dallas cop. I wondered: was he the same man who had killed Kennedy?

ONE OF THEIRS

At 4:15 p.m. ET, NBC announced that a suspect in the Kennedy assassination had been arrested. His name was Lee Harvey Oswald. I had never heard of him. All over America conservatives were checking their membership and donor lists. Then a reporter said, quoting the Associated Press, that Oswald was a member of the Fair Play for Cuba Committee.

"Praise the Lord!" I said.

"What is it?" Judy asked.

"The Fair Play for Cuba Committee is pro-Castro and pro-communist. Oswald isn't one of ours—he's one of *theirs*."

I learned later that Ed Butler of the Information Council of the Americas (INCA) in New Orleans had provided the information about Oswald's ultra-left background. Ed had debated Oswald on a New Orleans radio station in August. Following the debate he had put out a press release giving Oswald's personal history, including his defection to the Soviet Union and his public admission, "I am a Marxist."

Ed had sent an information packet about Oswald to a Washington friend, bald, burly Eugene Methvin of *Reader's Digest*, who set it aside for future reading. Now, on the afternoon of November 22, when Methvin heard the name Lee Harvey Oswald, he said to himself, "I know that name—he's got a communist connection."

He began leafing through a two-foot-high stack on the table behind his desk and found the INCA folder. He scanned it quickly and ran down the stairs to the first floor of the National Press Building, where the AP had its offices. He grabbed the arm of a reporter friend and said, "Do you know who Lee Harvey Oswald is?"

"No, and everybody in the world is trying to find out."

"Read this," said Methvin, thrusting the INCA folder into his hands. "He's a pro-Castro communist."

At first skeptical, the reporter skimmed through the news release and other material and his face lit up. "Gene, I owe you a roast beef dinner at Duke Zeibert's."

I refrained from thinking about what the media would have done to us had Oswald been the New Orleans secretary of the John Birch Society. Even so, Kennedy's death was almost certainly a fatal blow to our chances to win the presidency. I accepted the political calculus—Americans wouldn't want three presidents in one year.

But capturing the Republican nomination was different. Clif had been on the road for months, visiting state after state, traveling thousands of miles, lining up convention delegates who were as committed to Goldwater as they were to their church. With a little bit of luck and a couple of primary victories, we could win the nomination. And that would be a giant step toward establishing the conservative movement—and the anticommunist cause—as a viable political project in America.

"BE OUR DEFENSE"

By seven o'clock the Draft Goldwater office was as quiet as a confessional. The telephones no longer rang and the girls had put covers over their typewriters. We turned off the television and the coffeepot and the lights. Peter and Clif said that out of respect for Kennedy and until we knew the senator's decision, the committee would not engage in any political activity for thirty days.

Back in my apartment on Columbia Road, I turned on the television— it was JFK all the time—and called Anne.

"Saved by Fidel Castro," she said. "Who would have thought it?"

"You never thought it was one of us?"

"Most of the conservatives I know shoot from the lip. I hear Barry may not run, and who can blame him? His chances of winning the White House have gone from possible to impossible. Even the nomination is not the sure thing it was twenty-four hours ago."

I listened respectfully. I dated Anne as much for her brains as her beauty. "We have to convince the senator to run," I said.

YAF had already begun a national telephone-telegram-letter campaign pressing Goldwater to become a candidate. Anne promised to organize a letter-writing party in Suite 3505, Clif White's New York office in the Chanin Building, across from Grand Central Station. We said good night, each promising to share any promising news about the senator.

I fried myself a hamburger and washed it down with a National Boh. A little groggy, I turned off the television—tired of seeing Jack and Jackie smiling and waving in Dallas, a solemn Lyndon Johnson taking the presidential oath in Air Force One, Lee Harvey Oswald passing out Fair Play for Cuba leaflets on a New Orleans street corner—and got into bed.

Goldwater versus Kennedy would have been a hard-fought but fair fight. Goldwater versus Johnson would be no-holds-barred, with LBJ doing whatever was necessary to win. No matter. The senator had a *duty* to raise the conservative banner, to lead the nation down the road to liberty, to keep faith with those who had urged him and expected him to run. And if we didn't prevail in November, well, sometimes you win by losing.

My mind kept jumping around like a June bug, but at last things slowed down. I looked back over the day, examining my thoughts and my words, what I had done and had not done, resolving with His grace to do better on the morrow. I prayed:

Saint Michael the Archangel, defend us in battle.
Be our defense against the wickedness and snares of the Devil.
May God rebuke him, we humbly pray.
And do thou, O Prince of the Heavenly host, by the power of God,
Cast into hell Satan and all the evil spirits
Who prowl about the world seeking the ruin of souls.
Amen.

7

DECISION TIME

On Sunday morning I walked down Connecticut Avenue to attend the 11 o'clock Mass at Saint Matthew's Cathedral, where they were preparing for Kennedy's funeral Mass the next day. Behind the altar were the stacks of chairs that would be placed in the aisles and along the sides for the overflow of people. Seats were at a premium, and I was not on the list.

After Mass, I walked slowly home. Stores already had put photos of Kennedy framed in black in their front windows. I stopped to buy a twenty-ounce container of coffee, two strawberry jelly doughnuts, and the Sunday *New York Times*. Traffic was light even for a Sunday afternoon. I got to my apartment shortly before 1 p.m. I picked up the front section of the *Times* to see what they were saying about the senator and turned on the television.

Slack-jawed, I watched a replay of Lee Harvey Oswald, dressed in a dark sweater and dark pants, clutching his stomach and bending forward in pain as a gunman in a dark fedora fired once while shocked Dallas policemen in their white cowboy hats looked on, frozen in place. NBC, the only network at the police station for Oswald's transfer, showed the scene over and over—TV's first real-time murder.

I sat down heavily, the *Times* slipping from my hands. I took deep breaths and finally my racing heart settled into a normal rhythm. How could the killer get so close? Was he acting alone or was he a hit man for someone? Who wanted to silence Oswald—the Soviets? the Cubans? Was the killer part of some conspiracy?

That afternoon, following Jackie Kennedy's instructions that the ceremony emulate Lincoln's funeral, the president's dark mahogany coffin was carried up Pennsylvania Avenue on a horse-drawn caisson and placed on a black-draped catafalque in the Rotunda of the Capitol. I listened as Chief Justice Earl Warren, House Speaker John McCormack, and Senate Majority Leader Mike Mansfield took turns blaming us for Kennedy's death. Warren denounced "hatemongering," while Mansfield bemoaned "the bigotry, the hatred, prejudice, and the arrogance which converged in that moment of horror to strike [the president] down." Will they ever stop accusing us? I wondered. How could Goldwater run in such a hateful climate?

The next day, again a captive of television, I watched the solemn march of the Kennedys and honored guests—French president Charles de Gaulle towering above the tiny emperor Haile Selassie—from the White House to Saint Matthew's, where Cardinal Richard Cushing was the principal celebrant of the Latin Mass. After the final prayers, Cushing circled the bier three times, incensing the coffin and sprinkling it with holy water and praying, "Requiem aeternam dona eis, Domine, et lux perpetua luceat eis." David Brinkley translated for the non-Catholics and for many post–Vatican II Catholics: "Eternal rest grant unto them, O Lord, and let perpetual light shine upon them." Suddenly the cardinal, overcome with grief, cried out in English, "May the angels, dear Jack, lead you into Paradise!"

As they bore the casket down the aisle and out of the cathedral, the band struck up "Hail to the Chief," soldiers snapped to attention, and officers and policemen saluted. Jackie Kennedy leaned over and said something to little John standing beside her. He raised his right hand in a salute to his father, the fallen commander in chief. It was a good salute, his hand touching his hair, his left arm straight at his side.

I heard from "reliable sources" that Goldwater had decided not to run against LBJ, and not just because of the long odds. From his days in the Senate, he had watched Johnson do anything to win a vote, including allowing Bobby Baker, his handpicked clerk of the Senate, arrange afternoon "dates" for randy senators at the Alibi Club in the Carroll Arms Hotel.

We didn't know if our letter-telegram-telephone campaign would change the senator's mind. All we could do was wait for the outcome of Goldwater's December 8 meeting with his senior advisers in his Westchester apartment in Northwest Washington. I later learned from Denny Kitchel and others there how he had decided to run.

"I DON'T THINK YOU CAN BACK DOWN"

The senator began by saying, "Our cause is lost," arguing that no Republican could win in 1964 because Americans would not want three different presidents in barely one year. The idea of running against Johnson was abhorrent to him—Johnson was a wheeler-dealer, a hypocrite on civil rights, a dirty fighter. The plan that Goldwater and Jack had had of flying together from city to city and debating the issues was gone. Johnson would never agree to debate him. The campaign would be one not of ideas and issues but of half-truths and lies, as always in a Johnson campaign.

Like a Greek chorus, everyone at the meeting—Senators Norris Cotton of New Hampshire and Carl Curtis of Nebraska, Representative John Rhodes of Arizona, Peter O'Donnell, and John Grenier of Alabama—said the same thing: Goldwater had no choice but to run. This was the conservative hour—it was now or never. If Goldwater did not run, the Republican Party would remain in the hands of Nelson Rockefeller, George Romney, Richard Nixon, and the rest of the eastern liberal establishment. The last to speak was Senator Cotton, a large man with a dominating voice, who compared Goldwater to de Gaulle, the leader of the renaissance of postwar France. No one else had Goldwater's "mass appeal," Cotton said, his vision, his character, his ability to turn America in a conservative direction. "This is the hour, this is *your* hour," Cotton said. "This is your destiny. We will follow you. You have only to give the command."

Cotton's appeal brought tears to many in the room. They waited for Goldwater to respond, but he was silent. At last he asked them to let him "sleep on it" and thanked them for coming. He motioned to Kitchel to stay behind.

The two old friends sat silently in the fading amber light of a December afternoon. Goldwater turned on a table lamp, went to the liquor cabinet, and poured several inches of bourbon into two glasses, adding water for Denny. He remembered what he had said to his wife, Peggy: he didn't want to be president, but he wanted conservatives to have a voice. If no one challenged the Democrats, they would wreck the economy with their spending. And their policy of accommodation with the Soviets would only encourage the communists to keep slicing away at the free world.

Someone had to rally the conservatives to take over the Republican Party and start turning the nation around.

"What do you think?" Goldwater asked.

"What do *you* think?" retorted Kitchel.

"I know Norris and the others mean well, and I share their concern about the direction of the country. Hell, I've been talking about the dangers we face since I came to the Senate twelve years ago. I appreciate they've gone out on a limb for me, especially Norris up in New Hampshire. But damn it, this isn't our time. I can't win. No Republican can. And if I lose badly that would hurt the movement we've worked so hard to build."

Kitchel took a sip of his drink and said calmly, "Barry, I don't think you can back down."

The blunt words surprised the senator.

"You let the Draft Committee operate for more than two years," Kitchel said. "Hundreds of delegates have pledged themselves to you. You told me to set up a Washington office, which I did. You've talked to the press about the kind of campaign you would run—based on conservative principles. You've let just about everyone come to the conclusion that you are going to be a candidate. If you decided not to run now, a lot of good people like those here this afternoon would feel that Barry Goldwater has left them holding the bag."

"But everything has changed with Jack's death," Goldwater protested.

"The people who believe in you, especially the young people, have not changed. They've taken a stand for you—they expect you to stand up, too."

Goldwater knew what it would be like. Liberal Republicans would stop at nothing to deny him the nomination, because they were determined to retain control of the party that had been theirs for decades, from Willkie to Nixon. The press saw him as a wild cowboy from the West. Things wouldn't get any better if he were nominated. Landslide Lyndon would use every dirty trick in his big bag to win.

But there was no denying he had become the spokesman of the conservative wing of the Republican Party through the hundreds of speeches he had given, by publishing *The Conscience of a Conservative* (with Brent Bozell's help), by taking on Ike in 1958 when the president submitted an unbalanced budget that Goldwater had called "a dime-store New Deal." He had forged a bond with conservatives, especially young conservatives, that was just about unbreakable. How could he now let them down?

"All right, goddamn it," he said, "I'll do it." But, he added to himself, I'm going to run my way.

GOLDWATER FOR PRESIDENT

The first thing I did when I learned early the next day that Goldwater would run was to offer a prayer of thanksgiving at Saint Joseph's on Capitol Hill. I went to the Draft Committee office, still officially closed, and worked on a memorandum about the use of television in the campaign. I pictured Goldwater on a Florida beach talking about Communist Cuba just ninety miles away, Goldwater in front of a run-down public school in New York or Chicago challenging the local community to fix up the school and get the right books to students, Goldwater in the cockpit of a jet plane pledging to increase the defense budget and defend a free South Vietnam.

I did not know what my role might be with the Goldwater for President Committee. More experienced professionals were certainly available, but no one would work harder or had a better understanding of the senator and his record.

8

A CHOICE, NOT AN ECHO

On Friday afternoon, January 3, 1964, two days after his fifty-fifth birthday and on crutches because of an operation on his right heel, Barry Goldwater—Achilles in a dark blue suit—limped onto the patio of his hilltop home overlooking Phoenix to announce his candidacy for president of the United States. We had tried to persuade him to make the announcement in Washington, the center of the political universe, and anytime but Friday afternoon. But Phoenix was his home, and he didn't care how or whether the press covered his announcement. What he said was pure Goldwater, drafted by him:

> I have decided to seek the Republican presidential nomination because of the principles in which I believe and because I am convinced that millions of Americans share my belief in those principles.... I will not change my beliefs to win votes. I will campaign for limited government and individual responsibility and against regimentation that threatens to make us, our lives, our property, our hopes, and even our prayers... just cogs in a vast government machine. It was the young people who persuaded me to run. I felt that if I didn't make myself available, they might become discouraged.

The camera came in close on the senator's tanned face, with no hint of the double chin that marked most middle-aged men, set off by silvery white hair and bright blue eyes behind black horn-rimmed glasses. He looked straight into the camera and said, "I will offer a choice, not an echo."

This was the candidate we had been waiting for.

By late January, the Goldwater for President Committee had sixty-two people on its payroll at its two locations in Washington, D.C.: 1101 Connecticut Avenue NW and 1025 Connecticut Avenue NW. One slot still unfilled was director of information. I served as acting director, taking calls from reporters, drafting statements, accompanying the senator on a trip to Pittsburgh when his press secretary, Tony Smith, was sick and asked me to take his place. Then it was announced that Basil (Bud) Littin, a seasoned professional who had worked in Robert Taft's 1950 Senate campaign, would join us as public relations director. Of course I was disappointed, but I was relieved we now had someone in charge of communications. I looked forward to working with him.

In the meantime, I accompanied the senator and Mrs. Goldwater on a trip to Kinston, North Carolina, along with Tony and Jim Ellis, a Capitol Hill staffer familiar with Carolina politics. On the plane, I chatted with Goldwater, who after a few minutes said, "Well, I guess it's time to write my speech."

I recounted the trip in my campaign diary:

I looked at Tony who looked back at me and we gossiped about this and that (two ghost writers sitting on the sidelines) while the Senator wrote his own speech. It was a good speech about self-reliance and initiative and participating in politics and it was well-received by an enthusiastic audience of about 1,200. The Jaycee president told me they could have sold 5,000 tickets, but the Democrats warned him that if they held that big an event for a Republican, the Jaycees were dead in Kinston.

There was a reception afterward at the Kinston Country Club and a call came through for Goldwater and I took it. A Bob Seine (like the river in Paris, he said) was calling from Durham and he wanted to invite the Senator to come up to Durham the next morning, Saturday, to talk to the leaders in the Piedmont region of the White Citizens Council. They had heard George Wallace and Mr. Seine, who was a 100 percent backer of Goldwater, wanted them to meet the Senator. My first reaction was to wonder whether the call was some kind of trap and if our conversation was being recorded. After a few minutes I realized that Mr. Seine was indeed a leader of the White Citizens Council but totally unfamiliar with political reality. I begged off for the Senator, explaining he was scheduled to be in Fayetteville the following morning. I then excused myself when Mr. Seine invited me to address the Council. So much for the Southern (i.e., racist) Strategy the liberals insisted we were following.

Up the next morning at 6:30 A.M. After the Fayetteville breakfast, we flew back to Washington in what Goldwater called the Green Goose, a DC-3 that we used for short campaign trips up and down the East Coast. The Senator flew the plane for 20 minutes or so and then played gin rummy with Peggy. He was kidding all the time, and they kept laughing. A wonderful sound and sight—after 30 years of marriage.

Because Littin decided to work from New York City, I had to do a lot of coordination at committee headquarters. I usually put in twelve-hour days Monday through Friday and spent most of Saturday catching up on what I hadn't done during the week. Sunday was reserved for Mass and rest.

At times my inexperience was exposed. I wrote the copy and okayed the design for a campaign postcard titled "Ten Reasons Why We Should Select Goldwater President." One side was a full-color photo of a smiling Goldwater; the other side listed the ten reasons, which had been approved by Tony Smith, Kitchel, Littin, and others. Jack Morris, who did most of our printing and had an artist at his firm, sent me a final proof. The first batch of two hundred arrived and they were beautiful, all blue and gold, with a marvelous photo of the senator.

Everyone loved it, and then our office manager, Jim Day, called me into his little office and said, "Lee, I've been looking at your card and I have a question: where is the authority line?" I realized we had omitted the obligatory "By Authority Of" and a name. Every piece of campaign literature of a declared candidate for president or vice president must carry the name of his campaign committee and the name of a committee officer. I almost cried.

I immediately called Jack Morris, who said he would see what he could do. Within a couple of hours, Jack called to say that he had reserved twelve Heidelberg hand presses to run the 250,000 postcards by hand and imprint the required authority line. The cost—$325. I was so relieved I would have paid it out of my own pocket. The following day, Jack delivered the now-legal postcards, which became an early staple of the committee.

On an average day, I talked with Dave Broder of the *Washington Star*, Bob Boyd of the *Chicago Daily News*, Robert (Robin) MacNeil of NBC, Bob Pierpoint of CBS, John Goldsmith of ABC, Wally Mears of the Associated Press (the political reporter whose leads were frequently paraphrased by other reporters), columnist/author Ralph de Toledano, Carl DeBloom of the *Columbus Dispatch*, Lyn Nofziger of the *San Diego Union*, and my father, Willard Edwards of the *Chicago Tribune* (the last three being the only daily reporters sympathetic to the senator and our cause).

Over a Sunday dinner, Dad gave me some good advice about countering bad press. Personally cultivate reporters, he said, so as to dull their coolness or hostility. Don't complain, ever, about what they have written, but get them on your side with quick, efficient service and a smile. Lunches for three or four reporters at a time can help, but large press parties with lots of booze are a waste of time and money.

Sometimes our bad press was the result of careless remarks by our candidate. On his first visit to New Hampshire the first week of January, Goldwater said two things that provided our opponents, Republican and Democratic, with themes they used to try and sink us.

At a Concord news conference, the senator was asked whether he favored continuing the Social Security system. He replied that for years he had said the system was actuarially unsound and a pseudo–insurance program that was inadequately funded. He would suggest "one change"—that participation in the program be made voluntary. "If a person can provide better for himself, let him do it. But if he prefers the government to do it, let him."

Social Security was and still is a third-rail issue that prudent politicians avoid. But not Barry Goldwater. He might have survived the "voluntary" suggestion if he had not added—a bad habit of his—that people could "get a better Social Security program" through private insurance. That seemed to place him in the "It's time to replace Social Security" camp—which is where the pro-Rockefeller *Concord Monitor* newspaper put him. A *Monitor* headline read: GOLDWATER SETS GOALS; END SOCIAL SECURITY, HIT CASTRO. Within forty-eight hours, the Rockefeller organization had distributed a reprint of the *Monitor* article to every Republican household in the state and later to every recipient of Social Security in New Hampshire, of whom there were many thousands.

That was not all. In another news conference the same day, Goldwater was asked about his foreign policy, specifically NATO. There was this exchange:

Q How about nuclear weapons?

A I have said, the commander should have the ability to use nuclear weapons. Former commanders have told me that NATO troops should be equipped with nuclear weapons, but the use should remain only with the commander.

Goldwater was clearly referring to *the* commander of NATO and to the use of *tactical* nuclear weapons. But several reporters wrote that Goldwater wanted to turn over the authority to use nuclear weapons to *commanders* in the field. The *New York Times* got it right, thanks to its correspondent Charles Mohr, who reported that Goldwater specifically denied that he favored the authority for local NATO commanders. But spurred on by Rockefeller's disinformation machine, voters got the impression that Goldwater backed the use of nuclear weapons, period. A Dr. Strangelove image was created, and the seeds of a key question were planted: "Who do you want in the room with the Bomb?"

Six months later, *U.S. News & World Report* disclosed that what Goldwater had suggested in New Hampshire had been established policy under Presidents Eisenhower and Kennedy. The NATO commander did have the authority "under certain carefully defined circumstances" to use "battlefield atomic weapons" without the express consent of the president. Among the circumstances was a full-scale tank-led invasion of Western Europe by the Soviet Union. But the confirmation came too late. The idea of Barry Goldwater as a trigger-happy cowboy had been planted in the minds of many Americans. As Peter O'Donnell put it, Goldwater picked up "an atomic thorn in his foot" in New Hampshire that harried him throughout his campaign for the presidency.

In my campaign diary I wrote:

> You never do enough. The magnitude of a national campaign is staggering to the mind and to the body. We are putting together a national organization—the only ones to do so. Rocky is banking (!) all on a few primaries. He is pouring money into N.H., Oregon and California.... But BG has done so much for the Party, met so many people, raised so much money that Rocky can't make inroads into every state and region. N.H. is now so split with BG, Rocky, Sen. [Margaret Chase] Smith, and Wes Powell that a clear-cut winner is unexpected. Unless Rocky can overcome the [New Hampshire] reticence with $ and organization or we can dissolve New England reserve with Western charm and candor....

How silly it is really that so much time, money and effort [are] being expended in New Hampshire which has about 110,000 registered Republicans. BG said again that the crucial primary would be California. He is really scheduled to tour that monster—in fact his schedule is a back breaker, all over the 50 states, including Hawaii. That's one trip I wouldn't mind making!

Instead I traveled north.

PRIMARY TIME

The sidewalks and the streets of Concord, New Hampshire, were clear, but the snow, still white, was thigh-high in the front yards of the homes we drove by. The sun was supra-bright and the sky was as blue as a mountain lake. I wished I had brought my sunglasses. As long as I stood in the sun, I didn't need an overcoat, but when I stepped into a shadow I immediately felt the cold. We were headed for Katie's Kitchen, where the senator would pretend to have lunch while the photographers took pictures and the reporters recorded what he said to the customers who were willing to play their part.

"Hi, I'm Barry Goldwater, and I'm running for president."

"Hi, I'm Sam Adams, and I'm eating lunch. But I have a question for you. Are you going to increase my taxes?"

"Sam, there's as much chance of my increasing your taxes as there is that it won't snow again in New Hampshire."

"Well, if you stick to that—and I hear you're a man of your word—and if you promise not to mess with Social Security (my mother depends on it), I may vote for you."

"Sam, you have my word," the senator replied, smiling, and went on down the counter shaking hands and saying a few words to each person until he stopped in front of Katie and had a bite of her coconut cream pie. He passed on the coffee, explaining that "our mother told us that drinking coffee and smoking cigarettes would stunt our growth. She never said anything about alcohol."

I was in New Hampshire as the senator's traveling press secretary because Tony Smith's stomach was acting up again. "Don't worry about the press," Tony said. "The most important thing is to make sure they have a bed to sleep in. And don't worry about handouts—Barry will give them plenty to write about."

How true. Despite the hundreds of speeches he had given and the years of campaigning, Goldwater was engaged in something new—running for president. For the first time in his political life, he was the object of an unblinking, unending scrutiny by the press, the public, and members of his own party. The Mayo Clinic couldn't have been more thorough in its examination.

In Arizona, his profanity was dry-cleaned and his bloopers rewritten by reporters who worked for friendly newspapers like the *Arizona Republic*. But in the first primary of a presidential campaign, everything mattered—a careless phrase, a puzzled look, a fit of anger. Everything was disseminated by the national press—SEND IN THE MARINES, SENATOR URGES—and exploited by opponents. The adjustment to a national campaign would have been difficult under the best of circumstances, but Goldwater was still looking back at the campaign that might have been.

And he had not expected it would take him so long to recover from foot surgery. Wearing a heavy walking cast, he limped from a factory gate at 6 A.M. to a midmorning coffee in someone's front parlor to a lunch counter at noon to a midafternoon coffee to a pre-speech drink with donors to an evening talk in a meeting hall or school auditorium, as many as twelve appearances in a day. Such a schedule would put a normal person in bed, perhaps a hospital bed, but presidential candidates can't afford to be normal. They have to keep ticking like a Timex watch.

"I'll remember every step of this campaign," the senator said at the end of another marathon day, sipping from a water glass half-filled with bourbon. Glancing at Norris Cotton seated across from him, he said, "What are you trying to—kill me?"

"This is how we campaign in New Hampshire," Cotton replied.

"One damn vote at a time."

And there was the problem of getting the senator to stick to a script. One day, at the first stop, he said he would be inclined to withdraw from the United Nations if Communist China were seated. Midmorning, he said the United States should remain in the UN despite China's entry. At the next stop he said that if the mainland Chinese replaced the Nationalist Chinese in the UN, it would blow U.S. participation in the UN to pieces. In his evening talk, he digressed from the prepared text to protest, "I've never said, 'Let's get out of the UN.' I don't know how that rumor ever got started."

When a reporter asked me why Goldwater kept changing his position on the UN at every stop, I tried to make light of it: "He gets bored making the same speech every time."

"The man's running for president," the reporter responded. "When is he going to get serious?"

When I brought up the exchange with the senator, he smiled and said, "Lee, you don't know how much trouble I'm going to cause you."

From my campaign diary:

We flew high over the White Mountains in our DC-3 (nick-named the Green Goose because it was painted green) to Berlin, a depressed town in a depressed area reminiscent of West Virginia before Sen. Robert Byrd began pouring in the federal dollars. Four hundred friendlys turned out for us at the evening rally although we were competing with a high school basketball game and a concert by the Tucson, Arizona Boys Chorus of which, believe it or not, Goldwater is a trustee. We stayed overnight at the Costello Hotel where we dined late and surprisingly well on rare roast beef with a touch of garlic accompanied by an excellent burgundy. The Senator was upset—we forgot to bring along some Old Crow for post-rally sipping. I got to bed about 1 A.M., because I had to make sure all the reporters had rooms. I didn't sleep well—my first time on the road as the press secretary to a presidential candidate.

The next day we were at the University of New Hampshire in Durham where the Senator had dinner with a dozen awed YRs— the girls glow when he looks at them—and then spoke in the field house to about 1,800 ecstatics, easily outdrawing Rocky when he was here. The leftwing students with their scraggly beards and torn jeans passed out anti-Goldwater literature.

It had been a long always-on-the-go day, but the Senator shook the hands of every student. I noticed that the women, young and old, moved in close when they could. He was relaxed but reserved. "I'm not one of those baby-kissing, blintz-eating candidates," he explained. "I don't like to insult the American intelligence by think-ing that slapping people on the back is going to win you votes." I think his laid-back style goes well in a state where people can be as granite-like as the ground.

That night in the large Keene High School cafeteria, the Sena-tor was never better calling for a rebirth of strength and integrity in America. He is right out of the Old Testament, I thought, warning the people that things are perilously wrong and they must repent and reform their wasteful ways. I wish he'd pause to let the crowd cheer the good lines, I said to myself. "At home," Goldwater said, "our crime rates soar, rising four times as fast as our population. The quick buck, the dime novel romances, morality that works on a sliding scale depending on your position. These have replaced what Teddy Roosevelt called Americanism—'the virtues of courage, honor, justice, truth, sincerity and hardihood'—the virtues that made America."

I think, no, I *know* we are going to win.

TV AND TVA

"That's not what I hear," Anne said on the phone.

"From whom?" I asked sharply.

"Please, Lee, don't shoot the messenger. Charlie Wiley is up in New Hampshire working the phones and talking to people, and he figures Goldwater will be lucky to get 30 percent."

"I don't believe it," I said defensively.

"Did you hear about the two Republican women discussing who they're going to vote for?" Anne asked.

The first woman says, "I'm not going to vote for Goldwater."

"Why, Marie," says the second woman, "you've been a conservative all your life and Goldwater is a conservative. Why ever not?"

"He's going to take away my TV."

"No, no, Marie," says the second woman, "he's going to sell TVA, not your TV."

"Well," says the first woman, "I'm not taking any chances. I'm voting for that nice-looking Lodge."

"Very funny," I said to Anne.

"I love Barry Goldwater," Anne said. "I fell in love with him the first time I heard him speak at the National Federation of Republican Women luncheon in the Waldorf. He was so honest he took my breath away. But you don't have to be 100 percent conservative all the time."

"Then he wouldn't be Barry Goldwater."

"In which case," she said, "there may never be a President Goldwater." We talked a little longer, but Anne could tell my mind was elsewhere.

"You're tired," she said. "We'd better say good night."

"I've got a meeting with Denny tomorrow morning about the director of information. He's promised to make a decision."

"He'll make the right decision," Anne said. "You."

THE ONE LEFT STANDING

Denny and Tony had grown increasingly frustrated with Bud Littin, who insisted on directing our public relations and advertising from New York rather than Washington. He had missed a couple of meetings and sometimes did not answer phone calls. As deputy director I filled in as best I could, but we were falling behind on critical deadlines, including reserving time for our TV programs in New Hampshire. To help fill the gap, our New York advertising agency, Fuller Smith Ross, loaned us a veteran publicist, John Crider. John was high-energy with lots of ideas, some of them doable, but it soon became obvious that he had a drinking problem.

A problem became a crisis in mid-February, with just three weeks until the New Hampshire primary. We were at a meeting of our state chairmen at the O'Hare Inn in Chicago when Crider, after spending most of the afternoon in the bar, began talking loudly in the lobby, flirting with our girls and the receptionists, and offering to buy drinks for everyone. It was decided, on the spot, that Crider had to go.

At the same meeting, Littin stumbled over words and hesitated several times as he presented our communications plan for New Hampshire and beyond. I could see people in the room looking at one another and shaking their heads.

The following Monday, I was in New Hampshire traveling with the senator when Tony Smith phoned to tell me to start acting as the director of information. The last obstacle to my elevation disappeared when Littin suddenly resigned because of what he called a "heart condition." I wondered whether his trouble was not physical but psychological—his heart never seemed to be in the campaign.

With his hearing aid and grizzled hair, Denny Kitchel looked older than his fifty-some years. With my unlined face and ready smile, I looked a decade younger than thirty-one. As he talked, Denny ticked off my youth, my comparative inexperience, my habit of trying to do everything myself. He conceded I was a good writer and someone who knew Barry's record backward and forward.

"What I'm trying to say, Lee," explained Denny, "is that we need a director of public information, and while you are not my first choice, you are in place. Tony has confidence in you and Barry likes you. I'm not sure I want to use the phrase, but let's say you are the man for the time being. We can't afford to wait any longer."

"I will work eighteen hours a day to get the job done," I promised.

"Remember," Denny responded, "you can't do it all yourself."

I understood that I got the job because I was the only one left standing.

There is always one more thing to do in a presidential campaign: newspaper clippings to read, phones to answer, releases to approve, people to see, commercials to review, brochures to produce, campaign themes to decide on, and all the time you're trying, after all the coffee you have drunk, to get to the bathroom. At the center of my responsibilities was the handling of the press. Bob Humphreys, who had directed public relations for the 1952 Eisenhower-Nixon campaign and whom I met through Dad, compared the press to little baby birds who had to be fed every hour and whose mouth was almost as large as their body.

I was on the go all the time. One week I traveled four thousand miles, with trips to Chicago, North Carolina, and Delaware and multiple visits to New Hampshire and New York City, where I met with our ad agency about the thirty-minute documentary film and two five-minute TV spots they were preparing. I was drawn deeper and deeper into the campaign. How did you maintain perspective? How did you know if you were up or down, gaining or losing? The national press was negative about us, but the crowds were large and passionate.

We picked the theme for the last week in New Hampshire: "Moral Leadership and National Honor." It was a twofer, contrasting us with LBJ's wheeler-dealing and Rockefeller's divorce and remarriage (although the senator never mentioned Rocky's marital slips and slides).

I spent the last week of the campaign in New Hampshire, traveling with the senator. If I had any doubts about the outcome, they were swept away by the last day of campaigning in Manchester—the largest city in the state—when he rode in an open red Corvette in an old-fashioned torchlight parade with brassy bands, prancing drum majorettes, briskly moving World War II and Korean War veterans, homemade banners and signs—"Goldwater in '64," "Au H2O," "Live Free or Die," "Impeach Earl Warren"—and hundreds of young people eager to join a crusade.

At night, he addressed a "We Want Barry" rally in the city armory filled with four thousand foot-stamping, hand-clapping conservatives, who fell silent as he explained he was running to pay back America for all it had given him and his family. He brought the crowd to its feet when he said, "You are wrong, Mr. Khrushchev, our children will not live under Communism. Your children will live under freedom!" I recalled what the political historian Teddy White had said on the press bus earlier: "Goldwater sometimes makes more sense than any other public official in America today." If we get less than 35 percent, I thought, it will be a shocker.

On Tuesday, March 10, despite a blizzard that left fourteen inches of snow in its windy wake, 95,000 determined voters found their way to the polls. It was a bad day for the declared candidates: 33,521 people wrote in the name of Henry Cabot Lodge, a Massachusetts neighbor, giving the noncandidate who never left the ambassador's residence in Vietnam 35 percent of the vote. Goldwater was a weak second, receiving 21,775 votes, 23 percent of the vote. Rockefeller earned a miserable return on his sizable investment, placing third with 19,496 votes, less than 21 percent. Former vice president Nixon, peeking coyly from the wings, got 15,762 write-in votes, about 17 percent.

That evening, in the five-star Madison Hotel in Washington, where we had expected to have our victory party, reporters pressed Goldwater to explain what had happened. Standing in an almost empty ballroom amid congealing crab puffs, cold pigs in blankets, and untouched glasses of white and red wine, he said, "I goofed."

That was Goldwater, taking the blame. He vowed he would not repeat the mistakes of New Hampshire. There would be changes in the organization, he said, starting with a bigger role for Clif White.

Clif stepped forward and reminded reporters that New Hampshire was one primary. Winning the nomination was a marathon, he said, not a hundred-yard dash. He predicted that "Senator Goldwater will come back from this defeat to win the nomination in San Francisco." Some reporters did not bother to suppress their snickers, but Clif (and I) knew what they did not know: every day we drew closer to the magic number of 655 delegates to gain the nomination.

9

THE REAL
BARRY GOLDWATER

I was convinced we might have won or at least come closer to winning New Hampshire had people known the whole Goldwater story. How he flew supplies over the Himalaya Mountains, with the most dangerous peaks in the world, during World War II. How in the 1930s, long before he got into politics, he dropped food and supplies from his single-engine plane to snowed-in Navajos who otherwise might have starved to death. His black-and-white photographs of the Navajos and the Hopis and the Arizona desert and mountains had hung in the Royal Photographic Gallery in London and other prominent galleries. He was a tinkerer in the tradition of Thomas Edison, having built his own ham radio and turned a JX Javelin car into a four-wheel phenomenon with a jet fighter altimeter, a musical horn that played sixty-four songs, and a fire extinguisher. He had rafted down the Columbia River, paid the bills of the Phoenix Urban League when it got started, and written with Brent Bozell's help the most successful political manifesto of the twentieth century—*The Conscience of a Conservative*, which sold 3.5 million copies.

He was a man of many contradictions, inspiring and infuriating. He said of his presidential race, "I know I am going to lose, but I am going to lose my way," based on principles.

He was courageous and stubborn, announcing, "I did not come to Washington to pass laws but to repeal them."

He was profane and profound. A favorite maxim was "Any government big enough to give you everything you want is big enough to take away everything you have."

He delighted in challenging conventional wisdom, but always with the Constitution as his guide. He insisted, for example, that the federal government had no business in education, which was a local responsibility, but later changed to endorse federal action to ensure educational opportunity for blacks.

He was a man of plain tastes (a cheeseburger supreme with a slice of raw onion and a chocolate shake) and old-fashioned virtues like patriotism, hard work, and faith in God. He was a man of enormous charm and self-deprecating humor. On the wall behind the desk in his Senate office was a framed inscription that read, in pseudo-Latin, *Noli Permittere Illegitimi Carborundum*—"Don't let the bastards grind you down."

I prepared an elaborate public relations campaign to tell the Barry Goldwater story to the American electorate and scheduled a meeting with the senator. It was my first formal presentation to him as director of information of the Goldwater for President Committee. I had barely begun talking about his helping the Navajos and flying over the Himalayas and building a ham radio when he raised his big right hand and almost stuck it in my face. "Stop!" he said sharply. "Lee, if you try any of that Madison Avenue crap, I will kick your ass out of this campaign. This will be a campaign of principles, not personalities. Understood?"

What could I, a specialist fourth class, say to my commander in chief but "Yes, sir, understood." I was devastated, and I knew he was dead wrong. You didn't get in the ring with Rocky Marciano with one hand tied behind your back. You didn't tee it up against Arnold Palmer without your driver. Most people voted with their hearts rather than their minds. Even if they didn't agree with the senator on all the issues, they might vote for him if they liked him. But how could they know him well enough to like him if he wouldn't let us tell his story—his *whole* story? I never directly disobeyed him, but when I was sure he wasn't looking we planted stories about Goldwater's nonpolitical side. Of course, the mass media rarely picked them up, preferring to concentrate on the "dark" side of our candidate.

Over the next ten weeks, until the pivotal California primary, I shuttled between Washington and New York City and Los Angeles, overseeing the production of our TV and radio ads. I wrote and rewrote a dozen issue papers and most of the official Goldwater for President literature. I dictated dozens and dozens of letters, talked to donors large and small, suggested "Bucks for Barry" as a fundraising theme, and tried to come up with an overall campaign theme. I argued that we ought to be open about what we were offering the American people and adopt the slogan "The New Conservatism." That was too ideological for Bill Baroody, on leave as president of the American Enterprise Institute and the arbiter of all the senator's speeches and campaign literature. We never did settle on a central theme until after we had won the nomination.

I kept the press releases flowing and attended strategy sessions with Denny Kitchel, Dean Burch and Dick Kleindienst (members of the so-called Arizona Mafia), Bill Baroody, Wall Streeters Bill Middendorf and Jerry Milbank (whom we named the Brinks Brothers for their fundraising prowess), Clif White, and sometimes the senator, who remained confident about California, saying he had made about five hundred speeches there over the past decade. "They know me," he said. "They know I am not some right-wing nut."

Since there were thousands of John Birch Society members in Southern California, the trick was keeping them enthusiastic about the senator along with regular conservative Republicans. The senator stuck to a strategy of making only one major speech a day, limiting his press conferences, giving interviews to sympathetic reporters, and letting Clif White and the other professionals go about their delegate gathering at state and district conventions. Denny and Karl Hess accompanied Goldwater on the road. Denny could relax the senator and tell him to do things he didn't want to do—like meet a local group of donors. Karl turned out speeches almost as fast as the senator could deliver them.

REINFORCEMENTS

One reason why I was able to keep abreast of the never-ending demands for information was my new chief assistant, the redoubtable Mary Ann Ford of Reno, Nevada. Shortly after New Hampshire, our office manager, Jim Day, came to me and said, "I know you're shorthanded so I'm giving you some help. They are not charity cases, although they may look it, since they just arrived this morning after driving straight through from Nevada, napping in their station wagon and eating at truck stops. They know politics, they've worked in campaigns. They're probably Birchers, but our guy in Nevada, Uncle Frank Whetstone, vouches for them." He walked to the door and beckoned two women into my office.

"Lee," he said, "Mary Ann Ford and Joan Sweetland. Ladies, Lee Edwards. I know you'll do great things together."

Mary Ann could have passed for a Marine drill sergeant. She had short brown hair, steel-gray eyes, deeply tanned muscular arms, and an attitude of "Don't mess with me." She wore jeans with a large turquoise buckle, a checkered cotton shirt, and worn sneakers.

Joan was short and blonde with brilliant blue eyes and weighed far more than she should have. When she smiled, which was often, you didn't notice how heavy she was. I could not conceal my uncertainty at the sudden appearance of two unknown women from the Wild West. Before I could say a word, Mary Ann took charge.

"Look," she said, her voice half a tone deeper than mine, "we know this is sudden and you may have other people in mind, but all we ask is that you give us a chance. We're not beautiful or sophisticated or Harvard graduates, but we have worked in eight campaigns, six of which we won, and we love Barry. We will get the job done, whatever it is, even if it means cleaning the johns. So, what needs to be done?"

"Well," I began, and it was as if a great weight had been lifted from me, "we've got three policy papers that have to be distributed. Our newsletter is one week behind schedule. We have to place all our internal calls through the switchboard rather than to each other. We're short two desks, three typewriters, and four telephones. The coffee machine makes lousy coffee. The bottom right drawer of my desk is stuck. I am fielding so many press calls I can't get to the john, and Pearl Norman, who is a big donor, is driving me nuts with her thirty-minute telephone calls."

"We'll take care of it."

"I have to be in New York City; Raleigh, North Carolina; and Springfield, Illinois, in the next week."

"We'll take care of it."

"I haven't taken a columnist to lunch in a month."

"We'll take care of it."

"I don't get enough sleep."

"We'll get you out of here by eight, nine at the latest."

"We may lose California."

"That," said Mary Ann, smiling, "Barry will take care of."

Nothing seemed to slow Mary Ann down, not even the cancer she had fought for years with surgery, radiation, and chemicals. Her doctors said her cancer was in remission—she called it submission. Mary Ann and Joan were a remarkable team who I learned could get done whatever needed to be done. As Clif and his team accumulated delegates week after week, the attention of everyone at headquarters turned to the one remaining obstacle to our victory at the national convention in San Francisco.

10

THE MUST PRIMARY

California was Valley Forge, the Battle of New Orleans, the Alamo, Gettysburg, San Juan Hill, Normandy Beach, Pork Chop Hill. It was the New Right versus the Old Left; Goldwater volunteers versus Rockefeller hired guns; the Constitution versus Rocky's BOMFOG (the Brotherhood of Man and the Fatherhood of God); paperbacks like *A Choice Not an Echo* and *None Dare Call It Treason* versus CBS, NBC, and ABC; the man who didn't want to be president versus the man who thought he deserved to be president. We had to win California, or at least the senator thought we did, to warrant the nomination. Stan Evans would later describe the 1964 California primary as the most important primary for conservatives since the birth of the movement in the 1950s.

To gain what he considered to be rightfully his, Rockefeller resolved to spend whatever was necessary. His people said publicly their campaign would cost about $1.5 million but privately admitted the figure would be more than $2 million. Clif estimated that Rocky would spend at least $3.5 million and as much as $5 million. Five million dollars in one state in one month was more than we would spend on our entire campaign to win the nomination. (According to our treasurer, Bill Middendorf, our total expenditures were $4.75 million.)

Although we couldn't match Rocky's money, we had significant assets—thousands of volunteers, issues like smaller government and victory over communism, a candidate who had hit his stride, and adequate financing. We felt good about our chances until we held a strategy session in Washington with less than three weeks to go.

"If the election were held today," Dean Burch said slowly, standing beside an easel in our conference room, "we would lose California by about 200,000 votes."

His words stunned us, seated around a long laminated table crowded with coffee cups, yellow writing pads, blue Bic pens, and black three-ring binders filled with suddenly useless information about the national convention. Dean traced two colored lines on a chart, the black for Goldwater, the red for Rockefeller. They showed that although Goldwater had had a solid lead through April and the first part of May, it disappeared following Rocky's win in Oregon. Rockefeller now led the senator in California, 47 percent to 36 percent.

"That's a twenty-point shift."

"Impossible."

"Southern California is Goldwater country," said our polling expert, Jay Hall. "Our polls confirm it."

"Barry spends every vacation on his boat at Balboa Bay."

"My God, are we going to have another New Hampshire?"

"Our campaign is being run by the far right," Dean said quietly. "Good Republicans are excluded. Our billboards and radio and TV and newspaper advertising don't begin to match Rockefeller's. We've got money but we're not spending it right. Our main asset is our volunteers, but they're getting conflicting orders. Meanwhile, Rocky is going up and down the state saying Barry will destroy Social Security and get us into a nuclear war. And we're pulling our punches because Barry still thinks he's chairman of the Senatorial Campaign Committee and doesn't want to say anything negative about a fellow Republican."

It couldn't be. Both the California Republican Assembly, a liberal group, and United Republicans for California, a conservative group, had endorsed Goldwater. Robert Gaston, the Young Republican firebrand who liked to accuse other conservatives of not being conservative enough, had promised to direct his fire at Democrats. Our campaign consultants Baus and Ross had handled more than seventy state campaigns, most of them successfully. How could we be losing?

"We have about three weeks until the primary," Denny said, cutting through the sputtered questions and remonstrations. "What do we do?"

"Take over the campaign," Dean said. "Set up an operation in Los Angeles drawing on the talents of the Washington team and our New

York agency and turn this thing around. We can do it—it's not too late, but we have to do it now. The California people will be furious—some of them may even walk. But unless we launch an all-out, last-minute effort with us in charge, we will lose."

"We'll have to talk to Barry."

"I already have," Dean said coolly, "and he's okayed the switch."

"It's a big gamble."

"What we're doing isn't working."

"What choice do we have?"

"Let's do it!"

California, I thought to myself, here we come.

LOS ALTOS

A specter haunted the shabby halls of the Los Altos Apartments on Wilshire Boulevard where we were headquartered—not that of the reclusive Greta Garbo, who had lived in the Los Altos in her Hollywood days, but the grinning, backslapping Nelson Rockefeller. The spacious corner suite on the fourth floor of the Los Altos, said to have been Garbo's hideout, was our command center as we attempted the most difficult thing in politics—turning around a losing campaign.

On a late May morning, the sun had not yet burned away the brown haze covering the city. Everywhere you turned there was Rockefeller— on billboards; in TV and radio commercials; on buttons, bumper stickers, and yard signs distributed by Rockefeller workers. The New York governor's campaign had compiled lists of registered Republicans for mailings and telephone calls. Operatives had assigned automobiles, station wagons, and vans to precinct captains who would get Rockefeller supporters to the polls. The Rockefeller machine was up and running smoothly like a new Cadillac. We were still filling up the tank of our Chevrolet campaign.

A steady flow of people went in and out of our suite, up and down the steps of the sunken living room, back and forth in the bedrooms and on the balconies overlooking a small swimming pool none of us had time to swim in. Uniformed messengers carried bulky boxes and large padded envelopes through the always open door of our suite. The temp secretaries typed like automatons.

With sheets of paper and a row of pencils and pens laid out neatly before him, cheerful, cherubic Gene Hooker deftly sketched newspaper ads, drawing on his twenty-five years of Madison Avenue experience. In one corner, Steve Shadegg, who had managed the senator's two successful Arizona campaigns, was editing, on a Wollensak reel-to-reel recorder, the radio spots he had prepared for the Oregon primary but never used after Goldwater withdrew. Typing as quickly as the temps, Karl Hess, who never graduated from high school, was writing the senator's Memorial Day speech.

I was at the other end of the table from Gene Hooker talking to a reporter from the *Herald-Examiner*, outlining the candidate's schedule for the next couple of days. Dean was in one of the bathrooms talking to Bob Gaston, who listened politely to suggestions about how to use the Goldwater volunteers. Denny was just off the phone with golden donor Henry Salvatori, who had agreed to put another $50,000 into the campaign. "My money is just as good as Rockefeller's," Henry said truculently. Rus Walton, a creative California publicist, announced that the campaign had already distributed 23,731 copies of Phyllis Schlafly's *A Choice Not an Echo*, including in alleged Rockefeller precincts. "We get more bang with Phyllis's little book than Rocky does with all his bucks," Rus said. He expected to distribute another 25,000 copies by primary day.

For our thirty-second and sixty-second TV spots, we were cutting up the film *The Goldwater Story*, on which I, along with George Lyon and Cal Gingerich of our New York ad agency, had spent many hours. For a final TV program, Steve suggested that the senator appear with the whole Goldwater family in a living room setting and explain why he was running and what he would do if elected president. Denny objected, saying it sounded too "corny." Steve pointed to the powerful contrast between Barry, Peggy, and their handsome grown-up children, Joanne, Barry Jr., Mike, and young Peggy, and an all-alone Rocky in California and his very pregnant wife, Happy, in New York City.

From my campaign diary:

Twenty congressmen are flying in to explain why they call Barry Goldwater "Mr. Republican." So far we have lined up John Wayne to greet them in San Diego and are working on other Hollywood stars like Ronald Reagan to join them in other cities. I wonder if Reagan will wear his vanilla ice cream suit and white suede shoes. We could have had Billy Graham give the invocation at the Memorial Day rally at Knott's Berry Farm, but Baus vetoed Graham for fear he would detract from the Senator. Doesn't Baus know that politics is a game of addition, not subtraction? No wonder we're behind. Nobody is getting more than a few hours of sleep a night, but that hasn't prevented considerable extracurricular activity. I haven't heard so much talk about sex since I was in the Army. And not just among the younger guys. Karl Hess has a ready explanation: "Sex relieves tension."

The Senator has been a magnificent candidate this whole week, affable with the press, enthusiastic on the stump, ridiculing Rockefeller's spending proposals. Our crowds have been much larger than Rocky's.

I have been far from idle but I am frustrated. Most of the creative work is being done by others. I am essentially a traffic manager, although the Senator approved my idea of a post-convention "summit meeting" with all the Republican leaders and chaired by Ike. It got a good play in the press.

I had dinner with Teddy White in a rooftop restaurant overlooking Santa Monica gleaming like a diamond necklace on the dark edge of the ocean. Teddy said he wanted to know what it was like to work for a candidate who was so blunt, so honest, seemingly indifferent to public opinion. I explained how the Senator had captured the hearts of young conservatives like me, that it was like a first love, pure and passionate, sweeping away all questions, doubts and uncertainties, filling us with the conviction that with him we could change history. We knew the Senator was far from perfect, but who looked better in a pair of jeans or on a horse? Who made more sense talking about rolling back Big Government and defeating Communism? He inspired us, he challenged us, he made us feel we could do anything, including defeating the Liberal Establishment with all its money and power. When I finished, Teddy smiled his gentle smile and said it sounded like what young men and women had said when he asked them what it was like to work for Jack Kennedy.

I don't know whether he will use anything I said or not, but it was an evening I won't forget.

With a week to go, the Los Altos gang took political inventory. We had generous donors like Henry Salvatori and other wealthy conservatives who had given nearly $2 million. Salvatori liked to tell the story of the small luncheon at his club for which Patrick J. Frawley, the impulsive, alcoholic president of the Schick Razor Company, showed up an hour late. Frawley was no sooner seated than he interrupted Salvatori's low-key pitch, slurring loudly, "We all know why we're here, Henry." He pulled out his checkbook and scribbled something. "Here's my check for $50,000. How much are the rest of you guys putting up?"

We had an army of perhaps 50,000 unflagging volunteers, the largest number of unpaid workers in any primary in American politics. They had proved themselves in March when they gathered more than 85,000 signatures to put Goldwater's name on the ballot—only 13,000 were required. Almost all the signatures were valid. Rockefeller's hired hands took nearly four weeks to round up 44,000 signatures, of which 22 percent were found to be invalid. When Bob Gaston learned that the Rockefeller campaign was paying fifty cents a signature, he ordered his troops to collect 7,000 names in Orange County and turned over the $3,500 to our campaign.

BARRY'S BATTALIONS

There was no questioning the IQ (Intensity Quotient) of our workers. Rockefeller's campaign director, Stu Spencer (who later directed Reagan's gubernatorial campaigns), complained, half-vexed, half-admiring, "They keep coming at us like the Chinese army." One Saturday, 8,000 of our people took to the streets of Los Angeles County—almost as big as the state of Delaware—to canvass 600,000 registered Republicans. By primary day, they had compiled a list of 300,000 pro-Goldwater voters, all of whom they telephoned and urged to vote for the senator. Ten thousand volunteers got them to the polls.

I remember saying to Steve Shadegg, whom I admired as the ultimate professional, "We're still behind, by about nine points, but we're gaining fast."

"The Rockefeller people will start swinging harder and lower," Steve said. "It's what I'd do if the other guy was gaining on me."

Their attempted bolo punch was a glossy brochure, mailed to every Republican in California, that suggested Rockefeller had the endorsement of Republican leaders. On one page, a large picture of a smiling Rocky was placed alongside smaller photos of Nixon, Lodge, Romney, and William Scranton under the headline "These Men Stand Together on the Party's Principles." On the opposite page was a solitary photo of a frowning Goldwater with the headline "This Man Stands Outside—by Himself."

On another page was the headline "Which Do You Want? A Leader? Or a Loser?" Anne came up with a classic rejoinder, "Our answer is simple: 'We want a leader, not a lover.'" The brochure backfired: first Romney, then Nixon, and finally Scranton all denied they were for or against anyone in California. Still, the establishment kept trying to bring us down.

A front-page article in the liberal *New York Herald Tribune* quoted General Eisenhower as calling for a Republican nominee who would endorse "responsible, forward-looking Republicanism." He almost seemed to be spelling Rockefeller. To make certain everyone got the point, the paper ran a front-page sidebar by their house columnist Roscoe Drummond that began, "If former President Eisenhower can have his way, the Republican Party will not choose Sen. Barry Goldwater as its 1964 presidential nominee."

The senator calmly turned the attack on its head, or rather its back. Speaking at a California rally, he tucked the feathered shaft of a long arrow under his arm so that it seemed to be embedded in his back. He paused during his remarks to explain that the arrow illustrated "some of the problems I've had in the last few days." The audience broke up. Newspapers and TV stations across the country ran a picture of the "shafted senator" and the country joined in the laughter.

One person who was not amused was the supreme commander of the Allied Forces in World War II, who had not intended his remarks to be used as anti-Goldwater propaganda. On Monday, the day before the primary, General Eisenhower held a New York City press conference at which he sternly told reporters, "You people tried to read Goldwater out of the party, I didn't."

We also survived a problematic appearance by the senator on ABC's *Issues and Answers*. Since New Hampshire and the constant distortion of his remarks about nuclear weapons, Goldwater had refrained from giving any lessons on the art of modern warfare. But during a discussion of the Vietnam War, he was asked by Howard K. Smith how communist supply lines along the Laotian border with South Vietnam might be interdicted. Sitting in the ABC control booth and watching the interview, I was tense but confident the senator would skirt the question as he had for almost three months. But he suddenly reverted to the Goldwater of old:

> Well, it is not as easy as it sounds, because these are not trails that are out in the open.... There have been several suggestions made. *I don't think we would use any of them* [emphasis added]. But defoliation of the forests by low-yield atomic bombs could well be done. When you remove the foliage, you remove the cover.

If only he had stopped with the words "I don't think we would use any of them." I dreaded what the press would do with the senator's remarks. Within minutes both the Associated Press and United Press International ran stories saying that Goldwater had "called" for the "use" of nuclear weapons in South Vietnam. UPI went so far as to report that the senator had "proposed" the use of atomic weapons to defoliate the forests along the South Vietnamese border. It later retracted the story, but it was too late. I remembered Mark Twain's line: "A lie can travel halfway around the world while truth is putting on its shoes." (I later learned that Jonathan Swift wrote something very like those words about three hundred years ago.)

"Goldwater's Plan to Use Viet A-Bomb," cried the liberal *San Francisco Chronicle*, falsely quoting the senator as saying, "I'd risk a war." The *Chronicle* misquote was typical of the bias we contended with all year. We corrected the distortions and misstatements, but for every falsehood we struck down, new ones immediately sprang up.

When I talked to the senator after the ABC program, he admitted he should have kept his mouth shut. "But damn it," he said, "he asked me a question and the people have a right to know about the options our military is considering. Johnson keeps saying I will get us into a war, but damn it, we're already in a war in Vietnam."

As it had previously, the Rockefeller campaign overplayed its hand, mailing an expensive color brochure to two million registered California Republicans. The cover asked, "Who Do You Want in the Room with the H-Bomb?" It ripped Goldwater quotes out of context and fairly screamed that if Goldwater were elected, nuclear war would surely follow. Republicans read the shrill language of the brochure and considered the man who had spoken for years at their meetings, campaigned and raised money for their candidates, and taken most of his vacations in their state, and decided that, amid all the charges and countercharges of a rancorous campaign, Rockefeller had gone too far. Barry Goldwater had his flaws, but he was not Dr. Strangelove.

In the final frantic days, the race tightened and tightened again. Ten days after his victory in the Oregon primary, Rockefeller led us by nine points. The Friday before voting in California, he was still ahead by seven points, but the following Monday—the day before voters went to the polls—his lead was cut to two points. On Tuesday, June 3, primary day, we were tied. The momentum had swung sharply to us.

THE RELIGIOUS RIGHT

It so happened that Governor Rockefeller was scheduled to speak at
Loyola University of Los Angeles, a staunchly Catholic institution, in the
final week. We asked Dick Herman, a prominent Catholic layman back
in Nebraska, to call on Cardinal James McIntyre, the conservative arch-
bishop of the Los Angeles archdiocese, to discuss the Rockefeller talk, of
which, it turned out, the cardinal was unaware. Dick suggested that the
appearance of a divorced politician like Rockefeller at a major Catholic
institution might be interpreted as an endorsement of his candidacy—
and his attitude toward divorce and marriage. Six hours before Rockefeller's scheduled talk, Loyola withdrew the invitation, explaining that
the governor's visit was being "generally interpreted" as an endorsement.
Cardinal McIntyre's office told the press that His Eminence did not
want anyone to think that the Catholic Church was giving its blessing to
someone who had divorced his wife of many years and then married his
former secretary. The cancellation was the lead item on many radio and
TV stations in Southern California.

I had been calling Anne almost every night. Although we had broken up in February at my doing—I felt she was getting too serious and
I was all campaign all the time—she agreed to take my calls as long as I
kept them political. I told her about the cardinal's statement and asked
what impact she thought it might have on the Catholic vote. She replied,
"For good Catholics, it's always been Mater Si, Magistra Si."

The same week, a dozen Protestant ministers in Los Angeles issued
a statement suggesting that Rockefeller should withdraw from the presidential race because of his demonstrated "inability to handle his own
domestic affairs." It was the first time in California politics that Catholic
and Protestant leaders had united publicly against a presidential candidate. The denouement was the birth of Nelson A. Rockefeller Jr., on Saturday afternoon, May 30, three days before the primary polls opened in
California. Rocky was delighted and so were we, because he had given
ministers and pastors throughout the state the theme for their Sunday
sermons.

On primary day, thousands of Goldwater volunteers—Young Republicans and YAFers, housewives and retirees, small businessmen and blue-
collar workers, churchgoers and orange growers—fanned out across the
state with maps and lists of Goldwater voters circled in red. If they found
no one at home, they dropped off a circular ("Don't Forget to Vote for
Goldwater!") and made a note to return later. They kept coming back

until someone opened the door and promised they would go to the polls. If they needed a ride, they got one.

CBS News was using Lou Harris's new exit poll projections so that it could call the race in prime time back east. It didn't matter that the California polls would still be open. NBC had beaten CBS by several minutes in the Oregon primary, and the network of Edward R. Murrow, William L. Shirer, and Eric Sevareid was not going to come in second again.

At 7:20 P.M., with Harris's assurances echoing in his ears, Walter Cronkite surprised viewers by predicting that Barry Goldwater would win the California Republican primary with about 53 percent of the vote and take all 86 delegates, bringing him close to the 655 delegates needed for nomination. The wire services, which counted votes as they came in, had Rockefeller ahead because the liberal precincts in Northern California reported first. No other network had called it yet, but Cronkite was the most trusted man in America. His prediction confirmed that we had done the nearly impossible.

There were Indian war whoops and pounding on backs in the Presidential Suite of the Beverly Hilton Hotel, where the Los Altos gang had gathered to celebrate with the senator. The high spirits were fueled by beer, bourbon, and victory.

"We did it, by God, we did it."

"Congratulations, Barry."

"Congratulations, Goldie."

"It's no landslide but we won."

"I said we would beat Rockefeller by about 50,000 votes," Clif said. (The actual margin was a little over 68,000 votes, 51.5 percent of the 2.1 million votes cast.)

"Eighty-six delegates. I love winner-take-all states. How many does that make, Clif?"

"We now have more than enough to win on the first ballot."

"That was a great speech at Knott's Berry Farm, Barry. Nearly 30,000 people. You really had them going."

The senator nodded in appreciation and looked over at Karl Hess.

Someone began quoting from the speech: "The greatest day in history will be when an American president tells Khrushchev—'You are wrong! Our children will not live under socialism or communism!'"

We all joined in: "Your children will live under freedom!" There were more whoops and olés.

"I want to thank all of you for what you did," the senator said. "It was a great day for the forgotten Americans who work forty hours a week, feed and clothe their families, pay their bills, go to church on Sunday, and try to live by the Golden Rule. They're the heart and soul of America, and we have given them a voice. Goddamn it, listen to me, I'm still making speeches." He lifted his glass. "Here's to the greatest country in the world. As Harry Golden says, only in America would the first Jewish presidential nominee be an Episcopalian."

We could now start preparing in earnest for the national convention, but first there was a Senate vote on a bill that millions of Americans had waited for all their lives.

11

CIVIL RIGHTS AND
THE CONSTITUTION

Senator Goldwater wanted to vote for the Civil Rights Act of 1964 as he had for the civil rights measures of 1957 and 1960. He had said so publicly and privately to me and others. He was very aware that, if he didn't vote aye, everyone would get the wrong idea. Liberals would call him a right-wing extremist, black Americans would brand him a racist, white southerners would welcome him as one of their own, Republicans would make excuses for him, LBJ would say he was trying to turn the clock back one hundred years, and only he and conservatives would understand that his decision was not political but constitutional.

But he would vote for the act *only* if Title II on public accommodations and Title VII on employment were removed or amended significantly. Title II, the so-called Mrs. Murphy clause, was unacceptable because it said that a landlord could not refuse rental to anyone. Hell, Goldwater thought, I would not rent my home to a lot of whites. As for Title VII, he feared it would produce a regulatory state that would dictate a hiring-and-firing policy for seventy million working Americans. He was not impressed by the solemn promises of the bill's voluble floor manager, Hubert Horatio Humphrey.

Humphrey said during debate that the legislation "does not require an employer to achieve any kind of racial balance in his work force by giving any kind of preferential treatment to any individual or group." Democrat Pete Williams of New Jersey insisted that an employer could continue to hire "only the best qualified persons even if they were all white." When Goldwater expressed skepticism, a grinning Humphrey promised that if anything in the bill required the kind of preferential hiring that Goldwater predicted, "I will start eating the pages [of the bill] one after the other."

Goldwater did not smile back. He told his colleagues that if the government "can forbid [hiring] discrimination based on race, the same government can *require* people to discriminate in hiring on the basis of color or race or religion." He quoted Milton Friedman that it was no more desirable that "momentary majorities" decide what characteristics are relevant to employment than what speech is appropriate. He borrowed language from both Robert Bork, a Yale professor of law who had given him a lengthy memorandum criticizing the legislation, and William Rehnquist, an associate of Denny's law firm in Phoenix (and a future chief justice of the United States).

I marveled at the senator's courage in standing up for the Constitution when many were willing to bend it almost beyond recognition. At the same time, I was moved by the passionate arguments of Dr. King and the other civil rights leaders. How long did they have to wait for justice and equality?

A resolute Goldwater continued to present his case for principled dissent although he knew that most of his colleagues had made up their minds. Someone other than a southern Democrat had to express his opposition to a bad bill.

"The problems of discrimination can never be cured by laws alone," he said on the Senate floor, "but I would be the first to agree that laws can help—laws carefully considered and weighed in an atmosphere of dispassion, in the absence of political demagoguery, and in the light of fundamental constitutional principles...but not law that embodies features like these, provisions which fly in the face of the Constitution and which require for their effective execution the creation of a police state."

Senator Humphrey no longer had a happy face.

"If my vote is misconstrued, let it be," Goldwater said slowly, "and let me suffer its consequences. Just let me be judged in this by the real concern I have voiced here and not by words that others may speak or by what others may say about what I think." He knew what a firestorm his vote would ignite.

"My concern extends beyond this single legislative moment. My concern extends beyond any single group in our society. My concern is for the entire nation, for the freedom of all who live in it and for all who will be born into it...."

"This is the time to attend to the liberties of all."

Here was the Barry Goldwater we loved, guided by principles and not politics. On June 19, after eighty-three days of debate filling 2,890 pages of the *Congressional Record*, the Senate passed the Civil Rights Act of 1964 by a vote of 73–27, with twenty-one Democrats and six Republicans, including Barry Goldwater, voting against it. Forty-six Democrats and twenty-seven Republicans, including Senate Republican leader Everett Dirksen, voted for it.

The reaction to the senator's "No" vote was swift and sweeping.

Martin Luther King Jr. saw "dangerous signs of Hitlerism" in Goldwater and said that if he were elected president the nation would erupt into "violence and riots, the like of which we have never seen before."

NAACP secretary Roy Wilkins said that a Goldwater victory "would lead to a police state." Baseball icon Jackie Robinson, a registered Republican, said that Goldwater was "a hopeless captive of the lunatic, calculating right-wing extremists."

Oracular columnist Walter Lippmann wrote that Goldwater intended "to make his candidacy the rallying point of the white resistance." If elected, editorialized the influential *Christian Century*, "Mr. Goldwater could very well be the *last* president of the United States."

"Of course, liberal Republicans can't allow *that* to happen," Clif told me sarcastically. He was leaving the next morning for San Francisco, where he would oversee the nomination of the senator and the conservative takeover of the Republican Party that he and the other members of the "hard core" of the Draft Goldwater Committee had been working toward for three years.

"What the liberals don't understand," Clif said, "is that it's too late. Lodge, Rockefeller, Romney—we've beaten all of them. Now they're left with Bill Scranton, who looks as convincing on a white horse as my grandmother. Our house is built on solid rock. Our delegates will not be swayed, deterred, bullied, or bought off," he said. "Barry is going to be nominated—on the first ballot."

BIRCHERS

I must confess that the members of one organization had been singularly important in ensuring the nomination—the John Birch Society (JBS).

Conservative frustration with President Eisenhower and modern Republicanism had manifested itself in the 1958 formation of the JBS.

John Birch had been a Protestant missionary in China who had served in U.S. Army intelligence gathering in the Far East during World War II. A few days after Japan surrendered, Chinese Communists murdered him on suspicion of spying for the United States. The JBS described him as one of the first casualties of the Cold War. From its beginnings, the JBS used shock slogans like "Impeach Earl Warren!" and "Get the U.S. Out of the UN and the UN Out of the U.S."

Founder Robert Welch, a successful candymaker for most of his life, subscribed to the conspiracy theory of history, arguing that a secret group of powerful bankers, industrialists, publishers, and politicians was responsible for the spread of collectivism in the twentieth century. In his privately printed book, *The Politician*, Welch went over the edge and asserted that President Eisenhower either was "a mere stooge" for the communist cause or "had been consciously serving the communist conspiracy for all of his adult life." Welch insisted that the United States was coming increasingly under communist control. The society's monthly magazine, *American Opinion*, carried a scoreboard that routinely reported that America was more than 50 percent "controlled" by communists and their fellow travelers.

I met Welch at a Washington luncheon in very early 1958, when he was publishing *American Opinion* but before he started the society. Always looking for new outlets, I agreed to write a piece about a congressional hearing on the Kohler strike in Wisconsin. My article appeared in *American Opinion* in the spring of 1958. That fall Welch launched the JBS, and I immediately wrote Welch that I would no longer be a contributor to his magazine. I later discovered I was doing the same thing as my favorite senator.

Before starting the society, Welch visited Goldwater in Phoenix and asked him to read a draft of *The Politician*. After skimming through the manuscript, the senator told Welch that his theory about Ike's being either a dupe or a communist agent was crazy and that printing the work would harm not only Welch personally but also the anticommunist cause. "Welch never sought my advice again," Goldwater recalled. Nevertheless, Welch privately endorsed Goldwater for president and encouraged society members to work for his nomination and election.

The senator was always careful to differentiate between Welch and members of the society. Some of his best friends were members or former members, like Denny Kitchel, who dropped out after reading *The Politician*.

All during the campaign, I feared that Denny's brief JBS membership would come to light. I could see the headline: "Goldwater Campaign Manager Ex-Bircher." Some papers might not have bothered with the "ex." It never happened, proving that some political secrets can be kept, at least then. Such a secret could not kept in the Age of the Internet and today's omnipresent social media.

12

CONVENTION

They came from Dixon, Ashland, Lincoln, and Fargo, the heartland of America. They filled the high school bleachers for Friday night football and the church pews on Sunday morning. They stood at attention with hand on heart when they played the National Anthem, and they said grace before meals. They bought their suits and dresses and washing machines at Sears, and they wore their father's watch and the locket that had belonged to Grandma. They were grateful for what God had given them, but they were worried about the taxes that kept going up and the government's spending more than it took in every year. They resented faraway bureaucrats telling them what to do and what not to do. They were worried about the Russians, who kept boasting they would bury them. They knew there was no such thing as a free lunch—somebody always paid and it usually turned out to be them. And so they came to San Francisco to nominate a patriot who would roll back big government and win the Cold War and preserve the American Dream for their children and their children's children.

Although Clif was confident we had the votes to nominate the senator on the first ballot, he left nothing to chance. Jim Day had been in San Francisco since early May lining up rooms for delegates and alternates, working with the telephone company to install a communications system that would have impressed the National Security Agency, and preparing a bright green-and-white, fifty-five-foot steel-and-aluminum trailer at the rear of the Cow Palace that would serve as Clif's command center.

Inside the trailer, Clif sat before an electronic console resembling the cockpit of Air Force One. There were buttons for seventeen phone lines to key delegations on the convention floor. There were buttons for thirteen phone lines to the main switchboard at the Mark Hopkins Hotel, where we had our headquarters, and at the other major hotels housing Goldwater delegates. There was a direct line to the Presidential Suite on the seventeenth floor of the Mark and another to staff headquarters on the fifteenth floor, where I had my office. There was a special "all-call" button that allowed Clif to call everyone at the same time. He also approved a shortwave radio network that linked the trailer to several dozen walkie-talkies carried by delegation leaders and Goldwater staffers manning the convention hall.

In his pursuit of a perfect convention, Clif told Jim Day, "I want back-ups for the backups." Mobile radio equipment had failed or had been deliberately interrupted at crucial times in previous conventions, so Jim turned to the ever-resourceful Nicholas J. Volcheff of Pacific Telephone and Telegraph, who installed under the roof of the Cow Palace a powerful jamming-resistant antenna that produced a signal superior to that of anyone else at the convention, including the TV and radio networks. Because such a signal had never before been used at a political convention, the federal government assigned a unique frequency to the Goldwater system.

The senator was enthralled by all the technological wizardry. Anticipating Steve Jobs by thirty years, he mused, "If we had a couple more weeks, we could put a mini-phone in the pocket of every delegate."

THE BUDDY SYSTEM

Conventions are prone to outbursts of high emotion that, like tornadoes, sweep away everything in their path. That had happened at the 1940 Republican convention when outsider Wendell Willkie was nominated for president and, as we have seen, in 1960 when the delegates almost stampeded in favor of Walter for vice president. Even the most reliable delegate can go wobbly.

So we set up a "buddy system" whereby Goldwater delegates were paired off, an unshakable delegate with one who might waver. Leading up to the convention, the two people on each team were instructed to be in contact at least once a week. When they arrived in San Francisco—many of them aboard the transcontinental "Freedom Special" train that started in Washington, D.C., and picked up delegates along the way—they ate, slept, and moved around the city together. A card file of each Goldwater delegate with name, occupation, age, home address, telephone number, meal preferences, hotel, and other information was scrupulously maintained. "In case any reporter asks," Clif told me, "emphasize there is not one item of deleterious information about any delegate. Contrary to what has been written, our people don't have to be coerced into voting for Goldwater."

When Clif said he wanted to know where everybody was, he meant everybody, including me and every other staffer. We used locator boards with plastic overlays to sign in and out when we left the hotel—which was not very often during our two weeks in San Francisco. A closed-circuit TV camera was trained on the boards so that Denny, Dean, and Clif could use the TV sets in their rooms to locate anyone.

San Francisco has narrow streets and heavy traffic, so a fleet of limousines with two-way shortwave radios was reserved for key staffers. "I even have a train on standby," Jim confided to me, "to get our delegates to the Cow Palace in case the streets are blocked. We're ready for anything—except maybe an earthquake."

Inside the Goldwater trailer and flanking Clif were six regional directors, his commanders in the field. Wearing a headset, each director manned a post that linked him by telephone or radio to the delegations he was responsible for. Above each position was a TV set that allowed him to see what was happening on the convention floor. Behind each director was a personal assistant ready to step in if he had to leave the trailer to deal with a situation on the floor—or go to the john. All but one of the directors—Steve Shadegg—was a member of the original Draft Goldwater Committee.

And then there was my operation, the most sophisticated mass communications system ever put together for a national political convention. To guarantee that every Goldwater delegate and alternate received timely reliable information about the convention proceedings, we bought time on KFRC, a local radio station, starting Monday morning, July 13, at 6 A.M. We instructed Goldwater delegates to carry transistor radios so that they could tune in to the sixty-second bulletins broadcast every half hour and the five-minute programs aired every hour over what we called the Goldwater Radio Network. We produced the news bulletins and programs in our broadcast studio on the fifteenth floor of the Mark Hopkins.

In the same studio, run by broadcasting veteran Jack Buttram, we produced five-minute TV programs featuring Goldwater campaign officials like Denny Kitchel and Goldwater delegates like Clare Boothe Luce. We distributed the TV programs to local San Francisco stations as well as the national networks over the Goldwater Television Network. The networks ignored us at first but discovered they had to tune in to KFRC to get the latest delegate count and to our TV programs because we had exclusive interviews with Goldwater delegates like Senator Dirksen.

In my nightly report to Anne, I recounted how we had lined up Dirksen for an interview. "I told our people to meet him at the airport and explain we needed him for an exclusive interview on the Goldwater Television Network. And could he please do it even before he checked into his hotel?"

"You kidnapped the Republican leader of the Senate," Anne said, pretending to be shocked.

"Well, sort of. Dirksen chuckled all the way in from the airport."

"Enjoying yourself?" she asked.

"I love being in the eye of the storm."

CENTER STAGE

From my campaign diary:

> Our communications center in suite 1502 of the Mark Hopkins Hotel on Nob Hill is Grand Central Station from dawn to midnight. Phones ringing. Delegates coming and going. Old friends and new trying to get on the 15th floor. Patriots and hucksters pitching the idea that will assure the nomination and/or the election. "Thank you but we already have a campaign song." "Thank you for your research on how President Johnson stole his first Senate election." "Thank you for the first edition of Robert Welch's *The Politician*. We'll make sure Senator Goldwater sees it." Conferences large and small, important and insignificant, in the bedroom, in the solarium, in the bathroom where the never-silent AP and UPI tickers vie for attention. In the last three days, we have produced 54 sixty-second radio bulletins, 36 five-minute radio programs, ten five-minute TV programs, six four-page newsletters, 38 news releases, and a topless delegate in the lobby of the Mark. Actually, she was for Scranton— or so we insisted.
>
> By a remarkable coincidence—or is it?—our headquarters on the 14th and 15th floors are sandwiched between Scranton's HQ

on the 13th and 16th floors. We sleep on the 14th, which is rarely, and work on the 15th, which is perpetually. We have blocked off the elevator exits on the 15th so everyone has to get off on the 14th and walk up one flight. We have a guard at the top of the stairs who admits only staffers and others who wear the necessary presidential seal lapel pins we had made. Besides overseeing TV, radio and print production, I have held twice-daily briefings for the news media, at 10 A.M. and 3 P.M. I have had breakfast and lunch with key reporters every day, including Sunday. My best leak was suggesting that the Senator would go to Vietnam if elected just as Ike said in 1952 that he would go to Korea if elected. The *Examiner* put it on the front page. The Senator was amused.

Pinkerton guards in gray are at every exit—six per eight-hour shift around the clock, all paid by us of course. Reporters and photographers prowl up and down the hall. Nobody knows how they got presidential pins. I persuaded Denny to let it go, pointing out they can't access the floor where the Senator and the inner circle gather. The perils of campaigning: Vern Stephens, one of the Senator's two private bodyguards—only the President gets Secret Service protection—was "accidently" kicked in the groin by a CBS cameraman because he wouldn't let him get close to Goldwater. The Senator is an accomplished escape artist. He leaves the hotel every day through an underground passage that emerges more than a block away. He goes flying to relax—one afternoon he buzzed the Cow Palace. He has had installed a portable shortwave radio in his suite on the 17th floor. "This is K7UGA, portable 6," he says, "from the top of the Mark Hopkins Hotel, San Francisco. The handle is Barry, Baker Able Robert Robert Yankee." The media complain about tight security—I heard someone mutter "Gestapo"—but we're keeping the lid on until we have the nomination in hand.

My most unforgettable visitor showed up at 9:30 A.M., Friday, three days before the convention began. I was talking to a reporter, gulping coffee and smoking my seventh cigarette of the day, when the fourteenth-floor receptionist called to say that a young man wearing a white tuxedo with a red rose in the lapel and identifying himself as Mark Sunday, the grandson of the celebrated evangelist Billy Sunday, wanted to see me. He said he had a proposition that would generate worldwide publicity for the senator. "Send him up," I said. How could I resist talking to the grandson of the man who could not shut down my hometown, Chicago?

Sunday was in his late twenties, blond and fair-skinned with almost invisible eyebrows. His smile was wide and toothy like a shark's. His white tux was spotless and the red rose in his lapel was fresh.

"I have the exclusive rights," he began, "to something that will put Senator Goldwater on the front page of every newspaper in America and around the world."

"He's already on every front page in the world," I responded.

"I call it Outdoor Video," Sunday said. "It's a powerful slide projector that throws images—the senator's face, your campaign slogan, anything—on the sides of large buildings. Depending on how far away you place the projector, the image can be fifty feet high. You can see it for blocks and blocks. It's never been used in San Francisco or as far as I can tell at any political convention."

"Interesting," I said, already thinking where such a King Kong image would have the greatest impact, like the front of the Mark Hopkins. "How much are we talking about?"

"The Scranton people offered me $2,500," Sunday replied, "but I turned them down because I admire Senator Goldwater and what he stands for and so would my grandfather."

"Especially the senator's call for morality in government."

"Especially."

After a little bargaining, I offered Sunday $1,500, which he accepted so readily I realized I could have bought the "exclusive San Francisco rights" for $1,000. We made thick glass slides of the senator's official campaign photo as well as campaign slogans like "Au H₂O" and tested the projector Friday night on a couple of vacant buildings at the other end of the city. The images were as sharp and cinematic as Sunday had promised.

At dusk on Saturday we began projecting Goldwater photos and slogans seven stories high onto the front of the Mark Hopkins. People began to gather and point. Traffic slowed and stopped. The police became agitated. *Life* magazine photographers snapped and network cameras recorded. I was a little nervous about the senator's reaction—too Madison Avenue?—but I knew he never left the hotel by the lobby entrance. We kept it up for four nights, drawing some of the largest outdoor crowds on Nob Hill since V-J Day in 1945.

We put our mark on the Mark thanks to Mark. For a week San Francisco was Goldwater country. *Life* led its convention coverage with a two-page spread of a smiling sixty-foot-high Barry Goldwater covering the front of the Mark Hopkins Hotel. The headline read, "The Big New Face of the GOP."

13

THINGS THAT MATTER

Party platforms matter to conservatives because they are based on ideas, and ideas are why conservatives are in politics. Unlike most nominees, Goldwater did not dictate the contents of the 1964 Republican platform. He went before the hundred-member platform committee and said, "You know the great basic principles on which we agree." He urged them to draft a document "that will unite us on principle and not divide us." Then he took questions, something no other presumptive presidential nominee had ever done. When he was asked by a black member of the committee whether he would use the power and prestige of the presidency to enforce the Civil Rights Act of 1964, he answered, "As president I would take an oath to uphold all laws. It is the president's duty to administer the law, not change it." He described his lifelong opposition to segregation and added, "Unlike some politicians, I have done more than just talk about it," a jab at LBJ.

YAF was everywhere at the convention, providing the bodies for rallies and demonstrations; blanketing the city with Goldwater buttons and bows (seen everywhere was the pin of a gold elephant wearing black-rimmed glasses); visiting the hotels housing the delegates to pass out YAF literature, copies of *National Review*, *Human Events*, and the *New Guard*, and material from the Committee of One Million (Against the Admission of Communist China to the United Nations) and other conservative organizations; and transporting the YAF Dixieland Band around the city on a flatbed truck. YAF even had its own folk group—the Goldwaters, all in red, white, and blue jackets and pants, four young men from Indiana University who sang satirical songs.

A YAF highlight of the pre-convention was the airport arrival of William F. Buckley Jr., who was greeted with a two-hundred-voice chorus of "We Want Buckley!" while the YAF band played, "Won't you come home, Bill Buckley?" As he was driven away, a delegate asked a YAF member, "Was that a senator?" "No, sir," came the solemn reply, "a philosopher."

I named Mary Ann Ford and Joan Sweetland the Indefatigables. They kept all our machines running, made sure everyone met deadlines, never lost their temper, and put up with me—Mary Ann dubbed me "Our Benevolent Dictator." Sometimes I was not very benevolent when we missed deadlines.

I had never done a formal press briefing until San Francisco. I relied on my memories of Pierre Salinger's White House briefings and Bob Humphreys's stories—he handled the weekly press conferences of Senate Republican leader Everett Dirksen and House Republican leader Charlie Halleck. I quickly realized that the fifty-some reporters in attendance for the daily briefings were so eager for news I could tell them what Goldwater had for breakfast—as I did one day—and they would use it. At the conclusion of my last afternoon briefing, a senior reporter said after about twenty minutes of Q and A, "Thank you, Mr. President." I took his sarcasm as a compliment.

From the opening of the convention, anti-Goldwater demonstrators had organized outside the Cow Palace—college girls with dirty hair and dirty jeans, college boys in Fidel Castro T-shirts, bearded beatniks, and blacks chanting, "Aunt Jemima [*clap clap*] must go! Barry Goldwater [*clap clap*] must go! Uncle Tom [*clap clap*] must go!" They carried signs that read "Defoliate Goldwater" and "Goldwater for President—Jefferson Davis for Vice President."

Nightly, the neatly dressed, good-natured Goldwater delegates made their way through the chanting demonstrators into the Cow Palace, where on Tuesday evening they had their first real opportunity to let loose. General Eisenhower delivered a predictable address larded with ghostwritten language about U.S. history, Republican accomplishments, and the increase in centralized government and the decrease in liberty under the Democratic occupants of the White House. Toward the end of his remarks, almost as an afterthought, he said, "Let us particularly scorn the divisive efforts of those outside our family, including sensation-seeking columnists and commentators, because, my friends, I assure you that these are people who couldn't care less about the good of our party."

Like water pouring through a broken dam, the indignation and resentment of conservatives who had been described as extremists, right-wing radicals, and neo-Nazis burst forth. Loud, angry boos bounced off the press stands flanking the speaker's platform. Some delegates shook their fists at the startled TV anchormen in their glassed-in aeries high above the convention floor. One delegate jumped up and down yelling, "Down with Walter Lippmann! Down with Walter Lippmann!"

A surprised Ike hesitated and then incited the delegates some more: "Let us not be guilty of maudlin sympathy for the criminal who, roaming the streets with switchblade knife and illegal firearms seeking a helpless prey, suddenly becomes, upon apprehension, a poor, underprivileged person who counts upon the compassion of our society and the laxness of weaknesses of too many courts to forgive his offenses." Delegates roared their agreement. The ex-president was endorsing a favorite Goldwater theme—the urgent need for law and order in the streets and in the courtrooms. If Ike is with us, I thought, who can be against us?

Eisenhower ended by pleading for unity and urging fellow Republicans not to "drown ourselves in a whirlpool of factional strife and divisive ambitions." Within two hours, the anti-Goldwater gang within the GOP, led by Nelson Rockefeller, throttled any hope of party unity.

As I sat in our communications center at the Mark Hopkins and monitored the proceedings with an eighteen-inch TV set, I reflected that Rocky had lost the nomination but not his ability to goad conservatives into paroxysms of loathing and hostility. Standing at the podium, a stern-faced Rockefeller called on the convention to pass a resolution denouncing right-wing extremism and compared the John Birch Society to the Ku Klux Klan and the Communist Party, although no Bircher had ever hanged anybody or called for the violent overthrow of the government. Rockefeller spoke of "threatening letters, smear and hate literature, strong-arm and goon tactics, bomb threats and bombings, infiltration and takeover of established political organizations by Communist and Nazi methods."

That was how liberals saw conservatives, I thought, how Rockefeller and Scranton and the others saw the Goldwater delegates—as Nazi storm troopers who would unleash a Kristallnacht on those who opposed them. He did not mention the vicious anti-Goldwater literature his campaign organization sent to every Republican household during the California primary. And he skipped over the eleventh-hour letter Scranton sent to every convention delegate, which called Goldwater the leader of "right-wing extremists" and described "Goldwaterism" as a "collection of absurd and dangerous positions." What was dangerous about trying to strengthen Social Security? I thought. What was absurd about trying to win the Cold War?

We had warned the Goldwater delegates that liberals would try to provoke them, and they remained in their seats despite Rockefeller's words, seething but silent. But the galleries contained hot-blooded conservatives who had not traveled a thousand miles to be called Communists and Nazis. Rockefeller was interrupted by boos followed by chants of "We Want Barry!" underscored by rhythmic beats on a bass drum.

Rocky smirked, the galleries roared louder, and the bass drum thumped. "This is a free country, ladies and gentlemen," he said. "Some of you don't like to hear it, but it's the truth." The truth was that the new Republican Party didn't want Rockefeller as its nominee, and he didn't like being rejected. I knew his charade would have no impact on the outcome—the senator would be easily nominated—but I worried that the booing would reinforce the impression of many Americans that Goldwater conservatives were what the liberals said we were—out of control and scary.

PEDDLER'S GRANDSON

On the morning of his nomination, the senator got up at 5:30 A.M., cut himself shaving, had a hearty breakfast of fresh strawberries, bacon, eggs, and milk but no coffee, and talked in his basic Spanish with radio hams in Venezuela and Mexico City. He left the hotel to address a Captive Nations rally of several thousand ethnic Americans and pledged to crack open the Iron Curtain and let in the "sunlight of freedom" on a continent too long darkened by communist imperialism. That night, along with Peggy, Denny, Dean, and Jay Hall (the General Motors lobbyist turned senior campaign consultant), he watched the nominating and seconding speeches on television, lounging in an easy chair, his white shirt open at the collar, his blue-gray jacket draped over a chair. I was at the Mark, in our communications center—I had given my Cow Palace pass to Mary Ann.

The primary nominating speech was delivered by Senator Dirksen, an old-school golden orator who had persuaded a majority of Republican senators to vote aye on the Civil Rights Act of 1964, ensuring its passage.

He called Goldwater "a peddler's grandson" who had based his political career on "blazing courage." It was fashionable today, he said, to sneer at patriotism and "to label positions of strength as extremism, to follow other nations' points of view more often than our own." But through firmness and a sure hand, he proclaimed, Barry Goldwater would retrieve the self-respect of America.

Grasping the nettle of racism, Dirksen described Goldwater's vote against the Civil Rights Act as an example of "moral courage not excelled anywhere in any parliamentary body of which I have any knowledge." As for the GOP's swing to an unabashed conservatism that alarmed some in and out of the party, he declared: "Delegates in this convention...the tide is turning! Let's give 190 million Americans the choice they have been waiting for!"

It was the moment Goldwater delegates had been waiting for. The convention exploded. Gold tinsel fell from the ceiling (the tinsel an invention of "Rally Don" Shafto, a YAF member). A huge banner unraveled from the roof with the senator's name interwoven with the names of the states. The band struck up "When the Saints Come Marching In." Joyful delegates flooded the floor—Californians in gold bibs, Nevadans in red silk shirts, Texans with longhorns. Gold balloons slowly rose from the floor to disappear in the golden rain. Signs danced above the crowd: "A Choice Not an Echo," "Au H2O in '64," "Wojeichowicz and All of Brooklyn Are for Barry," "La Louisiane Dit Allons Avec L'Eau d'Or!" Cowbells and police whistles and squeeze horns joined the band, creating a cacophony that rendered everyone speechless. The Goldwater delegates set a record for the longest and loudest demonstration in Republican convention history.

Back in the Mark Hopkins, the senator nibbled chocolates as the roll call began. At 10:35 P.M. South Carolina, which had placed his name in nomination at the 1960 convention, carried Goldwater over the 655-delegate mark to give him the 1964 Republican presidential nomination. "I didn't think it would come so fast," Goldwater said and placed a call to Clif in the Goldwater trailer.

"Clif, you did a wonderful job, all of you fellows. I can't thank you enough. See you down here a little later."

"Thank you, boss," Clif said.

In the Presidential Suite, the phone rang, and Denny said it was Rockefeller wanting to offer his congratulations. "Hell," the senator said, "I don't want to talk to that son of a bitch."

"Thank you, governor," Denny said. "I'll let Barry know you called."

At a midnight news conference at the Mark Hopkins—I was given fifteen minutes to set it up—the senator was asked why he wanted to be president of the United States. His answer surprised many, although not me.

"Well, I don't know if it's a case of wanting to be," he said. "I think it's a case of responsibility. I felt and I feel tonight that the Republican cause needs a chance and the conservative cause needs a chance. And this is the only way that we can find these things out—is to put them to the voter. If the voter says he agrees then I'll be elected. If he says he doesn't agree then I guess I won't be elected, but I would have given it a chance."

Did he think he could beat President Johnson in November?

"Well, I wouldn't be in this thing if I thought I was going to lose, because as I've said, I'm too old to go back to work and I'm too young to get out of politics. A Democrat has never defeated me, and I don't intend to start letting him at this late date."

He did not mention that earlier in the evening, while watching his nomination, he was given the latest national survey of his Princeton-based pollster, Opinion Research. President Johnson was favored by almost 80 percent of the public, the senator by barely 20 percent, not because the people loved Johnson but because Rockefeller and other liberals had convinced them that Goldwater would destroy Social Security and get us into a war.

Turning to Kitchel, the senator said, "Christ, we ought to be writing a speech telling them to go to hell and turn it down, let someone else do it."

"It doesn't have to be all or nothing," Denny said. "Arizona law says you can seek reelection to the Senate and run for president."

"I won't do what Lyndon did in 1960," growled Goldwater, "covering his bet by running for vice president and his Senate seat at the same time. It would look like I didn't think I had a chance to win the presidency."

"Do you?"

"Not much of one, but it's the hand I've been dealt and I'll play it. Even if it means giving up the only thing I've ever wanted in politics."

14

EXTREMISM AND LIBERTY

I was not among the few who helped write the most controversial acceptance speech in national convention history. The process began on Saturday, July 11, with a working luncheon in the Presidential Suite on the seventeenth floor. Present beside the senator were Bill Baroody, AEI president on leave; Warren Nutter of the University of Virginia; Harry Jaffa of the Ohio State University; Stefan Possony of the Hoover Institution; Richard Ware, head of Earhart Foundation; and Karl (Shakespeare) Hess, the senator's chief speechwriter. Much of the discussion was about Hess's draft, which had not generated much enthusiasm.

When the group met Monday morning after the scurrilous Scranton letter had been delivered to every delegate the previous night, the Hess draft, conciliatory in tone, was discarded. The group decided to focus on one idea: the conservative movement aimed to take the country and the party in a new direction, a conservative direction.

The senator was so impressed with Jaffa's memo on extremism prepared for the platform hearings that he asked him to write his acceptance speech. Although Jaffa had never written a political speech, he readily agreed. He and Warren Nutter worked through the day and into the evening on a draft they presented to Goldwater on Tuesday. With Baroody acting as editor in chief, the group went over every word. They listened as Goldwater read each line aloud, including the two at the end that would make political history. There was unanimous agreement that the sentences about extremism and moderation said what Goldwater and the campaign wanted to say.

Like most of the staff, I did not know the content of the senator's address until he accepted the nomination Thursday evening. I got a copy of his remarks from Joan Sweetland just minutes before he began speaking, as did Clif White, Steve Shadegg and the other regional directors, Tony Smith, and anyone else with political experience. The inner circle did not want rank politics to intrude into their principled deliberations. My one and only brush with the speech came Tuesday afternoon, when I had to talk to Denny and was admitted into the presidential suite. In his shirtsleeves, Goldwater sat with Jaffa, Baroody, Nutter, Ware, Possony, and Hess, clearly enjoying the seminar.

"Freedom must be balanced," I heard him say, "so that order, lacking liberty, will not become a slave of the prison cell. And liberty, lacking order, will not become the license of the mob."

"Lincolnian," Nutter said softly. Jaffa nodded in acceptance of the compliment.

I was impressed by the elevated tone of the discourse but noted the absence of any reference to taxes, the price of wheat, or the Warsaw Pact. After all, the acceptance speech was a political speech, not a university lecture. I took advantage of my visit to ask Denny whether any decision had been made about a vice-presidential candidate.

"Barry," said Kitchel, turning to the senator, "we have to decide on your running mate."

"I told you, Bill Miller. He drives Lyndon crazy. As a former national committee chairman, Bill can pull the party together. Plus he's a Catholic and a strong anticommunist."

"What about the chairman of the national committee?"

"Dean."

"Not Clif?"

"Oh, Clif's young—he'll get his chance. Besides, he's a little too East Coast—you know he worked for Dewey. Dean's the man."

"It's your call."

"Damn right."

EXTREMISM IS NO VICE

On Thursday evening, July 16, in prime time, the senator was introduced to the convention and the country by the great unifier, Richard Nixon, who predicted that when Barry Goldwater got through, Lyndon Johnson would be singing "Home on the Range." He urged the faithful to ignore the polls and the columnists, reminding them that "Mr. Gallup isn't going to be counting the votes on November 3." Far from being weaker than it was in 1960, Nixon said, the Republican Party had more congressmen, more senators, more governors, and more state legislators. Ever the bridge builder, he mentioned Scranton and Rockefeller, and such was their respect for the man who had put Alger Hiss in jail that the Goldwater delegates applauded the liberal governors politely.

Nixon continued:

America needs new leadership. It needs a man who will go up and down the length of the land crying out, "Wake up, America, before it is too late!"

This is a time, my fellow Republicans and my fellow Americans, not for the New Deal of the 1930s or the Fair Deal of the 1950s or the Fast Deal of Lyndon Johnson but for the Honest Deal of Barry Goldwater.

Make your decision tonight about a man who has been called Mr. Conservative, a man who is now, by the action of the convention, Mr. Republican, a man who after the greatest campaign in history will be Mr. President—Barry Goldwater!

Watching from our communications center at the Mark Hopkins, I saw my hero, deeply tanned and silver-haired, ensure his defeat with his acceptance speech.

Goldwater walked slowly down the flag-draped catwalk to stand at the rostrum, where he was met by the martial notes of "The Battle Hymn of the Republic." Red, white, and blue balloons poured down from the rafters while a chorus of voices more powerful than the Mormon Tabernacle Choir chanted, "We want Barry! We want Barry!" The Cow Palace seemed ready to explode. The senator waited patiently while the convention chairman pounded and pounded his gavel until at last the great hall fell silent. I placed a copy of his address in my lap and followed along.

"I accept your nomination with a deep sense of humility."

(He earned it the old-fashioned way, I thought, one delegate at a time, with a little help from Clif and the rest of the Draft Goldwater gang.)

"The Good Lord raised this mighty Republic to be a home for the brave to flourish as the land of the free—not to stagnate in the swampland of collectivism, not to cringe before the bully of communism."

(He would inspire a free society, not guarantee a Great Society.)

"The tide has been running against freedom. Our people have followed false prophets. We must, and we shall, return to proven ways—not because they are old, but because they are true."

(Ways based on the Ten Commandments and the Constitution, not Freud and the editorials of the *New York Times*.)

"This party, with its every action, every word, every breath, and every heartbeat, has but a single resolve, and that is freedom."

(So hard to gain and so easy to lose, I thought.)

"Tonight there is violence in our streets."

(There had been Harlem riots, again.)

"Corruption in our highest offices."

(Everyone knew Bobby Baker was not only the clerk of the Senate but the panderer of the Senate.)

"Aimlessness among our youth."

(Rebels whose only cause was themselves.)

"Anxiety among our elderly."

(Who could blame them, with runaway federal spending and a Social Security system ready to implode?)

"We are at war in Vietnam. And yet the president, who is the commander in chief of our forces, refuses to say whether or not the objective over there is victory."

(President Goldwater would direct the Pentagon to win the war with overwhelming air and sea power and without nuclear weapons or U.S. ground troops.)

"Anyone who joins us in all sincerity is welcome. But those who do not care for our cause, we don't expect to enter our ranks in any case. What is needed is focused and dedicated Republicanism that rejects unthinking and stupid labels."

(Like "Goldwaterism" and "right-wing extremism.")

The senator paused, his face stern. The next words were underlined in the text: "And I would remind you that extremism in the defense of liberty is no vice!"

The delegates jumped to their feet, hollering their approval, while the conservatives in the galleries blew their horns like the Israelites marching into battle.

Then he offered the other half: "And let me remind you also that moderation in the pursuit of justice is no virtue!"

Future U.S. senator Trent Lott said the words were "a call to arms." Vic Gold, Goldwater's traveling press secretary in the general election, shouted, "Terrific!" Richard Viguerie, the future guru of conservative direct-mail fundraising, embraced the extremism line. But Richard Nixon recalled that he felt "almost physically sick" as he listened.

Liberals, Republican and Democratic, lashed out at Goldwater. "Senator Goldwater's remarks about extremism," Rockefeller said, "are dangerous, irresponsible, and frightening." "Those who say that the doctrine of ultra-conservatism offers no menace," said the NAACP's Roy Wilkins, "should remember that a man came out of the beer halls of Munich and rallied the forces of Rightism in Germany." "The stench of fascism is in the air," said Governor Pat Brown of California. "The Republicans have *Mein Kampf* as their political bible," said San Francisco mayor John Shelley. "If a party so committed were to take public office in this country," wrote the *Washington Post*, "there would be nothing left for us to do but pray." "If Goldwater is elected," wrote C. L. Sulzberger in the *New York Times*, "there may not be a day after tomorrow."

I sat before the TV set watching our delegates exult in the words that sealed our defeat four months before Election Day. The firebrand in me hailed the senator for throwing the gauntlet before the liberals while the pragmatist in me winced.

From my campaign diary:

> The acceptance speech was a disappointment to me. It was too literary, too long, too general, and contained that "extremism-moderation line" which will continue to haunt us throughout this campaign.... It was written for posterity which because of that speech and what it portends will not include BG as President. I learned later that Clif, still manning our trailer, said, "I wonder if they realize out there on the floor that they are hailing disaster and defeat."

In those days there were no spin doctors to work the news media and declare that the senator's speech was one of the most brilliant and evocative speeches in convention history. I did not hold a news briefing the next day; nor did Denny Kitchel or Dean Burch or Clif White or any of our other senior officials. If we had, we could have pointed out its Lincolnian and Churchillian accents. We could have placed the extremism line in perspective with references to Patrick Henry ("Give me liberty or give me death!") and Martin Luther King Jr., who had endorsed extremism in his celebrated "Letter from a Birmingham Jail." Goldwater stood by his words, remarking thirty years later when I interviewed him, "I'd make that speech again, anyplace, anytime—I think it's the best statement I ever made." But he never used the "extremism" line again in the campaign.

To heighten anticipation and encourage speculation, we had not passed out advance copies of the speech to the news media. "It hit them like a bolt of lightning," I said to Anne. "I heard one reporter say, 'My God, he's going to run as Barry Goldwater.'"

Advising Senator Goldwater and running mate William E. Miller during the 1964 campaign

15

ANYTHING GOES

I n the six weeks before the Democrats nominated President Johnson at their Atlantic City convention, Goldwater vacationed at Balboa Bay aboard a converted PT boat named *The Sundance*; we took command of the Republican National Committee and fired everyone but the cleaning lady; George Wallace withdrew his candidacy for president, explaining that the Republicans had passed a platform he could support (ignoring that we had endorsed and pledged to implement the Civil Rights Act); and the GOP held the "unity" summit I had suggested in Hershey, Pennsylvania, presided over by General Eisenhower, at which an overweening Nelson Rockefeller demanded that Goldwater repudiate extremism, racism, and the use of nuclear weapons (as though the senator had embraced all of them). Ike and Nixon both stressed their strong support of Goldwater, but Rockefeller kept kvetching. His behavior telegraphed what he would do in the fall—walk away from us.

Between the national conventions, I suffered intoxicating highs and excruciating lows. Following *Life*'s publication of my photo, along with those of Kitchel, Burch, and others, with the caption "Will handle public relations and advertising in the campaign," I was in fact director of public relations of the campaign—for ten days. Then Dean brought me into his office and said he was appointing L. Richard Guylay as PR director. "I have to," explained Dean. "I can't take the chance. Neither you nor I have ever been responsible for a $5 million national advertising campaign."

He asked me to serve as Guylay's deputy. Guylay was a soft-spoken New York professional in his fifties who favored gray flannel suits and black knit ties and had worked in Taft's 1950 senatorial campaign and Eisenhower's 1952 presidential campaign. He knew political PR and advertising but had never read *The Conscience of a Conservative*.

On the last day of July, when I was still acting director of public relations and before Guylay's arrival, I was called into a meeting with Leo Burnett, the legendary head of the Leo Burnett Agency in Chicago, which had been acting as the advertising agency of the Republican National Committee. Believing it was the professional thing to do, Burnett had directed his agency to come up with a slogan for the Goldwater campaign. The old master (then in his early seventies) personally made the presentation to Dean, deputy chairman John Grenier, and me. Politics is all about emotions, Burnett said, and he believed his team had come up with a slogan that was politically on target and appealed powerfully to emotion. He paused for effect and uncovered a mock-up of the slogan on a billboard:

IN YOUR HEART YOU KNOW HE'S RIGHT

Dean, John, and I looked at one another and nodded. "We like it," Dean said. "In fact, we love it."

Burnett responded that he knew the perfect place to introduce the slogan to the American people—the Democratic National Convention in Atlantic City. An enormous billboard across from the convention hall was available. It would cost $12,500 but would generate enormous free publicity and media coverage.

"It will drive Johnson and the Democrats nuts," I said. "Be sure to use a full-color photo of the senator."

That was the last time we saw Mr. Burnett, the wise old man of advertising, because his agency was replaced by Erwin Wasey, a small New York agency, on Guylay's strong recommendation. They dismissed the Burnett slogan as corny and old-fashioned and promised to come up with a better one. After a month of "intensive" research and "creative" thinking, Erwin Wasey presented their new slogan at a special meeting of the national committee. It was:

IN YOUR HEART YOU KNOW HE'S RIGHT

They had tried, Erwin Wasey said, but could not improve on the Burnett language. So much for Madison Avenue creativity, I thought. "In Your Heart You Know He's Right" reflected the strengths and weaknesses of our campaign. It appealed strongly to those on the right who believed in Barry Goldwater and his conservative ideas, but it failed to assure those in the middle who believed that Goldwater was too far to the right.

On his first day, Guylay invited me to a quick lunch at a nearby coffee shop and asked me to run the day-to-day operations while he concentrated on how to spend the $6 million (the figure kept going up) set aside for advertising. How ironic, I thought: the senator had prohibited me from using what he called "Madison Avenue crap" but had approved a quintessential Madison Avenue man as his PR director in his presidential campaign. I brooded for a day but reflected I was near the top in a presidential campaign run by a conservative on conservative ideas. I resolved to be the best damn number two I could be.

From my campaign diary:

> We spent days choosing the official campaign photo of the Senator. Smiling or not smiling? Gray suit or dark blue suit? White shirt or blue shirt? Bold tie or muted tie? With glasses or without glasses? The last gave us the most trouble. As handsome as the Senator is, he does not look good in glasses. But everyone knows he wears glasses with heavy black frames. One of our most popular items is a miniature brooch with a "gold" elephant wearing black frame glasses. Would it look like we were trying to make him over if we omitted the glasses? In the end we went with the glasses (although Citizens for Goldwater-Miller, run by Clif, selected a photo of him without glasses). It wasn't until after we released the photo and Republican groups were ordering it by the thousands that Jim Day pointed out that the glasses were a little crooked.
>
> Tony offered me the job of assistant press secretary traveling with the Senator on the road. I declined. I never liked baby-sitting and taking care of the reporters covering the Senator would be nonstop handling of the biggest babies in Washington. Vic Gold will fill the position. They call him Old Faithful (although he's only in his thirties) because he blows up every 14 minutes. But Vic is a consummate pro—he will feed, house, and transport the press, pick up their dry cleaning, memorize their favorite drink, do whatever is required to keep the boys on the plane happy.
>
> They are putting new ceiling lights in my office and the telephone men have begun their eighth rewiring in the last two weeks. The Republican National Committee has been a madhouse because we fired all the hacks who have been hanging around for years and brought in our gang—we are now two hundred strong. The

politicos—Burch, Grenier, the regional directors like Shadegg and Wayne Hood and Dick Herman—and everyone in communications are on the second floor. The *philosophes*—Baroody, Jay Hall, and so forth—are on the third floor. And rarely do they meet except on Sunday afternoon when we have our weekly strategy sessions.

We have a War Room with maps and phones and TVs that the Joint Chiefs of Staff would find familiar. We have a battery of TWX and DATA teletype machines that can send 1,050 words a minute to Republican offices across the country. We have WATS long-distance lines and auto-dial phones. It's a coast-to-coast version of Clif's convention trailer, and there's been nothing like it in campaigns until now.

One of our daily polls reported that only 9 percent of the people rate Johnson an "excellent" president while 39 percent rate him "fair to poor." Another poll said that about three-fourths of the independent voters like the Senator's straight talk—less than 25 percent are worried that he "acts without thinking." Sixty percent question Johnson's judgment. Even Gallup says that if the election were held today, the Senator would get 34 percent, up from 20 percent in June.

We can win, or come close, I know we can, but there are only 64 days until Election Day.

STUDY IN CONTRASTS

It would be difficult to find two candidates more opposite in their politics, philosophy, and personality than Barry Goldwater and Lyndon Johnson.

Goldwater's favorite president was Thomas Jefferson, Johnson's FDR. Goldwater's favorite philosopher was F. A. Hayek, Johnson's Machiavelli. LBJ was once described as "Machiavelli in a ten-gallon hat."

Goldwater believed in individuals, Johnson thought in electoral blocs. Goldwater swore by the Constitution, Johnson by the New Deal.

Goldwater was interested in many things besides politics. Johnson was interested only in politics.

Even his enemies conceded that Barry Goldwater was an honest man. Even his closest friends admitted that Johnson was a wheeler-dealer.

Goldwater was content to be respected by his friends and peers. Johnson was desperate to be loved, or feared, by everyone.

As president, Goldwater would have followed Eisenhower's policy of balancing economic stability and military strength. As president, Johnson would institute a policy of guns and butter that would produce a tragic defeat in Vietnam, with 58,000 Americans dead and 304,000 wounded, and a pyrrhic victory in the war on poverty.

As different as they were, Goldwater and Johnson were bound by the same basic elements of a political campaign—Money, Organization, the Candidate, Issues, and the Media. I referred to them as MOCIM, an acronym I would use in my writing and university teaching for the rest of my life. MOCIM is my semioriginal contribution to political theory—I learned about the first four elements from Clif White.

Money: In 1964 there were almost no regulations about raising funds for a national campaign aside from the requirement that you had to register with the office of the Clerk of the House of Representatives the name and address of anyone who gave more than $50. We calculated that we would have to raise at least $13 million, probably most of it in small contributions, because almost all the big givers, with a few exceptions like Henry Salvatori and J.D. (Stets) Coleman, were backing LBJ. We ended up raising more than $14.4 million from about one million individuals. No candidate had ever received such widespread support before—ever. By comparison, Nixon had received gifts from fewer than fifty thousand people.

Organization: As in the campaign for the nomination, it was a contest between our volunteers—about a half million across the country—and the trained professionals of the AFL-CIO, who had been winning elections for Democrats for thirty years.

The Candidate: Goldwater campaigned in the general election as he had in the California primary, giving one or two major speeches a day in populated areas and depending on the news media to carry his message beyond. Johnson on the road was a primal force, giving eight and ten talks a day, slowing down the open presidential limousine (open at his instructions despite Kennedy's assassination) so that he could shake the hands of those who reached out to him, always an hour late for a rally, talking too long, asking over and over again, "What has Barry Goldwater ever done for [fill in the name of the town or city]?"

Issues: Goldwater talked about the "forgotten American" who was alarmed at his loss of freedom in a society becoming a welfare state. He talked about lawlessness and immorality, and the 500 percent increase in crime over the past four years. He appealed to those who resented being told what to do and not to do by bureaucrats in a far-off city. He cited Johnson's failure to recognize the true threat of communism. He promised to fight to restore to the states their constitutional powers. But he did not talk about civil rights for fear of inciting demonstrations and worse.

Johnson had a simple message: the Great Society will have something for everybody.

Media: I learned from Vic Gold and from my father, traveling with the candidates as he had done since the 1940s, that the sixty or so journalists covering Goldwater were nearly unanimous in their personal like of the senator and as unanimous in their rejection of his "radical right-wing" positions. As one reporter put it, "How can he think that way?" Robin MacNeil of NBC, Charles Mohr of the *New York Times*, and Walter Mears of the Associated Press were national correspondents who had traveled with the senator from the beginning, even before Kennedy's assassination. They once asked themselves, "If you were climbing a mountain, who would you rather be roped to—Jack Kennedy or Barry Goldwater?" They all agreed—Goldwater.

Political advertising was still evolving, and there was nothing remarkable about our sixty-second ads. But our half-hour programs, including *Brunch with Barry* (the senator talking with half a dozen housewives about pocketbook issues) and *Conversation at Gettysburg* (the senator one-on-one with Ike) anticipated the thirty-minute polymercials of Ross Perot in 1992. According to one academic, we elevated the use of electronic media to raise funds to "an art form." Every one of our longer programs included an appeal for funds, usually by Hollywood stars like Raymond Massey and John Wayne—and once by a semiretired film actor named Ronald Reagan.

Paperback books were a major means of communication and commitment for conservatives in 1964. Never before had political paperbacks been distributed in such volume: an estimated total of fifteen to seventeen million. The top bestsellers were *A Texan Looks at Lyndon*, by the respected historian of the Southwest J. Evetts Haley (six million); *None Dare Call It Treason*, by former Young Republican John Stormer (five million), who was still writing right-wing exposés fifty years later; and *A Choice Not an Echo*, by Republican conservative activist Phyllis Schlafly (three million). All three books became bestsellers through word of mouth and the efforts of conservative groups like the JBS, which moved thousands of copies of all of them. They were written by conservatives for conservatives who did not trust the establishment media to tell the truth about Johnson and certainly not about Goldwater.

For his part, LBJ was determined to use any means to the end of a landslide triumph. For him extremism in the pursuit of victory was no vice. He instructed his campaign directors to make sure that the American people understood that Barry Goldwater was too dangerous to vote for. The result was a series of brilliant but vicious anti-Goldwater TV and radio spots like the "Daisy" commercial.

"DAISY"

A small, golden-haired girl is standing in a sun-speckled field, pulling petals from a daisy. In her high voice, she tries to count: "1, 2, 3, 4, 5, 7, 6, 6, 8, 9, 9..." When she reaches "9" a deep bass voice overrides her childish treble and begins a countdown, "10, 9, 8, 7, 6, 5, 4, 3, 2, 1, 0," as the camera comes in close on the child's face. At zero, it dissolves from the pupil of her eye to the explosion of an atomic bomb that fills the screen with a deadly mushroom cloud. Like a doomsday prophet, President Johnson's voice solemnly intones, "These are the stakes—to make a world in which all of God's children can live, or to go into the dark. We must either love each other or we must die." On a black screen are the words "Vote for President Johnson on November 3." A voice repeats the phrase and concludes dramatically, "The stakes are too high for you to stay home."

I was furious and yet admiring. Although they never mentioned his name, the message was clear: President Goldwater would get us into a nuclear war. I was struck by the integration of the ad's elements—the little girl among the flowers creating a mood of peace and beauty, the sudden switch to the bomb and the ominous mushroom cloud wiping everything away, the apocalyptic language. The ad played on the fears of Goldwater the "warmonger" created by Rockefeller in the primaries and reinforced by the president in his campaign speeches.

Dean Burch protested to the Federal Election Commission. We called on the Johnson campaign not to run the ad again. We later learned they had no intention of running it more than once—on CBS's *Monday Night at the Movies*, which drew an estimated fifty million viewers. They didn't have to. There was so much talk about "Daisy" that all three networks, CBS, ABC, and NBC, showed the commercial over and over on their newscasts, increasing the number of people who eventually saw it manyfold. *Time* followed with a cover story, "The Nuclear Issue," that used "Daisy" as a leading example. The Cuban Missile Crisis with its threat of nuclear confrontation was less than two years old. The popular film *Dr. Strangelove*, which ends with a nuclear exchange between the United States and the Soviet Union, had been released in January.

As Tony Schwartz, the Madison Avenue creator of the "Daisy" commercial, later explained, he deliberately played off the public's memories, vague and otherwise, of the senator's statements and his opponents' distortions about nuclear bombs and weapons. "The Daisy commercial," he said, "evoked Goldwater's pro-bomb statements. They were like the dirty pictures in the audience's mind." That Schwartz, a liberal Democrat, would equate dirty pictures and Goldwater's words reveals his own mind.

"Daisy" and another TV spot that suggested the senator would end Social Security (the camera focused on two large hands that picked up a Social Security card and tore it in half) were part of what the Democrats called the Anti-Campaign. It was run out of the White House, which would not be allowed under present campaign law and ethics.

LBJ'S ANTI-CAMPAIGN

Managed by veteran Washington-based Democrats, the Anti-Campaign churned out clandestine "black propaganda" about Goldwater. The group met in a small conference room on the second floor of the West Wing of the White House, almost directly above the Oval Office. Its members included Daniel Patrick Moynihan, then an assistant secretary of labor and later a U.S. senator from New York; Leonard Marks, who would become director of the U.S. Information Agency; and Hyman Bookbinder, a labor lobbyist and future Washington representative of the American Jewish Committee.

Typical of their black-bag politics was scheduling Democratic speakers before and after the senator's appearance in a city, smothering his message with pro-Johnson, anti-Goldwater rhetoric. Advance knowledge of Goldwater's travel schedule and advance copies of his remarks were provided by a spy the CIA had planted in our headquarters. E. Howard Hunt, later convicted for his part in the Watergate break-in, told a congressional committee a decade later that his CIA superior ordered him to infiltrate our headquarters. When Hunt questioned the order, he was told that President Johnson "had ordered this activity" and that White House aide Chester L. Cooper "would be the recipient of the information." In congressional testimony, CIA director William Colby confirmed Cooper's role in the illegal surveillance. That the CIA is prohibited by law from operating within the United States did not matter to President Johnson in pursuit of his historic landslide. We never suspected that one of us was a spy for the Democrats.

One of the Anti-Campaign's writers was John Roche, later a syndicated columnist and president of Americans for Democratic Action.

"We used to get advance texts of Senator Goldwater's key speeches," he admitted, enabling them to have speakers primed to reply "before Goldwater had even opened his mouth." When Roche asked how they got the speeches, "the reply was 'Don't ask.'"

That's not all. The Anti-Campaign enlisted the FBI, even though the bureau is supposed to limit its investigations to individuals and institutions considered to be risks or dangers to national security. That would not include the presidential nominee of a major political party who happened to be a sitting U.S. senator and a two-star general in the Air Force Reserve. Barry Goldwater was many things but not a Manchurian Candidate.

Nevertheless, the FBI arranged for widespread wiretapping of the Goldwater campaign. We suspected as early as the middle of September that the telephones at our national headquarters in Washington were bugged. Although our offices were periodically swept for listening devices, important information still leaked to the Democrats. Once, at a private meeting in John Grenier's office, regional political directors discussed the possibility of the senator's making a campaign stop in the Chicago area. Sam Hay suggested that East St. Louis be added to the itinerary and called the Republican chairman of Cook County, who agreed. Within the hour, a reporter called Hay to say he had heard Goldwater would be coming to East St. Louis and he would like the details. To protect themselves, the regional directors began making confidential calls from a pay telephone outside our headquarters. Steve Shadegg confessed that resorting to such tactics fostered feelings of "uncertainty and mutual distrust" among the Goldwater staff—precisely what the Johnson people hoped to foster.

The senator told me that two correspondents questioned him about a proposal he had not made public—that if elected, he would ask General Eisenhower to go to Vietnam to examine the situation and report his findings to him. He insisted that he discussed the possible Eisenhower visit with only two close advisers—Kitchel and Baroody—and only on the campaign plane. And yet the reporters swore they heard about it from the White House.

FBI BUGS

At the center of the Anti-Campaign was President Johnson, who illegally ordered the FBI to conduct security checks of Goldwater's Senate staff. The evidence of the president's personal involvement is convincing.

Cartha (Deke) DeLoach, the FBI's liaison with the White House and a longtime top aide to Director J. Edgar Hoover, denied at a 1975 congressional hearing that the bureau had investigated Goldwater aides. Some thirty years later, through the Freedom of Information Act, I obtained copies of FBI memoranda that detailed the results of the bureau's illegal file check of fifteen Senate staffers. "No derogatory information was located concerning" any of the people in Goldwater's office, stated one memo that bore DeLoach's initials, indicating he had read it.

J. Edgar Hoover later admitted that the FBI had bugged the Goldwater campaign plane at the direction of President Johnson. In 1971 Robert Mardian became the new assistant attorney general for the internal security division. During a two-hour conversation with Hoover, Mardian asked about the procedures of electronic surveillance. To Mardian's amazement, Hoover confessed that in 1964, the bureau, on orders from the White House, had bugged the Goldwater plane. When Mardian asked Hoover why, the FBI director replied, "You do what the president tells you to do." William C. Sullivan, the bureau's number-two man, verified to Mardian the FBI's spying operation against the Goldwater campaign. In a 1992 interview with me, Mardian said that Sullivan had told him about the bugging because "he was a Goldwater man" and was appalled at the president's partisan use of the bureau.

The senator assumed that he was under surveillance of some kind. "I never got upset about it," he told me years later. "Oh, I guess [I] should have, but knowing Lyndon as I did, I never did."

As author Victor Lasky later wrote about electronic surveillance in Washington, "It didn't start with Watergate."

16

LET GOLDWATER
BE GOLDWATER

Our crowds in the first weeks of the campaign were impressive: 53,000 in Los Angeles, 15,000 with an overflow of 3,000 in Seattle, 11,000 with 5,000 left outside in Minneapolis. The rallies resembled old-fashioned tent revivals. The people cheered when Goldwater chastised them for looking to government to solve their problems. They applauded when he declared that each individual is responsible for his own actions. "Let this generation light a lamp of liberty," he urged, "that will illuminate the world." They even clapped for his contrarian positions on the issues and his refusal to pander to special interests.

Not as receptive were the liberal academics who boycotted his plenary address at the American Political Science Association conference in Chicago. The professors who did not attend missed a perceptive analysis of the uses and abuses of political power. The senator praised the American system of federalism, with its genius for combining "the size and power of a great empire with the freedom of a small republic." But the system was endangered, he said, by the prevailing doctrine of the Democratic Party—that the Constitution means "only what those who hold power for the moment choose to say that it means." Indefinitely expanded federal power will crush the states, he said, "until the states have no will, and finally no resources, moral or financial, of their own." The federal system, he declared, is "the very foundation of our greatness—yesterday, today, and tomorrow."

It was political rhetoric at a high level and rarely presented in a presidential campaign. Some professors applauded, some jeered, some walked out, some stood in grudging appreciation at the end of his address. The senator enjoyed it all. There was nothing he liked more than baiting a hostile audience of liberal intellectuals.

From beginning to end, he would not pander to anyone, inspiring me and other young conservatives to be similarly principled, and persevering.

In Winston-Salem, North Carolina, he attacked Defense Secretary Robert McNamara and the administration's no-win policy in Vietnam and never mentioned tobacco or cotton. In St. Augustine, Florida, he spoke of the rising crime rate, terror in the streets, and the evils of Medicare but uttered not one reassuring word about Social Security. In Knoxville, Tennessee, he appealed for Democratic support and ignored the TVA.

Republican senators Karl Mundt of South Dakota and Milton S. Young of North Dakota were convinced that Goldwater's showing in the Midwest depended on his delivering the right address at the annual plowing contest in Fargo, North Dakota. For ten days, they worked closely with us on a statement that denied President Goldwater would make any immediate or drastic changes in farm policy. His goal was the gradual elimination of government price supports and an ultimate return to the free market.

On the day of the plowing contest, with Mundt, Young, and other prominent Republicans sitting on the platform behind him, the senator roundly condemned the administration's farm program. He reminded the several farmers in front of him that 17 percent of their income, amounting to $2.1 billion annually, was a federal subsidy. Raising his voice, he demanded, "Do you want that to continue?" He paused and then said reluctantly, "I have no intention of stopping supports overnight." A tiny group near the platform applauded, but the rest of the vast crowd that stretched to the horizon was so quiet you could hear the cows chewing their cud.

FLYING HIGH AND LOW

The senator's seat on the campaign plane faced forward against a bulkhead with three clocks showing the different time zones and with two small signs: "Re-Elect Goldwater in 1968" and "Better Brinksmanship than Chickenship." The wall beside him was hung with dozens of keys to the hotel rooms in which he had slept. Denny sometimes sat next to him, but in the closing days of the campaign, the senator preferred to sit alone in his shirtsleeves, going over what he was going to say at the next stop.

Sometimes he piloted the plane because it relaxed him. One time he sent the plane into a steep dive before pulling out as the ground rushed toward the passengers. Another time, he landed the plane so hard that the reporters in the back were almost jolted out of their seats.

"Jesus Christ!" yelled the *Baltimore Sun*. "What are you trying to do—kill us?"

"It never entered my mind," the senator said, smiling, when the reporter's cry was relayed to him.

He proved how different a candidate he was when, in the last weeks of the campaign, the D.C. police caught White House aide Walter Jenkins in the men's room of the YMCA, two blocks from the White House, fondling the genitals of a retired soldier.

Jenkins was arrested on Wednesday, October 7, but no reporter checked the police blotter that day and there was no immediate story. A cop finally leaked the arrest to us, and on Monday, October 12, Dean informed the senator.

If any other presidential candidate had been speaking about corruption in Washington and his opponent's most trusted assistant had been arrested for a homosexual act, the candidate would have gone into full attack mode. He would have called a news conference, pointed an accusing finger, called for a congressional hearing—Jenkins attended National Security Council meetings—ordered a TV spot denouncing the scandal, and told his campaign staff to squeeze the issue dry.

Dean and the other members of the inner circle wanted to do all of that, but the senator directed his campaign organization to remain silent. He had known Jenkins as a member of the Air Force Reserve Unit on Capitol Hill that he commanded. He ordered us not to try to take any political advantage of Jenkins's disgrace.

On Wednesday morning, October 14, a full week after the arrest, the *Washington Star*, an anti-Goldwater paper, called the White House to check the story. Within a few hours, Abe Fortas and Clark Clifford, close friends of the president and among the city's most prominent residents, visited the editors of the *Star*, the *Washington Post*, the *New York Times*, and other media and begged them not to publish the story to spare the forty-six-year-old Jenkins and his wife and six children. Editors agreed to delay but not to kill the story.

"Jesus Christ, Barry," Dean said, "they're trying to cover it up. They know this story is dynamite and could materially affect the campaign. It's what you've been talking about since day one—the need for morality in government—and here the president's closest aide, who has top security clearance, is arrested practically in the backyard of the White House on a 'morals' charge. We've got to say *something*."

"I know what Lyndon would do," the senator said, "but I'm not Lyndon and I am not going to use poor old Walter to get votes."

"Suppose we don't mention Jenkins but say there's a cover-up involving national security?"

"All right," the senator said reluctantly, "but I don't want anyone and I mean anyone in our campaign using this thing for political purposes."

At 8:02 P.M., October 14, seven days after Jenkins's arrest, we released a statement: "The White House is desperately trying to suppress a major news story affecting the national security."

United Press International responded by running a story (which UPI had already written) about the Jenkins scandal that made the front pages of every newspaper and the newscasts of every TV network. But our hopes that the scandal would make a difference, shift votes, and move us up in the polls were dashed when Nikita Khrushchev was suddenly replaced as the leader of the Soviet Union, Communist China exploded its first nuclear bomb, and the Conservative Party of the United Kingdom was defeated after thirteen years in power. The Walter Jenkins scandal disappeared, never to be seen or heard again.

17

LANDSLIDE

On October 26, 1964, I wrote the following entry in my campaign diary:

There are all kinds of campaigns—brilliant campaigns and dumb campaigns, expensive campaigns and bargain-basement campaigns, lucky campaigns and star-crossed campaigns, happy campaigns and grim campaigns, runaway campaigns and nail-biting campaigns. Our campaign is unlike any other presidential campaign because our candidate is unlike any other presidential candidate in history.

There are campaigns in which the candidates spend most of their time attacking and tearing down each other. But the Senator ignores Johnson's smears, slurs and attacks, including the TV commercials he calls "electronic dirt."

There are campaigns in which the press is scrupulously balanced in its coverage and campaigns in which it sides openly with a candidate. Everyone knows who the press wants to win this time. As the Senator says, "I wonder where Christianity would be today if some of these reporters had been Matthew, Mark, Luke, and John."

You've got to give Johnson credit. This past week, he went campaigning and covered 10,000 miles in seven days—hitting Phoenix, Reno, Helena, Denver, Cleveland, Louisville, Philadelphia, and

New York. He is a modern-day Machiavelli, all things to all men. He stopped seven times on the way in from the Phoenix airport to exhort the faithful, ten times on the way out. He'd love to carry the Senator's home state. On the motorcade into Denver, he yelled to crowds along the road, "Come on down to the speakin'. I want you all there. There's going to be a hot time in the old town tonight. It's Democrats all the way. We're going to have a party. You don't have to dress. Just bring your kids and your dogs and anything." In Peoria, he urged the Illinois State Federation of Labor to get out the vote. "You and I have a job to do on November 3, and we are going to do that job. The first job is to get back home, quit our big talk and bragging, get down to work, and get our friends and our uncles and our cousins and our aunts to the polls and elect Lyndon Johnson by the greatest landslide in history!"

Surprise. The press was captivated. "To describe this week's work as 'effective campaigning,'" gushed the *Washington Star*, "is like calling Hurricane Hilda a 'bit of a blow.' He is no longer John Kennedy's successor. He is a towering political figure, with a constituency that is his, and his alone." And because the press is convinced that a President Goldwater would endanger the country and the world, it looks the other way when Johnson is less than presidential. In Evansville, he came reeling out of his campaign plane and delivered a rambling incoherent speech.

"Is that man drunk?" CBS asked a Secret Service agent.

"If a fifth of aged Scotch will make you drunk, he's drunk," the agent replied.

The CBS reporter sent a memo about the drinking to New York City but never got a reply. He told Teddy White about it, knowing it would not be used until the campaign was over, if then. "Here was the man whose finger was on the nuclear button as drunk as you can be in a campaign centered around responsibility. But none of us reported it." The reporter repeated the story to me in the Mayflower bar probably because he knew no one would believe me if I tried to peddle it.

I also heard that en route to Detroit, Johnson, in violation of national security, moved to another plane the military aide carrying the codes that launch a nuclear war—in order to make room on his plane for a cash-laden VIP. The other plane almost crashed, but reporters overlooked it.

What they are reporting about the Senator is as far removed from the truth as a *Pravda* article about the Pope. TV cameras pan slowly over picket signs on the fringe of Goldwater rallies: "Down the Drain, Goldwater" "Fascist Lip in the West." In Montana, 10,000 of our people stood in the freezing rain to welcome the Senator, but the press put the crowd at 2,500 and described it as "unenthusiastic." In Atlanta and Memphis, one reporter so underestimated the crowds that Vic Gold tracked him down and gave him a trophy of a hand with an erect middle finger. Vic told the Senator, who laughed and said, "Hell, if all I knew about Goldwater was what I read in the press, I'd vote against the son of a bitch myself."

"Thank God for Lyndon Johnson," the *St. Louis Post-Dispatch* reporter said in Cleveland as the president leaned into the microphone and excoriated the Senator as a "ranting raving demagogue who wants to tear down society."

With one week to go until Election Day, I visited the men's room and looked in the mirror: was this the face that launched a thousand quips? There were dark pouches under my eyes and sharp creases from my nostrils to the corners of my mouth that had not been there two months ago. I had a double chin from all the pizza, cheeseburgers, and fries I had eaten. I hadn't done my usual regimen of push-ups and sit-ups for weeks. To save time, I took a taxi to headquarters. Gone were the walks up and down Connecticut Avenue, checking the new books in Kramer's, walking past the Golden Parrot and recalling the icy-smooth taste of a Bombay-all-the-way martini, watching the chess players—black versus white just like the pieces—at Dupont Circle, glancing down Rhode Island Avenue at Saint Matthew's and remembering the memorial Mass for Kennedy (was it only a year ago?). I looked again in the mirror. The only thing thinner was my hair.

Seven days, 169 hours, 10,080 minutes to go. I would have gone crazy if I hadn't been able to talk to Anne. Thank God she didn't cut me off, although I deserved it.

I walked back to my office, passing all the true believers who still felt that victory was possible. I wanted to share their belief, but the polls, including ours, wouldn't let me.

In Finance, volunteers opened the hundreds of envelopes that arrived every day and carefully recorded the name, address, and donation. Along with the checks and cash, there were rosaries and colored pictures of Jesus with biblical quotations, especially John 3:16 ("For God so loved the world that He gave His one and only son, that whoever believes in Him shall not perish but have eternal life"), and scribbled notes on kitchen pads. There were exhortations and imprecations, cries of hope and despair—the Forgotten American in full voice.

In the Political Division, Steve Shadegg, Wayne Hood, Dick Herman, and the other regional directors worked the phones and shared the latest depressing state poll or the editorial endorsement of Johnson by a rock-ribbed Republican paper, what a governor or a mayor or a county chairman or a senator or a congressman had said about Goldwater's chances, how many volunteers in Dallas and Spartanburg and Columbus and a hundred other cities had promised to get out the Goldwater vote on Election Day.

In the People's Room, campaign staffers listened politely as Mrs. Conquest, Dr. Gregorian, Captain Duvall, and other Goldwaterites outlined the one sure way to win the presidency. "Well, it would be very expensive to mail your book about the Illuminati to every household in America, but we will take your suggestion under advisement." "John Wayne, Raymond Massey, Ronald Reagan, and others are making speeches for the senator and appearing on TV, but we appreciate your willingness to go on national television and talk about the communist threat just ninety miles from our shores." "Thank you so much for your campaign song based on 'Hello, Dolly!' Several other people have had the same idea, but we will give your lyrics to our political people. Will you please sign this release form?" "Thank you for your suggested speech in which the senator promises to take down the Berlin Wall, invade Cuba, withdraw from the UN, and eliminate the income tax in his first one hundred days."

In Campaign Materials, volunteers shipped to our offices across the country gold-colored elephant cuff links, earrings, and pins; campaign buttons with the gold elephant wearing black glasses; inflatable red, white, and blue elephants in three sizes; clocks and playing cards with the senator's image; cans of the soft drink "Gold Water," which tasted like "piss," according to the senator; boxes of Goldwater Taffy, "a Golden Opportunity to sweeten your campaign fund"; elephant-print boxer shorts for men and elephant-print scarves for women; campaign photos of Goldwater that glowed in the dark.

In his office, Dean told me he had had it with Jay Hall and his doomsday analyses. He had been on the road with Barry, he had seen the crowds, he had heard the cheers and the chants—"We want Barry!" "We want Barry!" He had watched them grow larger and louder every day. Back in Washington, he passed along the good news, only to hear from Dr. Hall and his green-eyeshade associates that Goldwater was losing in more than forty states and would be damn lucky to get 35 percent of the vote. Dean almost slugged Hall. "I know we are gaining," he told me, "we can still win."

I wanted to believe him, I tried to believe him, but Goldwater wasn't Harry Truman. Too many voters were scared to death of the senator. We would do okay in the South, but the rest of the country would bury us. I didn't know anyone in politics or the press who thought we would win, including my father.

But we couldn't give up—the senator wouldn't give up; I wouldn't give up. The people who would vote for the senator on Election Day deserved that.

In Communications, we produced a daily newsletter with feel-good headlines like "Goldwater Widens Lead in Alabama" and "Nixon Calls Election Most Important Since World War II" and "Miller Socks It to LBJ." Bulletins were dispatched to the media and GOP offices twice in the morning and twice in the afternoon via our teletype machines. George McDonnell fed us action photos of the senator on the road, which we passed on to party offices. We communicated the air times of the Goldwater TV and radio programs. State and local committees could barely keep up with our information flow. Many did not try. They read the same papers and talked to the same experts as Dr. Hall and had reached the same conclusion—we were going to be buried, and deep.

From my campaign diary:

> Campaigns do things to people, especially those running the campaign. They eat too much, they drink too much, they smoke too much, they never get a good night's sleep. They lose their temper, they contradict themselves, they make mistakes that would embarrass a novice.
>
> Mary Ann has dropped the "benevolent" and now just calls me a "dictator." I don't have time to be polite. I keep saying we can win to keep everyone's spirits up, but it will take a miracle. My mind is on automatic pilot. My reflexes are mashed potatoes. I am a zombie in a suit and tie, one of the Living Dead. Ed Hunter was right that brainwashing starts with depriving the prisoner of sleep. What I wouldn't give for six hours of uninterrupted sleep. But I can't quit. As Churchill said, "Never give in, never, never, never, never, never, never!"
>
> Denny depends too much on Bill Baroody but how can you blame him? Denny's a corporate lawyer, not a political manager. He does one thing better than anyone else—talk back to the Senator.

"At the end of a day," he said to me, "we'll spend an hour together and he'll blow off steam and complain about this or that and I'll tell him to stop bitching and act like a presidential candidate and he'll tell me to go to hell and I'll tell him to go to hell and the next morning we're on the road again."

Good old *Human Events* never gives up. In the current issue: ads for Evetts Haley's *A Texan Looks at Lyndon*. The dates and times of the Senator's telecasts. Excerpts from a Raymond Moley *Newsweek* column in which he talks about the tepid support of Johnson, which along with the people's alarm about inflation, growing big government intervention, and communism "give Goldwater a far better chance than the polls show." A full-page article titled "What You Can Do to Prevent Voter Fraud," pointing out that the Cook County, Illinois, machine turned out 25,000 "ghost persons" for the Democratic national ticket in 1960. Kennedy carried Illinois by just 8,858 votes.

The most difficult thing in a political campaign is knowing when to say yes and when to say no. Relegated to the sidelines, Clif White—the man more responsible than any other for Goldwater's nomination—made only one serious attempt to affect materially the course of the fall campaign. He was inspired by the senator's argument that there was a "sickness of spirit" in America and that lack of national leadership had "turned our streets into jungles, brought our public and private morals to the lowest state of our history, and turned out the lights even at the White House itself." The senator mentioned the climbing divorce rates, juvenile delinquency, and street violence. "I charge with a sincerely heavy heart," he said, "that the more the federal government has attempted to legitimate morality, the more it has incited hatreds and violence."

Clif told the senator that he and Rus Walton, who had played a major role in the California primary, wanted to produce a documentary film that depicted the collapse of morality in America and how to restore it. From his campaign plane, Goldwater sent a note: "Agree completely with you on morality issue. Believe it is the most effective we have come up with. Also agree with your program. Please get it launched immediately." With the senator's okay, Clif and Rus produced what Teddy White called "a phantasmagoric film."

A STARK CHOICE

Titled *Choice*, the documentary film offered the viewer a vision of "two Americas" (this forty years before Democrat John Edwards made that phrase a theme of his ill-fated presidential campaign). On one hand there was LBJ's America, populated by gyrating female strippers, rioting blacks, models in topless bathing suits, fig-leaf-clad nude males, books like *Call Me Nympho* and *Men for Sale*, and a speeding black limousine with Texas license plates from which beer cans were thrown. On the other hand there was "Goldwaterland," in which the viewer saw smiling, white-blazer-clad youths, the American flag waving in the breeze, the majestic Statue of Liberty lit at night, and Barry Goldwater riding a horse, piloting a plane, exhorting the faithful to return to tried and true ways. Narrator Raymond Massey (whose rich voice recited the Gettysburg Address at Disneyland) intoned: "There are two Americas. One is words like 'allegiance' and 'Republic.' The other America is no longer a dream but a nightmare. Two Americas and you, you alone, stand between them. Which do you really want? Which?" With a rifle hanging on the wall behind him, John Wayne delivered the final on-camera message: "You've got the strongest hand in the world. The hand that marks the ballot. The hand that pulls the voting lever. Use it, will you? Use it."

A copy of the film was leaked to the press and to the Democratic National Committee, which called it "the sickest political program conceived since television became a factor in American politics."

Only hours before it was scheduled to be shown, the senator saw *Choice* for the first time and immediately said, "I don't want it used." The next day he publicly repudiated the film, saying, "It's nothing but a racist film." Once again, as he did with Walter Jenkins, Goldwater refused to be swayed by the prospect of immediate political gain in making his decision. He would not abandon his principles to get votes. *Choice* showed blacks in every possible bad light, rioting, smashing windows, looting and shooting. He would not offer that kind of choice to the American people.

He also decided the fate of another TV program that would alter the course of American politics. *A Time for Choosing* was a half-hour political address by the actor Ronald Reagan. Reagan and Goldwater had known each other socially for more than a decade, since Nancy Reagan's father had retired from his medical practice in Chicago and moved to Phoenix. The senator told me that when he first met Reagan, the actor was a New Deal Democrat but had steadily moved to the right during the '50s.

Never personally close, Goldwater and Reagan became political allies against big government.

As cochairman of Californians for Goldwater-Miller, Reagan had been campaigning for the senator up and down the state. Among his appearances was a talk to nearly a thousand Republicans at the Ambassador Hotel in Los Angeles. It was a variation of the speech he had given for years as a spokesman for General Electric but included an endorsement of Goldwater. Afterward, several Republicans, including Henry Salvatori and Holmes Tuttle, asked Reagan whether he would repeat the speech on national television. "Sure," Reagan said, "if you think it would do any good." Rather than delivering his remarks in a studio, Reagan suggested that he deliver the speech before a live audience in a campaign setting with Goldwater signs and banners.

The filming went well, and the talk was scheduled to be telecast on Tuesday evening, October 27, one week before Election Day. But the inner circle, led by Bill Baroody, dug in their heels. They argued that in the last week of the campaign, every dollar ought to be spent featuring the candidate and not a Hollywood actor last seen hosting *Death Valley Days*. Besides, Reagan discussed Social Security and farm subsidies, issues that would remind viewers of Goldwater's controversial positions.

They proposed a substitute program, a rebroadcast of the Goldwater-Eisenhower program, *Conversation at Gettysburg*, featuring a rather grim-faced Ike. But TV for Goldwater-Miller had already purchased time for the Reagan program. The wealthy California Republicans who underwrote the purchase, including Walter Knott, Salvatori, Tuttle, and others who would later become members of Reagan's Kitchen Cabinet, insisted they would buy time only for the Reagan talk, not the inner circle's alternative.

The day that *A Time for Choosing* was to air, Reagan received a telephone call from the senator, who sounded uncomfortable. "Ronnie," said Goldwater, "some of the guys here are concerned about your TV speech, especially the part about Social Security. They think it will bring up an issue that has dogged us all year long."

"Gee, Barry," responded Reagan, "I've been making the speech all over the state, and I have to tell you it's been well received, including what I say about Social Security. All I say is what you've said—why can't we put the program on a sound actuarial basis so that those who do depend on it won't come to the cupboard and find it bare? And at the same time, why not introduce voluntary features so that those who can make better provisions for themselves are allowed to do so? I can't cancel the speech,

Barry. It's not up to me. These gentlemen raised the money and bought the airtime. They're the ones you should talk to."

"Well," said the senator, "I haven't seen the speech yet. They've got a tape here, so I'll listen to it and call you back."

The senator and Denny, with Reagan's brother, Neil, also present, listened to *A Time for Choosing*. When it was over, Goldwater said, "What the hell's wrong with that?" and okayed the broadcast.

But the inner circle was not ready to give up. Just hours before airtime, Baroody and the others proposed a rebroadcast of *Brunch with Barry*, a half-hour program of the senator and a half dozen self-conscious women talking about rising prices and the Vietnam War. The Nielsen rating of *Brunch* had been so low it barely registered. The California group politely but firmly said no. The clock kept ticking. At last, Walter Knott called from California and told Baroody in his dry, whispery voice that he expected the national committee to approve the Reagan telecast or come up with the money for their program.

"We don't have any funds," Baroody admitted. "Cordiner won't write a check—he says it's not in the budget and it's your committee's responsibility." (Ralph Cordiner was our tightfisted finance chairman; he had been chairman of General Electric when Reagan hosted the weekly TV program *GE Theater*.)

"We will only underwrite the time for the Reagan show," Knott said. "And that's final."

There was a pause, and then Baroody said stiffly, "In that case, you have our permission to go ahead, but you're in for a big surprise."

"So are you, sir," Knott said, "so are you."

OVERNIGHT STAR

From my campaign diary:

> The Reagan TV show has elicited the greatest response of any program to date. We have received hundreds of telegrams, hundreds of telephone calls, and dozens of reports of undecideds and Democrats now declaring themselves for BG. Everyone has suggested, urged and demanded that the show be repeated. Last nite Ike called Ab Herman [one of the few national committee holdovers] from Walter Reed to say it was the best thing he has seen in the campaign and asked for a print.... The show's embarrassing to Mr. B[aroody], who

worked for hours to kill it, as well as our [ad] agency, which had nothing to do with it.

Why was it received so well? (1) Reagan is Reagan, a Hollywood TV star who commands interest and respect; (2) he was convincing and appealing; (3) he used statistics and specifics—he did not sling any mud or deal in generalities; (4) he preached conservatism without apologies; (5) he was a new face in the campaign, a respite from the same old theories and candidates....

Ronald Reagan is the man they wish Barry Goldwater was. Or perhaps I should say the man they wish he had been in this campaign. Listening to the Senator's [recent] speech from Madison Square Garden I was struck so forcibly by the utter dearth of facts and figures, concrete examples your mind and attention could cling to.... It was an exercise in conservative dialectic without the wit of Buckley, the eloquence of [Donald] Bruce, the fire of [Ed] Foreman, or, sadly, the blunt language of Goldwater. And that is why Ronnie Reagan, with his statistics and his awareness of today, has at last fired up the loyal, won the undecided and shaken the opposition.

Sitting before his typewriter in the Washington Star building, political reporter David Broder wrote that Reagan's speech was the most successful national political debut since William Jennings Bryan electrified the 1896 Democratic convention with his "Cross of Gold" speech. *Time* described it as the "one bright spot in a dismal campaign." In the seven days remaining in the campaign, Republicans showed the film over and over again on TV and at public meetings and for family and friends. More contributions arrived than we could count or spend—in the millions of dollars. Surveying the stacks of mail, Frank Kovac said to me, "This movement is the wave of the future."

In that last week of the campaign, Goldwater spoke in New York City; Bristol, Tennessee; Cleveland; Cedar Rapids, Iowa; Oshkosh, Wisconsin; Scranton, Pennsylvania; Las Vegas; Tucson; Los Angeles; Dallas; and Columbia, South Carolina. On the Monday before Election Day, he addressed a crowd of 250,000 in downtown San Francisco, the largest crowd of the campaign, inspiring Mary Ann (dispatched to California to coordinate the event) to call me and say excitedly: "Lee, they've gone crazy here. They won't stop cheering Barry. We had more confetti in the streets than when General MacArthur came here after Truman fired him. This is the headquarters of the liberal establishment of California.

This turnout means something. It means we can still win if we get our people to the polls."

How I wished that were true, but all the polls, including ours, said we were headed for a historic defeat. The liberals had been successful in scaring the people away from the senator. I kept hearing the narrator's voice on that damned "Daisy" commercial: "The stakes are too high for you to stay home."

Late on the afternoon of November 2, the last day of campaigning, the senator flew to the mountaintop village of Fredonia, Arizona, population 300, right on the Utah border, where he always finished his senatorial campaigns. He saw no reason not to do the same in his presidential campaign. There was an enormous crowd for Fredonia, over 1,800 people, waiting patiently in the deepening dusk. There were high school kids in Levi's and windbreakers, men in worn boots and women in calico dresses, Navajo and Paiute women in black hats and blue jeans. There, illuminated by two portable lamps and standing on the rear of a flatbed truck, the senator talked softly about hardworking people like those who lived in tiny Pipe Springs down the road:

> I think of the courage of those people who came here not knowing that the federal government could help them, but doing it on their own, standing off all kinds of abusive action, standing off the weather, but finally triumphing in raising cattle where cattle probably shouldn't have been raised, and living their lives as they felt God wanted them to. These were the things, the simple things I have talked about in this campaign, and I will continue to talk about as long as I live.

He stepped down from the truck, shook some hands, and went home, liberated at last from the campaign.

18

27 MILLION AMERICANS CAN'T BE WRONG

All day long the networks kept predicting a historic victory for President Johnson, and all day long I kept reassuring my people in communications that we had a chance, although I knew we did not. But that is what you are supposed to say, isn't it? I recalled that tears flowed when Bill Buckley told a YAF convention in September that the senator was likely to lose. So I dissembled. I knew there would be plenty of tears soon enough.

At 6:48 P.M. ET, four hours and twelve minutes before the California polls closed, NBC declared Johnson the winner.

The senator was at home with Peggy, Denny Kitchel, Karl Hess, and some family and a few close friends; he had opted against going to the Camelback Inn, where he usually received returns. Dean and other members of the national campaign, including me, were at the Shoreham Hotel in Washington, where the giant ballroom had been decorated with red, white, and blue bunting, "Goldwater for President" banners, and large color photos of the man. The bars were open and offered premium brands. Long tables were laden with rare roast beef, translucent shrimp, and plump meatballs simmering in chafing dishes. Along each side of the ballroom were color TV sets filled with the satisfied faces of political analysts explaining why the senator and conservatism had lost so badly. "One of the most inept campaigns in recent history." "No attempt was made to reach out to moderates and independents." "A brilliant campaign by the president." "We are seeing history made tonight with the impending landslide."

I wanted a drink and badly, but I had promised myself I would stick to ginger ale until the Illinois results at 8 p.m. If we didn't do well in Illinois, it was all over. I went back and forth between the suite—where Dean, John Grenier, and the regional political directors were already drinking—and the ballroom, which was never full even at the beginning of the evening and now was half-empty. Reporters pestered me for a statement, Lou Guylay having disappeared. Once again, by default, I was the spokesman for the Goldwater campaign.

At 8:01 p.m., all the networks reported that President Johnson would carry Illinois—the home of Lincoln, Everett Dirksen, and the *Chicago Tribune*—by more than a million votes. I poured myself a large scotch and water. Our in-house artist, Bob O'Connell, who at six foot two and more than two hundred pounds could have been a tight end for the Redskins, walked up to me and, tears streaming down his face, said, "Lee, we're not going to lose, are we?" A distraught Mary Ann called from San Francisco. "What happened to all those people who turned out for the parade? I was so sure things had finally turned around."

"Poor Barry," Steve Shadegg said to me upstairs. "Rocky said Barry wanted to end Social Security and it was so. Scranton said Barry was an extremist and it was so. UPI said Barry wanted to use atomic bombs in Southeast Asia and it was so. LBJ called Barry a demagogue and that, too, was so. He never had a chance, he never had a chance."

Out in Arizona, Goldwater said little as he sipped bourbon and watched his opponent's numbers climb higher and higher. Men and women; white and nonwhite; blue-collar and white-collar; under thirty and over sixty; rich, poor, and in between—just about everybody voted for the president by wide margins. Only two Republicans had ever received a lower percentage of the popular vote—John C. Frémont in 1856 and Alf Landon in 1936. Peggy dabbed at her eyes, and even Kitchel blew his nose.

"I'm sorry I didn't do a better job," Denny said.

"Hell, Denny, it wasn't your fault. It wasn't anybody's fault. No one could have won."

"We're going to carry the Deep South and Arizona, so it wasn't a shutout."

"How's Dean?"

"In shock."

"How so?

"He thought we could win."

"For Christ's sake, even Peggy knew I was going to lose."

"One thing," Karl said, "you did very well among college graduates, almost tied with Johnson, 48 percent to 52 percent."

"They got our message of freedom, even if no one else did. I got into the race because of them." He put down his glass. "I've had enough—I'm going to bed."

"Any statement?" Denny asked.

"I'll make one tomorrow. The press and Lyndon can wait."

Back in Washington, it was close to midnight when I went up to Suite C-240 of the Shoreham and asked Dean whether he wanted to issue a statement or talk to reporters. He shook his head. "Barry's gone to bed. Tell 'em he'll say something tomorrow."

I descended to the ballroom and told reporters there would be no statement by Chairman Burch or Senator Goldwater until the next day.

"So you're not conceding although you lost forty-four states?" one incredulous reporter asked.

"The only statement I will make," I said, slurring slightly, "is that the senator will make his statement tomorrow." Reporters shook their heads and began walking away. From the beginning to the end of his campaign, I reflected, Barry Goldwater did it his way.

THE END, THEY SAID

All over Washington, pundits were writing our obituary.

Walter Lippmann, the Delphic dean of columnists, wrote that "the returns prove the falsity of the claim that there is a great silent latent majority of 'conservative' Republicans who will emerge as soon as the Republican party turns its back on 'me-tooism' and offers them a 'choice.'" Robert J. Donovan of the *New York Herald Tribune* wrote that Republicans would remain a minority party indefinitely as long as they were or seemed to be the voice of "right-wing radicalism or extremism."

Richard Rovere wrote in the *New Yorker* that "the election has finished the Goldwater school of political reaction." Political scientists Nelson W. Polsby and Aaron B. Wildavsky stated that if the Republican Party continued to nominate conservatives like Goldwater it would continue to lose so badly "we can expect an end to a competitive two-party system." With quiet satisfaction, James B. Reston of the *New York Times* summed up that "Barry Goldwater not only lost the presidential election... but the conservative cause as well."

But the establishment's favorite political historian, Theodore White, offered a disclaimer: "One cannot dismiss Goldwater as a man without meaning in American history. Again and again in American history it has happened that the losers of the presidency contributed almost as much to the permanent tone and dialogue of politics as did the winners." Teddy was probably thinking of perennial presidential candidate Norman Thomas, many of whose socialist proposals were adopted by FDR and succeeding progressives. I believe that Barry Goldwater has had the greatest impact of all the losing candidates, which is why I call him the most consequential loser in American politics.

From my campaign diary:

Why we lost: (1) moderates voted for LBJ; (2) we didn't articulate the issues as we should have—due to the Third Floor's preoccupation with things theoretical; (3) LBJ made few mistakes and used his power as an incumbent Pres most effectively; (4) BG made too many mistakes; (5) BG never recovered from the SS and nuclear bomb smears; (6) the media killed us; (7) the mercenaries (AFL-CIO) beat the volunteers.

This was the last entry in my campaign diary. I have never kept another diary, although I took notes on my retreats at the Trappist monastery in Berryville, Virginia; on Anne's and my two-week trip to South Africa in the time of apartheid; when I stood in the middle of Red Square in Moscow and Tiananmen Square in Beijing; when I celebrated the two hundredth anniversary of Bastille Day in Paris; when I attended secret meetings of Le Cercle at which we plotted how to bring down the Evil Empire; after my first exclusive interview with Ronald Reagan, before he ran for governor; when we dedicated the Victims of Communism Memorial with President George W. Bush and a thousand other VIPs; at the rousing Captive Nations Rally on Liberty Island in New York Harbor, where I introduced New York mayor Abe Beame to thousands of anticommunists; and when I placed a tin of tuna fish in the begging bowl of a Buddhist monk in Bangkok.

The morning after the 1964 deluge, I walked to campaign headquarters, almost deserted, and called Anne, who offered solace and even hope. "Frank Meyer says we've witnessed the birth of a national political movement. Over twenty-seven million Americans voted for Goldwater despite all the lies and smears."

I remembered the shining faces of the people in New Hampshire and

California, the rallies that were more like revivals. I had witnessed the infinite variety of Americans, the wrinkled and the apple-cheeked, white and black and red and brown, Wall Streeters and Main Streeters, farmers and factory workers and teachers and cops, all yearning to be free. We had failed to make enough of them understand that government is not the solution but the problem.

"I don't care how many billions LBJ pours into the Great Society," I said to Anne. "Or how many promises he and McNamara make that they will not send American boys to fight in an Asian war. By the next election, people will look at the mess at home and abroad and say, 'You know something? Goldwater was right.'"

WHO WAS HE?

He was an unlikely revolutionary—the grandson of a Jewish peddler, a college dropout whose book *The Conscience of a Conservative* sold 3.5 million copies and was once required reading for History 169b at Harvard.

He raised issues like Social Security, a flat tax, government subsidies, welfare reform, privatization, affirmative action, and victory over communism, once dismissed as extreme, now mainstream.

He was not so much the candidate of a political party as the personification of a political movement.

He inspired thousands of young people like me to get into politics and form a national network committed to the advancement of conservatism. They included Ed Feulner of the Heritage Foundation; Ed Crane of the Cato Institute; commentator/presidential candidate Pat Buchanan; fundraising guru Richard Viguerie; American Conservative Union head David Keene; publisher Al Regnery; Fund for American Studies chairman Randal Teague; Young America's Foundation president Ron Robinson; Congressmen Phil Crane, Bob Bauman, Bill Sensenbrenner, and Bill Brock; and many others.

For the first time in national politics, he used direct mail and television to raise funds, attracting nearly a million donors. Ever since, conservative candidates and groups have been able to raise millions of dollars for their causes through the mail, giving them financial and political independence.

He broke the Democrats' hold on the Solid South, enabling the GOP to become a national party.

He persuaded 27.2 million Americans to vote conservative despite an unprecedented Anti-Campaign run out of the White House, laying the electoral foundation for Ronald Reagan's 1980 and 1984 landslide victories.

He approved Reagan's historic TV address *A sing*, which led directly to Reagan's running for governor of California. It's simple: no presidential candidate Goldwater, no President Reagan.

Barry Goldwater was our first political love, never forgotten, always forgiven.

19

ON MY OWN

"There is no such thing as a Lost Cause," T. S. Eliot wrote, "because there is no such thing as a Gained Cause." Conservatives will accept even a humiliating defeat as part of the human condition and resolve to carry on as a Remnant, if necessary. But 27.2 million people are not a Remnant.

In the wake of the Goldwater defeat, we bound up our wounds and continued to fight for ordered liberty, armed with the Declaration of Independence, the U.S. Constitution, *The Federalist*, *Democracy in America*, the Gettysburg Address, and the enduring ideas of F. A. Hayek, Richard Weaver, Whittaker Chambers, and Russell Kirk, among others. In 1960 Goldwater had urged us to get to work to take over the Republican Party, and we had taken a giant step with his 1964 nomination. It remained for us to turn his defeat into a national political movement and a presidential victory. We believed, naively, that if only we elected a conservative as president, all would be well.

The Goldwater campaign transformed my life. Before it, I was just another promising young conservative writer and political activist. Afterward, I was the creative publicist, featured in *Life*, who had projected the senator's fifty-foot-high face on the front of the Mark Hopkins Hotel during the Republican National Convention and had stunned the Democrats at their national convention by posting a giant billboard with a photo of a smiling Goldwater opposite their convention hall. Before

1964, I was stuck in the minor leagues; afterward, I always played in the majors.

The Goldwater campaign gave me the confidence to start my own Washington public affairs firm. The veteran political operative Ray Bliss had succeeded Dean Burch as chairman of the Republican National Committee in January and notified Goldwater appointees like me that our services would no longer be required, effective May 1, 1965. I was not upset, or surprised, at Bliss's decision: such are the wages of electoral politics. Bill Merriam of ITT invited me to join the Washington office he headed, and I suppose I would have made my way up the ITT ladder, perhaps even succeeding Merriam and becoming a vice president, someday. But when Bill mentioned in passing that I would have to fill out a ten-page questionnaire and be interviewed by the company psychiatrist, I decided that corporate life was not for me. "I wonder," Anne said, "if the ITT psychiatrist was one of the 1,189 psychiatrists who without talking to him said Barry was psychologically unfit to be president?" I decided to launch Lee Edwards & Associates, even though I did not have a single client or associate.

I had one unique qualification among all the public affairs and public relations firms in Washington—I was an unapologetic Goldwater conservative committed to helping conservative and only conservative clients. For the next two decades, I worked with every important conservative and anticommunist group in America. I wrote press releases and policy papers, directed seminars and conferences, created organizations and raised funds, produced documentary films and ghostwrote books.

All the while, I blocked out time to write in my own name, determined not to let my primary skill atrophy. I came to know the most influential conservatives and anticommunists in America—Bill Buckley, Milton Friedman, Ed Feulner, Richard Viguerie, Reed Larson, Vic Milione, Paul Weyrich, Lev Dobriansky, Tom Winter, Phyllis Schlafly, Morton Blackwell, Ron Robinson, David Keene, and Walter Judd. In the fall of 1965, while on assignment from *Reader's Digest*, I spent two days in California with a prospective gubernatorial candidate who would change history—Ronald Reagan.

LOVE AND MARRIAGE

But first I persuaded Anne Libby Stevens to marry me. Although we had broken up in February of the Goldwater year at my doing—I declared arrogantly that I was too busy with politics for romance—we stayed in touch, bound by politics. I shared with Anne the vicissitudes of the campaign. I discovered that when I listened to her and followed her advice, particularly about people, things went well. When I ignored her counsel and went my own headstrong way, I paid a price. She urged me not to overact when Dean or Lou made a decision without including me. In the middle of a campaign, she pointed out, decisions had to be made quickly, often without consulting everyone. Insecure for all my bravado, I complained when I was excluded, irritating the decision maker and causing him to keep excluding me.

Anne understood me very well and still loved me, *Deo gratias*. In early January 1965 I took out my yellow legal pad, headed a page "Reasons to Marry Anne," and divided it into two columns, one listing the pluses, the other the minuses. After an hour of thinking and writing, I added up the columns—the pluses outnumbered the minuses by ten to one. We were agreed on the two things that mattered most in our lives—our Catholic faith and our conservative politics. I wasted no more time on research and analysis and took the train to New York in late January during one of the worst snowstorms in East Coast history. I proposed to her at the Cattleman Restaurant following her favorite meal of a New York strip steak, medium; a baked potato, hold the sour cream; a Caesar salad; and two martinis. I had bought a gold band engagement ring at Erich Wolter on Connecticut Avenue (Mary Ann Ford helped pick it out), and I presented it to her with one of my best smiles.

"Okay," she said, after a pause, "but I don't believe in long engagements."

"How about May 1?" I suggested. "May Day is Workers' Day in every communist country and it's also the international distress signal."

"Perfect," Anne replied. She later told me she had been thinking of her mother's two divorces when she hesitated.

We were married on Saturday, May 1, 1965, in Saint Thomas More Catholic Church on New York City's East Side, Father Roger Pryor officiating, with Anne's teenage sister, Jane, as the maid of honor and Bob Bauman as our best man. As Anne came down the aisle on the arm of her father, Ray Costanzo, my smile was as wide as the senator's after winning the California primary. But Anne was not smiling. She seemed to be leaning heavily on Ray as she approached the altar. I took her hand, which held a sodden mass of Kleenex that I quickly stuffed in my pocket. Her eyes were red and puffy from crying. Who wouldn't be nervous, I thought, marrying me? But I was confident we were made for each other.

I kept smiling and praying, and once we knelt and Father Pryor began the service, I could feel Anne take a deep breath and let go of the apprehension that had gripped her.

In less than an hour, we were Mr. and Mrs. Lee Edwards and on our way to the rooftop reception at the National Federation of Republican Women building on Fifth Avenue. We danced and drank and posed for pictures with her parents and mine—the two mothers silently sizing each other up and deferring judgment. Anne had been told by one of her aunts to bring a satin purse to the reception, and people, especially her Italian relatives, kept giving her envelopes, which she put in the purse. When we got to the Plaza Hotel ("I've always wanted to spend my honeymoon night at the Plaza," Anne had once said) and opened the purse, a flood of tens and twenties came pouring out, assuring us of a far finer honeymoon than we had expected.

Two weeks later, after visits to Puerto Rico, St. Thomas, and Jamaica (including dinner at the Blue Mountain Inn, all rich foliage, lighted paths, white-jacketed waiters, and marvelous coffee), we moved into my small one-bedroom apartment on Columbia Road in Adams Morgan in Northwest Washington. After a quick survey, Anne said, "The bed has one pillow; the bathroom has one towel and one facecloth. You did know I would be living here, correct?" I blushed. The next day she and Mary Ann went shopping for the things that a newlywed couple needs, like pillows, sheets, towels, plates, cutlery, and glasses.

MY FIRST CLIENT

While they went shopping, I went looking for clients. My first call was on David Jones, YAF's omnicompetent executive director. Dave and I had been in frequent touch throughout the Goldwater campaign. I knew that YAF did not have a PR person, and it did not take long for Dave and me to agree that I would serve as the organization's public relations consultant for a monthly fee of $750 plus the use of a small office and telephone. I would handle the media and coordinate special events as well as select writing projects. I was ready to dance on the ceiling: I had not yet had lunch and I had my first client.

The next day, I visited Capitol Hill, offering my services to selected conservative congressmen who did not have a press assistant. In those days that was not uncommon. Today every member of Congress has one or two aides who handle press relations—there is no need for outside consultants. Also at the time, it was possible for someone like me to go on the congressional payroll as a part-time assistant.

My first interview was with a brand-new congressman, John Buchanan, a Goldwater Republican from Birmingham, Alabama. I explained that I would handle all his media communications, including a monthly newsletter, news releases, a weekly five-minute radio program, and a bimonthly TV program in which I would "interview" him about the issues of most concern to his constituents. John liked my Goldwater credentials. I liked his drawling, laid-back style. We agreed that for a monthly fee of $750 and a desk in his office, I would become his press assistant. I happily reported to Anne that her confidence in me was justified—we had a monthly income of $1,500 and could pay the $175 rent on our apartment.

This was the beginning of a nineteen-year career in Washington public affairs with more ups and downs than the Superman roller coaster at Six Flags.

Among my early House clients were Tim Lee Carter of Kentucky—I visited his backwoods district but failed to meet a single Hatfield or McCoy—Abner Sibal of Connecticut, the only "moderate" Republican I ever worked for; Clarence Miller of Ohio; and Robert Dole of Kansas, in his first senatorial campaign.

I ghostwrote Senator Strom Thurmond's first and only book, *The Faith We Have Not Kept*. I also helped former congressman Jim Gardner when he ran for governor of North Carolina, ghostwriting his book, *A Time to Speak*.

I secretly managed Republican James Gleason's campaign to become the first elected county executive of Montgomery County, Maryland, one of the most liberal counties in the state. Anne and I and Elizabeth, our first daughter, had moved into a small yellow stucco house in Somerset, Chevy Chase, just across the D.C. line. Gleason was already suspect because he had been Richard Nixon's chief of staff when he was vice president. Jim and I agreed that our opponent, Bill Greenhalgh, would be certain to highlight my Goldwater connection. I could see the *Washington Post* headline: "Gleason Campaign Manager Ex-Goldwater Aide." So I managed behind the scenes, communicating through my six-foot blonde assistant, Joan Lawton, whom we placed in Gleason's campaign office in Bethesda.

My most creative contribution to the Gleason campaign was the suggestion that in the interest of a nonpartisan campaign both candidates should pledge publicly to campaign strictly on the issues and not engage in personal attacks or negative advertising. To our delight, and relief, Greenhalgh agreed, depriving himself of an issue that would have surely affected at least some voters—depicting Gleason as a right-wing Nixonian Republican. We won by only a few thousand votes, but it was the most satisfying victory of my political career.

From 1965 through 1969, my main client was YAF. Much of what I did for YAF and other conservative clients was for a minimum fee. I tried to put the interests of the Movement first and my own second. Anne agreed as long as we could pay the rent and get the kids (Catherine followed Elizabeth in five years) through school, which we did until we fell prey to our two-faced, embezzling bookkeeper in the early 1980s.

In the fall of 1965, YAF's new national chairman, Tom Charles Huston, and other YAF leaders grew tired of seeing all the headlines and TV clips of the peaceniks and Vietniks demonstrating against the war in Vietnam and determined to launch a counteroffensive. They created the International Youth Crusade for Freedom in Vietnam (which evolved into the World Youth Crusade for Freedom, directed by James Taylor). The crusade was a two-month-long campaign with rallies in major cities in Southeast Asia, Europe, Africa, and the United States.

The rallies were scrupulously bipartisan—I doubt it would be possible to enroll as many prominent Democrats today as we did then. In Boston, for example, Democratic congressman Thomas (Tip) O'Neill, the future Speaker of the House, spoke, as did former Republican congressman Donald Bruce of Indiana. Democratic House Speaker John McCormack sent a message of support, as did Boston mayor John Collins, also a Democrat. In St. Louis, Democratic congressman Richard Ichord and Republican congressman Tom Curtis along with baseball star Lou Brock addressed a crowd of more than five thousand. In Long Beach, California, Barry Goldwater Jr., echoing his father, declared that America must continue to fight for freedom around the world.

LIGHT UP FOR FREEDOM

All these events led to a remarkable trifecta of ceremonies on January 8, 1966, in New York City, Philadelphia, and Washington, D.C. At an October meeting, someone suggested, in jest, that YAFers ought to run a "Torch of Freedom" from coast to coast as Greek runners had carried a burning torch from city to city to begin the original Olympics. Why not, I said, transport by car a Torch of Freedom from the Statue of Liberty in New York Harbor to Independence Hall in Philadelphia and finally to Constitution Hall in Washington? Dave Jones said, "Go for it."

The following detailed narrative reflects what the Army taught me—there is no substitute for painstaking planning and implementation. But you have to be ready to improvise.

Don Pemberton, YAF's New York State chairman, was put in charge of the initial ceremony at the Statue of Liberty. John LaMothe, YAF's Middle Atlantic representative, lived in Philadelphia and could be counted on, I knew, to make the Independence Hall event successful. Al Regnery, son of the famed conservative publisher Henry Regnery, was YAF's college director and coordinated the Washington rally. Al was responsible in large part for the crusade's success. He went on to head Regnery Publishing, which published dozens of *New York Times* bestsellers.

It was essential to have the right torchbearer of the Torch of Freedom. Dave Jones suggested someone who turned out to be perfect: Ron McCoy of Nogales, Arizona, the president of Boys Nation, the youth auxiliary of the American Legion. Ron was a handsome eighteen, a poised speaker, conservative and pro-YAF. Senators Thomas Dodd, Connecticut Democrat, and Karl Mundt, South Dakota Republican, agreed to speak at the concluding ceremony in Constitution Hall, as did the former commanders of the American Legion and the Veterans of Foreign Wars, ensuring good attendance by their organizations.

It would be wonderful, I thought, if we were joined by a beautiful young woman, preferably blonde, articulate, and patriotic, who had recently entertained the troops in Vietnam. Was there such a paragon? Indeed, there was: Dianna Lynn Batts, Miss USA World for 1965, and a member of the Bob Hope troupe that had visited Vietnam during Christmas. And she lived just across the Potomac River in northern Virginia. Providentially, her agent was Sid Sussman, with whom I had worked at *Broadcasting* magazine. Sid quickly grasped the PR possibilities and approved her participation without a fee. Dianna was in every photograph and story, including a large picture in the *New York Daily News*, which then had the largest circulation of any daily newspaper in the country.

In New York City, Don Pemberton was searching for the right person to light the Torch of Freedom at our Statue of Liberty ceremony. A fitting choice would have been the widow or mother of a serviceman killed in Vietnam. One widow agreed but then asked to be excused, saying the strain of the occasion would be too great. By mid-December we were becoming more and more anxious when Ken Gilmore of *Reader's Digest* called. He thought Mrs. Christopher O'Sullivan of Jackson Heights, Queens, might be willing. Ken had written an article about

Captain O'Sullivan, who had been killed on Memorial Day 1965. He had been impressed by Mrs. O'Sullivan's determination to honor her husband's sacrifice. She had to be brave, for she received dozens of telephone calls from unidentified callers who told her how "glad" they were that her husband had been killed in an "immoral" war. We contacted Mrs. O'Sullivan, who said she would be pleased to attend the ceremony. Could she bring her two sons, Steve and Michael? They were most welcome, we said, as were her husband's parents, Mr. and Mrs. William O'Sullivan, whose presence turned out to be a blessing.

Al Regnery and I visited the State Department and the old War Department Building to meet with aides about a message from President Lyndon Johnson or Vice President Hubert Humphrey. They were unfailingly polite but vague, never promising anything. I still don't understand the White House's turndown. While YAF was openly conservative and had backed Barry Goldwater in 1964, the rally was a bipartisan demonstration of public support for the war and our men in Vietnam. Our crusade was the *only* national youth effort for those goals in 1965 and 1966. Other Democrats were less skittish: in St. Louis, YAF director Michael Thompson persuaded the Democratic governor of Missouri, Warren Hearnes, to proclaim "Missouri Victory in Vietnam Week."

The final days before the rally were crowded with dozens of telephone calls as we double-checked every detail, from the special Constitution Hall parking for the speakers to the exact size of the band coming down from Philadelphia to the exact timing of the drive from New York to Philadelphia to Washington. Then came the inevitable crises.

Three days before the event, Senator Dodd's office informed us that he had been called out of town and would not be able to deliver his address. But he would send his son Thomas Dodd Jr., who was teaching at Georgetown University, in his stead. Tom Dodd turned out to be an excellent speaker, and several media organizations used the advance text of his father's remarks.

The second major crisis occurred when Mrs. Christopher O'Sullivan telephoned that her two boys were sick and she couldn't come to the Statue of Liberty on Saturday morning. We had to have the right person to light the torch and launch the day. Someone suggested Dianna Batts, but I vetoed the idea as smacking of Madison Avenue. (I appreciated the irony, recalling Goldwater's rejection of my "Madison Avenue" campaign to promote him.) We needed someone who would symbolize the sacrifice of our men in Vietnam. I remembered that Mrs. William O'Sullivan, Captain O'Sullivan's mother, had accepted our invitation. I called and asked whether she would be willing to light the torch. "Certainly," she said. Saturday morning, I discovered how much of a soldier's mother she was.

Have you ever visited New York City in early January? That January 8, the temperature was a crisp 25 degrees, and the wind roared at about forty miles an hour in New York Harbor. Still, 150 YAF members greeted us at the ferry dock that morning, all of them bundled up and covered with buttons, the most popular one reading "Bomb Hanoi." When I met the O'Sullivans, I learned for the first time that Mrs. O'Sullivan suffered so badly from rheumatism that she could walk only with a cane. Yet she boarded the ferry without complaint, and then, when we arrived at Bedloe's Island, the site of the Statue of Liberty, she walked several hundred yards to light the torch, which danced in the cutting wind. My favorite of the many newspaper photos was of Mrs. O'Sullivan, Dianna Batts, and Ron McCoy holding the lighted torch with the Statue of Liberty as a backdrop. We drank hot black coffee in the snack bar until the boat whistle sounded. I again thanked Mrs. O'Sullivan, who fixed her eyes on me and said, "I wanted to come."

Back at the dock, I congratulated Don Pemberton for the turnout of YAFers and public officials, and we were off for Philadelphia. Our driver got lost (on Interstate 95!) and the service at the Howard Johnson was slow, so we arrived at Independence Hall only a few minutes before the scheduled 2 P.M. ceremony. John LaMothe broke into a broad smile when he saw us pull up. It was cold in Philadelphia, but there was no wind and the American Legion band lifted our spirits with a Sousa march.

John had put together an impressive program that included officers of the Pennsylvania American Legion and VFW; Professor William Kintner of the University of Pennsylvania, a leading foreign policy scholar; and Gail Rothwell, Miss Philadelphia of 1966, who sang "The Star-Spangled Banner." The ceremony attracted almost a thousand people, who cheered when Ron McCoy held aloft the lighted Torch of Freedom. We quickstepped to our limousine and headed south, followed by several busloads of YAF members and the Legion band.

More than 2,500 young and old patriots jammed Constitution Hall. At 8:04, to the martial music of the American Legion band, the speakers and honored guests took their places on stage. The speeches were short and stirring. The folk songs got folks singing along. Dianna Batts, luminous in a white evening gown, brought tears to our eyes as she described her visits to the military hospitals in South Vietnam. I couldn't have been happier. Then, shortly before 9 P.M., Captain Lacey, in charge of the hall, drew me aside. Did we intend to light the Torch of Freedom? "Yes," I said. Had we checked with the D.C. Fire Department? After a pause, I truthfully replied, "No." "Then I'm very sorry," said Captain Lacey, "but I can't allow you to take that lighted torch on stage. It would be against fire regulations."

I was undone. I explained to the captain that the presentation of the torch to the representative of the South Vietnamese embassy was the climax of not only the Constitution Hall rally but other rallies across the country as well. We simply *had* to have a lighted torch. A flameless torch would be an insult to South Vietnam and a mockery of the rally and the crusade. Captain Lacey was sympathetic but firm. Responding to my entreaty (I may have teared up a little), he promised to telephone the fire department to see if an exception could be made. Unfortunately, the fire chief was out of town and could not be reached. Captain Lacey promised to keep trying to contact someone in authority but was unyielding—there had to be some kind of official permission.

I returned to my backstage post and watched the program we had so carefully constructed make its way toward a dark, anticlimactic conclusion. What could we do? *L'audace, l'audace, toujours l'audace.* I called aside two husky YAFers assigned to help in an emergency. I told them to be ready to hold Captain Lacey or anyone else who tried to stop Ron McCoy from going onstage with a lighted torch.

We were close to Ron's entrance, and I was preparing to light the torch when Captain Lacey approached me. He had not been able to contact any senior official at the fire department, but he said: "I have an idea. We have a fire extinguisher back here. Suppose I tell Riley to walk onstage right behind your torchbearer and be prepared to use the extinguisher if anything happens. I know how important this is to you. How about it?"

I considered his suggestion. Maybe my two big YAFers couldn't handle Captain Lacey, who was no lightweight. Maybe I didn't want to be arrested for assault and battery. Maybe it might work if Riley carried the extinguisher at port arms, across his chest, and didn't stand right next to Ron and the Vietnamese representative. "Okay," I said, "you have a deal."

Which is why, when Ron McCoy walked onto the stage of Constitution Hall, holding high a lighted Torch of Freedom, he was followed by a short little man holding an antique fire extinguisher to his chest. We dimmed the house lights for Ron's entry and hit him with a spotlight. Everyone was looking at the torch and listening to Ron talk about holding the flame of freedom high for the people of Vietnam.

The following week, our main speaker, Senator Karl Mundt, took to the Senate floor to praise YAF for an "inspiring and stirring program," calling it a "very dramatic rejoinder and refutation of the...teach-ins, the draft-card burners, and other misguided Americans, young and old, who have been publicly taking actions and making statements, giving aid and comfort to the aggressor in Vietnam."

As exciting as the "Light Up for Freedom" rally was, it was not the most consequential thing that happened to me in 1965.

ON THE ROAD WITH REAGAN

In mid-October, Anne and I spent two days traveling with Ronald Reagan in Los Angeles as he considered whether to run for governor of California. We were a foursome—Reagan, the driver, and the two of us. Anne sat up front and I was in the back, with my Wollensak reel-to-reel tape recorder, as big as a carry-on suitcase, on the seat between me and Reagan. I was researching for a profile of the potential candidate for *Reader's Digest*. Charles Stevenson, the *Digest*'s Washington editor, had given me the go-ahead at one of our monthly luncheons at the Cosmos Club.

Anne and I were with Reagan early and late—at a Rotary Club breakfast, at a Republican women's luncheon, at an evening speech before businessmen. We saw him dressed in spotless white, chocolate brown, and dark blue. We saw worldly women in Armani and Tiffany melt when he smiled at them. We saw skeptical businessmen jump to their feet applauding when he got through talking about what was wrong and right about America. We saw old politicians nudge one another and nod approvingly at his polished performance. We saw "little old ladies" in Keds and narrow-tied John Birchers line up to shake his hand. He never seemed to get tired or to perspire. There was about him the aura of a star and a leader. At the end of the first day, back in our motel, I looked at Anne and she looked at me and we said at the same time, "He's got it!"

I grilled Reagan on every state and national issue I could think of. He provided thoughtful answers, proof of his serious study of California's problems and possible solutions.

I asked him how we could prevent future riots like the recent one in the Watts section of Los Angeles, in which 34 people, most of them black, had died and another 1,032 had been injured. The solution, he said, was not more government money. "Private enterprise ha[s] more to offer than Big Brother government," he insisted. "I think that one of these days the [black American] must wake up and realize that his supposed friends in court, the Democratic administration, [are] simply trying to exchange one odious form of paternalism for another."

Why did Watts happen? I asked.

It was a combination of things, he replied: a lack of education, frustration over the inability to find a job, leaders who told them there are some laws "that are all right to break." He added, "What else could [you] expect but what happened?"

If elected, Reagan said, he intended to use the moral power of the governor to defend "state sovereignty" and resist federal encroachment on that sovereignty. Here was an early indication of Reagan's strong commitment to federalism, which would be a major theme of his presidency.

"I don't think the federal government can be completely oblivious to a governor who will be representing 10 percent of the population of the nation," he said. Referring to Washington bureaucrats: "I think their deeds and actions can be tempered." He acknowledged that such state opposition would be difficult, because the federal government had "usurped sources of revenue" through federal grants and aid.

When I asked about his political philosophy, he quoted a 1947 interview in which he had said that whether "it comes from management, or labor, or government, or the right, the left, or the center, whatever imposes on the freedom of the individual is tyranny and must be opposed. I don't think I have changed from that viewpoint today." I underlined his libertarian answer in my notes.

Looking back at the decisive Goldwater defeat and considering the dearth of conservative leaders, I said, "In one sense the future of the Republican Party may very well depend on you." He responded, "That's a frightening thought." But he smiled as he said it.

At the end of the second day, Reagan said we had been working hard and invited us to have iced tea and cookies at his home. We went up the steep winding road to Pacific Palisades and stopped at a surprisingly small house filled, it seemed, with every possible General Electric device. While he and Nancy were in the kitchen, we sat in the library den. Opposite us were several large bookcases filled with books. I got up and began examining the titles. They were, almost without exception, works of history, economics, and politics, including such conservative classics as F. A. Hayek's *The Road to Serfdom*, Whittaker Chambers's *Witness*, and Henry Hazlitt's *Economics in One Lesson*. There was also a book I had never read: *The Law* by Frédéric Bastiat, a nineteenth-century

French free-market economist. I was stunned. I had never read Bastiat. I opened several books—they were dog-eared and underlined.

Here was the personal library not of a shallow Hollywood actor dangling at the end of someone's strings but of a thinking, reasoning individual who had arrived at his conservatism the old-fashioned way, one book at a time.

That night I wrote in my notebook, "President Reagan?"

20

AUTHOR, AUTHOR

The memory of the August 1963 March on Washington and Martin Luther King Jr.'s soaring "I Have a Dream" speech remained with me. It seemed to me and others, conservatives as well as liberals, that Dr. King might be able to build a bridge between whites and blacks in America.

We knew it would not be easy. Most blacks looked to the federal government to solve their problems. Conservatives saw the government as the problem. We spoke very different languages, and there were few interpreters on either side. You could count on the fingers of one hand the young black conservatives in the 1960s. Jay Parker, who grew up in South Philadelphia and served on YAF's national board of directors, was an exception. Jay and I did our bridge building by forming a public affairs firm—the first integrated PR firm in D.C.—and serving black and white clients for more than a decade. Black intellectuals like Thomas Sowell of the Hoover Institution and Walter Williams of George Mason University were unknown to me until Jay educated me about them.

In 1965 I began to notice a turn in the words and actions of civil rights leaders, including Dr. King's increasing dependence on leftists for foreign policy direction. His criticism of our involvement in Vietnam broadened to include the military and capitalism. I was puzzled by his apparent odyssey, in a few short years, from Christian pastor and Gandhi disciple to strident prophet and antiwar activist.

What or who was behind the transformation?

Terry Catchpole was a talented young conservative writer and editor who had written for the *New Guard*. He approached me about collaborating on a little book that would consider the two kinds of civil rights leaders—moderates like Roy Wilkins of the NAACP, who believed in the Declaration of Independence and its promise of equality and the American political system, and radicals like Bayard Rustin, who used the banner of civil rights to promote a social and economic revolution. Given the extreme sensitivity of the subject, Terry and I decided to present the verbatim statements of eight civil rights leaders, including Martin Luther King Jr., drawn from their speeches, articles, TV and radio appearances, with only the barest commentary. We titled our eighty-page book *Behind the Civil Rights Mask*; the cover featured a sketch of Dr. King.

"We do not deny anyone his right to speak out," we wrote in the foreword, "for a 'negotiated settlement' in Viet Nam or even the socialization of America. But we do protest their cloaking such demands in the honorable mantle of civil rights." We hoped that the book would "help educate the American people as to the real goals and tactics of the extremists of the civil rights movement and, at the same time, serve the just cause of those Negroes seeking equality under law and redress of their legitimate grievances."

In his introduction to our book, the syndicated columnist John Chamberlain noted that leftists had tried unsuccessfully in the 1930s and '40s to infiltrate the American labor movement and were again at work in the civil rights movement. Will they succeed? he asked. "Not if a few honest men like Lee Edwards and Terry Catchpole can make themselves heard."

I was grateful to Chamberlain for calling us "honest." Other critics were not so complimentary, "racist" being one of the more frequent words. I stand by the accuracy of every quotation in our booklet. We checked and double-checked every word, especially those of Dr. King, who identified the civil rights movement not with the American Revolution but the French Revolution, in which, he said, "the streets had become a battlefield." (As though Americans had not fought in the "streets" of Trenton and New York and Yorktown.) He dismissed the FBI finding that there were communists in the civil rights movement with a quip: "There are as many Communists in the civil rights movement as there are Eskimos in Florida." But the presence of communists like Hunter Pitts Odell and Stanley Levinson in the King entourage was well documented.

Still, if I had it to do over again, I would not have coauthored *Behind the Civil Rights Mask*. As a conservative I was automatically suspect on the subject of civil rights. I had worked for Barry Goldwater, who had voted against the Civil Rights Act of 1964, putting me on the side of the segregationists. I had not previously published anything about the denial of American blacks' constitutional rights, except for one editorial in the *New Guard*. Anne agrees it was a mistake. As someone who had lived and worked in New York City and taught remedial reading to African American children in Harlem under the sponsorship of the New York City Mission Society, she had expressed her doubts about the book. But we were in the first year of marriage, and she was reluctant to be too adamant in her opposition. I wish she had been.

An unexpected outcome of the book's publication was an invitation from the famed American novelist John Dos Passos to lunch with him in his Northern Neck of Virginia home. I had read his bestselling trilogy *U.S.A.* as well as his most recent novel, *Midcentury*, which I had reviewed in the *New Guard*. Linked with Ernest Hemingway and Scott Fitzgerald in the 1920s and 1930s, he was no longer praised by establishment reviewers because of the explicitly conservative themes of his latest works. He was a gentle and genial host, amused by how Anne was pretending to eat the soft-shell crabs on her plate. "You keep chasing him," he observed with a smile. "Do you think you will catch him?"

REAGAN'S BIOGRAPHER

Both Anne and I were enthusiastic about my next book—*Reagan: A Political Biography*. I had published a ten-thousand-word article about Reagan in *Human Events* that the Reagan organization had reprinted and used extensively in the 1966 California gubernatorial campaign. When Ted Loeffler, the enterprising president of Viewpoint Books, suggested I expand the article into a paperback book—Ted published only paperbacks and very successfully—I quickly agreed. Appearing in October 1967, *Reagan* was the first political biography of Ronald Reagan and sold an estimated 175,000 copies, making me a bestselling author with my first real book. None of my subsequent twenty-five books have come close to selling as many copies. I am what they call a "midlevel" author, with sales usually ranging between 5,000 and 10,000. One exception is Anne's and my political handbook, *You Can Make the Difference*, which initially sold more than 16,000 copies and was reprinted a decade later.

I developed a method of research and writing for the Reagan biography that I have followed ever since. I begin with multiple personal interviews conducted face-to-face if at all possible. You have to be patient. I recall one three-hour interview that had produced nothing of value or interest, and then in the last five minutes the interviewee offered an insight that I featured. I visit academic and presidential libraries, historical societies, and other repositories and carefully go through the papers of the biographee and his colleagues, friends, and family.

I usually delay beginning to write until after six months or so of research. I want a solid foundation on which to build my book. I believe that the time spent on research should be as great as if not greater than that devoted to writing. I try to write every day to keep my conscious mind and my subconscious engaged. I am rarely troubled by writer's block, but when I am I put the manuscript aside and pick up an Agatha Christie or Laurie King mystery or watch TV programs like *Blue Bloods* or *Inspector Lewis*, confident that my little gray cells are working away. Almost always, the right words come to mind within twenty-four hours, usually while I am shaving. I cannot explain this process—it just happens. I subscribe to Hemingway's "iceberg" principle, that what the reader sees on the printed page is only the visible tip of months and even years of research, writing, and rewriting, especially rewriting.

For the Reagan biography, I made three lengthy trips to California. I talked to members of the Reagan family, like his brother, Neil, and people who had known him in Illinois, like his high school teacher Bernard Frazer. Particularly helpful was Earl Dunckel, who accompanied Reagan on the long train rides from plant to plant during the first General Electric years. I did more than a hundred interviews, including sessions with Reagan aides Lyn Nofziger and Ed Meese, and talks with political reporters like David Broder. I studied hundreds of newspaper and magazine clippings, speeches, news releases, and other bits of Reaganalia. Bruce Weinrod and Lo Anne Wagner combed the files and provided summaries. Bruce became deputy assistant secretary of defense under President George H.W. Bush. Fifty years later, he remains a good friend, adviser, and board member of the Victims of Communism Memorial Foundation.

After providing a summary of Reagan's first year as governor, I added an epilogue envisioning Reagan's nomination for president at the 1968 National Republican Convention. As it happened, Richard Nixon would narrowly fend off Reagan's eleventh-hour challenge for the presidential nomination at the 1968 convention.

I ended my biography by asking what kind of president Reagan might make and suggested that it depended upon the following: (1) Would he appoint sound, experienced people as his White House advisers and the heads of federal departments and agencies? (2) Would he work with both parties in both houses of Congress to achieve the best possible result for the general good? (3) Would he conduct our foreign policy with firmness and prudence? (4) Would he get more out of the American public by communicating the need for sacrifice, hard work, and cooperation? "In other words," I wrote, "would he be able to do in Washington what he is presently doing in Sacramento?" To those who protested that Reagan was too inexperienced and too conservative to be president, I offered Reagan's response: "I ran for governor without experience. Sometimes it helps— you don't know what you can't do."

President Reagan would do all of the above.

I sent a copy of the biography to the Reagans, who were so occupied with the events of 1968, including the Republican National Convention in Miami, that I did not hear from them until the fall, when Nancy wrote:

> Dear Anne and Lee:
>
> A belated thanks for sending us your book—you were most thoughtful and we do appreciate it. As soon as this election is over, we'll look forward to reading it. I think Ronnie has worked harder this time than he did in his own campaign!
>
> I'm so sorry we didn't have a chance for more than a brief visit in Miami—it seems a million years ago now. Do let us know if you come to Calif.—we'd love to see you.
>
> Our thanks again.
>
> Fondly,
>
> Nancy Reagan

THE OTHER '60S

For me, as for most young conservatives, the '60s were the decade not of John Kennedy but Barry Goldwater, not Students for a Democratic Society but Young Americans for Freedom, not the *New Republic* but *National Review*, not Herbert Marcuse but Russell Kirk, not Norman Mailer but Ayn Rand, not Gore Vidal but Bill Buckley, not Lyndon Johnson's Great Society but Ronald Reagan's Creative Society. We saw

Vietnam not as a civil war between north and south but as a critical battle in the protracted conflict against communism. It was the decade when conservatism was transformed from a debating society into a political movement, and I collaborated with almost every conservative leader who effected the transformation.

While I had many clients in the '60s, from the American Conservative Union to Strom Thurmond, YAF was number one, not because it compensated me the most—quite the contrary—but because it was committed to moving America to the right from the campus to the White House. I was with YAF when it helped Bill Buckley in his 1965 run for mayor of New York City, and I broke up when he said the first thing he would do if he were elected was to demand a recount. I was there when YAF collected food, medicine, and clothing for Vietnamese war refugees and sponsored "bleed-ins" (blood donation drives) and mail campaigns for U.S. soldiers serving in South Vietnam. After the fall of South Vietnam to the communists in 1975, I helped Vietnamese forced to flee their native land because they were anticommunist. I put Bui Anh Tuan, who had been one of South Vietnam's most popular novelists, on my payroll although it sorely tested our budget. Anne agreed that we should do it.

I was there when YAF, under Chairman Alan MacKay, began providing its chapters with the best conservative thought, understanding that "why" is as important as "how." Among the books distributed were Richard Cornuelle's *Reclaiming the American Dream* (a neglected classic), Phil Crane's *Democrats' Dilemma*, Russell Kirk's *The American Cause*, Frédéric Bastiat's *The Law*, and Max Eastman's *Reflections on the Failure of Socialism*.

YAF's second venture into presidential politics occurred in 1968 when it helped Clif White and other senior conservatives in their last-minute effort to nominate Governor Reagan at the Republican National Convention. Vic Gold and I published a daily satirical newsletter about a future Reagan administration that included such items as:

PRESIDENT REAGAN TO SELL P.O. TO AT&T
The Washington Post. WASHINGTON, D.C., March 15, 1969—President Reagan today announced that the United States Post Office will be sold to the American Telephone and Telegraph Company for $15 billion and that the money would be used to reduce the national debt by that amount.

SDS KAPUT

The Wall Street Journal. CHICAGO, ILL., June 15, 1969—Students for a Democratic Society today announced their dissolution.

"What's the use?" asked Carl Oglesby, the youthful-looking 48-year-old executive director of SDS. "Since Supersquare got in the White House no one listens to us any more."

CLARK WARNS AGAINST FILLING JAILS

The New York Times. NEW YORK, N.Y., May 12, 1970—Former Atty. Gen. Ramsey Clark today sharply criticized President Reagan's campaign against crime in the United States.

"Apparently, President Reagan is not concerned that while the crime rate is going *down* in this country, the number of arrests and convictions is going *up*. If this dangerous trend continues, the nation's jails will be filled with criminals," said Clark.

RON PUTS NIX ON U.N. PAYMENT

The Washington Post. NEW YORK, N.Y., Jan. 10, 1970—United Nations Secretary General U Thant today warned United States Ambassador to the U.N. Chet Huntley that he would resign as head of the international organization if President Reagan did not reverse his stand that the United States would not make up the $238 million deficit confronting the U.N. as a result of the Soviet Union and other communist nations not paying their dues.

When asked for comment, White House Communications Director Lyn Nofziger said, "U thant be therious."

Our eleventh-hour effort was too late. Nixon had already locked up conservatives Barry Goldwater, Strom Thurmond, and John Tower, who convinced southern delegates to stand by the more experienced Nixon. When Reagan called on Thurmond in Miami and asked for his backing, emphasizing his conservative credentials, Thurmond responded that he had already given his word to the former vice president. He told Reagan, a youthful-looking fifty-seven, "Don't worry, young man, your turn will come." Nixon later wrote me that without the help of Goldwater and other conservatives, he might not have won the first ballot, opening the way for a possible Reagan victory on a later ballot.

I worked for Nixon in the fall as a volunteer and celebrated, quietly, when he narrowly won, understanding that he would not be the apotheosis of conservatism or even anticommunism in the White House. I had not forgotten his telltale 1967 article in *Foreign Affairs* in which he wrote that it was time for the United States to establish better relations with what he now called, respectfully, the People's Republic of China. "Red China" was no longer an appropriate phrase, although Nixon had used it for twenty years.

CHAOS IN CHICAGO

The Republican convention was not my only national political convention that year. Anne and I traveled to Chicago, where the Democrats would select their national ticket, to promote our new book, *You Can Make the Difference*, the first political handbook written by conservatives for conservatives. Clif White, the most respected political consultant on the right, described our book as "unique," "well-written," and "comprehensive." I was excited about showing my hometown to Anne, who had never before visited Chicago. We headed in our rental car to Thirty-third and Union, where I had spent summers as a child with Grandmother and Grandfather Sullivan. It looked just the same—the same redbrick row house, the same porch, the same white Americans walking by, the same saloons on every corner. Bridgeport was a white enclave in a nearly all-black South Side. Mayor Richard Daley, who lived in the middle of Bridgeport, ensured its survival.

It was a hot summer day, and Anne and I went into a saloon to have a beer. We struck up a conversation with an old-timer at the bar.

"By any chance," I asked, "do you happen to remember my grandfather Arthur Sullivan, who lived just down the block?"

"Oh, yes," he said without hesitation, "the Republican!" It was twenty-three years since we had buried my grandfather, and yet he lived on in the memory of Irish Democrats like our new friend. We bought him a beer and toasted the Sullivans of both political parties.

Admiring a large poster of Mayor Daley on the wall, Anne said she would like to take one back to Washington. "No problem," said the old-timer. "I'll get one at the local party office. Don't go away. I'll be back in a jiffy." An hour later, we were still waiting, and then another forty-five minutes passed with no sign of our Democratic friend. We were about to leave when he came through the door with a rolled-up poster in one hand.

Smiling broadly, he said, "Sure and I forgot which saloon I left you in and I had to stop and have a little something at every one along the way."

"The Republican!": as a young boy with my grandfather Arthur Sullivan

He presented the poster to Anne with a little bow: "Here you be, little lady," he said, "with the compliments of the mayor."

Driving back to the Hilton Hotel on Michigan Avenue, I got confused and went the wrong way down a one-way street. A police car pulled us over. I braced myself for a bawling out and maybe a ticket, but the cop was smiling and readily accepted my apology and my story about revisiting my birthplace with my East Coast wife. "Welcome home," he said. It was the Friday before the Democratic convention began and before SDS and the rest of the left provoked the police and turned Chicago into a teargassed battleground.

Mayor Daley was proud, short-tempered, and without a sense of humor. He was taken in by the preposterous threats of Yippies like Abbie Hoffman, who said they would put LSD in the city's water supply, hire sexy males to seduce female delegates, and set off smoke bombs in the convention hall. The threats, along with SDS requests to demonstrate outside the convention and in the city parks, led Daley to assemble an army of security forces, including more than ten thousand Chicago police, five thousand National Guardsmen, and a thousand FBI and Secret Service agents. They faced perhaps eight thousand antiwar protestors from out of state plus five thousand leftists from the greater Chicago area.

Anne and I were staying at the Hilton Hotel across from Grant Park, and Tuesday evening we went outside and stood on the sidewalk, drawn by the sounds of the anti–Vietnam War rally in the park. Soon, rock-throwing leftists goaded the police into charging at them. Bottles flew and clubs drew blood. Clouds of tear gas drifted across Michigan Avenue, forcing us and other spectators to flee into the hotel lobby, where we could still smell the smoke. We jammed ourselves into an elevator and sought safety in our room overlooking the park, our eyes still stinging. Grant Park was covered in smoke. Demonstrators ran back and forth trying to evade the police, who freely used their clubs.

I agree with the findings of the federal commission appointed by President Johnson that the Chicago police used excessive force. It was obvious they had not been trained in the use of discriminate force to subdue rioters. I remembered how in Paris the gendarmes used lead-weighted capes to break up groups of student demonstrators, who quickly retreated before the mounted Garde Civile.

That week in Chicago, the antiwar movement was an irresistible force that collided with an immovable object, Mayor Daley. Television turned the collision into national theater and a national disgrace, ensuring Nixon's election and allowing YAF to present itself as a law-abiding youth alternative to SDS and the radical left. Most polls showed that a majority of Americans were appalled by the violence and the anarchy in Chicago and sided with the police. They agreed with former JFK adviser McGeorge Bundy, who said that whoever swung the clubs, the New Left was to blame.

I did not expect Nixon, regardless of his conservative campaign rhetoric, to chart a course to the right, but I was not prepared for détente with the Soviets; a historic visit to Communist China; wage and price controls; regulatory agencies monitoring the air, the water, and every other natural resource; and an unnecessary, inept political burglary. There was a bright side to the Nixon years. Watergate and the 1970s marked the emergence of two groups—the New Right and the neoconservatives—that altered American politics. I would play a consequential role with the former as an adviser to its founding father, Richard A. Viguerie, and as the first editor of its journal, *Conservative Digest*.

21

THE "VOICE" OF THE SILENT MAJORITY

My activist role in the conservative movement reached a peak on Veterans Day, November 11, 1969, when I served as the unpaid coordinator of a giant pro-Vietnam rally in front of the Washington Monument. For months I worked with veterans', civic, and other groups on our event, the idea of Slavics professor Charles Moser of George Washington University.

Our three-hour-long program was balanced politically, featuring both Democrats (including Congressman Mendel Rivers of South Carolina, chairman of the House Armed Services Committee) and Republicans (including Senator John Tower of Texas). We had an Eagle Scout lead the Pledge of Allegiance; a local Roman Catholic priest offer the invocation; a beautiful young black woman, Carmen Balthrop, sing "The Star-Spangled Banner" (Carmen later sang at the Metropolitan Opera); and a folk singer named Tony Dolan (who became President Reagan's chief speechwriter) entertain the crowd with patriotic songs. Thanks in large part to the American Legion and the Veterans of Foreign Wars, an estimated twenty thousand people turned out, the largest conservative gathering in the city's history to that time.

I was confident we would receive in-depth media attention—we were the only large pro-Vietnam rally on the East Coast. Among those who covered us was Nancy Dickerson of NBC News, who asked me to delay our start until her camera was in position. I was happy to oblige. I wanted something special to capture the media's eye—an enduring image. We had a limited budget and nothing for special effects—our one large gift of $10,000 came from the Texas millionaire Ross Perot, whose largesse was unexpected and unsolicited. I have always suspected that the White House encouraged Perot to help us. His generosity enabled us to buy ten thousand miniature U.S. flags, which we gave to people as they arrived.

I was the first speaker and my first words were: "Please join me in waving the American flag you are holding so that the nation and the world can see the real face of America." I shall never see a more beautiful sight than that undulating wave of red, white, and blue, with the gleaming white Washington Monument as a backdrop. *Time* magazine put our field of American flags at the base of the monument on the cover of its next issue, about the pro– and anti–Vietnam War demonstrations in Washington.

The morning after our rally, the *New York Times* described me as "The 'Voice' of the Silent Majority" in its "Man in the News" column. It listed some of the other "tough jobs he relishes doing for the conservative movement," such as producing *Tyranny*, a half-hour documentary film on communism; serving as executive producer of *The Square World of Ed Butler*, a syndicated TV variety program; and chairing the Everett McKinley Dirksen Forum, which would discuss current issues in the "Dirksen tradition." As I told the *Times* reporter about conservatism's impact on Washington, "The curve is up." The article carried a head-and-shoulders photo of me wearing a brown turtleneck sweater and corduroy suit and sporting long sideburns—me at my hippiest.

I confessed to the reporter that I did not always use the word *conservative* when explaining what I did and who I was. "There's so much happening, changing" in the world, I said. "It's not so much a matter of preserving but of extending freedom. Today, a conservative has to be a radical." By "radical" I meant returning to the philosophical roots of the American founding outlined in the Declaration of Independence and the Constitution. Driven by the memory of the Hungarian Revolution of 1956 and influenced by Walter Judd, with whom I was now working at the Committee of One Million, I sought however I could to extend freedom not only in America but around the world, especially to those people who lived, and not by their choice, under communism.

For the next fifteen years, until undone by an embezzling bookkeeper, I was a publicist, coordinator, and fundraiser for nearly every organization on the right, from YAF to the American Conservative Union, from the National Right to Work Committee to Life-Pac, from the Heritage

Foundation to the National Captive Nations Committee, from *Conservative Digest* to *Human Events*, from the American Council for World Freedom to the World Anti-Communist League, from Friends of the FBI to Americans for Agnew, from the American Security Council to the National Tax Limitation Committee, from the New Right of Richard Viguerie and Paul Weyrich to the moderate right of the Republican National Committee.

Lee Edwards & Associates never had more than a half dozen employees (including Anne) while often functioning as a mini–think tank. Whatever needed to be done to advance the conservative movement, I did or helped to do. At the same time, I kept writing. I syndicated my own weekly column, which led in time to a five-year association with the liberal *Boston Globe* as a monthly columnist. I ghostwrote a bestselling book about the New Right and a short biography of Dan Renn, a young North Carolina entrepreneur who became a millionaire selling fire alarms and preaching PMA (a Positive Mental Attitude) to his salespeople.

A good part of my business was to stay in contact with the Washington press corps, especially those whom I had met during the Goldwater campaign, including Dave Broder of the *Washington Post*, Wally Mears of the Associated Press, and Robin MacNeil of NBC and later PBS. I had learned from Dad that personal contacts (call them "sources," if you like) are the most important contacts.

When Theodore White published *The Making of the President 1968*, I wrote Teddy that he had written a "great book," especially the sections about Nixon, who had changed since the 1960 campaign and was receptive to ideas, and George Wallace, whom he had called "the GI candidate." I said I was amused by the reviews that had described White as "a reactionary" because he had been too soft on Nixon. Don't pay any attention to the "knee-jerk liberals," I wrote, who always become indignant and irrational "when the facts explode one of their favorite theories or clichés."

A week or so later, Teddy responded warmly, beginning, "What a pleasure to get that letter" and ending that it would be "fun" to have lunch in New York on my next visit. He said he had been trying to find a word to describe those who lived in the center of American thought and the word he liked best was *libertarian*. "I feel," he said, "that the word embraces both of us." It would have been fun to discuss with Teddy just how libertarian we were, but other things kept coming along and we never had that New York lunch.

THE RICHEST MAN IN AMERICA

Sometimes I sought business and sometimes I was sought, as when I received a telephone call from Dallas. Mr. H. L. Hunt would like to talk to you about a project he has in mind. Can you come to Dallas next week? Indeed I could. Mr. Hunt was the richest man in America as a result of his oil explorations and an outspoken conservative who, among other things, underwrote a daily radio commentary by former FBI agent Dan Smoot. He was known for signing his letters, "Constructively Yours."

Why had Hunt reached out to me? I wondered. Write his biography? Organize a patriotic rally in Washington? Surely he already had a public relations firm. Perhaps something in television? Maybe he had been told about my commentaries on Channel 9, the local CBS affiliate, which had generated considerable mail and an angry demand by Martin Agronsky, the longtime liberal host of a weekly TV program, that I be canceled, or else. Agronsky had more clout than I did—I was terminated after a half dozen commentaries. I was told off the record that Agronsky's insistence rather than my performance was the reason.

Arriving in Dallas, I made my way to the Hunt "ranch," which was dominated by an sprawling mansion—a Texas Taj Mahal—sitting all by itself in the middle of a thousand acres. I was escorted into a large wood-paneled room with bookshelves to the ceiling. "Mr. Hunt will be with you in a few minutes," a middle-aged secretary said. No tea or coffee was offered.

The door opened and a sharp-eyed man in his fifties looked me over but did not say a word. He turned and left, closing the door. A few minutes went by, and the door opened again. Another man, dressed in a tailored pinstripe suit and wearing brightly polished cowboy boots, stood in the door and examined me. Without saying a word, he, too, turned and left. Who were these people? The door opened again, and the secretary said, "Mr. Hunt will see you now."

The richest man in America was dressed in a dark suit, a white dress shirt, and a conservative bow tie. Jowly and overweight, Hunt was eighty years old but seemed years younger when he began talking. One of the sharp-eyed men sat in a corner, taking notes. Hunt wasted no time explaining what he had in mind: the setting up of chapters of patriotic Americans all over the country that would implement his "constructive" philosophy. He waved a copy of his book.

"I assume you have read it?"

"Yes, sir." Actually I had skimmed it, which was all that was necessary. It was a mishmash of laissez-faire economics, "rugged" individualism, the Protestant work ethic, and quotations of various Founding Fathers, especially Ben Franklin.

"You're the best conservative organizer in America," Hunt said, speaking softly, persuasively. "The *New York Times* says so and I think they're right. Will you do it?"

I was interested, but it was a very ambitious project, requiring weeks and months of planning and implementation, staff, and lots of travel. The telephone bill alone would be enormous.

I asked the key question: "How would it be financed?"

"Oh, you don't have to worry about that," Hunt responded. "The chapters will finance themselves. You can get the local people to help. You can pass the hat. You can sell copies of my book—I will let you have them at cost."

As we talked, he grew more and more enthusiastic, arguing that a network of patriots would reinvigorate America at a time of crisis. I kept circling back to the question of money, and he would respond, smiling, that money would not be a problem. For two hours, he tried to convince me to administer his national network of constructive Americans without any seed money from him.

Well, I said to myself, I was happy to organize the Veterans Day Rally without a fee, but I was damned if I would work for nothing for the richest man in America.

A disappointed Hunt finally allowed me to leave. In the foyer, the sharp-eyed men in their tailored suits and shiny boots were whispering to each other, satisfied, I am sure, they would not have to deal with me. They reminded me of sharks circling an old but still powerful whale. I did get something out of our meeting—an autographed copy of his book with the inscription "Constructively Yours, H. L. Hunt."

THE LUNCH BUNCH

To help bring Washington conservatives together in social as well as political settings, I hosted for nearly a decade starting in December 1968 a monthly luncheon and discussion group, "The Lunch Bunch." Bob Kephart, the libertarian publisher of *Human Events*, came up with the idea and asked me to act as host, preferring to remain in the background. Every month as many as one hundred conservatives crowded into the third floor of Freddy's restaurant on Massachusetts Avenue across from Saint Matthew's Cathedral to hear such speakers as Congressman Donald Rumsfeld, columnist James Jackson Kilpatrick, White House aide Lyn Nofziger, author Kevin Phillips, Nixon aide Pat Buchanan, Congressman Phil Crane, *New York Times* writer Tom Wicker, United States Information Agency head Frank Shakespeare, Senator James Buckley, arch-libertarian Murray Rothbard, columnist Bob Novak (not as conservative then as he would later become), author Richard Whalen, Governor Reagan chief of staff Ed Meese, journalist/author Stan Evans, activist/author Phyllis Schlafly, former Goldwater speechwriter Karl Hess, political operative John Sears, former Nixon aide Charles Colson, and *Washington Post* political reporter David Broder.

The speaker who touched us most and elicited a standing ovation—a rare reaction by skeptical Washington conservatives—was Chuck Colson. The hardened political operative who said he would run over his grandmother to win an election had just been released from jail. Chuck described how, sitting in a jail cell, full of shame and wondering what life held for him after his conviction for his role in Watergate, he began reading C. S. Lewis's powerful little book *Mere Christianity*. He experienced a Road to Damascus moment. After his release, he started a Christian prison fellowship for men like those he had met while in jail and introduced them to Jesus Christ. As Chuck finished, with tears in his eyes, we rose as one and applauded a fellow conservative who had risen high in politics and fallen to the lowest rung, only to find his true calling. He exemplified the adage that man does not live by politics alone.

Throughout the 1970s, the Lunch Bunchers included conservatives and libertarians on the way up or down who would exchange ideas and business cards, gossip and plot, and draw strength from one another in the uncertain era of Vietnam, Watergate, and Jimmy Carter. The lunch was a bargain: Freddy charged only five dollars for London broil and a dessert and coffee.

Frustrated that she and other wives could not attend the downtown luncheons and profit from the insights of the speakers, Anne suggested that Washington's conservative community sponsor an evening party every month or so at someone's home, as had been the custom in New York City during her years there. Anne and I hosted the first "soiree" in our home in Somerset, Maryland, just across the D.C. line. The women brought food and the men brought Coors beer and other potables, alcoholic and non-alcoholic. Drawing on her New York experience, Anne turned the evening into more than just another potluck supper by putting brightly colored candles on the tables and dressing up. Soon as many as 150 mostly young conservatives (in their thirties and forties) were coming. Teetotaler Morton Blackwell, the founder of the Leadership Institute, was responsible for transporting the unconsumed liquor from party to party.

With Reagan's landslide election in 1980 and the arrival of thousands of conservatives to serve in his administration, I realized there was no longer any pressing need for the Lunch Bunch, and I quietly shut it down, although some old-timers like Reed Larson of the National Right to Work Committee protested. But under Morton and the Leadership Institute, the "soiree" survives to this day as a patriotic Fourth of July picnic in northern Virginia that attracts hundreds of conservatives and their families.

COMMUNISM ON TRIAL

In 1967, when the Soviets and their satellites would celebrate the fiftieth anniversary of the Bolshevik Revolution, YAF and *Twin Circle*, the conservative Catholic newspaper edited by Daniel Lyons, SJ, one of the few traditional Jesuits left after Vatican II, decided to put international communism on trial for crimes against humanity. They asked me to be the coordinator.

After months of preparation and communication with anticommunists around the world, we were ready by February 1968 to present "International Communism on Trial" in the Hall of Nations at Georgetown University in Washington, D.C. Professor Lev Dobriansky, with whom I would collaborate on a number of anticommunist activities, including the Victims of Communism Memorial, was our university sponsor.

From the beginning we determined that our mock trial would be as close as possible to a real trial—like the Nuremberg Nazi crimes trial after World War II. We had a distinguished five-person tribunal, including two Cuban jurists who had helped write the 1940 Cuban constitution; a well-known Czech lawyer; a Chinese jurist who had studied in the United States; and as our "chief justice" Richard H. Slemmer, a well-known Columbus, Ohio, lawyer who had studied international law at Ohio State University. More than thirty witnesses who had suffered under communism testified during the three-day trial. One of the most dramatic was the Reverend Richard Wurmbrand of Romania, who removed his clerical shirt to reveal the deep scars left by fourteen years of torture by the Romanian secret police, the Securitate.

Our indictment accused the Communist parties and governments of the United States, the Soviet Union, the People's Republic of China, and twenty other countries of an international conspiracy to commit crimes against humanity that resulted in the deaths of an estimated 100 million people (an estimate that anticipated the conclusion of *The Black Book of Communism* three decades later). The indictment was issued by the World Court of Public Opinion, a concept that had been developed by Luis Kutner, a liberal Chicago lawyer whom I had met at the United Nations, and with whom I would collaborate (albeit unhappily) on Friends of the FBI.

Over the objections of a few hard-core anticommunists, I insisted that the communists have a defense counsel, whether they appeared in court or not. I argued that the prospect of an open clash between an anticommunist prosecution and a pro-communist defense would attract the mass media. We contacted the Washington office of the American Civil Liberties Union—I had met the Washington director, Irving Ferman, through my father—which located a lawyer willing to defend the communists. His name was Leonard Joseph Keilp, who, although only in his early thirties, was an experienced trial lawyer. Asked by a reporter why he had taken the case, Keilp replied that even communists deserved a defense.

Keilp's skillful defense made our trial come alive. He fought tenaciously for his clients, challenging the prosecution, led by Fred Schlafly, Phyllis's husband and a serious student of communism, for concrete evidence of conspiracy. Closely questioning every witness, he made the trial more than a predictable condemnation of communism.

On the final day of "International Communism on Trial," we received two telling compliments. NBC anchor Chet Huntley devoted several minutes of his newscast to our trial and praised our "balanced" examination of communism. And someone blew up a small wall in front of the Soviet embassy on 16th Street, NW, leading the Soviets to accuse us of fomenting violence by our "vicious kangaroo court." I still think it was the Soviets who blew up their own mini-wall in an attempt to draw public attention from the testimony of communism's victims in the Soviet Union, Eastern Europe, China, South Korea, the Caribbean, South America, and Africa.

If that was the intent, Moscow failed. Our trial generated extensive national publicity and reinforced YAF's reputation as a leader in the war against Marxism-Leninism. I do not think it an exaggeration to describe "International Communism on Trial" as a triumph. But we did not win every battle against the communists.

FREE CHINA

Founded in 1953, the Committee of One Million (Against the Admission of Communist China to the United Nations) was one of the most successful citizens' groups in America. It reflected the majority view of the American people, who did not want a government that played a major role in the Korean War and enslaved millions of its citizens to be admitted into the UN. Some politicians and policy makers argued that realism required the admission of Beijing. But the memory of the Korean conflict and the thirty-five thousand Americans who died in that war was still fresh. Throughout the 1950s and '60s, the American public stood firm against Communist China's admission into the UN and for the Republic of China (ROC) on Taiwan to represent China in the General Assembly and the Security Council.

The Committee of One Million was bipartisan at the insistence of its chairman, Walter Judd, who understood that if the organization were ever branded as the political creature of Republicans, its effectiveness would be severely impaired. The presence on the steering committee of leading liberal Democrats like House Speaker John McCormack of Massachusetts and Senator Paul Douglas of Illinois prevented pro-China partisans from characterizing the committee as a Republican or conservative front. Dr. Judd and committee secretary Marvin Liebman worked organizational and public relations miracles with an annual budget that never exceeded $100,000 until its last year. Marvin stepped down in 1968 and moved to Great Britain to pursue a long-held dream of being a theatrical producer in London's West End. I succeeded Marvin as secretary, thrilled to work with Dr. Judd and to manage the most respected anticommunist organization in the movement.

The fortunes of the committee were tied to the U.S. policy of containment, waxing in the 1950s, when President Eisenhower resisted communism from Guatemala and Lebanon to Quemoy and Matsu, and waning in the late 1960s and early 1970s, when President Nixon and Henry Kissinger pursued détente with Moscow and Beijing. Most of the original one million signatures against Communist China's admission into the UN came from the American Federation of Labor and the American Legion, both staunchly anticommunist in the wake of the Korean War. U.S. policy and public attitudes began to shift in 1961, when President Kennedy, who had said as a candidate that he was against the recognition of Communist China, accepted a subtle but significant change in strategy regarding Beijing's UN admission.

Instead of postponing any UN vote, the United States moved to have China's credentials considered an "important question," requiring a two-thirds majority of the General Assembly. Both Washington and Taipei were confident they could block a two-thirds vote for the foreseeable future. They were correct, but "foreseeable" came quicker than either anticipated as more and more Third World nations became UN members.

In 1964 both the Democratic and Republican party platforms included planks opposing the admission of Communist China, but in the spring of 1966 the House Committee on Foreign Affairs and the Senate Foreign Relations Committee both held hearings on "U.S. policy with regard to Mainland China." Harvard Sinologist John K. Fairbank testified that now was the time for the United States to reach out to China. But Fairbank and other apologists for Communist China fell silent when, within a few weeks of the congressional hearings, Chairman Mao launched the Great Cultural Revolution, plunging mainland China into political and economic chaos and bloodshed for almost a decade until his death.

With Nixon's election in 1968, it seemed that the Committee of One Million would enjoy a period of continuing influence. Dr. Judd and President Nixon had been political allies for more than twenty years. As the new secretary of the committee, I assumed we would have easy access to the White House and its national security advisers.

I was wrong.

Every attempt by Dr. Judd to see the president was blocked. We heard constant rumors of a possible rapprochement between the United States and Communist China. Travel and trade restrictions were relaxed, and in July 1971, Nixon told a surprised nation that he would soon be the first American president to visit China.

The Committee of One Million initiated a vigorous counteroffensive. Dr. Judd urged the president to ask the Chinese communists about the release of American servicemen still rumored to be in China; its role as an aggressor in the Korean War; its practice of genocide in Tibet; its responsibility for the deaths of American soldiers in Vietnam through its years-long supply of arms and ammunition to North Vietnam; and its habit of officially describing the United States as an "imperialist aggressor" surrounded by "running dogs."

I hired Hugh Newton, an experienced, high-energy public relations professional, to take charge of our communications program. We dramatically increased the size and distribution of our monthly newsletter and generated dozens of newspaper editorials and columns opposing any change in U.S. policy toward Communist China that would hurt free China (Taiwan). We raised the funds for a sixty-minute documentary film, *U.S.-China Policy: Danger at the Crossroads*, narrated by Bill Buckley—ever the obliging anticommunist—that presented the case for keeping the ROC in and Communist China out of the UN. Our central argument was simple: as long as Communist China refused to abide by the language of the Universal Declaration of Human Rights and to conduct itself as a law-abiding member of the international community, it did not deserve membership in the UN. When all the major TV networks refused to carry our documentary, accusing us of bias, we purchased time in key markets like New York City and Washington, D.C., and presented our film there.

Provoked by what I considered to be a betrayal of America's decadeslong commitment to the ROC and its embrace of a totalitarian country responsible for the deaths of countless Americans in the Korean War, I formed an anticommunist coalition that included YAF and the American Conservative Union. The coalition sponsored a weeklong series of events, including mock congressional hearings on Capitol Hill, a block party in Washington's Chinatown, and a demonstration in Lafayette Park across from the White House that used something rarely associated with conservatism—satire.

Two diplomats wearing masks identifying them as Nixon and Mao played a vigorous game of ping-pong in the park. Communist China had sent a signal to the United States by inviting an American ping-pong team to compete on the mainland, spawning the phrase "pingpong diplomacy." In our game, we made sure that no matter how hard he played, Nixon always lost to Mao. We attracted a large number of TV and other reporters, many of whom stated our objections to Nixon's trip. I was invited to appear on NBC's *Today* show, where I made the case for keeping the ROC in and Communist China out of the UN.

But all our efforts, including the introduction of a congressional resolution, were to no avail. The announcement that President Nixon was going to mainland China weakened the ROC's position in the United Nations. The U.S. delegation, led by Ambassador George H.W. Bush, insisted that the United States was 100 percent behind the ROC, but the delegates of the General Assembly took their cue from the travel plans of the American president.

On October 25, 1971, the UN General Assembly voted 76–35 to expel the ROC and seat Communist China.

We were devastated by the UN action, Dr. Judd feeling more disappointed and even betrayed than the rest of us. Nixon, the man who had almost picked him to be his running mate in 1960, had let Dr. Judd down badly. After a run of almost twenty years, the Committee of One Million closed its doors.

But I felt we could not quit: the Chinese people needed us more than ever. I immediately wrote a memorandum proposing the creation of a Committee for a Free China with Dr. Judd as chairman. Dr. Judd protested that at seventy-three he was too old to head a new organization, but I appealed to his abiding love for the Chinese and the need for a political counterbalance to the communist regime. He reluctantly agreed to help the new committee get under way with the understanding that he would step down in a year or two. I made the same limited commitment as committee secretary.

Under the succeeding chairman, Dr. Ray Cline, formerly a high-ranking analyst with the Central Intelligence Agency, and with the help of Jack Buttram and Hugh Newton, the Committee for a Free China helped keep alive in the minds of the American public the idea of a non-communist China.

A decade and a half later, Dr. Judd and I would be reunited when I persuaded him to let me write his story. His would be the first in a series of biographies of eminent conservatives—including Barry Goldwater, Ronald Reagan, William F. Buckley Jr., Edwin Meese III, and Edwin Feulner—I would publish in the 1990s and up to the present.

THE KGB AND ME

Not long after I became secretary of the Committee of One Million, I took a phone call from a heavily accented foreigner who identified himself as Gennadiy Domakhin of the Soviet embassy. He asked whether it would be possible for the two of us to have lunch one day—at the Mayflower Hotel. I was intrigued. I had never before been directly approached by a Soviet official and I agreed to meet. It was the first of a series of monthly lunches I would have with Domakhin from 1970 to 1975 and then from 1981 to 1985.

It was always the same. We would meet at noon in the Palm Court of the Mayflower, place our order, talk about the issues of the day, and part at about 1:30 P.M. Gennadiy always paid with a $20 bill. In the early period, he sought information about the new U.S.-Chinese relationship and how it might affect U.S.-Soviet relations. He knew of the committee's work and Dr. Judd's long-standing friendship with President Nixon. I told him nothing that could not be learned from reading the *Washington Post* or the *New York Times*. I assumed he was exploring how and whether the Committee of One Million and the rest of the so-called China Lobby could affect or perhaps deflect the U.S. opening to China.

A decade later, the central topic was President Ronald Reagan (Gennadiy had read my Reagan biography) and his intentions regarding the Cold War. I always replied that it was quite simple: the president wanted to talk with Moscow and would talk with Moscow but only after the United States had once again assumed a position of military superiority. I assured Gennadiy that Reagan believed in peace but in peace through strength.

Gennadiy was about my height, five foot seven inches, but much heavier, broad through the shoulders and with a thick neck. He usually wore a gray off-the-rack suit and a nondescript tie. I learned from FBI agents, whom I debriefed after every luncheon, that he was a colonel in the KGB and was in fact the head of the KGB in Washington, although his business card described him simply as a first secretary of the embassy. He was often on Capitol Hill to talk with congressional aides, most of whom would not meet with the FBI afterward or reveal what they had talked about.

The FBI was most grateful for my cooperation. The two agents who came to my office would suggest, for example, questions about the leadership of the Politboro (this was the period when Soviet leaders kept dying, first Brezhnev, then Andropov, then Chernenko), and I would report back Gennadiy's always guarded answers. Nothing that either he or I said or that I reported to the FBI was earthshaking.

Over time, Gennadiy and I began spending more time talking about ourselves, our family, and our children. We talked about Dostoyevsky, Goncharov, Tchaikovsky, Gogol, and even Solzhenitsyn. Over time, our relationship deepened to the extent that Gennadiy and his wife, Raisa, and their two children came to our home one Christmas week. Our children played downstairs in the family room while we had tea upstairs. Gennadiy's gift was a small painted box that our girls pretended contained a listening device. For a long time, whenever they walked by it they would say, "Hello, Gennadiy."

Another time my KGB "friend" came to my annual song recital at the Church of the Little Flower in Bethesda and applauded my American Songbook selections along with the parishioners. Our assistant pastor, Father Hurley, was in the audience. At the reception, Gennadiy asked

Anne, "Who is that priest? I know him." It turned out that before he became a priest, Father Hurley had been an intelligence officer stationed in Moscow. I was impressed by Gennadiy's memory. When I recounted his visits to our home and our church, the FBI agents were puzzled and could not explain them. They insisted he was hard-core KGB. Should I talk about defecting? I asked, half joking. They did not bother to reply.

I won't forget our last Mayflower luncheon in the summer of 1985. Gennadiy revealed he would soon be returning to Moscow for reassignment. He had been in Canada between his two U.S. stays but did not know where he was going. As usual our conversation was about Reagan, who had said he was looking forward to meeting the new general secretary, Mikhail Gorbachev. At the very end of lunch, as we took a last sip of coffee, Gennadiy leaned over and whispered about Gorbachev, "He's different." And so he proved to be.

Three years later, when I visited the Soviet Union for the first and only time on a tour arranged by the *Washington Times*, I first called the Soviet embassy in Washington to ask for Gennadiy Domakhin's contact information. I explained that he and I had often lunched and I wanted to see him when in Moscow. I waited patiently and at last a voice came on and said coolly, "We have no record of any such person." Click.

In Moscow I asked our Soviet hosts about Gennadiy Domakhin, explaining that I wanted to say hello to someone whom I had known in Washington. I received the same answer, "We have no record of any such person." I have often wondered where Gennadiy and Raisa and their children are and where Gennadiy has landed in the Putin era. I have gone online but to no avail.

WORLD ANTI-COMMUNIST LEAGUE

Because of my association with the Committee of One Million, in 1969 the World Anti-Communist League invited me to attend its annual meeting in Bangkok, the capital of Thailand. I decided to take advantage of the trip to visit Hong Kong and film interviews of the "freedom swimmers" who had risked their lives to swim the shark-infested waters of Hong Kong Harbour to gain freedom in the British colony.

Every one of the young men who survived the perilous hours-long swim gave the same explanation: they had fled mainland China because they were tired of being told by Communist Party members where to work and live, what to say and not to say, of being watched night and day. They wanted to live their own lives in their own way, and they had heard it was possible to have that kind of life in Hong Kong. I hoped to make a documentary film—a successor to *Tyranny*—out of the Hong Kong interviews and other footage I planned to shoot in Bangkok, where I would meet anticommunists from around the world.

I will remember Bangkok for its golden temples and saffron-robed monks and green-water canals and its smell of strange spices and its slender people so friendly and serene. I remember visiting a great square early one morning and watching the monks line up and wait for someone to fill their empty bowls. I noticed a vendor standing beside a table that held a pile of small wooden cages containing live birds. He smiled and said, "Only one dollar." "For what?" I asked. "Only one dollar," he repeated. Intrigued, I gave him a dollar and he gave me a cage, saying, "Open it." I did and the bird immediately flew out, circled above us, and then returned to its cage. I shook my head. "You see," explained the vendor, "you have made yourself happy by freeing the bird and me happy by giving me a dollar and the bird happy by giving it a minute of freedom." I had not expected to find a philosopher posing as a vendor.

At the World Anti-Communist League Conference, I interviewed people who had suffered under communism in mainland China, Vietnam, Ukraine, Hungary, and other East European nations. They told stories of secret police, forced relocations, prison camps, executions, rationing and famine, stories of parents and children separated and sent to different camps, stories that brought tears to my eyes. When I asked a Russian survivor of the Gulag how many victims of communism there had been, he replied, "Everyone who lived in the twentieth century was a victim of communism." Unfortunately, I was not able to raise the funds to finish the documentary.

After the conference ended, I flew to Taipei, where I was handsomely treated because of Dr. Judd's high reputation. I had tea with President Yen Chia-kan, the first ROC president I would meet. In the following years, I had audiences with Chiang Ching-kuo, the son of Chiang Kai-shek, and Lee Teng-hui, the first Taiwan-born ROC president. Yen sought assurances that the United States would continue to support the ROC's membership in the United Nations. I did not want to be the bearer of bad news to my host, so I was as optimistic as possible. I did not reveal President Nixon's unwillingness to give Dr. Judd an appointment.

The most dramatic part of my stay was the flight to the island of Quemoy, lying about a thousand yards from mainland China. Several of us World Anti-Communist League conferees boarded a DC-3 that headed west toward the mainland. Before long, I saw that the waves were getting closer and closer—soon we were almost touching them. An escort officer explained we were reducing altitude to fly under the communist radar. We landed (without any shots being fired) and were taken to a dugout facing the mainland. Through powerful binoculars, we could see a military installation and guards moving back and forth. They were probably looking at us. There had been no trouble (beside an occasional shell) since the Quemoy/Matsu crisis a decade before, when the Chinese communists had threatened to take what they considered to be theirs. President Eisenhower had ordered a couple of aircraft carriers into the Taiwan Strait, and the communists halted their threats. Nations had a way of behaving when Ike stopped smiling and grew serious.

There was a superb demonstration of manual arms by soldiers who looked fit enough to take any hill, followed by a long lunch, really a feast, of a dozen courses punctuated by many a "*Gambai!*" Before nightfall we were back in the Grand Hotel overlooking Taipei, where I reflected that I did not feel like a stranger in a strange land. Dr. Judd had taught me so much about China that I felt at home. Was it a coincidence that the Chinese version of my name is "*li awah*," which can be translated as "he who loves China"?

With President Chiang Ching-kuo of the Republic of China

22

SQUARE POWER

My most unforgettable client was Edward Scannell Butler of New Orleans and Los Angeles, debater of Lee Harvey Oswald ninety-three days before Oswald assassinated John Kennedy, author of *Revolution Is My Profession*, creator of the Square Movement, executive director of the anti-Castro Information Council of the Americas, adviser to Schick president Patrick J. Frawley and other corporate executives, drafter of the Declaration of Revolution that emerged from a Square Power Conference, and anticommunist extraordinaire.

Ed was convinced that "America was in the midst of a world revolutionary war" and the only way to victory for America and freedom and defeat for the communists and the enemies of freedom was through what he called "conflict management." Conflict management was a third way between a strategy of peace through negotiation and accommodation and a strategy of victory through military might and retaliation. It would be implemented by conflict managers like Ed who would operate outside the walls of government and within the private sector. Ed urged Americans to remember and recover their revolutionary past and to engage what he called "Tyrannists," especially Marxist-Leninists, on every front.

Revolution Is My Profession is a handbook, not a philosophical treatise, with practical examples of how to go about putting the enemy, communist or otherwise, on the defensive. It emphasizes the importance of graphics and language to win the revolution—such as a "thumbs up" borrowed from World War II heroes to counter the V sign of the peaceniks. Ed insisted that we cannot depend on governments, even liberal democratic governments like America's, because they operate so slowly and always within the law, while the communists (and terrorists) move across national borders and without regard for the law. "Only private professionals," Ed wrote, "can interrupt the vicious cycle" of the anti–South Vietnam, anti-America, anti–U.S. government campaign conducted by the Marxist-Leninists.

I never accepted Ed's thesis that *only* people in the private sector can carry the day against totalitarian forces on the other side. True, our bureaucracy, like all bureaucracies, is snail-like. But we know from Poland's Lech Wałęsa and other freedom fighters behind the Iron Curtain that the Voice of America and other Western broadcast services like the BBC played a vital part in encouraging Solidarity and bringing about the collapse of communism in Eastern and Central Europe in 1989. People in the East heard and saw what life was like in the West and decided they wanted no more lies, no more breadlines, no more secret police, no more denial of basic human rights and liberties.

I do believe there is an important role for private conflict managers, sometimes working with and sometimes working without the cooperation of government. I myself was a "conflict manager" in the 1980s, working with the British journalist Brian Crozier, one of the most creative anticommunists I ever met, and capable of operating effectively without CIA money, something Brian was frequently and inaccurately accused of taking. Anti-anticommunists probably said the same thing about me, but I was never on the CIA payroll.

Ed Butler was in his midthirties when I met him, about six feet tall and athletic-looking (I learned later that he worked out regularly), with a soft New Orleans drawl and an inviting smile. He studied closely the attitudes of young people. I admired Ed for challenging the counterculture, and I can attest that he made a difference among college students in the late 1960s with his concept of Square Power. I organized well-attended student leader conferences at Haverford College outside Philadelphia and Lake Forest College near Chicago. At the time, Chicago was the home base of the far-left Students for a Democratic Society (SDS), and we picketed SDS headquarters, daring them to come out and debate us. No one responded to our chants or banging on the front door. Score one for the Squares.

Ed chose the word *square* to contrast with the anything-goes philosophy of the left. He created a square logo with the outer line ending in an arrow pointing up, distinct from the formless psychedelic image of the hippies. At the age of seven, our daughter Elizabeth attended the Square Power Conference at Haverford and ever after referred to Ed as the Thumbs-Up Man. A by-product of Haverford was the Declaration of Revolution, adopted by the students (after editing by Ed and me) on the front steps of Independence Hall. I wondered whether the Founders would be amused at our choice of words and venue. The declaration challenged young Americans to rise up and oppose all forms of tyranny in the same liberty-loving, revolutionary spirit as that of the authors of the Declaration of Independence.

Ed also hosted a weekly TV show, *The Square World of Ed Butler*, that featured film and TV stars as well as political guests. His very first guest was the Hollywood legend John Wayne, who talked about all those who had fought and died at Bunker Hill, Gettysburg, the Alamo, the Argonne, Pork Chop Hill, and Da Nang that we might live in peace and prosperity.

The Square World and everything else Ed did depended financially on Pat Frawley, the Schick president and CEO. Frawley was impressed by Ed's high energy and fertile imagination but more impressed by his argument that if the heavily bearded antiwar hippies prevailed among America's youth, Schick would be out of business. For the sake of the country and his company, Ed argued, Pat should get behind the Square Movement and its clean-cut, smooth-faced members. Pat got out his checkbook and told Ed to get going and right away.

Pat Frawley was in his fifties when I met him, a nonstop talker, a recovering alcoholic and antismoking zealot who liked to test his guests in a unique way: he would take you outside to a set of monkey bars in the rear of his house, which was as big as a castle and had been previously owned by Bing Crosby. He would quickly swing from bar to bar and then invite you to do the same. I was able to make the third bar before my quivering arms gave out and I dropped to the ground. Pat did not hide his disappointment, but he did not object when Ed hired me, maybe because I was half Irish and did not smoke, although I liked a cocktail or two after five. The same day I flunked my physical, I spent about nine hours, one-on-one, with Patrick J. Frawley, at the end of which I was as exhausted as though I had hiked twenty miles with a large backpack. Pat was not a linear thinker or talker, jumping from thought to thought and word to word, leaving you to fill in the spaces.

I was persuaded by one of his pet theories—that alcoholism was connected to climate. He pointed out that the nations with the highest percentage of alcoholics were in the North, like Ireland, while the nations with the lowest percentage were in the South, like Italy. Pat would fix you with his blue eyes and begin expounding on the dangers of smoking, drinking, and not exercising and you could not look away. I marveled at Ed's ability to spend dozens of hours with Frawley and not go crazy, which I think Pat was, a little. If I had drunk as much as he had in his first forty years, I would probably have been crazy or dead.

If Ed Butler had only engaged in his debate with Lee Harvey Oswald in New Orleans, which led to Oswald's being identified as a man of the left just hours after President Kennedy's assassination, he would still warrant attention. But like many graduates of our Square Power Conferences— Republican congressman Dana Rohrabacher of California, for one—he made a difference. Ed died in 2005 at age seventy-three in New Orleans, managing a radio station and pointing out, in his daily editorials, the parallels between the Marxist-Leninists of old and the Islamic extremists of the present.

GOING HOLLYWOOD

Because of Ed, I was working in Brentwood, right next to Hollywood, and I guess it was inevitable I would come down with Hollywood fever. I began traveling back and forth between D.C. and L.A., seeking to link conservative film stars with my conservative clients. I was a successful matchmaker but paid a high price for one.

In the spring of 1970, I spent a magical day with film and TV star Loretta Young. My appointment at her home in Bel Air was in the late afternoon, around 4 P.M. A maid opened the door and led me into a large foyer. To my right was a large staircase curving down from the second floor. I did not have to wait long. Amazingly youthful and beautiful at fifty-seven, Loretta came down the stairs, almost floating. As she reached the bottom she spun around as she always did on her TV show, her dress swirling around her. "Hello, Lee," she said, her voice warm and vibrant. "How nice of you to come all this way." She looked into my eyes and smiled.

We sat in her living room drinking tea, and I explained the important work of Americans United for Life, a new pro-life legal aid organization headquartered in Chicago. I talked about the rise in abortions and the likelihood that a Supreme Court decision would come in the near future (the *Roe v. Wade* decision was three years away), and I suggested that her support of Americans United for Life, still a young organization, would significantly enhance its influence.

We taxied to the Beverly Wilshire Hotel for dinner at Hernando's Hideaway. The maître d' gave us a quiet table in the corner. Loretta and I talked about her films and her Academy Award for *The Farmer's Daughter* and the three Emmys for her dramatic TV roles. We had martinis and wine and several flambé dishes. We talked about Richard Nixon and Ronald Reagan, for whom she had voted for governor, and about other Hollywood Republicans like Fred Astaire and Bing Crosby, and about a convent she supported, and about "God and His children," which we all were.

I had the good sense, despite the martinis and the wine, not to mention Clark Gable, with whom she had had an affair in the mid-1930s, or the resulting child she later adopted. Somewhere along the way, without any preamble, she said she would be happy to serve as honorary chair of Americans United for Life. We were the last to leave Hernando's.

In the late spring of 1971, I met with Efrem Zimbalist Jr., the actor who at the July 1963 rally in Washington, D.C., had delivered some well-received remarks I had drafted. Because Zimbalist was in the middle of production on his popular TV show, *The FBI*, he asked me to meet him on the set. What struck me was how small the set was—a roofless wooden structure of small rooms in which Zimbalist and the other actors moved back and forth. There were occasional gunshots but nothing like the fusillades (or the blood) that fill today's detective programs.

During a break in filming, Zimbalist came over to where I was sitting. I told him about the Friends of the FBI, the nonprofit group I had recently formed along with Pat Gorman and the liberal Chicago lawyer Luis Kutner. The FBI in general and J. Edgar Hoover in particular were undergoing sharp criticism at the time. In view of Hoover's unparalleled anticommunist credentials—I much admired his *Masters of Deceit: The Story of Communism in America and How to Fight It*—I thought he ought to be honored and not pilloried for his service. A bipartisan group of political and other leaders had agreed to serve as advisers, including Senators Robert Byrd of West Virginia, a Democrat, and Strom Thurmond of South Carolina, a Republican.

I explained to Zimbalist that we intended to counter the negative publicity and stress the remarkable record of the FBI and its longtime director with a book, a national conference, and a newsletter, among other things. I did not have to do a lot of selling. Picked personally by Hoover to play the lead in the series, Zimbalist was aware of the anti-

Hoover, anti-FBI barrage. I said that his endorsement and name on a fundraising letter would help us raise the needed funds to carry out our program. Zimbalist agreed to serve as honorary chairman and gave me two samples of his signature. An assistant director came over and said, "We're ready for the next scene." Efrem and I shook hands, and I promised to stay in touch. Our meeting did not last thirty minutes.

A Friends of the FBI letter, with Zimbalist's signature, elicited an extraordinary response, raising an initial $380,000 from fewer than ten thousand donors, as I recall, for an unbelievable $38 per response. Everything worked together—the name of the organization, Zimbalist's name, the prolonged anti-FBI rhetoric in the press, the deep respect conservatives have for the FBI. I immediately began making plans for the book and the conference. I should have remembered that pride goeth before a fall.

I bragged about our success everywhere, including at a party attended by Ben Bradlee, the executive editor of the *Washington Post* and the second most powerful man in Washington. I taunted Bradlee, whom I barely knew, describing how we intended to counter the *Post*'s anti-FBI propaganda and there was "nothing" he could do about it. Anne wasn't with me or she would have warned me to keep my big mouth shut. Bradlee said little but lost no time showing me what he could do: he assigned ace correspondent Nick Kotz, a Pulitzer Prize–winning reporter, to do an exposé of Friends of the FBI.

I was still riding high from the results of the mailing when Kotz visited our office. I blithely said we had nothing to hide and gave him access to all our files and correspondence. My only caveat: he could not take any files out of our office—he had to read them there and then. I recall that he sat in our tiny foyer for hours going through a foot-high stack of folders. He found at last what he was looking for—a letter from me to Kutner and Gorman, proposing that we form Friends of the FBI and calling it "a natural." Voilà: Conspiracy proven.

On May 21, 1972, in its Sunday edition, the *Washington Post* carried a front-page article by Nick Kotz headlined "The Troubled 'Friends of the FBI.'" It detailed the problems I had been trying to resolve, including escalating fees from Kutner, whose tax-exempt organization we were using until Friends of the FBI received its own tax ruling; invoices from Gorman for everything from printing and postage to list rentals and caging returns; letters from the IRS and the Postal Service about our tax status; questions from Zimbalist about our use of the funds raised; and finally a request, through his lawyers, to stop using his name. As liberal members of Kutner's board demanded to know why they were defending the FBI and Gorman asked for an increase in his monthly fee, I decided it was time to reorganize.

An agreement was reached under which Gorman received $138,000, Kutner $47,000, and I $7,500. The *Post* article led one self-righteous social conservative to accuse me of "enriching" myself at the expense of the FBI and the just-deceased J. Edgar Hoover, who had died on May 2, 1972. When I confronted my erstwhile friend and explained how I had barely covered my expenses, he admitted he had not read the entire story, only the lead paragraph, which referred to a partnership that had "produced a Niagara of dollars." Only a trickle found its way to me.

A word of explanation about the $138,000 payment to Gorman, about 37 percent of the money received. Thirty-seven percent sounds like a lot, but the initial, or "prospect," mailings of a new organization are fortunate to break even—most lose money. A net of $245,000 from the first Friends of the FBI mailing was unprecedented and provided adequate funds for the organization's planned activities. Given that Gorman had guaranteed all the mailing costs, his expenses and fees were reasonable.

Kutner's demands were pure greed. They reminded me of Humphrey Bogart in *The Treasure of the Sierra Madre*, who went crazy with gold fever. Kutner kept demanding ever higher fees for services that amounted to no more than the loan of his tax-exempt group.

Determined to keep faith with our donors, I turned Friends of the FBI over to my friend and colleague J. A. (Jay) Parker, the respected black conservative who with the help of Frank Carrington and Americans for Effective Law Enforcement published an excellent study of the FBI's impressive record. It also sponsored a Washington conference, "Law Enforcement and the Media," featuring a keynote address by Senator Robert Byrd, and conducted a national poll to determine young people's attitudes about the Bureau. The results revealed a highly negative opinion of the FBI along with a profound ignorance of the Bureau's very real accomplishments over the years.

I learned several lessons from Friends of the FBI:

1. Never provoke a media baron like Ben Bradlee.
2. Never rely on a liberal in a crisis—Kutner folded like a cheap chair when his liberal colleagues pressured him to abandon Friends of the FBI.
3. Keep up-to-date, accurate records of all financial transactions, especially donations. We were not prepared to process

thousands of gifts in a timely fashion; we fell behind and never caught up.

4. Never give into hubris—it will chew you up and spit you out.

BLACK AND CONSERVATIVE

The person who saved Friends of the FBI—and our objective of disseminating the truth about the Bureau—was Jay Parker, whom I had met in the early days of YAF. Born in South Philadelphia, in one of the city's most depressed areas, Jay never went to college but became the first black conservative to head his own public affairs firm in Washington, D.C., serving U.S. and foreign clients like the government of South Africa. For a decade, Jay and I shared offices and staff at 1735 DeSales Street across from the Mayflower Hotel. We formed the Edpar Company, the first integrated public affairs firm for conservatives. Always impeccable in a gray or dark blue striped suit and vest and matching fedora, Jay became a respected leader of Washington's nonprofit world, the first African American president of the Washington Kiwanis Club, the most prestigious service organization in the nation's capital, and a board member of the Salvation Army, Goodwill, and the Columbia Lighthouse for the Blind.

Over the years, he developed a national network of black conservative writers and thinkers that included the author Thomas Sowell of the Hoover Institution and the economist Walter Williams at George Mason University. In 1979 he founded the Lincoln Institute (a name Anne suggested) and began publishing the *Lincoln Review*, a quarterly that examined issues and ideas from the perspective of conservative black Americans. Allan Brownfeld did most of the editing. A good friend and protégé of Jay's was Supreme Court justice Clarence Thomas.

"My name is Clarence Thomas," the deep voice said. "I like what you have to say!" It was Christmas Eve morning, 1979, and Jay was sorting through his mail when the phone rang. For the next forty minutes, Jay mostly listened as Thomas, a legislative assistant to Senator John Danforth, Missouri Republican, talked about politics, black-white relations, and how much he enjoyed reading the *Lincoln Review*'s positions on free enterprise, limited government, and traditional moral values. "I thought I was the only one out there," Thomas said several times. It was the beginning of an enduring friendship between the young black lawyer on Capitol Hill and the founding father of the contemporary black conservative movement in America.

Following Ronald Reagan's 1980 presidential victory, transition coordinator Ed Meese asked Jay to head the team looking at the Equal Employment Opportunity Commission (EEOC). Jay invited Thomas to join the team. The hardworking Thomas wound up cowriting the EEOC report, which led first to a post in the civil rights division of the Department of Education, next chairman of the EEOC, and then judge on the U.S. Court of Appeals for the District of Columbia.

His 1991 nomination to the U.S. Supreme Court became a cause célèbre when Anita Hill, a former colleague at the Education Department and the EEOC, accused Thomas of "sexual harassment" (actually, using problematic "sexual" language). Other female witnesses, black and white, who had worked with Thomas told the Senate Judiciary Committee they had never been harassed by their boss. Following a sharp Senate debate, Thomas won confirmation by a vote of 52–48, becoming at age forty-three the youngest member of the court. Since then Justice Thomas has become an influential and consistent conservative voice on the Supreme Court. And it all began with his reading a little conservative journal with a circulation of a few thousand.

Thomas once told a college audience how much he admired Thomas Sowell and Jay Parker for refusing to give in to "the cult mentality that hypnotizes" so many black Americans. "I can only hope," he said, that "I can have a fraction of their courage and strength." He insists that blacks, like any other group in America, should be free to think for themselves and not be obliged to follow racially prescribed lines. Jay Parker believed there were thousands of conservative black Americans who once thought, like Clarence Thomas, they were all alone but discovered in the *Lincoln Review* a place to share their ideas and dreams of a better, color-blind America.

AMERICANS FOR AGNEW

After the travails of Friends of the FBI, my experience with Americans for Agnew was almost uneventful. In late 1971, Washington was full of rumors that President Nixon was seriously considering dropping Vice President Spiro Agnew as his 1972 running mate and replacing him with John Connally, a liberal carpetbagger from Texas. Our goal was simple: to keep Vice President Agnew, a hero to conservatives for his alliterative assaults on the media and his sturdy defense of traditional institutions like the family, on the ticket. We believed that the best way to do that was to produce an impressive write-in vote for Agnew in the March New Hampshire primary. Nixon was always sensitive to political winds, and a strong Agnew showing in New Hampshire, I was sure, would help convince the president to keep his VP on the ticket.

In the fall of 1971, I turned to Hollywood again. I wrote John Wayne asking him to serve as honorary chairman of Americans for Agnew and sign a fundraising letter, the proceeds to be used for a New Hampshire write-in campaign. After not hearing anything from Wayne for several weeks, I was ready to abandon the project. Then I received in the mail the fundraising letter with a scrawled "Okay" alongside "Duke's" signature.

With Pat Gorman again underwriting the production costs and postage, we began mailing in November. The early returns were modest, nothing like the phenomenal response to Friends of the FBI, but they were good enough to keep mailing. Because we were a political action group, we did not seek or claim tax-exempt status. We created a write-in ballot and mailed it to as many Republican households in New Hampshire as we could.

On March 4, 1972, Spiro Agnew received 45,524 write-in votes for vice president, a record high for write-in votes for the office. The rumors that Nixon might drop Agnew died almost overnight. The Nixon-Agnew ticket won a historic landslide in November.

Given Agnew's subsequent fall and forced resignation, do I regret organizing Americans for Agnew? No. At the time, it was the right thing to do for the advancement of the conservative movement.

Ironically, in the middle of our write-in campaign, I was visited by a large, stone-faced gentleman from the vice president's office. Leaning forward in his chair, he warned me, in a menacing voice, that I had better not do anything to "hurt" his "guy" or I would regret it. I was speechless. I was working to save the vice president from being dumped from the ticket, and some overly protective political operative was threatening me. I do not believe the vice president or his chief of staff initiated or approved the visit or the threat. I never heard again from the visitor. With our mission accomplished, I closed down Americans for Agnew.

ENTER THE NEW RIGHT

I admit that I was starstruck by meeting and working with actors like Loretta Young, Efrem Zimbalist, and John Wayne. But I decided, with counseling from Anne, that show business was a dangerous distraction.

Washington, not Hollywood, was my kind of town. I resolved to stick to what I knew best—the making of public policy. My resolution resulted in my contributing to one of the most influential political movements of the 1970s and 1980s—the New Right.

Concerned about the uncertain state of the conservative movement—following Representative John Ashbrook's poor showing against Nixon in the 1972 Republican primaries and George Wallace's strong show-ing—I sent Richard Viguerie a memorandum outlining a plan of action for conservatives. I argued that it was up to professionals like us "to recap-ture and revive the spirit which transformed conservatism into a national political force in 1963 and 1964." I proposed:

- A national conference of experts in all aspects of domestic and foreign policy that would produce "A Conservative Platform for America," to be presented to the platform committees at both the Republican and Democratic national conventions.
- Assistance to conservative candidates in selected U.S. Senate campaigns. I mentioned that I was a director of the Com-mittee for Responsible Youth Politics, organized by Morton Blackwell, and that we were providing youth directors to North Carolina Senate candidate Jesse Helms, Representa-tive James McClure of Idaho, and Senator Carl Curtis of Nebraska. (All were elected, and Helms would become one of the most effective constitutional conservatives in the Senate.) The Committee for Responsible Youth Politics would evolve into the Leadership Institute, which has trained thousands of young conservatives in every aspect of electoral politics.
- A national conservative/patriotic "Congress" on July 4, bring-ing together groups and organizations of "all hues and shades of conservative opinion." I had in mind as a model the suc-cessful July 4, 1963, rally for Barry Goldwater.
- A newsletter that would give the facts without editorial comment about the right, from the American Conserva-tive Union and *National Review* to Ronald Reagan and Fred Schwarz. "There never has been one, to my knowledge," I wrote, "and there should be." Later that year I would begin publishing a newsletter, the *Right Report*.
- A documentary film company that would turn out profes-sional, philosophically sound films about the conservative movement. I said I would be happy to participate and pointed

out that I had produced three documentaries in the past three years: *Tyranny*; *U.S.-China Policy: Danger at the Crossroads*; and *Proudly They Came*, a film about the 1970 July 4 celebration that featured a cavalcade of Hollywood stars and other personalities, including Bob Hope, Red Skelton, Kate Smith, Fred Waring, and Billy Graham. The key to success, I said, was distribution.

• A television station in Washington, D.C. I said that one was now available—the former WFAN-TV, Channel 14, "which went dark about two months ago." The license could be purchased for "amazingly little," I wrote, but it would take "several millions more to keep the station going until it began to make money."

Twenty years later, Paul Weyrich persuaded businessman Joseph Coors to underwrite National Empowerment Television (NET), which operated out of Paul's Free Congress offices on Capitol Hill. NET offered solid programming and attractive conservative personalities, but cable was in its infancy and not enough independent stations picked up NET. After spending more than $20 million, NET was forced to close down in 1997. It was a brilliant idea but before its time. CNN started in 1980 and Fox News Channel in 1995, the latter made possible by the backing of billionaire Rupert Murdoch and a viable cable system.

23

THE RABBI AND
THE PRESIDENT

Like everyone else in Washington, with the exception of Bob Woodward and Carl Bernstein, I did not anticipate in late 1972, following Richard Nixon's landslide reelection victory, that the nation would soon be immersed in a constitutional crisis that permanently changed American politics. The Watergate scandal and Nixon's forced resignation had the following impacts:

One, the American people's attitude toward government was altered from healthy skepticism to deep cynicism. Following Watergate and into the present, every poll has found that a majority of the public no longer trusts the government to tell the truth or to act in their best interests. The distrust, born out of Watergate, was reinforced by Lyndon Johnson's lies about the course of the Vietnam War; the early cover-up of Iran-Contra by Oliver North and other National Security Council aides; Bill Clinton's public denial of the Monica Lewinsky affair; and the repeated references to nonexistent weapons of mass destruction to justify the Iraq War. This cynicism has produced a corrosive anti-Washington attitude that prevents Republicans and Democrats from presenting bipartisan solutions to problems ranging from health care and Social Security to campaign finance and immigration. Pandering to public distrust, Republicans portray Washington and the federal government as the enemy of the people. Obedient to progressive ideology, Democrats offer Washington and the federal government as the best answer to our problems.

Two, in pursuit of greater circulation and ratings, the news media have dramatically increased their coverage of government scandal, inefficiency, and abuse, thereby strengthening the public's mistrust of government. At the same time, government as the locus of our ills is the main theme of countless TV dramas and feature films. It is ironic that although the media are generally thought to be liberal in their politics, their muckraking emphasis on a dysfunctional government strengthens the Republican argument against centralized authority and weakens the Democratic proposal for a greater role for Washington.

What did the Founding Fathers have on their minds when they assembled in Philadelphia in 1787? They came together because the Articles of Confederation had created near anarchy in the new republic, allowing the thirteen states to issue their own money, establish tariffs on products from other states, and conduct their own foreign policy with sovereign nations. Wise men like George Washington, James Madison, Benjamin Franklin, and Alexander Hamilton agreed that a new governing document based on the idea of ordered liberty was urgently needed. The result was a political miracle—the U.S. Constitution with its intricate checks and balances and carefully divided government. At root, it acknowledged that a federal government, carefully limited, was needed because men were not angels.

Wise presidents from Lincoln to Reagan have followed this philosophy. We must remember that while President Reagan said, in his first inaugural address, that "government is not the solution to our problems; government is the problem," he then said the following: "It is not my intention to do away with government. It is rather to make it work—work with us, not over us; to stand by our side, not ride on our back. Government can and must provide opportunity, not smother it; foster productivity, not stifle it."

This prescription for limited government is consistent with Adam Smith, F. A. Hayek, and the other classical liberals who helped to build the philosophical foundation on which the modern conservative movement rests. A modern conservative like Walter Judd, Bill Buckley, or Barry Goldwater accepts the need for limited constitutional government. Implicit in such a position is a respect for the highest office in the land, the presidency, if not necessarily for the particular occupant.

I was willing, therefore, in late 1973 to meet with Rabbi Baruch Korff, chairman of the Committee for Fairness to the Presidency, who said he had an urgent matter to discuss with me. We met in his suite in the Mayflower Hotel, which he was quick to explain was being rented to him at a bargain rate. He stressed that he was serving without salary as head of the committee. He seemed an ordinary sort of man until he began speaking, when he was transformed into an Old Testament prophet. He was mesmerizing as he argued that Nixon's enemies were out to destroy him and in the process would seriously weaken and damage the presidency. He wanted my help, he needed my help, he could not move ahead without my help. He knew of my organizing and particularly my fundraising abilities. Would I agree to raise the funds to run the newspaper ads, sponsor the rallies, publish the book that would save not Richard Nixon but the presidency? There were tears in his eyes and he reached out and held my hands.

I knew that you could not separate the office and the man. Whatever I did would help both. How much did I owe Richard Nixon? I remembered that Nixon had been the one congressman who believed Whittaker Chambers and put Alger Hiss in jail. I remembered Dad's stories about the 1960 campaign and the vicious media attacks against Nixon. I remembered my 1966 meetings with Nixon and his brilliant tour d'horizon of the world. And I reflected that whatever Nixon had done— the "smoking gun" would not be revealed for several months—many if not most Democrats wanted to bring down Nixon because he had won reelection in a landslide and had humiliated them. If they couldn't defeat him in the voting booth, they would defeat him through congressional hearings and impeachment. Yes, there had been the trip to China and the wage and price controls and all those regulatory agencies. But in the end Nixon and the conservative movement were tied together because of Alger Hiss, whose conviction for perjury (and in effect espionage) was one of our greatest and most timely victories. How could I say no?

Rabbi Korff broke into a huge smile when I said I would help and without a fee, my contribution to the cause. As I recall, I raised close to $100,000 for the Committee for Fairness to the Presidency over the next few months. True to his word, Rabbi Korff used the money to place ads, hold a rally that drew well over a thousand people, and publish a book, *The Personal Nixon: Staying on the Summit.*

My only compensation came in April 1974, when Korff arranged for me to meet the president in the White House. When the rabbi introduced me, Nixon quickly responded, "Of course I know Lee—I practically raised him." I was shocked at Nixon's appearance—he was puffy-faced and his hair was streaked with gray.

I know that Korff kept urging Nixon to keep fighting and that many Americans still supported him, but when Barry Goldwater visited him in the Oval Office in early August and said it was time for him to go, Nixon went.

How strange, I reflected at the time, that I had been involved with both Nixon and Agnew, who had won reelection by a historic margin but who had then left office in disgrace. Their fate validated Lord Acton's dictum that power tends to corrupt. Ever the conscience of the conservative movement, Bill Buckley urged conservatives not to make the mistake of defending Agnew as liberals had defended Alger Hiss in the 1950s. They should separate the "valid ideas" Agnew had espoused from the misconduct of the man. Buckley did not try to make the same argument about Nixon, most of whose presidential actions were counter to conservatism.

With President Richard Nixon and Rabbi Baruch Korff in the White House, 1974

24

THE NEW RIGHT

The two men most responsible for the birth of the New Right were Jerry Ford and Nelson Rockefeller.

On the morning of August 20, 1974, Richard Viguerie turned on his television set to learn that newly sworn-in President Ford had made his decision regarding his vice president. There had been intense speculation about his choice. A majority of conservatives favored the man that many of us called Mr. Conservative, Barry Goldwater, while others preferred Ronald Reagan, in his last year as governor of California. I would have been happy with either man. Instead, Ford picked the man he knew was anathema to us. When he was asked later that year to list the achievements of his first hundred days as president, Ford replied, "Number one, nominating Nelson Rockefeller."

Viguerie was dumbfounded. Rockefeller? The liberal whose venomous misrepresentations of Goldwater during the 1964 Republican primaries had been used by Democrats to bury the Republican candidate in the general election? The liberal who had forced Nixon to sign the infamous Fifth Avenue Compact in 1960, placing a liberal label on the GOP platform that helped defeat Nixon in the fall? The high-flying, wild-spending leader of the eastern liberal establishment? Richard could not have been more upset if Ford had selected Teddy Kennedy.

Something had to be done. The following night, Richard invited fourteen conservative friends to dinner to discuss how to stop Rockefeller from becoming vice president. The group included political activists, Capitol Hill aides, journalists, and a couple of lawyers—but no elected officials. They came up with good ideas but quickly realized they did not have the necessary leadership on or off the Hill to block Rockefeller. Congressional Republicans, although far from enthusiastic about the New York liberal, had no stomach for a hard fight so soon after Nixon's resignation as president. Many were still in shock, wondering whether their party had a future.

"Most Republicans chose to put party above principle," Richard later said to me. Not so these tough-minded younger conservatives who were tired of compromise, tired of accommodation, tired of losing. They began to coalesce. Some shared Richard's outrage at the Rockefeller nomination. Others were frustrated by their experience with the Nixon administration, which talked right in the 1968 election but governed left when in office. Some were just impatient and spoiling for a fight, unwilling to wait for older conservatives to start leading.

These ambitious, aggressive young conservatives had four things in common: proficiency in practical politics, mass media, and direct mail; a willingness to work together; a commitment to put political philosophy before political party; and a conviction that they could win elections and lead America. They had the same self-confidence as the founders of YAF, who did not know what could not be done, like filling Madison Square Garden and nominating Barry Goldwater for president.

While never a member of the inner circle of the New Right, I was its chronicler as editor of *Conservative Digest* and collaborator with Richard Viguerie on his first and most influential book, *The New Right: We're Ready to Lead*.

Political analyst Kevin Phillips first used the term "New Right" when discussing "social conservatives," and he was the first to use it to describe the collective efforts of Richard Viguerie, Paul Weyrich, Howard (Howie) Phillips, and John (Terry) Dolan, the four founders of the New Right. They wanted, Kevin Phillips wrote, "to build a new coalition reaching across to what elite conservatives still consider 'the wrong side of the tracks.'" They were a group of antiestablishment, middle-class political rebels more interested in issues like "abortion, gun control, housing, ERA, quotas, bureaucracy and the grassroots tax revolt than in capital gains taxation or natural gas deregulation."

They were a diverse and yet harmonious quartet, middle-class yet blue around the collar. They had all attended college, but they were political activists, not intellectuals. They believed in the power of ideas but were committed to putting ideas into action. They were true believers, firmly conservative and fiercely anticommunist. They saw as their enemy the four bigs of modern America—Big Government, Big Business, Big Labor, and Big Media.

Each of the four contributed different talents—Richard, fundraising; Paul, long-range strategy; Howie, grassroots organizing; Terry, media skills. All of them were media-savvy. They knew how important the front page and the evening newscast were to modern politics. They learned how to wind up in the headlines by attacking the establishment, in and out of the Republican Party. They were young men in a hurry to change history.

Viguerie declared in *Conservative Digest*, of which I was the founding editor, that conservatives would have to look to someone other than Barry Goldwater, the man who had ignited the conservative counterrevolution in 1964, to lead "the swelling conservative sentiment in America." While conceding that Goldwater had voted right on issues ranging from the Anti-Ballistic Missile Treaty to prayer in schools, Richard charged that Goldwater too often placed party before principle, as with his broad hints that he favored Ford rather than Reagan for the GOP's 1976 presidential nomination. Ever the party loyalist, Goldwater described Reagan's bid as "divisive." Equally telling for Viguerie and other New Rightists, Goldwater refused to consider, let alone join, their attempts to forge a coalition between economic and social conservatives.

Conceding that Goldwater had done great things for the conservative movement in the past, Viguerie wrote that "we must look for someone else to lead the new majority of the 1970s and 1980s."

Actually I wrote those words and much of the article, which was cosigned by Richard as publisher and me as editor. Why did I coauthor it? Ego. I knew the article would generate serious public and media attention, and I wanted to bask in it.

I rationalized the article's critical tone by noting that Goldwater had said he didn't want those 27 million who had voted for him in 1964 "to think I'm trying to lead them.... I never for any moment assumed I had a position of leadership over anybody." I took him at his word. In drafting the article, I stuck to the facts about Goldwater's frequent absences from the Senate and softened Richard's language. I did not consider how Goldwater might react to our criticism, especially mine, one of the young conservatives whose pleas had persuaded him to run reluctantly for the presidency.

A few days after the article appeared, the senator was asked on national television how he felt about it. He said that the most disappointing thing was that someone who he thought was a friend (an obvious reference to me, although he did not mention my name) had written something so unfair and misleading. It was said more in sorrow than in anger, which made his remarks all the more painful. I had hurt the man who had changed my life, leaving me hurt as well.

The article created a breach between the senator and me that lasted until the early 1990s, when I approached him about writing his biography. Without saying a word about the *Conservative Digest* article, Goldwater gave his permission and told his family, friends, and former colleagues to cooperate fully with me. It is a measure of the man that he never asked to see my manuscript before it was published. Barry Goldwater was a mensch through and through.

FUNDING FATHER

Richard Viguerie has rightly been called the Godfather of the New Right because he brought and kept together the diverse talents and personalities of its principals, much as Bill Buckley did in the early years of *National Review*. But Richard's contribution to modern American conservatism involves far more than his leadership of the New Right. Since 1962, he has been the fundraiser for almost every major conservative political figure and organization; his first client was YAF. He is passionate about doing all he can to preserve and protect America and Western civilization against all enemies foreign and domestic, particularly communism. He agrees with Fred Schwarz that "you can trust the communists—to be communists." He has raised billions of dollars for his clients, more than any other political fundraiser in America.

Not every client has been a winner. Viguerie did the fundraising for Congressman John Ashbrook of Ohio when he challenged President Nixon in 1972 for the Republican presidential nomination. Richard estimates that he lost $250,000 but learned an important lesson: it is not enough to run a candidate of high principle in a national campaign. You have to surround him with an experienced political organization, a creative communications team, and sufficient money for a national effort, all things Ashbrook lacked.

Viguerie often refers to himself as "003," meaning that he has been active in the conservative movement at the national level longer than all but two people—the late Phyllis Schlafly, "001," and me, "002." I am flattered, but with the honor comes the realization that I have been active in the anticommunist conservative movement since 1958, almost six decades. I decline to accept the title of 001 now that Phyllis is gone.

Richard is one of the most generous people I have ever known, host of July 4 celebrations and Election Night parties, movement breakfasts and luncheons, formal dinners at his Great Falls home, casual shindigs at his Rappahannock farm. One Fourth of July, he sat suspended above a large barrel of water while conservatives tried to hit the target and dump him. When they did, he came up soaked and smiling. There is something about Richard that reminds you of a favorite uncle who always has a funny story to tell and something in his pocket for the children.

The chief strategist of the New Right was Paul Weyrich, a working-class German Catholic whose father tended the boilers of a Racine, Wisconsin, Catholic hospital for fifty years. A former newspaperman and radio-TV journalist in Milwaukee, Paul came to Washington in 1967 as press secretary to Senator Gordon Allott, Colorado Republican. He quickly gained a reputation as a stern "don't waste my time" organizer, who cut off extraneous discussion in any meeting he chaired. If someone brought up a problem, he wanted to know if the person had a solution. From his first day in Washington, he emphasized the importance of social issues; he played a central role in the formation of the Moral Majority in the late 1970s.

Like the other New Right founders, Weyrich was galvanized by the opposition. During Nixon's first term, he attended a meeting of key liberals planning the enactment of a public housing bill. Present were a White House official, a Washington newspaper columnist, an analyst from the Brookings Institution, representatives of several black lobbying groups, and aides to a dozen senators.

Everyone was given an assignment. The Senate aides promised that their bosses would make supporting statements and would contact other senators. The White House official said he would keep everyone informed of the administration's strategy. The columnist said he would write a favorable column about the legislation. The Brookings analyst promised to publish a study in time to affect the debate. The black lobbyists agreed to hold public demonstrations for the legislation at the most appropriate time.

"I saw how it could be done with careful planning and determination," Weyrich recalled to me. "I decided to try it myself." With funding from Joseph Coors and other conservative businessmen and direct-mail funds from Viguerie, Weyrich founded several of conservatism's core institutions, including the Heritage Foundation; the Committee for a

Free Congress (later the Free Congress Foundation); the Senate Steering Committee (composed of the Senate's most conservative members); the Moral Majority; the American Legislative Exchange Council (ALEC), which works with state legislators; and National Empowerment Television (NET), later America's Voice.

The New Right, Weyrich explained, was headed by radicals determined to transform the existing political structure commanded by liberals. "We are the forces of change. If people are sick and tired of things in this country, they had best look to conservative leadership for that change." The same radical spirit motivated fed-up grassroots citizens to form the Tea Party in 2009 and inspires Tea Party members of Congress and governors today.

BORROWING FROM LIBERALS

New Right leaders readily conceded that they imitated liberals. The Committee for the Survival of a Free Congress was started to rival the National Committee for an Effective Congress. The Republican Study Committee in the House of Representatives was launched to counter the Democratic Study Group. The Senate Steering Committee vied with the Wednesday Club, a group of liberal Republicans. The Conservative Caucus rivaled the lobbying of the leftist Common Cause. The Heritage Foundation challenged the Brookings Institution. "If your enemy has weapons systems working and is killing you with them," Weyrich told me, "you better have weapons systems of your own."

Paul was referring to "weapons" like the innovative National Conservative Political Action Committee (NCPAC), founded in 1975, which spent more than $1 million in cash and in-kind contributions in political races in its first five years, an impressive sum in those days. Under its aggressive young chairman, Terry Dolan, NCPAC specialized in primaries, believing that "a well-placed dollar" had more impact in a primary campaign, which is usually underfinanced and poorly organized. An emphasis on primaries was a major reason for the Tea Party's remarkable success some thirty-five years later. NCPAC also relied on research and polling.

NCPAC pioneered the independent expenditure campaign, which allows a PAC to spend as much as it wants for, or against, a candidate as long as there is no direct contact or coordination between the PAC and the candidate and his organization. In 1978, NCPAC ran independent expenditure ads in Iowa, Colorado, and Kentucky attacking Demo-cratic senators Dick Clark, Floyd Haskell, and Walter Huddleston for supporting the Panama Canal Treaties, which transferred the canal to Panama. Clark and Haskell were defeated. In 1980, NCPAC sponsored independent advertising campaigns costing about $700,000 against six of the most liberal Democrats in the Senate: George McGovern of South Dakota, Frank Church of Idaho, John Culver of Iowa, Birch Bayh of Indiana, Thomas Eagleton of Missouri, and Alan Cranston of Califor-nia. Four went down to defeat, only Eagleton and Cranston surviving.

The ads were not subtle. One anti-Church commercial showed an empty missile silo and stated that because they were empty "they won't be of much help in defense of your family or mine. You see, Senator Church has almost always opposed a strong national defense." Accused of being too negative and careless with facts, Terry responded that he was not after "respectability"; the only thing he cared about, he said, was whether "we're effective." "Effective" meant defeating liberals. I was reminded of Terry's "take no prisoners" philosophy when Lee Atwater was criticized for his tactics in George H. W. Bush's 1988 presidential campaign, espe-cially the controversial Willie Horton ad.

While Paul Weyrich was organizing conservatives in Washing-ton, Howard Phillips was organizing conservatives at the grassroots. A founder of YAF at age nineteen, Howard (or Howie, as we knew him then) started the Conservative Caucus with a tiny staff and a list of 11,200 names provided by Viguerie. He persuaded antitax New Hampshire governor Meldrim Thomson to become his national chairman. Howie's organization grew faster than any other political group of the time. By 1980, the Conservative Caucus had 300,000 contributors, chairmen in half of the 435 congressional districts, and an annual budget of almost $3 million. Much of the organizing was personally done by Howard, who seemed to have an endless supply of energy and dark pin-striped suits. "We have three basic jobs," he explained to me, "to recruit and train local leaders, to lobby at the grassroots level, and to help set the agenda for national debate." Four decades later, Heritage Action is doing the same things with its grassroots leaders called "Sentinels."

IRON FIST

Born out of Watergate, the New Right channeled its disillusionment with Nixon and the Republican Party into a movement independent of the GOP. Most traditional conservatives like Bill Buckley (and myself) preferred to stick with the devil we knew, the Grand Old Party. In place of "blind Republican partisanship" (Howard Phillips's words), the New Right sought to build a movement of all strains of conservatism. As Howard put it, "I think both the New Right—the iron fist—and the Old Right—the velvet glove—are necessary." In his later years, however, Howard rejected the Republican Party, which he considered to be a traitor to conservative principles; he berated President Reagan, for example, for sitting down with Soviet leader Mikhail Gorbachev.

In its early years, the New Right was more pragmatic, believing as I did that it was possible to fuse principle and effectiveness. Long-time Reagan aide Lyn Nofziger praised the New Right's emphasis on winning, and grassroots conservatives responded enthusiastically to its can-do approach. In mid-1975, after a decade of politicking, the more traditional American Conservative Union had forty thousand members. The Conservative Caucus, in its first eight months, had almost the same number.

Inevitably, friction developed between old and new conservatives as they competed for members and money. *Human Events* editor Tom Winter, an American Conservative Union director from the beginning, publicly parted with Richard Viguerie about the potential size of the conservative universe. "Richard feels the more groups the better," Winter said. "I disagree. I think that what happens is you get smaller pieces of perhaps a slightly expanding pie."

The continuing expansion and influence of conservatism over the past fifty years suggests that Viguerie, not Winter, had the better strategy to build a national movement. But growth brings problems, such as how to achieve and sustain a consensus among different factions. True believers can get carried away. Infuriated by President Ford's selection of Nelson Rockefeller, for example, New Right leaders began considering other political playing fields, even a third party.

"I want to strengthen the Right wherever I can," Richard explained to me. Because he considered George Wallace a man of the right, despite his racist policies, he helped him retire his 1972 presidential debt, raising about $7 million for the governor from 1973 to 1976. He suggested that Wallace was "the first national candidate since Goldwater" that conservatives could get excited about. But Richard was roundly, and properly, criticized by many conservatives for helping a prominent Democrat and arch-segregationist. The criticism deepened Richard's disaffection with the establishment.

After Nixon resigned as president in August 1974, Richard stepped up his populist, antiestablishment rhetoric. He argued that in the minds of most Americans, "Republican" meant depression, recession, Wall Street, and Watergate. "It's easier to sell an Edsel or Typhoid Mary," he declared. He predicted that "in ten years, there won't be a dozen people in the country calling themselves Republicans." I pointed out to Richard that experts had said the same thing about Republicans after FDR's landslide victories in 1932 and 1936. But he was on fire with the idea of starting a third party.

He found an intellectual ally in William Rusher and his new book, *The Making of a New Majority Party*. Rusher called for a "new vehicle" that would include a winning coalition of existing forces—that is, economic and social conservatives. He was frustrated and mystified by the seeming unwillingness of Republican leaders—with the exception of Ronald Reagan—to reach out to Democratic social conservatives.

The key to launching a new political coalition, Rusher wrote, was an "attractive and believable" presidential candidate in 1976. For him, the choice was obvious—Reagan. Richard agreed and promoted what he called a "dream ticket" of Reagan and Wallace. I and others argued that such a ticket would require a serious and almost impossible compromise by Old Right and New Right. Traditional conservatives would have to get in bed with a once and perhaps future segregationist and an enthusiastic advocate of government programs. New Right leaders like Howard Phillips were not sure that Reagan was conservative enough. They pointed out that as governor of California, Reagan had signed the most liberal pro-abortion state law in the country and had allowed California's annual budget to more than double from $4.6 billion to $10.2 billion.

Reagan later explained that he had signed the abortion law because he had been told that it would decrease abortions in California. In fact, the number of abortions soared, leading Reagan to rethink his position. As a presidential candidate and as president, Reagan was emphatically pro-life, always sending a message to the annual March for Life in Washington and authoring an antiabortion book titled *Abortion and the Conscience of a Nation*, the first book to be written and published by a sitting president.

New Rightists like Phillips wanted Reagan to be 100 percent philosophically pure. That was asking the impossible of a practicing politician. Reagan had deep-rooted principles, but as governor of California, he had gained a sense of when to give in to get something that would advance personal liberty and reduce government. A good example is his welfare reform, achieved through his tough bargaining with the Democratic General Assembly. Reagan's reform produced a net decrease of 301,000 persons on Aid to Families with Dependent Children (AFDC); estimated savings of $2 billion in state, federal, and local taxes; and increased grants to the truly needy of 43 percent. Reagan's prudential approach to welfare was adopted by many other states, including New York, and contributed significantly to the welfare reform that the U.S. Congress passed two decades later.

As president, Reagan remarked to aides that while he admired Senator Jesse Helms, he was not about to follow him "marching off the cliff with flags flying and the band playing" on every issue. He preferred to take 70 percent of what he wanted and come back later for the other 30 percent. That was the case with his Economic Recovery Tax Act of 1981, when he proposed a 30 percent across-the-board reduction in personal income taxes but settled for 25 percent (the final compromise figure was 23 percent).

In early 1975, Richard and other New Right leaders were encouraged by Reagan's speech at the Conservative Political Action Conference (CPAC) when he asked, "Is it a third party that we need, or is it a new and revitalized second party, raising a banner of no pale pastels but bold colors which make it unmistakably clear where we stand on all the issues troubling the people?" Notwithstanding Reagan's implicit rejection of a third party, diehards within the ACU appointed the Committee on Conservative Alternatives (COCA) to research the election laws of the fifty states, necessary organizational information for a new party.

In April, Reagan informed a deeply disappointed Rusher at a private dinner in his Pacific Palisades home that he was not inclined to go "the new party route." He believed that a coalition of economic and social conservatives could and should be forged under the aegis of the Republican Party. Rusher countered that such a populist coalition could not be formed under the Republican banner. Nor did he believe that Reagan could be nominated by a party that accepted Nelson Rockefeller as its vice president. Reagan was not persuaded, retaining his commitment to the Republican Party. It was a momentous decision that would lead to Reagan's challenging President Ford for the 1976 Republican nomination for president, and almost winning.

Shrugging off Reagan's rejection, Rusher, Viguerie, Phillips, and others formed the Committee for the New Majority and set about putting the American Independent Party (AIP) on as many state ballots as possible. They hoped to get Reagan, assuming he would fail to win the

Republican nomination, to carry the AIP banner. The obstacles were for-
midable. They had to deal with all the different state requirements. They
had to raise money for a party that had no history and no candidate. And
they found themselves allied with people and groups whose backgrounds
and motives differed widely from theirs.

The resulting coalition was part New Right Republican, part southern Democrat, and part kook. My initial skepticism about the project
turned into open alarm. I didn't want good friends to be badly hurt by
associating with racial and religious extremists. The *Twilight Zone* tone
of the 1976 AIP convention in Chicago was set by the keynote speaker,
John M. Couture of Wisconsin, who declared, drawing on the infamous
(and fabricated) *Protocols of the Elders of Zion*, that "atheistic political
Zionism is...the most insidious, far-reaching murderous force the world
has ever known, which plotted two world wars, undermined countless
governments, dictates the policy of numerous others." His poisonous
words brought cheers and flag waving from many of the three hundred
delegates and shocked Rusher, Viguerie, and other New Rightists.

Rusher et al. had hoped to forge a new party that would attract a
new majority of conservative Republicans and Democrats who no longer
felt an allegiance to their parties. Given their political experience, they
were, I thought, surprisingly naive. Their hopes were dashed by the blatant anti-Semitic atmosphere of the convention and the conspiratorial
fantasies of the delegates ("We know who killed Kennedy! LBJ!"), who
selected Lester Maddox, the segregationist former governor of Georgia,
as their presidential candidate. Bitterly disappointed, Rusher and the
others (including me) marched out of the convention hall before Maddox
was nominated. I didn't have to say, "I told you so."

25

THE CHANGING FACE
OF CONSERVATISM

At about the same time that the New Right emerged because of what it considered the treachery of moderate Republicans, a series of events forced a small but influential group of old-fashioned liberals to move out of their no-longer-comfortable Democratic digs. The happenings included the 1972 presidential candidacy of George McGovern, the willingness of modern liberals to let South Vietnam and other nations fall into the hands of communists, and the revolution in sexual and social relations that produced what Lionel Trilling called the "adversary culture."

The neoconservatives were "mugged by reality," in Irving Kristol's pointed phrase. They attacked the radicals as despoilers of the liberal tradition. Kristol called for a return to the "republican virtue" of the Founding Fathers and invoked the idea of a good society. Echoing Russell Kirk as well as Adam Smith, he endorsed the notion of a "moral and political order" and conceded that the idea of a "hidden hand" had its uses in the marketplace. Conservatives like *American Spectator* editor R. Emmett Tyrrell warmly welcomed Kristol. Bill Buckley said that the godfather of neoconservatism was "writing more sense in the *Public Interest* these days than anybody I can think of."

The neoconservatives were, as Theodore White put it, "action intellectuals" with close connections to leading universities and the mass media, direct access to officeholders and the political elite, good relations with major elements of organized labor, and strong roots in influential foundations and think tanks. They were uniquely qualified to carry the conservative message to places where no conservative, not even Bill Buckley, had gone before.

Kristol and his colleagues spawned institutions as Viguerie and Weyrich did on the New Right—journals like the *Public Interest* and the *New Criterion*, and organizations like the Coalition for a Democratic Majority, founded in the wake of McGovern's capturing the Democratic nomination.

The New Right and the neoconservatives were not natural allies. The New Right was deeply suspicious of government while the neoconservatives accepted government. The New Right loved the mechanics of politics while the neoconservatives preferred the higher plane of public policy. But both hated communism and despised liberals—the New Right for what liberals had always been and the neoconservatives for what they had become. In the end, it was the neoconservatives' tough anticommunism and resistance to the counterculture that won the approval of conservatives and led to a marriage of convenience. The minister who presided over the nuptials was Ronald Reagan, who needed the brainpower of the neoconservatives and the manpower of the New Right, especially the Christian Right, to win elections and enact good public policy.

During the 1970s and '80s, I interviewed most of the leading neoconservatives and befriended Midge Decter, the wife of Norman Podhoretz and a perceptive writer on social issues and foreign policy. She was my kind of anticommunist, with no illusions about the means or the ends of communists. In time (and I think because of her decades as a trustee of the Heritage Foundation), Midge became a conservative without any prefix. She even was elected president of the Philadelphia Society, the leading organization of conservative intellectuals in America. Once asked how she could be friends with Phyllis Schlafly, the slayer of the Equal Rights Amendment and the first lady of American conservatism, Midge replied, "It's easy—she's been doing my dirty work for years."

CONSERVATIVE DIGEST

In my 1972 memo to Richard Viguerie, I had proposed publishing a newsletter detailing what was happening on the American right. That idea came to fruition later that year, when I started the *Right Report*, a six-page newsletter that appeared twice a month. In a letter to Bill

Buckley, I characterized the *Right Report* as "an insider's newsletter on the conservative/anticommunist/libertarian movement in America."

The newsletter's circulation was modest, with never more than a thousand subscribers. But it was read by Washington insiders, left and right; I know because I received frequent telephone calls from political operatives as well as reporters about its contents.

I enjoyed writing the *Right Report*, but it never came close to breaking even financially. In 1976, I was content to sell it to Richard Viguerie, who turned over the editorship to Morton Blackwell, a rising star of the New Right. I turned my editorial attention to a more promising project.

For years, I had been thinking about starting a magazine like *Reader's Digest* that would reprint articles by traditional conservatives, libertarians, and anticommunists, as well as some political moderates and even liberals who opposed communism, such as George Meany of the AFL-CIO. It would be mostly but not exclusively political, with pieces about education, health, and culture. But I never met anyone with the necessary resources until, one day late in 1974, I mentioned my magazine idea to Richard Viguerie, who lit up. He had had the same idea for some time and agreed to underwrite the magazine, with himself as president and publisher and me as editor. I suggested that it be called *Conservative Digest*. Richard added the line "A Magazine for the New Majority."

The first issue appeared in May 1975 and covered the political spectrum, featuring conservative columnist James J. Kilpatrick on Reagan as a presidential candidate, liberal Senator William Proxmire opposing "government domination of our economy," British journalist Malcolm Muggeridge reviewing Bill Buckley's book about his time at the United Nations, conservative state legislator H.L. (Bill) Richardson of California warning against "government medicine," anti-gun-control partisan John Snyder, and a maiden column by Richard Viguerie, who wrote that it was time for a new mass-based conservative monthly with a "vigorous editorial policy." He added, "We don't intend to be deferential to conservative 'leaders' who are mentally retired and for all intents and purposes have given up the fight." His blunt language anticipated the controversial article about "Mr. Conservative" (Goldwater) that he and I would coauthor later in the year.

INTERVIEWING THE GREAT AND NOT-SO-GREAT

While running *Conservative Digest*, I had the opportunity to interview people like Bill Buckley, Governor George Wallace, and Herman Kahn.

The interview with Kahn, founder of the Hudson Institute, was like being in the room with the ten smartest people in the world. He was funny, profound, measured, provocative, ready with an opinion on any subject from nuclear war ("we don't believe that either [the United States or the Soviet Union] believes in nuclear weapons as a method of achieving positive gains") to overpopulation ("Paris has a population density of ten thousand a square mile and is not an 'ant heap' in any sense of the word") to the role of religion ("One of the reasons why I have great faith in the United States is because it is a religious country"). After the interview, I could not get my mind to stop racing from thought to thought for hours. I could have sat there, on a high bluff overlooking the Hudson River, asking Kahn questions until he said "*no más*." I am not sure he would have.

The interview with Governor Wallace was different. In a wheelchair and in constant pain from the attempted assassination two years earlier, he tended to repeat himself, his vocabulary was limited, perhaps deliberately, and he tired noticeably during our interview. Although he made the case for his populist Jefferson-Democrat philosophy, the fiery politician from Alabama was no more. I felt sorry for him. Wallace still harbored dreams of the presidency, but moderate Jimmy Carter was a more appealing candidate in 1976 than the liberal Hubert Humphrey had been in 1968, when Wallace received ten million votes.

In November 1975, I traveled to New York City to interview Bill Buckley, just turned fifty, in his *National Review* office overflowing with books, many of them written by him. In his shirtsleeves with his tie pulled down, Bill sat on his legs in some vaguely yoga position. He gestured frequently with a ballpoint pen as he talked about the conservative movement and his magazine, without which there would have been no movement.

Has *National Review* done more or less than he expected, I asked, when he started it twenty years ago? More, he replied, in dispelling the notion that "conservatism is an illiterate creed." Less, he admitted, in becoming "an extremely important and ubiquitous voice in the academy." He pointed out that at present, no publication, left or right, had that kind of influence.

I brought up *NR*'s annual deficit, which ran close to a half million dollars. Thanks to its readers, I had been told, the magazine was able to handle all but $100,000 of that amount. How was the difference covered? Although he mentioned only "sacrifices of all kinds," I knew that Bill personally made up the difference with his lecture fees ($2,500 per appearance), which he donated to the magazine. I also knew that Bill served as *NR*'s editor pro bono, although the magazine did provide editorial assistance and research for his books, newspaper columns, and TV program, *Firing Line*.

He elaborated on the deficit, saying, "If we had a capitalist class that was less than in deep torpor…this wouldn't be a problem. But they're much too busy advertising in *Playboy* and *Penthouse*, which is one-half sex and one-half derogation of American institutions, to feel any sense of responsibility for a journal which they think is mildly disreputable because it defends their way of life."

National Review, he said, was his single most important activity—more important than his syndicated column, which appeared in 350 newspapers; his weekly TV program, carried on 230 stations; and the speeches, articles, and books he produced to the delight of friends and the consternation of adversaries.

What an extraordinary communicator, I reflected, reaching hundreds of thousands of readers and viewers every week. I asked whether he thought he would ever win a Pulitzer Prize. "You have to be nominated first," he replied. What a travesty, I thought, recalling that the 1974 Pulitzer winner for editorial commentary had been the predictably liberal columnist Mary McGrory.

I had one last question. Earlier in the year, out of curiosity, Bill had attended the annual Bilderberg gathering, whose highly placed members, in the opinion of hard-core conservatives, were intent on fashioning a world under the socialist banner. What is a Bilderberg meeting really like? I asked. "To judge from my own experience," he said, savoring the words, "were any such conference held at Princeton or Harvard it would be thought of as mildly and stuffily right-wing." And with raised eyebrows and gleam of white teeth, Buckley was off for his harpsichord lesson and a little Bach.

MEETING REAGAN AGAIN

Perhaps the most memorable interviews I conducted were with Ronald Reagan. For the debut issue of *Conservative Digest*, in 1975, I secured an exclusive interview with Reagan, who had just completed his second term as governor of California and had not yet said whether he would challenge President Ford for the 1976 Republican presidential nomination. But you could tell he was thinking about it by his answers to my questions.

When I asked him whether he agreed with what many people were saying, that the Democratic and Republican parties were very much the same thing, he disagreed sharply. He said that Republicans had been put on the defensive for so long, despite presidential victories, they had failed to tell people what their party stood for—a philosophy of limited government and individual freedom. "We're with the people," he said, but the people didn't realize it. And he disagreed with Bill Rusher's call for a "new majority party," saying that what we needed instead was "a new second party." The third party was already there, in that "great group of independents that have become disenchanted with both parties."

He said that Republicans should appeal to this third group by raising a bold banner based "on an end to fiscal irresponsibility, on balanced budgets, a reduction of the federal budget, a reduction of the power of the federal government, reducing that bureaucracy, getting more autonomy back to the local and the state level, an end to permissiveness in our dealings with social problems." Asked to evaluate the performance of President Ford after six months in office, he carefully sidestepped, remarking it was too early for a judgment about someone who was what he called an "instant president."

I noted that President Ford often compared himself to President Harry Truman. Given that Reagan had campaigned for Truman in 1948, I asked, how did he feel the two men compared? Reagan's answer provides insights into his foreign policy philosophy of peace through strength. "I thought [Truman] had a lot of guts," Reagan said, "and he could have been a great president. And where he missed was across the water in Korea.... If Harry Truman had been the one who said ... as long as [Americans] are going to die fighting for their country, why then I'm going to give them a chance to hoist a victory flag and [do] whatever it takes to win."

Reagan linked the stalemate in Korea to the U.S. defeat in Vietnam. "I don't think there would have ever been a Vietnam if we'd won in Korea. I don't think there would have been a Berlin Wall and I don't think maybe there'd be a [communist] Cuba."

He anticipated the rules for conflict laid down by his future secretary of defense Caspar Weinberger when he said that America "has never had a history of asking men to die uselessly." He thought that when our government asks young men to fight, it "has a sacred obligation" to do so only "for a cause so important that you want them to win it just as quickly as possible and you will do everything as a country to help them do that."

When I asked him under what circumstances he would run for president, he responded: "I don't really understand these people who just go out and say, 'I'm going to be President of the United States.' ... I just have always believed that the people more or less determine who tries. . . . Then you have to estimate is this just a faction or does this represent widespread thinking and can I contribute?"

I interviewed Reagan again in early 1976, after he had announced his intention to run for president. We talked about what he hoped to do in his first hundred days in the White House.

He began by saying that no other candidate had gotten to the heart of the matter, that "it is Washington itself that is wrong, that Washington is trying to do things that Washington should not be doing." This foretells Reagan's language in his 1981 inaugural address: "In this present crisis, government is not the solution to our problem; government is the problem."

When I asked how he would deal with a liberal Congress and an entrenched bureaucracy, he replied, "A president has got to take the truth to the people, over the heads of the Congress, tell the people what he is trying to accomplish, what's standing in the way, and then depend on the people." As president, Reagan went to the people again and again, starting with his Economic Recovery Tax Act, which would not have gotten congressional approval without intense public pressure on House Democrats and Reagan's personal lobbying of some twenty-five southern Democrats.

He was particularly critical of U.S. foreign policy, saying, "I don't think that anyone in the world believes anymore that the United States has the guts to really be the leader of the free world and to do what has to be done." When I pressed him to be specific, he answered that we should let the Soviets know "we're not going to accept number two [in military strength], we accept the leadership of the free world, and we're going to stand behind our allies." He added, "Too many American presidents have been going to Moscow and Peking too often. It's time maybe for some of their leaders to come here." Here was another early indicator of the Reagan policy of peace through strength. He would let the Soviets know that a new kind of president was in the White House.

Reagan talked about the need for Republicans and Democrats to meet on common ground and form a New Majority that would be "basically what is called conservative." Clearly, Reagan was thinking about reaching out to what would be called "Reagan Democrats," who would help him win landslide victories in 1980 and 1984.

He said that as president he would seek to simplify the federal income tax code and adjust tax rates to account for inflation (he did not mention "supply-side economics"); remove controls on the price of crude oil and natural gas; balance the budget; support the Human Life Amendment;

eliminate forced school busing; become number one in military strength, because "to be second is to be last, and that invites war"; and propose a systematic transfer of federal authority and resources to the states.

Reagan believed that the American people were ready for a politics of common sense and that a New Majority coalition would help him govern. As we know, the people were not ready in 1976 for Reagan conservatism, but after four years of President Carter they were eager for a change in November 1980.

THE REAGAN CONVENTION

I was in Kansas City for the Republican National Convention as editor of *Conservative Digest* and a member of the press. Either as a political aide or a journalist, I had attended every convention since 1960 and would attain a string of twelve consecutive Republican conventions through 2004, when George W. Bush was renominated. I skipped the 2008 and 2012 conventions but traveled to Cleveland in July 2016 as Heritage Foundation media fellow to watch Donald Trump accept the Republican presidential nomination. I also attended three Democratic conventions—the revolutionary 1968 meeting in Chicago, when Hubert Humphrey was nominated to a smattering of cheers; the 1976 convention in New York, when the outsider Jimmy Carter was nominated; and the 1992 meeting, again in New York City, when Bill Clinton secured a nomination that had seemed earlier in the year to be almost worthless.

In Kansas City, we promoted a special issue of *Conservative Digest* that had a striking cover photo of Reagan in black tie and Nancy Reagan in a red gown, under the headline "My First 100 Days" (the cover story resulting from my recent interview with the governor). On the first evening of the convention, I and several editorial assistants stood outside the entrance to the convention hall, handing out copies of the magazine to the delegates. The delegates divided like the Red Sea, with Reagan delegates gladly accepting the magazine and Ford delegates turning away, often with a frown or a grimace. You could tell the delegates by what they wore: the Reagan delegates were Middle American, often in polyester and worn cowboy boots; the Ford people were country-club Republican, decked out in Gucci and tasseled loafers.

After passing out all our copies, we made our way to a location opposite the convention hall where we had set up an outdoor slide projector—a 1976 version of what I had used so successfully in 1964 at the San Francisco convention. As dusk settled over the convention, we began projecting slides of the *Conservative Digest* cover as well as other photos of Reagan and a Reagan for President poster. As I had expected, the news media began using our Reagan slideshow as filler during their early programming. Within five minutes, a golf cart with two stern-faced men came racing up to us.

"What do you think you're doing?" one man demanded, not bothering to identify himself. He was either a White House aide or a Secret Service agent.

"Promoting our magazine, *Conservative Digest*," I explained.

"Well, you'll have to stop. You're defacing the convention center. Who gave you permission?"

"The mayor of Kansas City," I replied.

"Who?" responded the man, his jaw dropping.

I reached inside my coat and showed him the letter of approval we had received from the office of the mayor, whom we had written months before.

The agent turned away and began whispering into a walkie-talkie. After a minute, he looked at me and said, "Well, it looks like it's okay for you to go ahead, but we'll be watching you."

"Thank you, sir," I said. I turned to our operator: "Okay, let's run that cover again."

We returned the next two nights to present our "Ronald Reagan's First 100 Days" show. There was no sign of Ford people, but I knew they were watching.

COMMUNISM, AGAIN

At the end of 1976, I stepped down as editor of *Conservative Digest*, proud of what we had accomplished. During the two years of my editorship, our circulation soared to 150,000, more than that of any other conservative magazine, including the longtime leader, *National Review*. We developed major writing talent like Mark Tapscott, who would become an editor at the *Washington Times* and the *Washington Examiner* before rising to executive editor at the Daily Caller News Foundation. But Richard kept narrowing the magazine's editorial focus and turning it into a vehicle for the New Right. I agreed that the New Right had every right to have its own magazine—I just didn't want to be the editor. Richard and I parted amicably. Four years later, he asked me to help with the writing and publication of his first book, *The New Right: We're Ready to Lead*. Four years after that, he asked me to return as editor of *Conservative Digest*, which I did for two years, until Richard sold the magazine. *Conservative Digest* made a significant contribution to the conservative movement, giving voice to "social conservatives" and concerns that were ignored by the establishment press, left and right.

Without the demands of *Conservative Digest*, I was able to spend more time on the subject closest to my heart—the clear and present danger of communism. Easily half of the weekly columns I wrote from 1974 to 1978 dealt with communism.

Starting in January 1975, I wrote with mounting concern about the communist violations of the so-called cease-fire in South Vietnam. My visit to Saigon the previous year and my talks with naive South Vietnamese officials who thought they could depend on the United States intensified my determination to support their cause. Twenty years later, the Vietnamese American community, of all the ethnic communities in America, was the strongest supporter of the Victims of Communism Memorial.

In my January 12 column, I wrote that North Vietnam had captured Phuoc Binh, the capital of Phuoc Long Province—the first South Vietnamese capital to be captured and held by the communists since January 1973. Hanoi was able to step up its offensive because the Soviet Union preached détente but practiced a policy of supporting "wars of national liberation," including Vietnam. I pointed out that Congress had authorized $1 billion in military assistance to South Vietnam but had appropriated only $700 million. The very least the new Congress could do was to release the other $300 million in a supplemental appropriation.

In late March, I reported that approval of the $300 million supplemental for Saigon was problematic because many congressmen were saying, "South Vietnam is a lost cause. Why throw money down a rat hole?" When you mention that "20 million South Vietnamese are depending on us," I wrote, "you are usually confronted with a shrug or a scornful look."

I noted that a group of prominent liberals and conservatives, led by Paul Nitze and Edward Teller, had signed a *Washington Post* ad urging Congress to approve the $300 million. Professor P. J. Honey of London predicted that if Saigon fell, "on the basis of past communist deeds, and given the size of South Vietnam's population, the minimum number of those to be butchered will exceed one million and could rise to several times that figure." The professor's prediction turned out to be painfully accurate: *The Black Book of Communism*, published by Harvard University

Press, put the number of South Vietnamese who died under communism following the end of the Vietnam War at one million.

After the South Vietnamese cities of Huế and Da Nang had fallen to the communists and Saigon's fall was clearly imminent, I asked, "Who lost Vietnam?" I started by listing the army of South Vietnam (ARVN), which finally gave in "after so many years and so much blood." Next came the U.S. Congress "for its failure to provide the aid which the U.S. promised it would give to South Vietnam." Next came Secretary of State Henry Kissinger, for "it was he and President Nixon who engineered an agreement...they knew would not be kept" by North Vietnam. Or at least, I said, they should have known.

President Ford warned America's "adversaries" that they should not feel that "the tragedy of Vietnam is an indication that the American people have lost their will or their desire to stand up for freedom any place in the world." Unfortunately, I wrote, the people of South Vietnam could not hear the president—"his words are drowned out by the sound of North Vietnamese bullets, shells, airplanes, and tanks."

In late April, I wrote of a new captive nation. With the fall of Phnom Penh to the Khmer Rouge, Cambodia had become the twenty-eighth nation under communist control. I quoted from the once-classified State Department report known as the Quinn Report, which noted that Cambodian communists had for years used terrorism, brainwashing, and murder to create a communist society. The report concluded that the Khmer Rouge's programs "have much in common with those of totalitarian regimes in Nazi Germany and the Soviet Union." According to *The Black Book of Communism*, one-fifth of Cambodia's population of seven million died at the hands of the fanatical Khmer Rouge.

The sound of falling dominos in Southeast Asia grew louder when Vietnam became Captive Nation #29 in June 1975 and Laos #30 in September 1975.

The Ford administration seemed unable or unwilling to respond to these tragedies. I joined other conservatives, including Ronald Reagan, in criticizing President Ford for not meeting with Aleksandr Solzhenitsyn when the great writer and Soviet dissident came to Washington, although the president took time to confer with the leaders of Communist Romania, Falangist Spain, and Marxist Zaire.

Referring to a bipartisan colloquy on the floor of the U.S. Senate, I reported that Cuba had stepped up its campaign to export revolution. Cuban-trained guerrillas were active in the Dominican Republic, Uruguay, and Argentina. Cubans had trained the militia and the air force of far-left South Yemen. An additional thousand Cuban troops arrived in Angola to aid the so-called People's Republic against the opposition; the total number would reach thirty thousand. And all the while Secretary of State Kissinger insisted that the United States could do business with the Soviet Union, which was underwriting and directing all the Cuban forays.

In October 1976, I flew to London at the invitation of the British journalist and resolute Cold Warrior Brian Crozier, highly regarded for his shrewd analysis of Soviet leaders and policy, and for his in-depth biographies of Charles de Gaulle, Francisco Franco, and Chiang Kai-shek. He was an unofficial but influential foreign policy adviser to the chair of the Conservative Party, Margaret Thatcher, whom Brian said could well be Britain's first woman prime minister.

I also knew Brian as the head of a private intelligence service—to which I was a contributing editor—that, when necessary, sponsored non-violent measures against the communists and their dupes. A few years later, when a far-left coalition held a rally in London's Trafalgar Square to protest the deployment of our Euromissiles, Brian arranged for large loudspeakers to be placed on the roofs of buildings surrounding the square. As the emcee prepared to introduce the main speaker, all the loudspeakers began playing the British national anthem, causing many in the crowd to stand and sing along, disrupting the meeting and short-circuiting its militant mood.

At about the same time and with Brian's financial support, which depended heavily on the generosity of Pittsburgh philanthropist Richard Scaife, I hosted a visiting delegation of European parliamentarians, including an Italian Socialist, a British MP, a French politician who would later become deputy mayor of Paris, a retired Belgian general, and a member of the German Christian Democratic Party. They vigorously and effectively defended the idea of Euromissiles in debates at Georgetown University and Columbia University and in editorial board sessions at the *Washington Post* and the *Wall Street Journal*.

While in the UK, I witnessed the formation of the National Association of Freedom and its newspaper, *The Nation*, filled with articles about the growing public resistance to socialism in Great Britain. Proof of the association's impact was the dedication of a 120-foot monument to the Katyn Massacre of 1940, when some twenty-two thousand Polish officers, intellectuals, and other prominent citizens were murdered on the direct order of Joseph Stalin. (I remembered the Katyn monument years later when we discussed what kind of monument the Victims of Communism Memorial Foundation should build in Washington.) Following my week in London, I wrote with measured optimism that although Britain remained in critical condition, "she can recover" with "a sufficiently large transfusion of freedom." And so she did, with Margaret Thatcher leading the way.

In late November 1976, the bipartisan, philosophically diverse Committee on the Present Danger was born. The principal threat to America and the world, the committee stated, was "the Soviet drive for dominance based upon an unparalleled military buildup." The committee called on President-elect Carter to approve "high levels of spending" for "our ready land, sea and air forces, our strategic deterrent and above all the continuing modernization of those forces through research and development."

Confirmation that ordinary citizens as well as sophisticated foreign policy experts recognized the danger of growing Soviet military power came the following April when a national survey showed that (as I wrote in a column) "the American public as distinct from the Eastern Establishment is still firmly anti-communist and does possess the will to resist Soviet expansionism." I reported that all groups, whether liberal, conservative, or moderate, agreed that the United States should turn back communism and be stronger militarily than the Soviet Union.

Now is the time, I wrote, for anticommunists to explain that it is in the national interest of the United States not to recognize Cuba, to press for strict compliance with the Helsinki Accords in Eastern and Central Europe and the Soviet Union, and to call for retention of our treaty and diplomatic relations with the Republic of China. I would address all these issues in the decade ahead. I noted that the Committee on the Present Danger stressed its bipartisan nature, which encouraged the media to cover its activities. From the beginning, I insisted on the same bipartisanship for the Victims of Communism Memorial Foundation.

26

CAPTIVE NATIONS
AND PEOPLES

The years between 1968, highlighted by the Prague Spring, and 1979, when the Soviets invaded Afghanistan, were years of trial and trouble for America and the free world. Communism, led by an expansionist Soviet Union, seemed to be on the march everywhere.

The communist world grew significantly, spreading from Eastern and Central Europe, China, North Korea, and North Vietnam to other parts of Asia (Cambodia, Laos, and all of Vietnam), Africa (Angola and Mozambique), and Latin America (Nicaragua). Political and intellectual elites in industrialized countries openly voiced their preference for the policies of Moscow and Beijing rather than Washington and London. The nonaligned world often sided with the communist bloc in the United Nations while presenting itself as neutral.

Here in America, the bipartisan consensus on the Cold War that had prevailed for twenty years from Truman to Nixon was coming apart. Antiwar demonstrations were increasing, and congressional hawks were turning into doves. Vietnam was a major but not the only cause of contention. So was the issue of nuclear parity, promoted by those who argued that limited means and domestic needs required it. President Nixon and Henry Kissinger, first as national security adviser and then as secretary of state, agreed on the need to accept the world as it was and to make the most of it. Kissinger, the apostle of realpolitik, insisted it was in the interest of the United States to encourage a multipolar world and move toward a new world order based on "mutual restraint, coexistence, and ultimately cooperation."

I marveled that someone so respected for his pragmatism could be so starry-eyed. Didn't the Soviet Union's aggressiveness show that it would take advantage of every weakness, every "restraint" by the United States, to advance its goal of communizing the world? Wasn't it clear that for the Soviets "coexistence" was just another form of warfare? Had not Moscow demonstrated by every broken treaty, every "war of national liberation," every KGB operation around the world, that it sought not cooperation but conquest? I rejected the Kissinger Doctrine as well as the Brezhnev Doctrine, under which no communist country could be allowed to become noncommunist. I resolved to challenge the Brezhnev Doctrine in every way I could.

In 1970 I formed the American Council for World Freedom (ACWF). The council's directors were a Who's Who of anticommunists in America, including retired U.S. Army lieutenant general Daniel O. Graham, former director of the Defense Intelligence Agency; Dr. Lev E. Dobriansky, Georgetown University professor, chairman of the National Captive Nations Committee, and later a cofounder of the Victims of Communism Memorial Foundation; Dr. Walter Judd, honorary chairman of the Committee for a Free China; retired U.S. Navy admiral John S. McCain Jr., former commander in chief of the Pacific Area Command, U.S. Navy (and father of future U.S. senator John McCain); Ronald Pearson, vice president of YAF; Dr. Stefan T. Possony of the Hoover Institution; and Fred Schlafly, ACWF chairman. As ACWF secretary I was responsible for all its activities, including fundraising, for which I received, when there were funds, a modest monthly fee.

In short order, ACWF became the U.S. chapter of the World Anti-Communist League (WACL). The league was an outgrowth of the Asian People's Anti-Communist League, founded in the early 1950s by Chiang Kai-shek of the Republic of China (ROC) on Taiwan, Syngman Rhee of South Korea, and other anticommunist Asian leaders. Each year, WACL held an international conference, and ACWF agreed to host the April 1974 meeting in Washington, D.C. I am proud of that conference. Never before had there been such a congregation of eminent right and left anticommunists.

The conference featured a luncheon address by AFL-CIO president George Meany; remarks by Franz Josef Strauss of West Germany (and an almost certain future chancellor except for his early death); a luncheon talk by Senator Barry Goldwater; an address by General Anastasio

Somoza Debayle of Nicaragua, whose security guard was only slightly smaller than our president's; and an address by Bill Buckley at the concluding banquet. In between there were panels of scholars and experts such as Robert Conquest of the Hoover Institution, former UN General Assembly president Dr. Charles Malik of Lebanon, scholar-author Lin Yutang of the ROC, dissident author Mario Laza of Cuba, and Dr. Hoang Van Chi of South Vietnam.

But as I traveled about meeting WACL chapter leaders and discussing the program agenda, I became uneasy. Some chapters were led by men who were openly anti-Semitic. The Catholic head of the Mexican chapter, Raimundo Guerrero, said to my face that Pope Paul VI was not a true Catholic and denounced Vatican II as the work of the devil. I recall a meeting at which one of his associates made a point of displaying the revolver tucked in his belt. Some of the Eastern Europeans had ties to extremist groups that had fought on the side of Nazi Germany in World War II, albeit against the Soviets. When I brought my findings to the WACL secretariat—dominated by Asians—they admitted they knew of the extremist ties and positions but preferred to stress the anticommunism. They promised to address the problem later and urged me to concentrate on the Washington conference. I reluctantly agreed.

Following the successful conclusion of the WACL meeting, Stefan Possony and I drafted a letter to WACL president Ku Cheng-kang. We expressed our deep concern about the leadership of the Mexican chapter and the background of other chapters, and recommended they be removed from membership. We said that if such action were not taken, ACWF would be obliged to resign as the U.S. chapter of WACL. All the ACWF directors approved the letter. To our deep disappointment, WACL did not take any meaningful action, and ACWF resigned from WACL in 1975. Later, under the leadership of retired U.S. Army major general John Singlaub, a new U.S. group joined WACL, which had changed its name to the World League for Freedom and Democracy (WLFD) and removed the most blatant extremists. As WACL and then WLFD, the league helped expose the Marxist-Leninist objectives of the Soviet Union and its allies and helped anticommunists around the world realize they were not alone in their struggle against the ism responsible for more deaths than all the wars of the twentieth century.

A natural outlet for my anticommunist efforts was the National Captive Nations Committee, headed by Lev Dobriansky. Lev asked me to serve as executive director, which I did for nearly a decade and without compensation. He had drafted the original captive nations resolution in

1959, worked with members of Congress in both parties to obtain passage, and persuaded President Eisenhower to sign the first presidential proclamation in 1959 declaring the third week of July to be National Captive Nations Week. Since then, every U.S. president has faithfully issued a proclamation recognizing National Captive Nations Week, although the rhetoric varied with the conduct of the Cold War. President Carter almost declined to issue a proclamation, but a broad-based coalition made up of liberal Democrats, labor leaders, and neoconservative intellectuals as well as prominent conservatives "persuaded" Carter to honor precedent and recognize the existence of such captive nations as the Soviet Union, China, Cuba, Vietnam, North Korea, and Cambodia. The resolution is proof of the power of an idea and the perseverance of one man.

A LIBERTY RALLY

In 1976, in addition to the proclamation and parades in New York (up Fifth Avenue) and Chicago (down Michigan Avenue), the Captive Nations Committee held a rally at the Statue of Liberty (where in 1965 YAF had begun its daylong transport of a Torch of Freedom from New York to Philadelphia to Washington). We decided to hold the event on Sunday, July 11, only a few days after the two hundredth anniversary of the Declaration of Independence and the day before the Democratic National Convention began in New York City's Madison Square Garden. As I had been for the Veterans Day rally in November 1969, I was the volunteer coordinator of the Captive Nations rally, although unlike most of those in attendance, I had never lived in a captive nation.

Several thousand of us gathered beneath the Statue of Liberty to hear speeches by Democratic mayors Abe Beame of New York and Richard Daley of Chicago, who arrived in a wave-jumping Coast Guard patrol boat minutes before they were scheduled to speak; the junior U.S. senator from New York, James L. Buckley; Democratic congressmen Ed Koch (later New York City mayor) of Manhattan and Mario Biaggi of Brooklyn; and Sol (Chick) Chaikin, president of the powerful International Ladies' Garment Workers' Union (ILGWU). Chaikin's participation reflected the broad-based nature of our "Bicentennial Salute to the Captive Nations," whose sponsors included the New York City Central Labor Council, the Catholic War Veterans, the Military Order of the Purple Heart, the A. Philip Randolph Institute, and every ethnic group imaginable. Leading up to the rally, I worked out of the ILGWU offices in lower Manhattan and discovered that we agreed on just about everything—from communism's continuing threat, to the centrality of the family—except for the right to work.

At our Liberty Island rally, we were entertained by a head-tossing Chinese dragon, vaulting Ukrainian athletes, thigh-slapping Bavarians, sinuous Turkic dancers, and Tchaikovsky's *1812 Overture*, performed by the fifty-five-piece Staten Island Musicians Society Military and Concert Band. Our hearts were moved by the remarks of three foreign visitors— Tran Van Don, the last vice premier of South Vietnam; Dr. Ku Cheng-kang of the ROC, who flew ten thousand miles to be present; and Avraham Shifrin of Israel, who had spent ten years in the Gulag. My biggest challenge was affording every ethnic group time for their presentation, and not favoring anyone. If the Czechs had three minutes, the Slovaks insisted on three minutes. If the Tibetans had four minutes, then the Uyghurs wanted the same. A couple of times, voices were raised, but I managed to satisfy all parties.

We had a lot of competition that Sunday afternoon: a VIP brunch for selected Democratic delegates at the famed 21 Club; a block party in lower Manhattan; a Jimmy Carter party at Pier 88; a march down Broadway by more than ten thousand right-to-life supporters; and a demonstration by several hundred gays proclaiming, "Sodomy Is Good."

In his talk, Lev Dobriansky, an economist by profession and an optimist by nature, reiterated that the captive nations, especially the non-Russian peoples within the USSR, were our best allies. The non-Russian areas inside the Soviet Union accounted for 50 percent of the population. Some thirty-two key natural resources were located in non-Russian areas like Ukraine (never "the" Ukraine), Georgia, and Byelorussia. Without those resources and non-Russian peoples, Lev argued, the Soviet Union was no longer a superpower. He quoted approvingly from President Ford's 1976 proclamation: "We do not accept foreign domination over any nation...[and] renew our support for the aspirations for freedom, independence and national self-determination of all peoples." Unfortunately, Ford forgot what he said in his proclamation when he debated Democratic challenger Jimmy Carter that fall. Asked about the Soviet Union's role, he insisted, "There is no Soviet domination of Eastern Europe."

Recapping the rally in my weekly column, I suggested steps that the United States could take to keep faith with the captive nations: make further trade conditional on democratization within the Soviet empire; require the Soviets to live up to the 1975 Helsinki Agreement, allowing families and friends to cross borders and exchanging journalists, academics, and scientists; and call on the Soviets to allow Jews as well as Christians, Muslims, and others to leave the Soviet Union if they wished. "We could do many things if we put our minds to it," I wrote, "if we decided that there must be no more captive nations, realizing that if we do not act we run the risk of one day becoming a captive nation too."

Among those who might have read about our rally—the *New York Times* and Associated Press published short articles—was the former California governor turned radio commentator, Ronald Reagan. He devoted a 1978 program to human rights and what he called the "Iron Curtain countries" of Eastern and Central Europe. He pointed out that for forty years "we have proclaimed a captive nations week to remind the world and ourselves that the Soviet Union holds millions of people in bondage." He dismissed President Carter's captive nations message as "weak" and "meaningless." He criticized the White House's decision to return the Crown of Saint Stephen to the communist government of Hungary even though the United States had promised at the end of World War II that we would hold the crown in trust "until Hungary was once again free." Why, asked Reagan, were we giving legitimacy to an illegitimate government? "Are we really serious about human rights?" he asked.

As president, Reagan demonstrated he was very serious about human rights by holding the first Rose Garden ceremony marking National Captive Nations Week. Along with Lev and other ethnic leaders, I was honored to be present and to thank President Reagan for his leadership and his willingness to name the Soviet Union as the reason for the existence of captive nations and peoples.

In July 1984, the president hosted a captive nations ceremony in the East Room of the White House. He detailed how his administration had begun an initiative to "bring words of truth and a message of hope to millions of imprisoned people throughout the world." It would, he said, modernize the Voice of America, expand the reach of Radio Free Europe and Radio Liberty, and establish Radio Martí to broadcast "the truth to the people of Cuba." We burst into applause—I suspect the East Room had not resounded with such applause and enthusiasm in a long time.

PRIMARY VEHICLE

As important as the National Captive Nations Committee was, the ACWF was the major vehicle for my anticommunist activity in the 1970s.

For example, in November 1976, shortly after Mao Zedong's death, we sponsored the conference "The United States and China After Mao," with an array of Sino experts. Our luncheon speaker, former U.S. ambassador to the ROC Walter P. McConaughy, warned us about Beijing's demands that the United States sever diplomatic ties with the ROC. There were alarming signs that the Carter administration intended to establish diplomatic relations with Communist China. Which is what Carter did in December 1978, when Congress was not in session and could not object.

In 1977 I coordinated ACWF conferences on détente and human rights. It seemed appropriate to explore two issues that mattered so much to President Carter. I practiced what Marvin Liebman had taught me— get the commitment of a prominent person and use him to get participants of similar stature. Ex-CIA official Ray Cline of the Center for Strategic and International Studies was highly respected by liberals as well as conservatives. Ray was perhaps best known for briefing President Kennedy on the U-2 photos of the Soviet missile sites during the Cuban Missile Crisis. I knew Ray through Dr. Judd and the Committee for a Free China, and he agreed to serve as honorary chairman of the conferences. With his sponsorship, I was able to line up former CIA director William Colby, former NATO head General Andrew Goodpaster, Russian dissident Vladimir Maximov, and union leader Joseph T. Power, among others. Lev persuaded the AFL-CIO Executive Council to be a cosponsor. And so just one week after President Carter's inauguration, we presented "The U.S. and the USSR After Détente," which took a hard look at the Soviets' inhumane treatment of dissidents. Some thirty years later, we followed a similar policy of nonpartisan research and analysis in the public events and publications of the Victims of Communism Memorial Foundation.

ACWF also became involved in the debate over the Panama Canal Treaties, which would have turned the canal over to Panama, headed by the corrupt dictator Omar Torrijos. The treaties proved to be one of the most galvanizing issues of the decade, pitting the conservative movement against the Carter administration and, surprisingly, Bill Buckley, who favored the transfer. ACWF was firmly against the treaties, as was Ronald Reagan, who said of the canal, "We built it, we paid for it, it's ours!"

Seeing the enormous potential of an issue that aroused the patriotic fervor of most Americans, I drafted an educational campaign that besides the usual communications devices included applying grassroots pressure on Congress. I got carried away, because the Internal Revenue Service— the Carter IRS—charged ACWF with engaging in political action and violating our tax-exempt status. We challenged the ruling and fought a years-long battle with the IRS. We ultimately won, but the victory so drained our modest resources that by 1980 we were struggling to keep the council alive.

ACWF's last major project had an impact. It was a thirty-two-page study, edited by Stefan Possony, that urged the incoming Reagan administration to adopt a strategic "Pentad" of offensive missiles, bombers, submarines, defense weapons, and space weapons to achieve strategic superiority over the Soviet Union. The Pentad's space weapons would intercept Soviet long-range ballistic missiles. I do not claim that the study led to Reagan's Strategic Defense Initiative (SDI), but a prominent member of our task force was General Daniel Graham, a key Reagan adviser on national defense and an ACWF director throughout the 1970s. Two years later, with the financial support of the Heritage Foundation, General Graham launched his High Frontier project, which called for an antiballistic missile system. High Frontier drew on the research of the ACWF study.

I am proud of what ACWF was able to do on an annual budget that never approached $100,000, publishing timely studies like "Hands Off the Panama Canal," by Isaac Don Levine; "The Strategic Dimension of East-West Trade," by Miles Costick; and "International Terrorism: The Communist Connection," by Stefan Possony and Lynn Bouchey. The last study documented that starting in the 1950s the Soviets trained, financed, and directed early terrorist groups. Later terrorist groups like al-Qaeda and the Taliban copied their techniques, demonstrating the connection between international terrorism and communism. Without Moscow and its terrorist training camps, there might have been no 9/11 terrorist attacks and some three thousand innocent people in New York City, Washington, and Pennsylvania might not have died.

ACWF echoed Barry Goldwater's uncompromising anticommunism with a call to monitor the Gulag in the Soviet Union and abandon SALT until "genuine peace-insuring arms control becomes feasible." It anticipated the multifaceted Reagan Doctrine with a recommendation that the United States eliminate all trade practices that favored the USSR, such as interest rates below world market rates, and cut off exports of new American technologies to Moscow.

KEEPING BUSY

Blessed with abundant energy and good at what is today called multitasking, I served clients in a variety of ways in the 1970s. I wrote press releases and contacted reporters, editors, and columnists for the National Right to Work Committee, YAF, the American Conservative Union, the Committee for a Free China, the Church League of America, and the American Legislative Exchange Council. I created a series of educational ads about the legal cases of the National Right to Work Legal Defense Foundation and the Public Service Research Council, which won a Freedoms Foundation award. I introduced the American Security Council to the wonders of direct-mail fundraising, despite the initial skepticism of president John Fisher, who became a direct-mail enthusiast, raising millions of dollars for his organization through the mail.

I wrote *Rebel Peddler*, the biography of Dan Renn, a young, charismatic North Carolina entrepreneur who built a company filled with ambitious young salesmen like himself and made millions of dollars selling home fire alarms, many of them to mobile homes. An apostle of positive thinking, Dan first operated out of his two-bedroom apartment; within three years his company was grossing $10 million in sales. At thirty-two, he commanded three thousand salesmen, a staff of thirty-six young men and women (I don't think I ever met anyone over forty), and a full-time pilot for the company plane. He was a conservative Republican in love with America and the American Dream who said of his company, "We believe in the positive—in man's humanity to man. I see my obligation as motivating people to do something with themselves." But Dan could not counter the competition of cheaper transistor alarms produced by giant stores like Walmart. Renn Enterprises went out of business a decade and half later. Dan died in 2004 of congestive heart failure, but I think the real reason was the failure of his dream, not his heart.

From time to time, I suggested newspaper column/radio commentary ideas to Reagan and his chief writer, Peter Hannaford. I provided Pete with a foreign policy memo on Cuba, Taiwan, and the Panama Canal, for example, describing the canal treaties as "a prime symbol of the Ford/Kissinger give-in and give-away foreign policy." In August 1978, Reagan wrote me that he would consider doing a column on the role of the National Right to Work Committee in blocking the "misnamed labor reform bill." "Bless you for what you are accomplishing," Reagan said.

In January 1971, I offered White House chief of staff Don Rumsfeld, at his invitation, some advice on how to deal with conservatives who were growing visibly restless because of Nixon initiatives at home (the Family Assistance Plan, regulatory agencies like the Environmental Protection Agency) and abroad (SALT I and the China initiative). "Don't take the conservatives for granted," I wrote, advising the White House to reach out to them. "A little oil this year will insure a smoother running machine next year." And don't assume, I warned, that conservatives have no place to go "and will automatically support RMN come what may. I know that some people in the White House hold this opinion, but they are in for a rude awakening." And so they were.

In August 1971, twelve prominent conservatives led by Bill Buckley announced they were suspending "support of the [Nixon] administration" because of its "overtures to Red China" and the "deterioration of the American military." Several of them backed Congressman John Ashbrook's quixotic but principled primary campaign against Nixon. Ashbrook never received 10 percent of the vote in any of the states in which he campaigned—New Hampshire, Florida, and California. But he was hailed by hard-core conservatives, who argued that Ashbrook had forced Nixon to veto the liberal Child Development Act, keep Spiro Agnew on his ticket, and address the explosive social issue of busing in the Florida primary.

Richard Viguerie, who financed the Ashbrook campaign through his direct-mail efforts, was inspired by Ashbrook's example to take a more activist role in the movement. "I felt isolated and frustrated," he later said. "I kept looking for people who could lead, who could make things happen. Finally, reluctantly, I began to call my own meetings." The meetings led to the formation of the New Right.

PARIAH NATION

As I had since my Army years in West Germany and my bohemian year in Paris, I traveled extensively in the 1970s, visiting Taiwan, Mexico, South Vietnam, Brazil, Great Britain, and France. The most fascinating country was South Africa, the land of apartheid and arguably the most castigated nation in the world. Anne and I spent almost two weeks there in the summer of 1974 as the guests of South Africa's Department of Information, whose director had read our political handbook, *You Can Make the Difference*, and apparently thought we might be sympathetic to his white-led government. Before accepting his invitation, we made it clear that as conservatives we believed that all men were created equal and were entitled to certain unalienable rights, whether they lived in America or South Africa.

The first thing we learned was that not everything was black and white in South Africa. There were 16 million black Africans representing eight tribes, the largest the Zulus. There were also 2.5 million "coloreds"—

primarily people of mixed race—located mostly in and around Cape Town. There were 700,000 Indians in Durban, who had come from India the previous century to help build the railroads. And finally there were 4 million whites divided unequally between a majority who spoke Afrikaans and a minority who spoke English.

The second lesson was that there were two kinds of apartheid or separate development—the grand and the petty. The former was based on the granting of separate, independent "homelands" such as KwaZulu, Transkei, and Ciskei to the eight African tribes. The white government insisted that the homelands would be sovereign and independent. To Anne and me, the plan looked like a policy of divide and keep conquered. Much in the news was the chief minister of the Transkei, Paramount Chief Kaiser Matanzima, who set 1976 as a target year for full political independence while conceding that economic assistance from the South African government would be necessary for years.

The white government believed that its homelands policy would satisfy the political aspirations of the black majority, but based on our interviews, we concluded that no more than half the blacks would be satisfied with the plan. What of the other half? We visited Percy Qoboza, the influential young editor of *The World*, the number-one newspaper in Soweto, the all-black suburb of Johannesburg. Percy said that the five million urban blacks had no interest in moving to the "homelands." Their home was Soweto and the other urban areas. They wanted equal pay, property rights (they lived in government-owned houses), and the vote. They were not interested in a distant, often barren, predominantly rural province. They wanted a black government, not a white government, and they wanted it now.

Our hosts did not limit our interviews and meetings in any way, arranging for us to talk with a wide range of citizens—including liberal English and conservative Afrikaans members of parliament, colored and black African leaders, academics and journalists, businessmen and government officials. At Anne's insistence—I was preoccupied with examining every possible aspect of the country—we spent a weekend at Mali Mali, a luxurious private game reserve next to Kruger National Park, where we slept in our own air-conditioned "hut" complete with a shower and bath and double wash basin. We ate fork-tender impala steak under the stars while being served icy-cold martinis by African waiters in immaculate white uniforms. We saw giraffes and hippopotami ("Do not get out of the jeep," warned our guide, "they can move very quickly") and watched lions feeding on dead impalas from behind a secure wall.

We also spent one freezing, sleepless night in the best motel in Umtata, the capital of Transkei, wrapped in our coats, gloves, socks, and sweaters. Anne would not let me turn on an ancient electric heater for fear it might explode and start a deadly fire. We flew from Umtata to East London in a four-passenger, single-engine bush plane that was so buffeted by wild wind and rain and bolts of lightning that we feared we would never land safely, leaving our two young daughters in Chevy Chase orphans. It was the most terrifying plane ride I have ever been in. We both set personal records for saying the Rosary. When, by the grace of God, we finally touched down, the veteran pilot, who had said little during the stormy flight, remarked, "I think that's all the flying I am going to do today."

As we took leave of South Africa—beautiful, complex, exotic, disturbing—Anne and I were filled with foreboding. Whites, blacks, coloreds, and Indians were trying to build a multiracial nation in the face of tremendous odds, lengthened by the impatient and the adamant within and without the country. It seemed an almost impossible goal, and time was not on their side. Looking back, I realize that no one mentioned the man sitting in a cell on Robben Island, Nelson Mandela, who, along with the Afrikaans leader F. W. de Klerk, later accomplished a miracle—a peaceful rather than a revolutionary transition from apartheid to democracy.

THE POPE UP CLOSE

Late in the decade, in cooperation with the Archdiocese of Washington, I edited a handsome full-color picture book of Pope John Paul II's visit to Washington, D.C. I arranged for a team of photographers to accompany him everywhere he went during his thirty-six hours in Washington. I was within a few feet of the pope many times, but never formally met him—I was too busy making sure that our photographers captured his many moods.

My enduring memory is of his visit to Trinity College, a women's college next to Catholic University in Northeast Washington, where I noticed a line of perhaps twenty people of all ages in wheelchairs hoping to catch a glimpse of the Holy Father. His long black limousine slowly approached the college and then abruptly stopped. I could see the pope trying to get out of the backseat, but the cardinals on either side did not move, concerned, I guessed, that they were far behind schedule. Suddenly the pope climbed over one cardinal and out of the limousine. He went over to the line of wheelchairs and, leaning over, said a few words to each one. I moved closer and heard one say, "Pray for me, Your Holiness," and the pope reply, "And you must pray for me."

He was and is a pope for the ages.

27

LEAVING THE ARENA

The presidency of Jimmy Carter was a time of economic misery for the American people and of communist gains around the world, but they were golden days for conservatives. Following Watergate, Republicans had been told and some conservatives agreed that the party was finished. But in the 1978 off-year elections, after two years of Carter, the GOP gained three seats in the Senate and thirteen seats in the House of Representatives, most of them conservatives. Several, like Senator Orrin Hatch of Utah, owed their victory to the New Right.

Because of Carter's ineptitude, things got even better for conservatives, although not for the country, in the next two years. By the end of 1979, the inflation rate stood at 13.3 percent, the highest since the Korean War and nearly double the rate that Carter had inherited from Ford. Confronted by mounting economic woes, Carter refused to blame himself or his administration's maladroit decisions. Instead, he faulted the American people, who, he said, were deep in the throes of a spiritual "crisis of confidence."

Things were no better abroad. The pro-West shah of Iran was ousted. Marxist regimes were established in Angola and Mozambique, and the Soviets invaded Afghanistan. Casting about for an explanation of communism's global aggression, UN ambassador Andrew Young went Orwellian, asserting that the thirty thousand Cuban troops in Angola brought "a certain stability and order" to the country.

What better time for a conservative to run for president and for conservatives to rally to his cause? In 1976, I wrote frequently about Ronald Reagan in *Human Events* and other journals, praising his leadership and his record as governor of California. In 1980, I helped Lyn Nofziger in the Reagan for President press office at the Republican National Convention in Detroit. I personally observed Barbara Walters obtain an exclusive interview with Reagan through unrelenting, infuriating persistence.

She began calling our office early Monday morning, the first day of the convention, and then every hour or so afterward. She never varied, saying, "This is Barbara Walters of ABC and I would like to talk to Lyn, please." When asked about what, she would reply, "An interview with the governor." Lyn took the first call and explained that Reagan was busy visiting delegations and working on his acceptance speech and wasn't giving interviews. An hour later, an undeterred Walters called and asked to speak with Lyn, who shook his head and did not take her call. Walters kept calling all day and into the next day until about 5 o'clock in the afternoon, when an exasperated Lyn literally threw up his hands and surrendered, giving Walters the first network interview with Reagan. I remembered Walters's persistence twenty years later when I was trying to raise the money for the Victims of Communism Memorial. I refused to give up, although there were times, as I will record, when I was sorely tempted.

My other contribution to the 1980 Reagan campaign was to revise and update my 1967 Reagan biography. Rewriting the book was one thing—getting it published was another. I cannot recall who suggested it, but I hired Lucianne Goldberg as my literary agent. Lucianne would become famous as the friend who encouraged Linda Tripp to tape-record her phone conversations with the most famous intern in White House history, Monica Lewinsky. Lucianne maintained she did not know it was illegal to record phone calls, and I believe her.

Lucianne was a smart, well-connected New Yorker who assured me—it was early 1980, after Reagan had won the New Hampshire Republican primary—she would have little trouble lining up a publisher. Two weeks later, a chastened Lucianne reported that she had been unable to find a mainstream publisher interested in a Reagan biography. The reasons varied from "He won't get the nomination" and "He can't get elected" to "There's no market for a conservative book about a conservative politician." She began contacting publishers outside New York and located Nordland, a small publishing house in Houston that agreed to publish *Ronald Reagan: A Political Biography* and offered a modest $10,000 advance. Their plan was to publish in the fall to take advantage of public interest in the presidential campaign.

I was skeptical about the timing but went to work, updating the book through the Republican national convention and suggesting what Reagan might do in his first hundred days, based on my study of the man. I listed such things as a 30 percent across-the-board cut in personal income taxes; a significant increase in defense spending; a freeze on federal hiring; increased military pay and benefits to make the voluntary military a more effective fighting force; a strengthened CIA and National Security Agency; and an easing of environmental controls to encourage more coal mining and oil drilling.

I said that Reagan would express his willingness to discuss arms control and reduction with the Soviets "but on a truly bilateral basis" and from a position of military superiority. This would be, in fact, Reagan's foreign policy as president, culminating in the Intermediate-Range Nuclear Forces (INF) Treaty and bringing about a peaceful end to the Cold War. Few analysts thought such an outcome was possible as Reagan took office.

Among the possible cabinet and other high-ranking appointments in a Reagan administration, I mentioned Caspar Weinberger, Alexander Haig, and Alan Greenspan, all of whom would serve under Reagan. As a strict interpreter of the Constitution, I said, Reagan would nominate jurists to the Supreme Court and the federal judiciary "with similar respect for that great document." And he did, elevating William Rehnquist to chief justice and naming the eloquent originalist Antonin Scalia to the court. Sandra Day O'Connor and Anthony Kennedy earned less praise among conservatives, although Reagan defended O'Connor as the kind of nonideological justice he sought. Reagan, I wrote, would reduce the role of government in the lives of Americans "whenever and wherever possible." As we know, one of his first acts as president was to end price controls on petroleum.

I noted that while campaigning, Reagan had often quoted the early Massachusetts Bay Colony leader John Winthrop, who had said that the eyes of all mankind were on the colonists as they landed and that they could be as "a shining city on a hill." Winthrop had referred to "a city on a hill" but Reagan added the evocative word "shining." Reagan asserted, I wrote, that the eyes of all mankind were still on America and wondered whether its people would give hope to all those who yearned for freedom. That was what Ronald Reagan wanted to do as president, I concluded—

help America fulfill her destiny and put her people once again "on the road to achieving the American Dream."

I thought we had a good, salable book. It included my research on the early Reagan years in Illinois and Hollywood, his gradual transformation from a liberal Democrat into a conservative Republican, how his famous TV speech in the 1964 presidential campaign was almost blocked, his acknowledged success as governor of California, his near capture of the Republican presidential nomination in 1976, and his winning the nomination in 1980. I suggested that we delay publication until after the general election, which I was confident Reagan would win. I was prepared to write a final chapter covering the campaign. But the publisher said he wanted to take advantage of the fall campaign and the fact that one-third to one-half of all books are sold in November and December.

We went to press, but to my sharp disappointment, Nordland was unable to line up a national distributor to handle the book. No one was interested in a one-book deal with a Texas publisher they had never heard of. There were modest sales in Washington and through Nordland's academic contacts, but the book never made it to most retail bookstores. A cash-strapped Nordland could afford only a limited advertising campaign. I could not help thinking that my 1967 Reagan biography had sales of 175,000.

NEW NEW EDITION

When Reagan won the presidency in an electoral landslide, however, I immediately contacted Nordland to argue that now was the time to come out with a new edition with a last chapter on how he won. At the same time, I called an old friend, publisher Jameson Campaigne Jr., to ask whether he would be willing to handle the national distribution. Jim said he would be happy to do so. New management at Nordland decided to reset the type and design a full-color cover (the earlier edition had a lackluster black-and-white photo of Reagan). I wrote a 9,600-word final chapter in less than a month. Nordland set a spring publication date, and I began compiling a list of reviewers and media contacts. And then in the early afternoon of March 30, 1981, a deranged John Hinckley tried and failed to end the Reagan presidency with a .22-caliber revolver and six Devastator bullets.

I called Nordland to suggest one more revision: a final chapter, "The Shooting of the President," that would cover Reagan's first hundred days in office and the day he was shot. I delivered a 7,800-word draft in three weeks. I was not happy with the new cover that featured, below a close-up of a smiling Reagan, a black-on-yellow banner that almost screamed, "Complete Through the Assassination Attempt." But I was assured the banner would help sales.

The book was hailed in the conservative press as "the best biography of our president" (columnist John Chamberlain), "must reading for aspiring politicians" (*Human Events*), "a useful and exceptionally detailed biography" (*Policy Review*), and "an important historical contribution" (Senator Paul Laxalt). It was dismissed in the liberal press as "hagiographic" (Nicholas von Hoffman in the *New York Review of Books*). I was flattered when von Hoffman wrote that my book "ought to be bound in white leather and sold to families who already have a white leather King James Bible." How often is your work compared to the Bible?

I was amused by the charge that my biography was "hagiographic" and that I idolized Reagan, coming close to nominating him for sainthood. I do not deny that I accentuated the positive in describing his extraordinary life, from son of a failed shoe clerk to Hollywood and television star to successful governor of our most populous state to a presidential victory to his near death at the hand of a demented assassin to his triumphant appearance before a joint session of Congress less than a month later. How else would you tell his story? Stress his initial nervousness as a radio announcer, his failed marriage to Jane Wyman, the cancellation of his TV drama series after "only" eight years of high ratings, his failure to capture the 1976 Republican presidential nomination? All of the above events are in my book, in their proper place.

Let me be clear. Those seeking absolute objectivity in my Reagan biography or any of my other books about the conservative movement will not find it. But then they will not find objectivity in Arthur Schlesinger's laudatory history of Franklin D. Roosevelt's presidency or William Manchester's deferential biography of John F. Kennedy with all its Camelot allusions. Pure objectivity is impossible in literature and life. We all have our biases, prejudices, and strong beliefs, and we carry them with us wherever we go. My books are works of scholarship, selection, and, I admit it, praise for a movement that has been transformed from a small group of isolated writers and intellectuals into a paramount political movement in my lifetime.

My Reagan biography was not my only 1981 book. I revised and expanded *You Can Make the Difference*, the political handbook that Anne and I had cowritten in 1968. I added a chapter about the right to life, highlighting the political savvy of blue-collar Democratic activist Joe Barrett, with whom in 1977 I cofounded Life-Pac, the first antiabortion political action committee. Another new chapter dealt with the right to keep and bear arms, featuring pro-gun advocate John Snyder and the National Rifle Association. I also wrote about Phyllis Schlafly's amazing defeat of the Equal Rights Amendment despite the backing of the entire liberal establishment, and the New Right's rise to political prominence.

READY TO LEAD

As pleased as I was with the revised Reagan biography, the book that had the greatest political impact was *The New Right: We're Ready to Lead*, by Richard Viguerie. The book was part autobiography, part history, and part political manual. Richard asked me to help with the production as well as the writing of his book, which he intended to self-publish, inspired by the success of Goldwater's *The Conscience of a Conservative* and Schlafly's *A Choice Not an Echo*, each of which sold more three million copies. We did not sell that many, but *The New Right: We're Ready to Lead* remains one of the most cited references in any examination of the New Right and its role in American conservatism.

From the opening sentences ("It's very simple. The left is old and tired. The New Right is young and vigorous") to its final words ("We're lean, determined and hungry to gain victories for conservatism and to renew our great country"), *The New Right* was intended to highlight a new dynamic leader and a new political force intent on changing the direction of American politics.

Richard described how the New Right got started in his home following President Ford's selection of Nelson Rockefeller as his vice president and kept growing with the battle to stop the giveaway of the Panama Canal. He chronicled the decline of liberalism as evidenced by the 1978 defeat of prominent liberal Democrats like Senators Dick Clark of Iowa and Tom McIntyre of New Hampshire. He also emphasized the New Right's resolve to put prayer back in the public schools and preserve the traditional family.

That Richard understood the importance of issues like school prayer was underscored by his asking the Reverend Jerry Falwell, the founder of the Moral Majority, to write the introduction to *The New Right*. Falwell agreed and in his introduction praised "Mr. Viguerie" for speaking up against liberals whose actions had occasioned America's "perilous condi-

tion." He urged moral Americans to band together and "make a difference in America." America's destiny, he said, depended on their action.

In November 1980, Dr. Falwell, the Reverend Pat Robertson of the
Christian Broadcasting Network, and several hundred conservative Protestant pastors urged their congregations to go to the polls and help Ronald Reagan win a decisive victory over President Jimmy Carter, a Southern Baptist and Sunday school teacher. Pollster Lou Harris estimated
that as many as six million white Protestants voted for Reagan, providing
the conservative Republican with a wide margin throughout the South
and the nation.

The New Right's success, Richard explained, was built on four
elements—single-issue groups like right to work and right to life; multi-
issue conservative groups like the American Conservative Union; coalition politics, based on the principle that politics is addition, not subtraction; and direct mail to raise funds and provide news and information
overlooked or omitted by the regular news media. "You can think of
direct mail," Richard wrote, "as our TV, radio, daily newspaper and
weekly newsmagazine."

Referring to the need to build a new majority in America, he quoted
Congressman Newt Gingrich, elected to the House in 1978 and already
a favorite of the New Right because of his audacity: "The way you build
a majority in this country is you go out and put together everybody who's
against the guy who's in. And instead of asking the question, 'What
divides us?' you ask the question, 'What unites us?'"

Fourteen years later, Gingrich would lead the House Republicans to
their first majority in forty years. I devoted two chapters to Newt in *The
Conservative Revolution*, my political history of American conservatism,
explaining why, despite his historic success, he was unable to carry out
the revolution promised in the Contract with America. Newt, I wrote,
was an inspiring revolutionary but an indifferent manager.

In the last chapter of *The New Right*, Richard urged the next president (presumably Ronald Reagan) to create a National Commission
to Restore America, made up of "our most distinguished conservative
citizens," who would single out the most critical challenges confronting
the nation and suggest how to overcome them. He tried to lessen the
commission's burden by suggesting fifty specific items for an agenda "by
which every American could attain the American dream." They included:

* A Taxpayer's Bill of Rights Act (already proposed by Senator
  Helms)

- Adoption of an educational voucher system (by 2016, school-choice programs operated in twenty-eight states and the District of Columbia)
- Putting SALT II on the back burner permanently (President Carter did, following the Soviet invasion of Afghanistan)
- Balancing the budget (part of the Contract with America)
- Approval of a constitutional amendment protecting the right to life from the moment of conception to natural death
- Holding a summit meeting of U.S. allies to coordinate countersubversion and counteraction against terrorism

While endorsing the longtime conservative emphasis on economic and foreign policy, Richard wrote, the New Right was convinced that conservatives could not become "the dominant political force in America" unless they also stressed the issues that concerned ethnic and blue-collar Americans, born-again Christians, pro-life Catholics, and Jews—issues like school busing, abortion, pornography, education, traditional moral values, and quotas.

Richard's book was an early articulation of the issues that led to the birth of the Tea Party movement thirty years later.

Richard noted how far conservatives had come since Goldwater's crushing defeat sixteen years earlier and wrote, "Yes, the tide is turning. It is turning our way—freedom's way."

A word here about ghostwriting, which has been an honorable profession since Alexander Hamilton wrote George Washington's celebrated Farewell Address more than two centuries ago. Beginning with my years as press secretary to Senator John Marshall Butler, I had drafted speeches and remarks of varying length and even books for a variety of public figures, including Senator Strom Thurmond; Congressmen Bob Bauman of Maryland and John Buchanan of Alabama; actors Efrem Zimbalist Jr. and John Wayne; presidential candidate Barry Goldwater; New Left analyst Phillip Abbott Luce; William Cardinal Baum of Washington, D.C.; North Carolina gubernatorial candidate James Gardner; Montgomery County, Maryland, county executive James Gleason; and direct-mail guru Richard Viguerie.

I studied their speeches and statements, noting their favorite words and phrases, the words they avoided, the rhythm of their rhetoric, and the pace of their speaking, and copied their natural voice as best I could. I received few complaints and many compliments about my ghosting. From the mid-1960s through the mid-1980s, I also continued to write in my own name (the Reagan and Renn bios, the political handbook) to satisfy a strong, even compulsive need to write. To paraphrase Descartes, *j'écris, donc je suis.*

OFF THE ROLLER COASTER

With Reagan's presidential victory in November 1980, two congruent feelings formed within me. I had enjoyed tremendously the exhilarating ride as a public relations consultant for nearly two decades, the political victories and the front-page stories, cheering crowds and Oval Office visits, exposing communism and raising the right. But politics was a young man's game, and I was approaching fifty. I wanted off the roller coaster.

I had made a difference as a conservative activist and publicist, but I no longer relished the constant demands and unrelenting pressure of political campaigns and causes. I wanted to lead a more measured life. I had managed to keep our little firm afloat, but we were increasingly buffeted by winds and waves that threatened to sink us, things like unemployment compensation, health insurance, pension plans, and taxes, federal and D.C. Most of what I earned went to pay the salaries of my staff; there was little left for Anne and me and our two daughters. We had been living in the little town of Somerset in Chevy Chase in an old stucco house that I loved, but we decided to move into the Springfield section so that Elizabeth and Catherine could go to Walt Whitman High School, the best school in the area. Our new house across River Road and near our church, Little Flower, was much larger and far more expensive, requiring a second mortgage and adding to my income concerns. I was tired of always worrying about my clients and their goals. What about Anne's and my goals? We had put almost nothing aside for our retirement.

I had long wanted to teach at a college or university and write full-time about the conservative movement. And Anne had long encouraged me to close down Lee Edwards & Associates.

I prayed for guidance, reinforced by our experience with the Charismatic Renewal within the Catholic Church. Anne and I had taken to attending Friday night prayer meetings at Saint Bernadette's Catholic Church in Silver Spring, where we made new friends and were baptized in the Holy Spirit. I had never paid much attention to the third person of the Trinity until joining the renewal. Although I had overlooked Him, He had been there all the time.

28

BACK TO SCHOOL

I n the fall of 1980, Kitty Scott, a friend from Young Republican days and president of the Friends of the Library at Catholic University, invited me to give a talk on the 1980 presidential race. I said yes, thinking it would afford an opportunity to test my MOCIM theory.

In my October lecture at Catholic University, I graded Governor Reagan and President Carter on the five major elements of electoral politics—Money, Organization, the Candidate (as a campaigner), Issues, and Media. I rated Reagan and Carter on a scale of zero to five, with twenty-five the highest possible score. I used the latest published reports about fundraising, talked to friends and experts about each man's organization, evaluated each candidate's campaign skills, determined the major issues and where each man stood on them, and noted how the mass media treated each, positively or negatively. It was no contest: Reagan topped Carter in every category by several points. Even the liberal media favored Reagan; Carter's sanctimonious attitude did not sit well with cynical reporters. My analysis suggested a landslide win for Reagan, although most polls showed a close race. (I have used MOCIM in every subsequent presidential race and have accurately predicted each winner, including in the 2016 election, when I picked Donald Trump to defeat Hillary Clinton, barely.)

I knew my Catholic University talk was a success because the question-and-answer period lasted for an hour and could have gone longer. A senior professor told me it was the best political lecture he had ever heard. I received invitations to repeat the talk. James P. O'Leary, a former chairman of Catholic University's politics department, said to me, "Why don't you try to get your PhD here at Catholic?"

Jim's suggestion and the favorable reaction to my lecture provided just the encouragement I needed to pursue a new life.

A week later, I was seated in Claes Ryn's office on the third floor of Marist Hall on the Catholic University campus. Claes, a conservative scholar whom I knew from Philadelphia Society meetings, was the current chairman of the politics department. I had brought along copies of my Reagan biography and *You Can Make the Difference*, and I put them on Claes's desk along with copies of my articles in *National Review*, *Human Events*, and selected newspapers.

"Claes," I began, "I want very much to teach and I know that I need a PhD to do that. I'd like to enroll in the program here. I brought along some of my books and writing to prove I can research and write and in the hope I can get some credit for them."

Claes reached over and pushed aside my little pile of books and articles. "I know you can write, Lee," he said, "but let's talk about what you need to do to earn a PhD here."

He outlined the courses I would have to take, the papers I would have to write, the two languages in which I would have to show fluency and proficiency, the written and oral comps I would have to take, and the doctoral dissertation I would be expected to write. Assuming that I would be a part-time student taking classes at night and on the weekends, he estimated it would take me four or five years to earn a doctorate. Claes was correct: I enrolled in my first class in the spring of 1981 and received my PhD in world politics in the summer of 1986. I picked world politics to deepen my understanding of communism. I opted against American government or political philosophy because there was little I could learn in the former and there was more than I wanted to learn in the latter.

I did well in my classwork, finishing with a 3.85 average and being elected to the national political science honor society, Pi Sigma Alpha. I got a B in Claes's political philosophy class—modern philosophers like Rousseau and Marx were no problem, but Plato and Aristotle were problematic—and another B in Theories of International Relations from O'Leary. Claes said my sentences were too short, the aftereffect of the hundreds of press releases and newspaper columns I had written. I learned to lengthen my sentences. I passed exams in French, rusty after twenty-five years but sufficient, and Spanish.

My 304-page dissertation, "Congress and the Origins of the Cold War," argued that the so-called Do-Nothing Republican Eightieth Congress of 1947–48 had helped lay the foundation for the foreign policy of containment that kept the Soviet Union out of Western Europe and at bay in much of the world until the 1980s, when President Reagan initiated a "win" policy for the Cold War. I called the 1947–48 period a "golden age of bipartisanship," led by President Truman, a Democrat, and Senator Arthur Vandenberg of Michigan, a Republican. My father pronounced my dissertation "impressive," a compliment I treasured.

I applied for a full-time teaching job at almost every college and university in the Washington area, including Catholic, Georgetown, George Washington, American, Maryland, even Hood College in Frederick, Maryland, but there were no openings. Competition was and is fierce for teaching posts at a university, with as many as 250 applicants for an assistant professorship. I persuaded Catholic University, starting in 1987, to hire me as a lecturer and then as an adjunct assistant, associate, and full professor of politics, the last one requiring faculty Senate approval. For the past thirty years, I have usually taught one undergraduate course a year at Catholic. For a couple of summers, I taught a graduate course at the Pentagon, "U.S. Foreign Policy Since 1945." My students, mostly captains and majors, were the best I have ever had, always prepared, smart, articulate, motivated to earn a master's degree to help them move up the ranks. My number-one Pentagon student was the chief of staff for General Colin Powell, then chairman of the Joint Chiefs of Staff. I have forgotten his name, but I am certain he will earn at least two stars by the time he retires.

Over the decades, I have taught, in addition to foreign policy, courses entitled "Mass Media and American Politics," "Mass Media and World Politics," "Congress and the Media," and my favorite, "The Politics of the Sixties." I begin that last course writing on the blackboard "John Kennedy" and "Barry Goldwater," "SDS" and "YAF," the "Port Huron Statement" and the "Sharon Statement." I let the students make up their minds as to which—the left or the right—was more important and has had a more lasting influence on American politics. Often, out of a class of thirty, as many as one-third will say the right. I require my students to write reviews of two works, *The Conscience of a Conservative*, by Barry Goldwater, and *Profiles in Courage*, by John F. Kennedy. Many will write, "You know, Goldwater makes a lot of sense."

I take teaching seriously and expect the same from my students. I do not allow laptops or iPhones except for disadvantaged students. The students seem to appreciate my old-fashioned lectures. My student ratings usually run plus 4 on a scale of 5. I frequently receive emails from former students asking for a letter of recommendation or bringing me up to date on what they are doing. I believe I would have been hired if I had applied to a college outside Washington, but D.C. is my home and I did not want to leave it. Neither did Anne.

A CONSERVATIVE MIND

I was trying to emulate an intellectual hero of mine, the historian Russell Kirk, who successfully mixed lecturing, writing, and teaching for years. I first met Russell in the early 1960s and featured his pro-Goldwater newspaper columns in the Goldwater campaign. I did not learn until later that he had ghostwritten two speeches for the senator, including one at Notre Dame on the importance of faith as well as reason in politics.

I still recall the 1964 rally for Goldwater in Madison Square Garden when I saw Russell in his customary vested suit and YAF cofounder Annette Courtemanche in a bright orange dress walking hand in hand toward me—she was radiant, he was grinning proudly.

"Why are you beaming so?" I asked.

"Oh, Lee," she replied, smiling, "I'm getting married!"

"To whom?" I asked.

"To Russell," she said, and my jaw dropped.

He was forty-five, she was twenty years younger, but it was a marriage of heart, mind, and soul. Russell converted to Catholicism before their wedding day, although he had been thinking of going over to Rome for some time. Russell and I would meet and talk at Philadelphia Society meetings and at the Heritage Foundation, where over the years he delivered more lectures—over forty—than any other outside speaker. He spoke quickly, too quickly in fact, and tended to mumble as graduates of Oxford and St. Andrews are prone to do. But he filled the Lehrman Auditorium at Heritage almost every time, always attracting young conservatives.

In private conversation, he was happy to talk about almost anything but politics. One evening, during the Reagan years, Anne and I and our younger daughter, Catherine, had dinner with Russell and Annette and one of their daughters in a downtown Washington restaurant. Russell sat next to twelve-year-old Catherine, who was clearly uninterested in the political gossip that Anne and I and Annette were sharing. Russell leaned over and said to Catherine, "Do you believe in ghosts?"

"Well, I'm not sure, maybe the Holy Ghost."

"Well, I do," Russell said, and began telling Catherine a story about the ghosts that haunted the old Victorian house in Mecosta, Michigan, in which he had spent summers as a child and where the Kirks now lived. Catherine was entranced and ever afterward remembered how Russell Kirk, one of the most famous intellectuals in America, had made her a part of the evening.

In his last book, *The Sword of Imagination*, published in 1994, Russell, who had received honors and achieved fame (although not fortune) beyond the reach of most men, asked a fundamental question: "Is life worth living?" He suggested that in our moorless age, many would shrug or shake their heads no. Contrary to this modern atmosphere of moral ambiguity, he offered an alternative, writing that life "ought to be lived with honor, charity, and prudence."

Looking back over his life at the age of seventy-five (he would pass away that year), Russell saw that he had sought three ends: to conserve "a patrimony of order, justice, and freedom" and a respectable moral order; to lead "a life of decent independence," necessary for kindling a rigorous mind and making his voice heard; and "to marry for love" and rear children who "would come to know that the service of God is perfect freedom."

By the grace of God and his own talents, Russell Kirk achieved all three goals and provided a raison d'être for those who reject the modern existential arguments that life is without meaning and who joyfully honor the permanent things.

BALANCING AND DOWNSIZING

The first half of the 1980s were some of the busiest years in my life as I sought to balance the demands of my graduate studies and my public affairs firm, whose only full-time employee now was me. Anne acted as my secretary and associate, typing letters, talking to clients, helping me to meet deadlines. We were always perilously close to operating in the red, and I never felt we could afford to pay her, not even a minimum wage. Anne never complained. Looking back, I am appalled at how I took her many essential contributions for granted.

When necessary, we would hire someone to do a particular job, like producing radio spots for the Republican National Committee or handling the details of the 1983 Freedom Conference in Rome, the first-ever gathering of free-market think tanks from Europe, Latin America, and Asia. The official host of the Rome Conference was the nonprofit Center for International Relations (CIR), a new nonprofit organization I created at the suggestion of Heritage Foundation president Ed Feulner. Ed argued that liberals had been applying for and receiving most of the government grants for ages. It was time for conservatives to receive a fair share. Heritage had a strict policy of no government funds or contracts, but a new organization like CIR could operate without such restrictions.

Reagan's United States Information Agency approved CIR's proposal for a 1983 Rome meeting as well as subsequent free-market conferences in Costa Rica, Washington, Guatemala City, and Bangkok. Emerging from these meetings was an informal international network of think tanks and individuals committed to fostering free enterprise and free societies. We had a knack for spotting winners: a participant at our first conference in Rome was the then unknown but future award-winning Peruvian economist Hernando de Soto.

VOICE OF AMERICA

Most of my income worries would have been solved if I had been selected to fill the one Reagan administration job I wanted and for which I believed I was particularly qualified—director of the Voice of America (VOA). I had extensive journalistic experience beginning with my days as a copy boy at the *Washington Times-Herald* and editor of two magazines (three, if you include the *Duke Peer*). I had been a frequent guest on VOA programs as a spokesman for the American Council for World Freedom and the National Captive Nations Committee. Whenever they wanted a strong anticommunist voice, they knew where to go. In the 1950s and 1960s, when the Cold War was at its hottest, VOA had been a key part of U.S. diplomacy, but under Nixon and Carter, VOA was told to lower its voice and follow the party line on détente. I was confident that under President Reagan, VOA would once again speak out forcefully for freedom and against communism. Who better to head up Reagan's VOA than his biographer and a recognized expert on communism working toward a PhD in world politics?

I filled out the usual multipage forms for the White House Personnel Office and asked friends on Capitol Hill like Paul Laxalt and Strom Thurmond, administration officials like Richard V. Allen (Reagan's national security adviser), and Reagan supporters like Bill Buckley to write in support of my selection as VOA director. Weeks went by, and I was told, by Reagan transition insider Neal Freeman, as I recall, that I was on the short list. More time passed, and at last the word came—the new director was Ken Tomlinson, a senior editor of *Reader's Digest*, a well-qualified journalist and a solid conservative, but not my equal in service in the conservative movement or my support of Reagan going back to his 1966 campaign for California governor. Ironically, as editor of the *New Guard*, I had published an article by Ken when he was an undergraduate at Randolph-Macon College.

I suspect that a major reason for my being passed over was that I had registered twice as a "foreign agent"—once for the World Anti-Communist League when we placed full-page advertisements in the *New York Times* and the *Washington Post*, reprinting the final communiqué of the league's annual meeting, and once for the Republic of Argentina, for which Lee Edwards & Associates placed a series of institutional ads in opinion journals like the *New Republic* and *National Review*, extolling the cultural and economic attractions of a "new" Argentina.

I never lobbied anyone in Congress or the executive branch. The World Anti-Communist League ads, while well-intentioned, were wordy and predictable. The Argentina ads contained anodyne language about Argentina's participation in the World Cup and its improving economy. Nevertheless, because Lee Edwards & Associates was the recipient of funds from a foreign source, I was required to register with the Department of Justice as a "foreign agent." The total cost of the newspaper and magazine advertising was less than $100,000, of which we received the usual 15 percent. So much for the myth of the million-dollar foreign agent.

I did not have time to brood because I was busy with new clients as a result of my Reagan biography and my longtime connection with the new president. I did not seek them out—they came to me. The new associate director of communications at the Republican National Committee (RNC) was Mark Tapscott, whom I had brought to Washington from Dallas in 1975 to be the associate editor of *Conservative Digest*. Mark had always been at the cutting edge of communications, and he persuaded the RNC, for the first time, to produce and distribute a series of radio commercials about the Reagan Republican Party, including the first ever Spanish-language spots. Mark asked me whether I would be interested in writing the copy and overseeing production. I said, "Yes, as long as I don't have to write in Spanish."

At the time, in the early 1980s, there were three major Hispanic groups—the Puerto Ricans in New York City, the Cubans in Miami, and the Mexicans in Southern California and along the Texas-Mexico border. I altered the copy slightly for the Cubans, inserting some anti-Castro language, but stuck with a limited government, free-market theme, consistent with Reagan's philosophy. I knew that the Spanish accent varied from group to group, and we hired an announcer who could imitate a Mexican, Cuban, or Puerto Rican accent. Anne drew up a chart of selected Spanish-language radio stations in the three areas, indicated which tape should go to which station, and gave them to the RNC for mailing.

We were satisfied we had done a good job at something new for us as well as for the RNC. And then—disaster. Within twenty-four hours, the committee was bombarded with telephone complaints. The mailing house had not followed our careful instructions but had mailed the wrong tapes to the stations, with Puerto Rican stations getting the Cuban tape, Cuban stations the Mexican tape, and Mexican stations the Puerto Rican tape. We immediately reproduced the spots and personally talked to the mailing house to ensure the right delivery. There were apologies all around. The mailing house did not charge for its error. Mark Tapscott was not fired. To my surprise, the RNC continued to use our services. The lesson: in any new project, do not assume anything—check every step of the process.

In the middle of this hullabaloo, I received a call from Dr. LeRoy Pesch, the son-in-law of W. Clement Stone, the master insurance sales-man who had become a billionaire by practicing PMA (a Positive Mental Attitude) and instilling it in his employees. Stone's daily morning mantra while standing in front of the mirror in his bathroom was: "I feel healthy! I feel happy! I feel terrific!" Pesch had seen my Reagan book and wanted to talk to me about two things: a possible biography of W. Clement Stone and a health-care organization he was launching—Health Resources Corporation of America (HRCA).

This was the beginning of an eighteen-month relationship that included a generous monthly fee of $6,000; the title of vice president for communications for the membership arm of the corporation, the Ameri-can Self-Health Association (ASHA), a name I suggested; a taste of the gilded life of the rich that included chauffeured limousines, company air-planes, and a guest bedroom in the Pesch mansion outside Chicago that was as large as Anne's and my living room; skyscraper offices in Chicago's Loop; and a six-hour interview with the seventy-nine-year-old Stone in his book-lined study.

Working with the creative commercial artist Don Sparkman, who had designed most of the brochures and newsletters for Lee Edwards & Associates, we produced a logo, letterhead, and bronze plaque for the Washington, D.C., office building on 16th Street, NW, that ASHA leased. I wrote a brochure for ASHA on the theme of "wellness," a new concept at the time, and rewrote the HRCA brochure. I edited a monthly newsletter, prepared an ASHA membership letter for a direct-mail campaign in Houston, and edited a four-hundred-page handbook filled with suggestions and success stories on how to become successful and stay healthy. For the handbook, I borrowed liberally from the large PMA literature, which stretched back to the 1930s and Napoleon Hill's classic *Think and Grow Rich*. I persuaded the syndicated columnist Nick Thimmesch to write a column about ASHA and its plans to revolution-ize health care in America by putting the individual in charge of his own health, a familiar theme today but revolutionary thirty years ago.

"One of the more interesting and respected wellness groups," Thim-mesch wrote, "is the American Self-Health Association, whose members pay $35 a year for a continuing flow of information about rules of healthy living, a detailed personal health profile, and use of a Self-Health toll-free number to call with questions about self-health problems." We're not for everybody, LeRoy Pesch told Thimmesch. "Nor are we an alternative to the medical system. We just feel it is better to enjoy the 99 percent of life you spend outside of hospitals or away from doctors than to focus on illness."

We used the ASHA fee to pay Lee Edwards & Associates' bills, which seemed to keep mounting, although we were careful to keep expenses, especially my salary, down. Our bookkeeper, Don Goodyear, reassured me we were in a good cash-flow situation and were just expe-riencing the normal ups and down of a small business. Although excited to be involved in a new concept of health care consistent with conserva-tive principles, I began to chafe under the layer of corporate rules. I had turned down offers from DuPont and ITT and had never regretted my decision. Had I made the right decision signing on with Pesch?

Furthermore, HRCA seemed to conduct its business in an unbusi-nesslike manner. It had offices in Chicago, Washington, and Houston, but there was haphazard communication between them. My memos went unanswered. Telephone calls were not returned. When LeRoy Pesch came to Washington, there was a great flurry of activity, topped by expen-sive dinners at which Roy would describe a new world of health care in the making, founded on the network of hospitals that HRCA planned to purchase and the million-plus members of ASHA. It all seemed possible when you were in Roy's presence. His voice was magnetic, his presence commanding. Like his father-in-law, he was a master salesman, but once he had departed, direction ceased and communications slowed to a trickle. I had no budget and no staff.

A highlight of my Pesch adventure was a trip to Houston, where W. Clement Stone purchased one of the most profitable private hospitals in the city and the nation—Houston Northwest Medical Center. The reception celebrating the new ownership was attended by several hundred of Houston's most important citizens, including city officials, doctors, lawyers, realtors, entrepreneurs, and insurance salesmen eager to meet and greet the Master of PMA.

W. Clement was not impressive physically, standing perhaps five foot five inches and resembling, with his wide bottom and narrow shoulders, a large penguin with colorful suspenders and spats. He had thinning hair dyed jet black and a pencil-thin mustache that Hercule Poirot would have dismissed with a flick of the fingers. But Stone more than made up for his unprepossessing stature with a stentorian voice that seized you and would not let go.

After being introduced fulsomely by LeRoy Pesch, Stone stood silently before the microphone, looking out at the expectant audience. At last he spoke, the words exploding out of his mouth: "I feel healthy! I feel happy! I feel ter-r-r-ific!"

There were startled looks throughout the audience.

Stone repeated the words: "I feel healthy! I feel happy! I feel terrific! Come on, everybody, repeat after me. I say them every day first thing in the morning in front of my mirror." His voice filled the large meeting room: "I feel healthy! I feel happy! I feel terrific!"

Slowly, hesitantly, a few people, then a few more, then a couple of rows, until finally the entire audience of Houston's finest was united in a ringing chorus of "I feel healthy! I feel happy! I feel terrific!" I found myself joining in. I have never been part of a healthier, happier, more terrific crowd, now caught up in a rush of laughing and hugging and applauding the little man with a big voice who had transformed them with nine words.

Not long after, on a Sunday afternoon in his Winnetka home, I had my six-hour interview with Stone. It would be, I thought, the first of many I would conduct while writing his biography. It was very near a monologue, filled with homely axioms (some would call them clichés) he had honed over the years:

- All I want to do is change the world.
- Give hope (the magic ingredient for success)—you will have hope and be made hopeful.
- Have the courage to say no. Have the courage to face the truth. Do the right thing because it is right. These are the magic keys to living your life with integrity.
- Regardless of what you are or what you have been, you can still become what you want to be.
- Strive to understand and apply the Golden Rule.
- Do it now!

Along the way, we talked briefly about Richard Nixon, whose 1968 and 1972 presidential campaigns Stone had generously supported, perhaps with as much as $10 million. He said he admired Nixon for overcoming his narrow loss to John F. Kennedy in 1960 and his much larger loss to Pat Brown for the governorship of California in 1962. Always seeking to be positive, he called the Watergate scandal a "wonderful thing," explaining: "Because of Watergate, attorney generals and states attorneys now will press charges against public officials, if they're warranted. Before President Nixon, they'd sweep those charges under the rug."

In later years, Stone publicly repeated his belief that Watergate had been a wonderful thing. An insight into Nixon's character can be gained from his attendance at a 1980 ceremony honoring Stone, when he said, with a smile, "Nobody gave me more and asked less than W. Clement Stone."

Following the interview, which left me but not the near-octogenarian Stone drained, I wrote him suggesting that (1) we collaborate on a new self-help book, revising and updating his 1962 bestseller, *The Success System That Never Fails*; (2) I begin his biography, incorporating the research and interviews we would do for the self-help book; and (3) I continue working on the *Reader's Digest* profile I had already begun.

As I accumulated material and conducted interviews with family members and associates, I noticed that Stone's enthusiasm about the biography waxed and waned. I had difficulty scheduling another interview and in fact never had another. Finally, one day I shared my frustration with his only daughter, Donna Pesch. Had I done something wrong? Had her father changed his mind? Did he want someone else to write his story?

"Well," Donna responded, "there is something we should have told you at the beginning."

"Which is?"

"My father is convinced that as soon as someone publishes his life story, he will die."

In fact, W. Clement Stone nearly lived forever, passing away in 2002 at the age of one hundred. Donna's belated revelation caused me to set aside the Stone book and focus on the communications needs of HRCA and the ASHA. Still feeling like an outsider, I soldiered on through 1982; the year was capped by a lavish Christmas party at the Pesch home. With eyes and hopes centered on him, Roy smoothly delivered an inspirational message about the future in which he singled out several people, including me, as those who had made special contributions. The words of praise and the eggnog elevated my mood, and I returned to Washington filled with good resolutions about HRCA and ASHA.

Two weeks later, I was ordered to go to the Chicago office. I was kept waiting for an hour and a half before meeting with the corporation's hatchet man, who told me that I had been terminated—after saying he never knew what I was doing for HRCA—and that a limousine was waiting to take me to the airport and out of their lives. I was shocked at being treated so rudely but relieved, despite the loss of the monthly fee.

I took stock on the plane ride home. A corporate life was not for me. The dismissal was another sign that I should shut down my office as soon as possible. I was about halfway through the PhD process at Catholic University and doing well. Henceforth, wherever I was, I resolved to stick to what I was good at—political writing and policy analysis.

I later learned that the parent corporation had been less than forthcoming. It seemed that a cash-poor HRCA had expected ASHA to generate big bucks quickly, signing up hundreds of thousands of members in the first year—a totally unrealistic objective. Such a scenario would have required mailing to many millions of prospective members. Who would have paid for the production, postage, and other costs of the mailings? HRCA, I learned, was close to broke and expected ASHA to bail it out. We thought HRCA would advance the necessary money. We were in a classic catch-22 situation.

What happened to LeRoy Pesch and his dream of a health-care empire was not surprising. With backing from his father-in-law, he bought three hospitals and in 1984 merged with one of the largest public hospital chains in America, Republic Health Corporation. The following year he urged Republic to go private through a leveraged buyout; with the backing of several junk bond companies, the buyout took place. But within two years, according to the *New York Times*, a company that had been turning a $22 million profit lost $293 million. LeRoy Pesch was removed as Republic's chairman and his personal $31 million investment disappeared. The master salesman with a revolutionary idea in health care proved to be a dysfunctional CEO, beyond even the power of PMA.

With Heritage Foundation president Ed Feulner

29

DEFALCATION

Despite my resolution to leave the PR business, by the spring of 1984, I had not yet closed the door of our small office. We were still servicing clients like the National Right to Work Legal Defense Foundation, the Republican National Committee, and the Center for International Relations. We needed the income to pay the mortgage and other bills at home, and I still enjoyed helping conservatives achieve their goals. We might have continued in that manner for another year or two until I earned my PhD from Catholic University. But God had other plans. (Much of the following narrative is taken from Anne's notes and correspondence with banks, lawyers, police, and the FBI.)

Donald Goodyear came to Lee Edwards & Associates in 1979 in response to our ad for a part-time bookkeeper. He described himself as an accountant retired from the GAO (then the General Accounting Office, now the Government Accountability Office), and he offered good letters of recommendation (which subsequently disappeared). He seemed to have other clients, and we assumed he was getting a GAO pension. He was very supportive of our operation even during the period when we trimmed our staff and moved into smaller offices but still used his services.

In 1981, we began to see some financial improvement. Don flattered me by waxing eloquent about my "amazing ability" to generate income—referring to the fee from Health Resources Corporation of America and the advertising buys for the Republican National Committee and the National Right to Work Legal Defense Foundation. I did not realize that such a cash flow was an irresistible invitation to an embezzler. Don drew up numerous plans and budgets for the day when, he said, we would be operating at a profit. I am pretty good at numbers but am easily bored by spreadsheets and financial statements. I was happy to let Don handle the financial planning—and the deposits.

About this time, he borrowed $4,200 from us to upgrade his computer accounting business, which he conducted in our office rent-free. We charged him no interest in exchange for 25 percent of his business. I do not recall that we ever received a single payment from him. But we were pleased to help someone whom we thought of as a member of the team.

Balding and in his late forties, Don looked like a down-at-the-heel Mel Tormé. He usually wore old jeans and sweaters (with holes in them) and dirty sneakers to work. He often rode his bike, which he would take up on the elevator and park outside our office. Anne said that he would wear a shirt and tie when I was in the office but would revert to his old ways when I was out or he didn't have an appointment with a client.

Anne spent a great deal of time with Don, who talked a lot and repeated over and over stories about the GAO, his ex-wife, and his four children (especially Judy, who had many health problems). In every story, he was the steady, long-suffering, blameless guy. We later heard a much different story from Judy and others.

He never seemed to take offense, even when I came down hard on him for not giving me the figures I needed to track our ad buys with radio stations and in public opinion journals. He would eventually produce what I wanted with promises that he would be more punctual. He always had excuses—a broken collarbone, emergencies involving Judy that inevitably occurred on weekends, tax work for his other clients, and multiple computer problems.

The tardiness with figures became more and more prevalent in the last part of 1983 and the first part of 1984. There were other signs we failed to recognize. He always grabbed the phone before Anne could. He was very nervous about the mail and would not go out of the office until it arrived—and he made sure he saw it first. Early in 1984 we decided to move into a smaller office and to do without Don. Anne informed him that she planned to take over the bookkeeping and asked him to get the books in order for her. He responded that it would take some time and he wanted to teach her about using the computer so that she could "just punch in the numbers" each month to get a balance sheet. Smooth and easy, he said. "Just as soon as tax season is over we'll work on the changeover."

A few days before Easter Sunday, Anne and I and our two girls, Elizabeth and Catherine, drove to Scranton to visit Anne's relatives. Before leaving, Don asked me to sign forms and checks for the federal income taxes and the D.C. taxes due. I looked over the figures he had prepared and they looked okay, so I signed the forms and the checks. We subsequently learned that he never mailed them. When we left, Anne noticed that Don's computer was missing but thought he was having it serviced after a busy tax season.

On Monday, April 23, 1984, Anne and I returned to Washington after our brief holiday and went to the office, where to our surprise there was no sign of Don. Anne thought it strange he did not call in—in the five years he had been with us he usually let us know his plans. On Tuesday, I went to our bank, National Savings and Trust Co. (NS&T), to arrange a $5,000 line of credit to cover some checks that had suddenly started bouncing. We were upset with Don for letting this happen because we were certain there were sufficient funds in our two bank accounts. His daughter Judy called to see if we had heard from Don because her mother was trying to locate him. Anne began to worry that something had happened to him—maybe he was in the hospital.

On Wednesday, Anne called his girlfriend, who said she hadn't heard from him since the previous week. And he didn't answer the telephone number she had. Anne began to worry more about us and less about Don. She had kept the checkbook of the Center for International Relations (CIR) and began going through it and discovered several missing checks with blank stubs. I called the Palmer National Bank, which handled the CIR account, and learned the worst—someone had been cashing checks against the account without our knowledge.

We began going through Don's desk and discovered it was empty—he had taken with him our financial records for the five years that he had been our bookkeeper. Anne called NS&T to let them know about the Palmer Bank fraud and the missing files. We were certain that Don had defrauded us at NS&T as well.

Because it was expensive to obtain copies of bank statements and checks from NS&T, we limited our reconstruction to one year, April 1983–April 1984. The loss to Lee Edwards & Associates during that year was $45,847.54. The loss to the CIR, of which I was president, was $31,000. The stolen monies were not profits but actual operating capital, leaving us with debts in excess of $50,000. Bank charges plus legal and accounting fees ran another $7,000. We do not know how much more Donald Goodyear stole from us in the five years he was our bookkeeper, but his removal of all the financial files for the period suggests it was far more than the $76,847.54 we could document.

I was urged to declare bankruptcy by our accountant, our lawyer, and numerous friends. But I think that a man should pay his debts, even if he is not directly responsible for them. Anne went along with my decision, admiring me but wondering whether it was a matter of principle or of pride. I borrowed $21,000 on my life insurance to pay advertising bills and arranged a payment schedule for other debts.

I deserved to be punished for being so careless, but Anne did not deserve her punishment, primarily although not exclusively psychological. While I sought the new business we urgently needed, she spent six months reconstructing our records and those of CIR. She developed stomach ailments and sleep problems. She handled irate calls from radio stations, magazines, and suppliers who wanted to know when they would receive payment. She protected me while I tried to line up new business to pay old debts. Even so, my blood pressure soared, and I experienced bouts of heart palpitations. On the advice of Dr. James Foster, our GP for many years, I began taking beta blockers (and still do). I wondered whether I had been wrong about not declaring bankruptcy.

I drew up a list of possible jobs for a fifty-two-year-old publicist who may have seen his best years. When everything seemed to be collapsing around us, old friends came through.

I asked Lyn Nofziger, who was directing the communications for the Reagan-Bush reelection campaign, if I could do something for the campaign. After I explained what had happened, he immediately said, "How would you like to edit the Reagan-Bush newsletter?" For the next eight months, I worked one day a week in the Reagan headquarters editing a weekly eight-page newsletter filled with pretty photos, large headlines, and happy stories about the president's approaching landslide victory. My fee was $2,500 a month, generous given the workload.

Lew Uhler, whom I had met while working on my first Reagan biography in the 1960s, retained me as a public relations consultant to the National Tax Limitation Committee at $1,500 a month. Reed Larson, the longtime head of the National Right to Work Committee, arranged for me to be a PR consultant to the National Right to Work Legal Defense Foundation at $1,000 a month. The American Conservative Union paid me $3,000 to handle the PR for CPAC '84. The CIR received grants from the U.S. Information Agency and the National Republican Institute to host free-market conferences in Costa Rica and Thailand. I worked with Ron Guberman of Media Reactions to produce two sixty-second TV spots for the National Rifle Association, starring movie cowboy Slim Pickens of *Dr. Strangelove* fame, who told the dirtiest stories I have ever heard—they would make a Marine blush.

CONSERVATIVE DIGEST, AGAIN

My next call was to Richard Viguerie, who revealed that he had just fired the editor of *Conservative Digest*. Would I be interested in taking up the editorial reins again? I said yes, not quibbling with the fee, and thus became the first and last editor of *Conservative Digest* when Richard was publisher and owner of the magazine.

The articles for the most part were antiestablishment columns by New Right leaders Paul Weyrich, Howard Phillips, Phyllis Schlafly, and Connie Marshner. The New Right still exerted some influence. When *Conservative Digest* celebrated its tenth anniversary in May 1985, we received congratulations from a wide range of conservatives, including President Reagan, White House communications director Pat Buchanan, Congressman Newt Gingrich, Senator Orrin Hatch of Utah, Interior Secretary Don Hodel, Senator Bob Kasten of Wisconsin, former UN ambassador Jeane Kirkpatrick, and Congressman Vin Weber (a member of the Gingrich Gang that produced the Contract with America). Reagan praised the *Digest* for "its clear voice in defense of free enterprise, a strong foreign policy and traditional values." The Reagan message was ironic, given that Richard had won many a headline criticizing Reagan for not being conservative enough.

But *Conservative Digest* no longer had the same impact. Our circulation was a fraction of what it had been back in the mid-1970s. The paper stock was no longer glossy but newsprint. I did my best to make the magazine current and readable, but it was not easy because Richard would get caught up in one of his enthusiasms—Pat Robertson for president!—and would brook few questions and no objections. Richard ended up selling *Conservative Digest* at the end of 1986.

With the help of Lyn, Richard, Lew, Reed, and others, Anne and I survived 1984 and began to think there was life after defalcation, albeit a different life. The D.C. police turned over our case to the FBI, which went looking for Goodyear and found him two years later. In the interim, we learned that he had robbed his sister down in Florida of $40,000, that he owed Nantucket Capital, a division of Gulf and Western in Springfield, Massachusetts, a "sizable" sum, and that he had spent much of his money (that is, *our* money) on visits to massage parlors in Northern Virginia. In July 1986, I wrote to Judge George Neilson of the D.C. Superior Court urging him to put Goodyear in jail where he belonged and where he could not commit future acts "of conning innocent people, stealing when given an opportunity, and feeding an obvious addiction which gives him pleasure at other people's expense."

We will never know what sentence Judge Neilson might have imposed, because Goodyear never showed up for sentencing and has been a fugitive from justice ever since. I have forgiven him, even making jokes about "looking for Mr. Goodyear," but Anne is Italian to the core and has neither forgiven nor forgotten. I can thank Goodyear for one thing: his embezzlement forced me to close permanently the doors (actually just one door) of Lee Edwards & Associates.

ROASTED AND TOASTED

One thing that sustained me during these dark and dreary times was a "roast" banquet organized by Peter Gemma and other friends, who told stories about the $5 luncheons at Freddy's, my brief career as a TV commentator, the *Conservative Digest* cover of John Connally in what looked like a wig, the *Right Report* predicting Ronald Reagan would win the 1976 Republican nomination, and the Reagan biography "complete through the assassination attempt."

I was touched, not least by a message from the White House:

> Recognition for the exceptional talents and achievements of Lee Edwards is both richly deserved and long overdue. Lee has always been more interested in promoting the causes he believes in than tooting his own horn. But he has played some pretty powerful blasts on that bugle of his, and the notes were always clear. No one ever accused him of being an uncertain trumpet.
>
> From the days of Barry Goldwater's 1964 Presidential campaign, Lee Edwards has always been in the forefront of the struggle to restore America, to bring it back to its ancient moorings. Come to think of it, I got my own political start in that Goldwater campaign. I was a supporting extra, saying a few words on television. Lee was in the thick of the battle as Director of Communications.

Since that time our paths have crossed quite a bit. Well, maybe that metaphor isn't quite right, because we were always moving in the same direction. And sometimes I'd spot Lee up ahead. I think he was running interference.

Lee has fought hard with uncommon intelligence and resourcefulness. But he has fought fair and always without rancor. That is why his friends cherish him and even his enemies respect him. Tonight I join with his friends who celebrate him. I salute Lee Edwards, not only a seasoned campaigner but, truly, a man for all seasons.... God bless you and those who honor you.

—Ronald Reagan

FROM CATHOLIC TO GEORGETOWN TO HARVARD

In 1985, things continued to improve professionally. I passed my oral PhD exams at Catholic University and wrote my dissertation, "Congress and the Origins of the Cold War," which won approval from my dissertation committee. I received my doctorate in world politics at the university's 1986 graduation.

In mid-1985 I visited an old friend, David Jones of the Charles Edison Memorial Youth Fund (later the Fund for American Studies), who, it turned out, had a summer job for me. He explained that the fund was thinking of adding a summer program on political journalism in addition to its present program on comparative political and economic systems at Georgetown University. Would I be interested in helping it get started? I loved the combination of teaching, journalism, and Georgetown.

As founding director of the Institute on Political Journalism, I created a curriculum of classes in economics and ethics, lined up internships at some fifty media organizations, including the *New York Times* and *U.S. News & World Report*, and persuaded Washington journalists such as Lou Cannon of the *Washington Post*, Ann Compton of ABC, Larry Barrett of *Time*, Walter Mears of AP, and Judy Woodruff of the *MacNeil-Lehrer NewsHour* to lecture on Wednesday evenings. I lectured once a week on the history of journalism, current trends in print and broadcast, and the qualities of a good journalist but quickly discovered that the journalism school students already knew most of the material. I shifted over to co-teaching the ethics course the following year.

In our first year, we had fifty-five students from fifty-three colleges and universities who, aside from complaints about the un-air-conditioned

Georgetown dorms (and the bugs), were well satisfied with the program. Although they had initially questioned the usefulness of the economics course, most admitted by graduation they were better off for the experience. I put it plainly to them in my first lecture: "You cannot be a political reporter in today's world without a basic understanding of economics." We scheduled site briefings at the White House, NBC News, and ABC News. We had a well-attended Saturday morning career session led by a half dozen journalists. I reported to Dave Jones at the end of summer that the institute had had an immediate impact—one student had accepted a position with the *New York Times* and five others were considering or had accepted jobs with Washington news organizations.

In August 1985, as I was wrapping up the first summer of the Institute on Political Journalism, I got an unexpected telephone call from Jonathan Miller, the director of the Institute of Politics (IOP) at Harvard University's John F. Kennedy School of Government. He invited me to be one of the six IOP fellows for the fall semester. The reason for the belated invitation was unspoken: they needed a token conservative to prove the institute's ideological evenhandedness. I didn't care that I was not the first choice. A semester at Harvard not only would look good on my résumé as I tried to find a teaching job but also would fulfill a long-held dream of attending the oldest and most celebrated school in America.

I headed off to Cambridge with Anne's blessing. As an IOP fellow, I was expected to participate fully in orientation week, lead a student noncredit study group, develop a piece of substantive research, and be an integral part of the IOP's social and collegial events. As compensation, I received a stipend of $2,000 a month for four months plus a housing allowance of $450 a month. The responsibilities were not onerous, the compensation was reasonable. Additional perquisites included membership in the Faculty Club, library and athletic privileges, an office at the IOP, typing assistance, and permission to audit Harvard courses without charge.

I took advantage of all privileges. I lunched at the Faculty Club with Harvey Mansfield, Richard Pipes, Adam Ulam, and Edward Banfield, all intellectual heroes of mine. I attended the classes of Michael Sandel and James Q. Wilson, marveling at Sandel's ability to hold the attention of seven hundred students with his lectures on moral reasoning. I did not miss any of the special IOP luncheons with liberal icons like John Kenneth Galbraith (when I mentioned I knew Bill Buckley, he replied, "Good skier, poor thinker") and Governor Michael Dukakis in his downtown

Boston office, where Kitty Dukakis personally served us ham and cheese sandwiches with chips and Coca-Cola.

I offered a seminar entitled "Reagan and the Conservative Movement: Past, Present, and Future." The class initially attracted well over fifty undergraduates, but to my consternation, half walked out during my talk. I later learned it was Harvard's custom to allow its students to go "shopping" the first week of classes, sitting in and then leaving the classroom if they so chose.

I struck up a friendship with IOP fellow John Wilson, a member and later chairman of the D.C. City Council, as liberal as I was conservative. National Public Radio station WGBH invited John and me to debate weekly the issues of the day. We had fun disagreeing on just about everything but spending, where he was quite conservative. His later death through suicide was a tragedy. Washington would have been a far better place with John Wilson rather than Marion Berry as its mayor.

At an IOP panel in the Kennedy School auditorium, I sketched the history of modern conservatism—from the early days of traditionalists, libertarians, and anticommunists coming together under the leadership of Russell Kirk, Bill Buckley, and Barry Goldwater; the 1964 Goldwater campaign; Nixon and Watergate and the rise of neoconservatism and the New Right and the Christian Right; the election and presidency of Ronald Reagan. I listed important political dates in my life: 1958, my first published article in *National Review*; 1964, when I joined the Goldwater campaign; 1965, when I first interviewed Ronald Reagan; 1975, when I became the founding editor of *Conservative Digest*; 1981, when I went back to school at Catholic University to earn a PhD; and September 9, 1985, when I arrived at Harvard as an IOP fellow and took up residence in Cambridge, the Forbidden City, "once closed but now open to me, your humble, obedient, and conservative servant."

At the end of the fall term, as I prepared reluctantly to leave Cambridge—my offer to stay on through the spring term was gently rejected— I wrote an op-ed revealing "The Truth about Harvard," which appeared in the *Boston Globe*. Here are a few myths about America's oldest and most celebrated university that I exposed.

It is *not* the most liberal university in America, I argued, but stands behind the University of California at Berkeley and the University of Michigan as well as smaller colleges like Haverford and Oberlin. Indeed, in response to the changed political atmosphere in Washington, Harvard had moderated its liberalism. I pointed to the presence of conservatives like Professor Samuel Huntington, director of the school's largest foreign affairs institute, and to the fact that the Harvard Republican Club was the largest student organization on campus, with more than three hundred members.

Harvard does *not* have the most brilliant students in America, I wrote, although I conceded that the great majority are very intelligent. But its intellectual rigor is no more and in some cases less than at other schools. As proof, I pointed out that an estimated 98 percent of its freshman class graduated. Such a percentage is possible only when there is an understanding among administration, faculty, and student body to keep marginal students who would, at some other school, be given their walking papers. More than one student told me, "The most difficult thing about Harvard is getting in."

Harvard is *not* an intellectual utopia, I said, that cares only about ideas and philosophy and *Veritas*. In fact, it is one of the most fiercely entrepreneurial institutions I ever encountered. "Every tub with its own bottom" is the rule, meaning that each school, department, and professor is encouraged and expected to raise the money for a book, a seminar, a conference, a library, a museum. In that sense, Harvard is a libertarian's paradise.

I ended by saying that I enjoyed immensely my stay at Harvard and the IOP, and I looked forward to the many luncheons and dinners at which I would explain what Harvard is really like. I would be watching closely to see whether, in pursuance of *Veritas*, Harvard would allow more conservatives, not just tokens here and there, to lecture and teach in its classrooms.

"Harvard need not fear a significant conservative presence," I wrote, "any more than the Soviet Union need fear the entry of hundreds and thousands of American students, professors, artists, and writers. After all, if you know the truth, you shall be free."

A NEW MAGAZINE

I returned as director of the Institute on Political Journalism in 1986, building on the success of the first year—AP editor Wally Mears described the program as "remarkable for the energy and intensity of the participants." But I left the institute at the end of that second year when I became the senior editor of the *World & I*, a mammoth (seven-hundred-page) monthly magazine published by the conservative *Washington Times*. I stayed with the magazine for more than a decade because my half-week with it allowed me to pursue my writing. As Washingtonians know, the *Times* and its affiliated publications were owned and heavily subsidized by the Reverend Sun Myung Moon and the Unification Church of South Korea. While the majority of the reporters and editors at the newspaper were not "Moonies," I was the only non-Moonie at the *World & I*, aside from the editor in chief, Dr. Morton Kaplan of the University of Chicago.

How I got the position was problematic. When I learned that a new magazine was looking for a senior editor, I expressed interest and was invited to be interviewed at a downtown hotel. I entered a long, narrow bedroom at the end of which two men were seated—a thin, professorial-looking American in an old sports jacket and a young, handsome South Korean who never said a word. Dr. Kaplan asked a series of questions about my interests and qualifications. I showed them my résumé with its list of publications and explained that I kept up with current events and felt I could contribute to the magazine. I was a little vague on details because I had never read the magazine. I was in and out in less than thirty minutes, feeling I had not impressed either Kaplan or the silent Korean sufficiently to get the job.

A week later someone from the magazine called and asked for a recent photo. When I asked why, the answer was "For the file." I looked for but could not locate a good shot of me, so I sent off a photo of me and Pat Buchanan at a recent book event. Two weeks passed and I got another call—I was hired and asked to start the following week.

I later learned that the photo of me and Pat had been sent to Reverend Moon, who prided himself on being able to determine the character and the ability of someone by looking at the person's photo. I always wondered: did Moon think he was hiring me or Pat Buchanan?

As for working for a Moonie publication, I was never told to publish or not to publish a particular author or article, never directed to build up Reverend Moon and the Unification Church or tear down his critics. If asked what it was like to work for someone who thought he was God, I would reply, "Reverend Moon is not the first publisher I've worked for who thinks he's God."

My *World & I* colleagues were not brainwashed or shuffling zombies. They laughed and cried and lost their temper. But for the most part, they exuded a certain calm that was catching. They were professionals who knew how to write and edit and select photos and lay out pages and line up authors to fill seven hundred pages of articles about current affairs, science, the arts, health, books, and every other imaginable subject. Our magazine was the personal favorite of Reverend Moon, who hoped we would be able to replicate similar journals that enjoyed wide circulation in South Korea. But our circulation was never mass because we never had a large enough promotion budget. Our few thousand readers loved us, and libraries did their best to find room for us.

I wrote mostly political articles with an occasional book review. In the February 2001 issue, I said that while a presidential election was usually a referendum on continuity or change, the "American people in 2000 seemed to vote for continuity *and* change." The desire for change frustrated Vice President Al Gore, who should have been able to win the presidency by promising to continue the unquestioned peace and prosperity of the Clinton-Gore years. But Clinton was so unwelcome in the living rooms of many Americans that Gore kept the president at arm's length in the campaign, insisting again and again, "I am my own man."

The desire for continuity hampered Governor George W. Bush, who promised to solve the problems that Clinton-Gore had not addressed while using nonthreatening rhetoric such as "compassionate conservatism." He was unable to use the character issue as much as he had planned after Gore decoupled himself from Clinton at the Democratic Convention.

The ambivalent mood of the electorate produced the closest presidential contest since 1960, when Kennedy defeated Nixon by two-tenths of 1 percent of the popular vote—the same margin by which Gore topped Bush. But Kennedy handily won the electoral vote, while Bush narrowly won the electoral vote, and the presidency, with 271 votes, one more than needed.

And yet, depending on your yardstick, the election was not that close. Bush carried twenty-nine of fifty states and more than three-fourths of the counties. On the other hand, Gore carried two-thirds of the largest cities and by as much as a three-to-one margin. The suburbs split evenly between the candidates, but Bush carried smaller towns and rural areas with 60 percent of the vote.

Truly, the nation was divided, politically, culturally, racially. And yet most Americans did not worry needlessly about the outcome. They knew there would be no military coup, no UN peacekeeping force, no new election. They knew there would be a winner, a transition, and an inauguration, and they were encouraged by the spirit of bipartisanship that seemed to emerge in Washington, led by the man who had offered himself as a unifier and not a divider during the campaign.

This was the first few months of 2001—before 9/11, before Osama bin Laden haunted our TV screens, before wars in Afghanistan and Iraq, before the Great Recession.

RED SQUARE

Although anticommunist to his core, Reverend Moon believed in academic, journalistic, and other exchanges between the East and the West and underwrote the work of the World Media Association, which in November 1988 invited me as a *World & I* editor to join a delegation of journalists who would spend ten days in the Soviet Union. It would be my first and only visit to the birthplace of the Bolshevik Revolution. On the flight over, I joined skeptics like Richard Grenier, Georgie Anne Geyer, and Steve Pejovich in pledging that we would not be taken in by Soviet propagandists and would seek the truth about the impact of glasnost and perestroika on our Cold War adversary.

It did not take us long to discover that while the Soviet Union was no longer Stalinist, it was still socialist.

We listened to Communist Party members routinely vilify Stalin and Brezhnev. We read articles in the *Moscow News* about the role of "market forces" in the Soviet economy. We roamed freely through the streets of Leningrad, Kiev, and Moscow, unaccompanied by Intourist guides or secret police. We were waved through customs at the Soviet-Finnish border. The proof of a more open Soviet society seemed to be all around us. I recalled what the KGB colonel Gennadiy Domakhin had said to me about Gorbachev: "He's different."

Several of us were invited to visit the unofficial Independent University in Moscow to hear a government-sanctioned talk by José Sorzano, former deputy U.S. ambassador to the United Nations under anticommunist extraordinaire Jeane Kirkpatrick. Sorzano's appearance was all the more remarkable because he was a Cuban exile who had never concealed his anti-Castro animus.

Even glasnost, however, had its limits. When Sergei Grigoryants, the Armenian dissident who had spent twelve years in the Gulag for "anti-Soviet" behavior, tried to introduce Sorzano, the local Communist Party secretary stopped him. The apparatchik, accompanied by a large but unarmed lieutenant colonel in the militia, declared there could be no meeting because no written permission had been obtained. University representatives protested they had received a verbal go-ahead, but the party official insisted he needed something on paper. Another dissident with a shoulder-held camera videotaped the heated debate.

At last, Grigoryants, who had not said a word, approached the party official. Might he ask a question? he said quietly. The communist nodded. Did the comrade think that General Secretary Gorbachev, who was traveling to New York City the following week, would like to see on American television a videotape of a distinguished U.S. diplomat being denied the opportunity to speak in Moscow, just before he met with President Reagan and President-elect Bush? The party secretary's face fell. Did the comrade think, continued Grigoryants, that such a denial was the image of glasnost that General Secretary Gorbachev was seeking to present to the world, especially in the United States? The party official hesitated and then, looking as though he had tasted something sour, replied that since verbal permission had been given, there was no deliberate violation, and the lecture could proceed.

José Sorzano told a spellbound group of some seventy intellectuals and students, ranging in age from their early twenties to their mid-fifties, about Cuba's limping economy and at the same time its material support of the Sandinistas in Nicaragua, made possible by Soviet aid of $5 billion to $7 billion a year. From the incredulous looks exchanged and the repeated inquiries during the question-and-answer period, I realized that it was the first time that the full extent of Soviet aid to Communist Cuba and Marxist Nicaragua had been detailed in the Soviet Union.

Despite glasnost, the Soviet Union was far from an open society. At a meeting with Leningrad journalists, we asked whether they had reported the recent U.S. news conference of Andrei Sakharov, who criticized some six areas in which glasnost was not progressing fast enough, including public meetings. After some hesitation, a gray-haired veteran communist said, "We are not familiar with this speech." I was disappointed at such an obvious lie: if there was one person whom the Soviet press kept track of, it was Sakharov.

If glasnost was exciting the Soviet intelligentsia, perestroika was depressing most of the Russian people. It was being judged at the dinner table, and after three and a half years, the people were not eating as well under Gorbachev as they had under Brezhnev. There were serious shortages in staples, not luxuries, like meat, coffee, and sugar. I saw a long line in Leningrad outside a candy store and asked why. There had been a sugar shortage for many months, I was told, because people were hoarding it to make bootleg liquor, their response to Gorbachev's anti-alcoholism campaign. The government was finally forced to reopen the liquor stores, and sugar again became available for candy.

I saw other signs of economic dislocation. The black market was as ubiquitous as the KGB used to be. We were warned by our guide not to do business with anyone who came up to us on the street—the police had been known to arrest tourists for trading in the black market. But we would no sooner step off our yellow Intourist bus than we would be approached by polite, well-dressed young men in their early twenties who offered to sell us lacquer boxes, caviar, and wood dolls, but most of all rubles for our dollars.

Once, standing in the middle of Red Square, with the Kremlin on one side, Saint Basil's Cathedral on another, and the GUM department store on yet another, I was approached by a smiling young man wearing a stylish Western overcoat and a Burberry scarf. "Would you like to exchange dollars for rubles?" he asked in excellent English. "I can offer an excellent rate—five rubles for one dollar." (The official rate was one ruble for $1.60.) I looked around—no one was within twenty yards. The Lenin Tomb with its guards was across the square. Was it a trap? Would a KGB agent appear out of nowhere and arrest me? Flashing a thick wad of rubles, the young Russian said, "One hundred rubles for a Jackson— it's a good deal." I took a $20 bill from my wallet, and we transacted our business without incident.

Such unrestrained street-corner commerce suggested that the need for hard currency, particularly U.S. dollars, was so urgent that Gorbachev was encouraging the black market, knowing that both the dollars and the rubles would wind up in the government's hands, it being illegal to take rubles into or out of the country.

Paradoxes abounded in Gorbachev's "new" Soviet Union. Modern airplanes took off and landed in blinding snowstorms, but modern hotel elevators often broke down. Newspapers, magazines, and TV channels poured forth a river of misinformation, disinformation, and noninformation. According to the Soviet media, Sakharov never held a U.S. news conference about glasnost, and José Sorzano never lectured about Cuba and Nicaragua in Moscow. Russians glorified the past, spending millions of rubles on refurbishing the glorious gold-leafed palaces of Peter the Great and Catherine II, but refused to learn from it. After seventy years of socialist economic failures, they were not yet persuaded that socialism did not work. Citizens were encouraged to start cooperatives—there were an estimated thirty thousand private ventures in the first two years—but the state abruptly announced there could be no privately produced books or posters, sale of icons, brewing of beer, cutting of diamonds, or videos. In November 1988, it was still illegal for a Muscovite to walk in off the street and photocopy a document. My hotel room had a telephone but no telephone directory.

At the GUM department store, I saw desperate shoppers roam the aisles like hungry wolves. Dozens of women lined up to buy boots; if they did not fit, they exchanged pairs with one another on the sidewalk out-side the store. In a computer world, shops used abacuses to total up what was owed. A nation with rich fertile land and almost endless natural resources imported wheat to feed its people.

Even after a visit of just ten days, you could see that the Soviet Union was breaking down; the KGB was no longer feared; the black market was rampant and attracting more marketers every day; glasnost and per-estroika were not strengthening socialism but weakening it; dissidents were growing ever bolder and more outspoken; and Gorbachev's attempt to "Westernize" a country that had never experienced the Renaissance, the Reformation, or the Industrial Revolution was doomed to fail.

FAREWELL TO THE *WORLD & I*

As we entered the year 2000, I sensed a growing concern among my *World & I* colleagues as to whether the church and Reverend Moon, now in his eighties, would be able to justify indefinitely our heavy subsidiza-tion. I had been dividing my time almost equally between the magazine and the Heritage Foundation since 1996, when Hugh Newton, the foun-dation's senior public relations counselor, invited me to write a history of Heritage. That assignment resulted in *The Power of Ideas: The Heritage Foundation at Twenty-Five Years*.

I pushed hard to become a full-time Heritage employee, and so it came to be in January 2002, beginning the most productive years of my life. My status as a Senior Fellow and then Distinguished Fellow in Con-servative Thought in the B. Kenneth Simon Center for American Stud-ies owed in large measure to the center's brilliant director, Dr. Matthew Spalding, now associate vice president and dean of educational programs at Hillsdale College. I like to think that the fact that Matthew is my son-in-law did not unduly influence him.

30

MISSIONARIES
FOR FREEDOM

My semester at Harvard in the fall of 1985 had proved pivotal for me. Harvard taught me that I could contribute in an academic atmosphere, that I could hold my own among professional intellectuals, that teachers with a conservative point of view were needed in the American academy.

I also noted the dearth of books about American conservatism, either from the left or the right. Emboldened by my Harvard experience, I decided I would try to change that. Borrowing from Churchill, I explained to friends and associates, "I know what history is going to say about the conservative movement, because I am going to write it."

I began my experiment in historiography by writing Dr. Walter Judd's biography. It was the first of more than twenty books about the modern American conservative movement.

"A MARVELOUS MAN"

I had worked with Walter Judd as secretary of the Committee of One Million (Against the Admission of Communist China to the United Nations) and its successor, the Committee for a Free China. I learned of his encyclopedic knowledge of foreign affairs. I discovered that he was not so much a twentieth-century conservative as an eighteenth-century

With Dr. and Mrs. Walter Judd on Dr. Judd's eightieth birthday

liberal, a disciple of Thomas Jefferson, whom he loved to quote. Dr. Judd believed in limited government, individual liberty, and the duty of government to help those who could not help themselves. Although a medical missionary in China for 10 years, he never flaunted his faith, preferring, as his New England mother had taught him, to let his deeds speak for his commitment to God and the Gospel. He was an American original with roots that went back 350 years to the freedom-seeking Pilgrims.

It seemed as though he had known every American leader of his time: presidents from Franklin D. Roosevelt to Ronald Reagan; secretaries of state from Dean Acheson to Henry Kissinger; politicians from Arthur Vandenberg to Barry Goldwater; generals from George Marshall to William Westmoreland. He knew foreign leaders like Chiang Kai-shek, Jawaharlal Nehru, and the Dalai Lama. During his twenty years in Congress, he had written or cosponsored historic legislation regarding the United Nations, the World Health Organization, the Voice of America, technical assistance to underdeveloped nations, and the removal of all racial discrimination clauses from U.S. immigration laws, the first civil rights law in eighty years.

After leaving Congress in 1963, he broadcast a daily radio commentary to more than a thousand stations at its peak; contributed to *Reader's Digest*, which had the largest circulation of any magazine in America; and lectured constantly to citizens' groups and at colleges, reminding students of their obligation to protect and pass on America's freedoms as preceding generations had done for them.

I joined with others in urging Dr. Judd to write his autobiography. We said he had a duty to tell his spellbinding stories about his year of house arrest under the Japanese, facing death at the hands of Chinese bandits, and his lifelong battle against skin cancer. He must, we said, record his reflections on how and why the United States emerged from its isolationist cocoon to become the leader of the free world in the post–World War II period. What advice could he, who knew Asia so well, offer America as we entered what many called the Pacific Century? Was the Cold War over? Could we now live in peace and harmony with the communist regimes of China, Cuba, Vietnam, Laos, and North Korea?

We gave him a thousand reasons to write his autobiography, and the answer was always the same: he had too much to do. Besides, he wasn't a writer—he agonized over every word that he wrote. The years went by. Finally, after my return from Harvard, I said, with some exasperation, that he was not getting any younger (he was then an amazingly youthful eighty-seven) and if he wouldn't write his life story, I would. To my delight, he agreed to work with me on an authorized biography, not, he emphasized, to perpetuate his name and his memory but to bring about a better understanding of the leaders and historic events with which he had been associated.

It was not an easy book to write. There was a Matterhorn of material, a researcher's dream and nightmare. The Hoover Archives at Stanford University held 313 boxes of Judd's correspondence, notes, speeches, clippings, pamphlets, audiotapes, and films. There were another fifty-plus boxes at the Minnesota Historical Society, which housed the Judd papers on local and state affairs. (Anne traveled to Minneapolis and spent a week there going through the papers.) And his home had filing cabinets overflowing with papers, letters, receipts, bills, and old diaries. Apparently, Walter Judd had never thrown anything away—I found lecture notes dating back to the early 1920s, when he was traveling around the country for the Student Volunteer Movement, urging young Congregationalists and other Protestants to become missionaries in Africa and Asia.

There was also the problem of Dr. Judd, the perfectionist, who said he wanted to read the manuscript before it went to the publisher to make certain there were no "errors." It was, after all, an authorized biography. For three straight days, an average of eight hours a day, we went over the manuscript page by page, line by line. Most of his corrections were reasonable, but he would not be hurried, insisting on reading every word. On the second day, my impatience flared up, and I said with some heat, "Is all this really necessary? We're very close to our publishing deadline." Dr. Judd replied emphatically, "It may be your book, but it's *my* life." I made no further objections.

At Dr. Judd's direction, I left out many details of his personal life: his musical performances as a student on the Chautauqua circuit; homely letters to his wife as a new member of Congress; acts of kindness and generosity to neighbors and friends. We agreed that I should concentrate on the public life of a public man who helped shape U.S. foreign policy in the twentieth century.

That was the story I told in *Missionary for Freedom: The Life and Times of Walter Judd*. It was the story of a man who understood, far better than most, the nature of the communist adversary confronting us. He made a difference in Congress because he was willing to work harder and longer than anyone else—he was always prepared for the debate of the day. He was eloquent, tireless, a perfectionist, who was never satisfied with his own work. He possessed remarkable foresight, predicting the war with Japan, the loss of China to the communists, and conflict in the Korean peninsula. He was not a saint: he liked a gin and tonic or two in the evening (the tonic a carry-over from his fight against malaria, which he contracted in South China). He placed the demands of his missionary work and later the anticommunist cause ahead of everything else, including his family. He had a monumental self-confidence that sustained him when the rest of the world did not accept his apocalyptic predictions about the coming conflict with Japan and the fall of China to Mao Zedong and his "agrarian reformers."

I believe that he inspired and informed more Americans longer—from the early 1920s through the late 1980s—with his speeches, radio broadcasts, TV appearances, and writing than any other public figure. Walter Judd was inspired by the words of Thomas Jefferson carved in giant letters on the corona of his great white marble monument in Washington: "I have sworn upon the altar of God eternal hostility against every form of tyranny over the mind of man."

My Judd book was published in 1990. I was honored when C-SPAN founder Brian Lamb invited me for one of the first *Booknotes* interviews, and when the book earned praise from the likes of Richard Nixon, Bill

Buckley, and Barry Goldwater ("Thanks for having done this marvelous job on a marvelous man").

MR. CONSERVATIVE

The success of the Judd biography convinced me to take up the story of Barry Goldwater, about whom there had been no serious study for nearly thirty years. I poured myself—heart, soul, and mind—into the project.

Adhering to my iceberg philosophy, I conducted 174 interviews, nearly all in person and audiotaped. (Along with my other interviews since 1965, more than 400 in all, they have been digitized and are available through the Hoover Archives at Stanford University, the repository of my papers.) Many of the people whom I interviewed are no longer living, including Senator Goldwater himself; Denison Kitchel, Goldwater's friend and colleague for fifty years; F. Clifton White, more responsible for Goldwater's being nominated than any other single person; Harry Jaffa, for his recollections about the most famous sentences in presidential acceptance addresses; William A. Rusher, without whom there would have been no rise of the right; and Theodore Sorensen, for his recollections about the John Kennedy–Barry Goldwater friendship. My Goldwater biography is the longest book I ever wrote—572 pages including the index, the endnotes, and the bibliography. I think it will be around for a long time to come, an opinion corroborated by publisher Regnery, which published a new edition in 2015, twenty years after the first edition. In a new introduction, I wrote that Goldwater's 1964 campaign "affected American politics more than any other losing presidential campaign in modern times."

My book received good to very good reviews in the *Washington Post*, the *Washington Times*, the *American Spectator*, and *National Review*, which called it "a full-length, massively researched biography...a definitive source."

THE NOBEL LAUREATE

Among my interviews for the Goldwater biography was the most influential libertarian in America—the University of Chicago economist and Nobel laureate Milton Friedman, who had been an informal adviser to the senator in his 1964 campaign. Friedman first met Goldwater in the late 1950s at a series of informal dinners held in the home of Bill Baroody, president of the American Enterprise Institute (AEI). Baroody brought together AEI scholars like Herb Stein, Charles McCracken, and Friedman with conservative politicians, trying to translate ideas into policy.

Friedman's most significant public contribution during the 1964 campaign was an article in the *New York Times Sunday Magazine* titled "The Goldwater View of Economics." At the invitation of the *Times*— and without running it by us—he wrote a clear, concise analysis of Goldwater's economic philosophy. He wrote that "freedom and opportunity are Senator Goldwater's basic goals for mankind: freedom of the individual to pursue his own interests so long as he does not interfere with the freedom of others to do likewise; opportunity for the ordinary man to use his resources as effectively as possible." Considering Goldwater's specific economic proposals, Friedman noted that Goldwater called for a 5 percent across-the-board cut in income taxes each year for five years—a total cut of 25 percent, precisely the reduction sought in Reagan's 1981 Economic Tax Recovery Act. As to "federal-state relations," Friedman noted that Goldwater suggested the consolidation of many grants-in-aid programs and making "lump-sum cash grants to the states and localities roughly equal to the amount that is now going to them. Local communities would then be free to use the funds at their own discretion." Again we see the outline of a federalist philosophy that Reagan attempted to implement in his presidency.

If only, I reflected many years later, we had presented Friedman's simple but powerful summing up of the senator's economic philosophy and its possible applications to the American people, who knows how many votes might have been switched? But Friedman, like so many other conservative intellectuals, was never invited to be part of the campaign.

I met Milton Friedman during the campaign and connected with him again in 1968 when Anne and I helped start the Robert M. Schuchman Foundation following Bob's untimely death at twenty-eight from a brain embolism. After graduating from Yale Law School, Bob had moved to the University of Chicago, where he was a protégé of Friedman, who had the highest expectations for him, as did we all.

In 1970, I organized a two-day conference titled "Private Solutions to Government Programs." Following Marvin Liebman's first rule, I first secured Milton's promise to participate; that helped me land other luminaries, including Yale Law's Robert Bork, University of Chicago economist Yale Brozen, and Harvard political scientist Edward Banfield.

In the 1980s, I worked closely with Milton when I was a consultant to the National Tax Limitation Committee, headed by onetime Reagan aide Lew Uhler, who relied heavily on Milton's advice as he attempted to guide tax and spending legislation through the Congress.

I caught up with Milton a decade later when I began interviewing people for my Goldwater book. The following are excerpts from our December 1992 interview, in which he offered insights into Goldwater and Ronald Reagan, whom Friedman also advised when he was governor and president.

LE: What are your first recollections of Goldwater?

MF: I was very favorably impressed with him as a sincere, honest, principled human being who really believed what he said.

LE: He was not regarded as a deep thinker. When you were talking ideas and concepts, how did he handle them?

MF: Well, he was very practical, very much down to earth, but he was interested in ideas. Let me put it this way. There are three levels. You can be interested in sort of the abstract ideas, basic values. You can be interested in the process of thinking about them. Or you can be interested in the process of applying them. And I would say that—this is almost thirty years later so don't expect too much from me or a photographic memory—my impression is that the first and the third were his strengths, he was not very much interested in the second.

LE: What did you think of his acceptance speech in San Francisco?

MF: I thought it was very good, including his phrase about extremism in the defense of liberty.

LE: That didn't bother you?

MF: Not at all. If [the senator] had prefaced that sentence with the comment, "As Seneca said in Rome many years ago..." it would never have raised any fuss whatsoever. It's always been a fascinating example to me of how much of a difference a few words can make. At the time I heard it, I thought it was fine. I agreed with it. I still agree with it. [Laughing]

LE: How important was the Goldwater candidacy?

MF: I do think, as everybody else does, that the 1964 convention marked a major turning point for the Republican Party, by taking it out of the hands of the eastern Republicans, and putting it in the hands of essentially the western populist Republicans as opposed to the eastern country-club Republicans.

LE: And the 1980 Republican convention?

MF: The greatest mistake Mr. Reagan made…was to pick George Bush as a vice president. That reinstated the eastern country-club Republicans in the driver's seat. He should never have done that. And I will never understand why he did it. I just say to myself how much different the world would be if instead of Bush, you would have had someone from the right group.

LE: Jack Kemp, perhaps?

MF: No, no. The right person would have been, you know, the fellow who was in Congress, who was defense [secretary] for Ford, who was then the head of—

LE: You mean, Donald Rumsfeld?

MF: He was my favorite candidate at the time…. I think he would have been ideal for the job. He would be president today.

LE: Since you have mentioned the two men, Reagan and Goldwater, how do you compare them?

MF: Both men had the one common feature, they had real principles. That's what distinguished them, I think, from any other candidate for the presidency during my lifetime. I always say that Reagan was the first president who was elected because the people came around to agreeing with him rather than because he was going out and finding what the people thought and then saying that was what he wanted…. Reagan said exactly the same thing in his wonderful speech in the '64 Goldwater campaign that he was saying in 1980. His theme didn't change. What happened is that public opinion moved around to agree with him. Everybody says he was elected because he was such a great communicator. I think that's a bunch of nonsense.

LE: Because?

MF: I think if Reagan had been running in '64 he would have been defeated as soundly as Goldwater was defeated.

Now as between the two men…I would say that Reagan is more analytical. In terms of the three stages I mentioned before, he's more interested in the middle stage…. You know he's gotten a very bad rap because of the whole intellectual community being so opposed to him. If you've ever had a serious discussion with Mr. Reagan, you know that he's perfectly capable of carrying on an extended abstract conversation. Whereas I think Goldwater is much more likely to jump from the first stage to the third. That has led Reagan to be more consistent.

LE: Supposing Barry Goldwater came along today, in 1992, with that directness of his, what do you think…

MF: If Reagan had been nominated in '64 and Goldwater nominated in 1980, each with the same platform that the other had, Goldwater would have been elected in 1980 and Reagan would have been defeated in 1964.... I think a Reagan identical to what he was in '80 would have a much harder time getting elected in 1996.

Milton Friedman died in 2006 at the age of ninety-four. He has become an icon of conservatives, who often quote his most famous maxim: "There's no such thing as a free lunch."

A CONSERVATIVE CANON

Following the Goldwater biography, I published fourteen books in the next two decades (plus four hundred-page monographs, or "little" books), all part of the canon I was writing about the American conservative movement. The next, published in 1997, was *The Power of Ideas: The Heritage Foundation at Twenty-Five Years*. In it, I argued that while many players had a hand in turning America away from the liberal welfare state of Roosevelt and Johnson and the world from totalitarianism, one of the most important was the conservative movement's "Ideas Central," the Heritage Foundation. Through Heritage's position papers ran the classic themes of American conservatism—limited government, free enterprise, individual freedom, traditional social values, and a strong national defense. Even liberals, I said, granted that the foundation played a key role in almost every major public policy debate of the past quarter century. As Richard Weaver wrote in 1948, ideas have consequences, and Heritage proved that the right ideas have the best consequences.

For my next work I turned to political history writ large. Published in 1999, the book was *The Conservative Revolution: The Movement That Remade America*. With the Free Press as my publisher and Adam Bellow, son of Saul, as my initial editor, with blurbs from Bill Buckley, William J. Bennett, and George Will, and with conservatism riding high in the political saddle, I had high hopes for this work. I told the story through Four Misters—"Mr. Republican," Senator Robert A. Taft of Ohio; "Mr. Conservative," Barry Goldwater; "Mr. President," Ronald Reagan; and "Mr. Speaker," Newt Gingrich. I noted that these men brought intellectual and ideological stability to an often fractious movement and held the high ground against the pragmatists who would compromise conservative principles for transitory political advantage. I hoped that reviewers would review my history and not me, but my hopes were not realized.

Why is it that liberals insist that a conservative historian cannot write an objective book about conservatism but never question whether a liberal historian can write an objective book about liberalism? Reviews of *The Conservative Revolution* in *Kirkus*, *Publishers Weekly*, and *Library Journal* began by mentioning my Heritage position, signaling my right-wing politics and thus presumably my inability to be "objective" about my subject. But I am certain that the same publications did not bring up the liberalism of Arthur Schlesinger Jr. and Robert Dallek when reviewing their glowing books about FDR and John F. Kennedy. *Publishers Weekly* described *The Conservative Revolution* as "partisan history." *Kirkus* was patronizing, saying that readers who dislike subtle analysis will find the book "an enjoyable read." Liberals love to warn the reader to beware of conservatives bearing opinions but never utter the same warning about liberals.

William Rusher, the longtime publisher of *National Review* and a distinguished fellow at the Claremont Institute, put the question of scholarship in perspective by quoting the eminent Columbia historian Alan Brinkley, who wrote in 1994 that American conservatism was "an orphan in historical scholarship." Brinkley had called on fellow historians to fill this intellectual vacuum. Conservatives had waited in vain, Rusher wrote, for a "thorough-going historical account of the entire [conservative] phenomenon, written by a professional scholar." Such a book, he said, has at last been published—*The Conservative Revolution*. Rusher praised the book's "extensive and meticulous" scholarship and its "striking balance and objectivity."

Almost a decade after the fall of the Berlin Wall, I grew concerned about the lack of public interest in why it fell. So I approached the Hoover Institution about publishing a collection of explanatory essays by leading academics on the right. Hoover director John Raisian quickly approved the project, and I lined up contributions from former national security adviser Zbigniew Brzezinski, Harvard historian Richard Pipes, Hoover senior research fellow Robert Conquest, UC-Berkeley historian Martin Malia, AEI social philosopher Michael Novak, British journalist Brian Crozier, UMass Amherst sociologist Paul Hollander, and UC-Davis economist Andrzej Brzeski.

In my opening essay for *The Collapse of Communism* (2000), I argued that when communist leaders in Eastern and Central Europe admitted they no longer believed in communism, they dissolved the glue of ideology that had held together their facade of power and authority. The communists also failed, literally, to deliver the goods to the people. They promised bread but produced food shortages and rationing. And they could not stop the mass media from spreading the desire for freedom among the people. Far from being an armed fortress, I wrote, "Eastern Europe was a Potemkin village easily penetrated by electronic messages of democracy and capitalism from the West." And communism failed to achieve its proudest claim—the creation of a New Man. Summing up *The Collapse of Communism*, I said, "Utopia turned out to be Nowhere."

That only a few thousand people read *The Collapse of Communism*, despite promotion by the Hoover Institution, reinforced my conviction that a permanent institution was needed to educate the American people about the ideology, history, and legacy of communism. I had started the Victims of Communism Memorial Foundation (VOC) in 1990 for just this purpose. I had maintained my conviction through the 1990s even as the foundation struggled to raise the funds for a memorial museum about the victims and crimes of communism. I knew that the U.S. Holocaust Memorial Museum had raised about $164 million through private sources. I thought a goal of $100 million for the 100 million victims of communism was apt for our museum. But by 1999, we had raised less than $1 million. Most of the wealthy anticommunists like Henry Salvatori, Charles Edison, and J. Howard Pew had died. Approaches to various ethnic communities had not uncovered any golden donors. Maybe, I thought, we were wrong. Maybe there was no real interest in our museum and memorial.

If we didn't do something soon, VOC was in danger of becoming one of those "good" ideas floating around Washington that remained just that—an idea.

WORLD FREEDOM DAY

My belief in our mission was strengthened when future Italian prime minister Silvio Berlusconi invited VOC to send a U.S. delegation to a Rome conference on postcommunist Europe. We got busy and the result for the June 1999 meeting was a distinguished group that included former vice-presidential candidate Jack Kemp, Harvard historian Richard Pipes, social philosopher Michael Novak, and anticommunist extraordinaire Arnold Beichman.

A conference highlight was an intense debate between the feisty Beichman and the equally combative Solidarity leader Lech Wałęsa. The issue was whether the Rome conference should approve a resolution urging the United States and other governments to declare November 9— the day the Berlin Wall came down—as World Freedom Day. Beichman had been lobbying for such a day for nearly a decade and urged conferees to sign a resolution in support of World Freedom Day.

When Wałęsa unexpectedly refused, an angry Beichman accosted the former Polish president in a hallway and, sticking his finger in his chest, demanded to know how Wałęsa could say no. What does the Berlin Wall have to do with Poland? Wałęsa asked. Poland, not Germany, led the way to freedom in Eastern and Central Europe. Introduce a resolution about Poland, Wałęsa said, and he would sign it.

For a moment I thought Arnold was going to throw a punch, but instead he replied loudly that whether Wałęsa liked it or not, the Berlin Wall was the symbol of the collapse of communism. Muttering something about pigheaded Poles, he walked away. In the end, thanks to the efforts of VOC and others, the Rome conference overwhelmingly endorsed World Freedom Day. Two years later, in his first year in office, President George W. Bush formally recognized November 9 as World Freedom Day.

In the balmy Roman evenings, the American delegates gathered around the pool of our comfortable motel on the outskirts of Rome to talk about a world without the Soviet Union and with America as the only superpower. We recalled memorable moments such as when the Russian historian Alexander Yakovlev, once a close adviser to Gorbachev, said flatly there was no difference between Lenin and Stalin— they were both "mass murderers." We agreed that such an assertion was rarely heard in the history classes of the American academy. I brought up the role that VOC could play in a post-Soviet world, quoting Santayana about the need to remember history, and received promises from everyone to help however they could. They kept their word, joining our national advisory board, providing information about foreign leaders, and suggesting contacts within ethnic communities in the United States.

As VOC struggled through the 1990s to match a realistic goal with the hard reality of fundraising, I kept writing about American conservatism.

THE ROAD TO LIBERTY

There are a few "indispensable" institutions in the conservative movement. At the very top are a journal of opinion, *National Review*; a Washington think tank, the Heritage Foundation; and an educational institute, the Intercollegiate Studies Institute. I had written a history of Heritage, and I intended to write a biography of *NR* founder Bill Buckley. So when ISI board chair Louise Oliver invited me to write a history of the Institute as it approached its fiftieth anniversary, I could not resist. I knew ISI well— I had first received ISI literature in 1954 when I was a senior at Duke, the result of my mother's enrolling me as a member. I even wrote a short libertarian essay about the efficacy of the free market for *The Individualist*, ISI's official publication.

ISI is the story of a small group of intellectuals who challenged the liberal zeitgeist on the campus and in the process built an educational pillar of the conservative movement. They were not arrogant about their intent, only serene in the knowledge they were building on 2,500 years of Western civilization.

ISI was founded in 1953 by the libertarian Frank Chodorov after he received a $1,000 check from Sun Oil Company president J. Howard Pew. Pew had responded to a Chodorov column in *Human Events* that called for the creation of a society of college students who would counter the campus trend to socialism by extolling the virtues of free enterprise and individual freedom. ISI's first president was Bill Buckley, who served in that role before he founded *National Review*. ISI's longest-serving president, Vic Milione, ensured that ISI would not get caught up in low politics or high finance by situating ISI in Philadelphia, midway between Washington, D.C., and New York City.

ISI focused originally on combating socialism, then resisting the cultural crisis of the 1960s and 1970s, next battling political correctness in the 1980s and 1990s, and finally answering the renascent anti-Americanism on college campuses following September 11, 2001, and the wars in Afghanistan and Iraq. ISI's mission from the Cold War to the war on terrorism, I wrote, was "to lay the intellectual and cultural foundation for ordered liberty in America and to help the West triumph in the clash of civilizations."

Among those who benefited from ISI programs were Heritage president Ed Feulner, Reagan national security adviser Richard Allen, Reagan secretary of the navy John Lehman, *Weekly Standard* cofounder William Kristol, author-editor M. Stanton Evans, libertarian historian

Leonard Liggio, author and historian Burton Folsom, Hillsdale College president Larry Arnn, and hundreds of college professors. ISI made a difference in the minds of many. After attending one of ISI's weeklong summer seminars, where teachers freely mixed with students at meals and late-night bull sessions, one young man said, "Why can't my college be like this?"

Both Chodorov and Milione, although differing widely in their political philosophy, agreed that the most effective way to influence a generation, and a nation, was to do so at the cultural level. "If you respect the integrity of students and the process of higher education," Milione said, "then you do not attempt to 'use' a student for short-term political goals." Milione subscribed to James Madison's idea that free people cannot remain free without the necessary culture, understanding, and mores. It was Milione who coined ISI's motto "to educate for liberty." In the face of radically changing higher education, I wrote, ISI remained tethered securely to the lasting ideas of Western civilization, avoiding academic fads like "safe spaces."

Regnery published the book, *Educating for Liberty: The First Half Century of the Intercollegiate Studies Institute*, in 2003. Robert Huberty wrote of my work in *Human Events*, "Edwards is our chronicler of conservatism's lives and times. We are in his debt."

Increasingly, I was described as a historian, not a political activist. I was achieving my goal: to become a historian of the conservative movement. *The* historian, of course, is the esteemed George Nash, who wrote the classic work *The Conservative Intellectual Movement in America Since 1945*, consulted by all.

ORIGINAL INTENT

Ed Meese may well be the perfect public servant. I learned this as I researched and wrote my next book, a biography of the former attorney general titled *To Preserve and Protect: The Life of Edwin Meese III* (2005).

From the halls of California's state capitol to the Oval Office in the White House, Meese was Ronald Reagan's most trusted aide. Once asked whom he would rely on if he faced a crisis, Reagan replied without hesitation, "Ed Meese."

Time and again, Reagan would turn to Meese after a far-ranging discussion among cabinet officers and policy experts. As usual, Meese had been taking careful notes on a yellow legal pad and would present

With Edwin Meese III, 1981

the arguments on all sides so fairly that no one objected. "Reagan valued Ed's mind," White House aide and Reagan confidant Mike Deaver told me, "his ability to sum up and recommend." His recommendations spanned the Reagan presidency, from the firm handling of the air traffic controllers strike and the passage of the Economic Recovery Tax Act to the scrupulous handling of the Iran-Contra affair, in which Meese made certain there was no cover-up à la Watergate.

Whereas liberal jurists routinely referred to a "living Constitution," Attorney General Meese in 1985 delivered a series of lectures calling for a "jurisprudence of original intention"—a return to the intent of the authors of the Constitution and the Bill of Rights. One scholar said that Meese was the first attorney general since Robert Jackson under President Franklin D. Roosevelt to enter the debate on how the Constitution ought to be interpreted and to recognize that "there is a central role for the executive branch in shaping the form of jurisprudence."

Selfless is a word one does not hear often in Washington, but as Reagan adviser Peter Hannaford wrote, the word accurately describes Ed Meese, whose life was "a series of jobs in which public service and policy fulfillment—not riches or glory—were his goals."

Ed's office at Heritage, where he was the Ronald Reagan Fellow in Public Policy for more than twenty years, was down the hall from mine. We would bump into each other in the small kitchen. I noted he made his own coffee and carefully cleaned up any spill from a previous user of the coffee machine. I learned from interns that he made his own photocopies. I never saw him upset or angry. Once after a management meeting, I remarked on his habit of taking notes. "Well," he said, "they usually come in handy, and besides it's a good way to stay awake."

To avoid the charge of hagiography, I kept looking for one discernible flaw in Ed Meese's character, one misstep in his public performance. But I discovered nothing significant until I interviewed Lyn Nofziger, Reagan's first press secretary when he was governor and a key political adviser in his presidential campaigns. I explained my dilemma to Lyn and asked, almost desperately, "Can't you think of *one* negative thing to say about Ed Meese?" Lyn reflected for a second and then responded, "Well, it's a good thing Ed isn't a girl, because he can't say no."

Other colleagues said the same: Meese would not turn down a friend or colleague who asked for his help. "There is no job too small, no effort too great, no place he will not go," said California judge Lois Haight, "if he can lend his name, his reputation, his prestige, or just his strong hands and stout heart."

REAGAN AND THE FOUR VIRTUES

Even before Reagan died in June 2004, a decade after informing the American people that he had Alzheimer's, I had decided to write a short book summing up all I had learned and observed about him through the years. In an era of big books, I decided to go small.

I built *The Essential Ronald Reagan* (2005) around the four classical virtues: courage, prudence, justice, and wisdom. I said that Reagan displayed physical courage in his handling of the attempted assassination by John Hinckley when he kept telling jokes—"I hope you're all Republicans," he said to the surgeons about to operate on him—to reassure his wife, his political aides, and the American people that he was all right. And he displayed political courage in 1981 when he insisted on tax cuts to get the economy going again rather than the tax increases liberals said were needed.

He was prudent in his use of force as commander in chief, declining to dispatch hundreds of thousands of American troops around the world

Interviewing President Ronald Reagan in the Oval Office, 1984

and instead assisting indigenous anticommunist forces in Nicaragua, Afghanistan, and Angola. He adhered to what he called the "70 percent rule," taking 70 percent of what he wanted at the time and coming back later for the other 30 percent.

Regarding justice, he insisted that his administration did not have separate social, economic, and foreign policy agendas but one agenda based on limited constitutional government, individual freedom and responsibility, peace through strength, and traditional American values derived from our Judeo-Christian heritage. He defended the rights of every American from the moment of conception to that of natural death.

He possessed wisdom to a rare degree, having the ability to see what others could not see. He anticipated the collapse of communism, predicting in 1982 that Marxism-Leninism was headed for "the ash heap of history." He was confident that his across-the-board marginal tax cuts would rejuvenate the U.S. economy, and before his presidency was over more than seventeen million new jobs had been created. He was certain that SDI—the Strategic Defense Initiative—would convince the Soviets they could not win an arms race with the United States and persuade them to seek to end the Cold War peacefully.

In his farewell address in January 1989, the president told the men and women of the "Reagan Revolution" that they had made a difference—they had made America stronger and freer and had left her in good hands. "All in all," he said with a twinkle in his eye, "not bad, not bad at all."

FORT BUCKLEY

I decided on a short biography again when I turned my attention to Bill Buckley, that other transformational leader of the conservative movement. I knew Al Felzenberg was writing an in-depth biography for Yale University Press, and Sam Tanenhaus was said to be writing a major bio for a New York publisher.

I limited myself to two themes about Buckley: an analysis of the four intellectuals who had the greatest influence on his thought, and a recounting of his political acts and decisions that made him the architect of the modern conservative movement. The resulting book was *William F. Buckley Jr.: The Maker of a Movement* (2010).

Bill's four "teachers" were Albert Jay Nock, the libertarian author and editor; Willmoore Kendall, the Yale professor of government who had Bill as a student; Whittaker Chambers, the American who spied for the Soviets but became America's premier anticommunist; and James Burnham, onetime Trotskyite and early neoconservative who was first among the senior editors of *National Review*.

In his last year at prep school, Bill began reading—at his father's urging—the works of Nock, a frequent luncheon guest at the Buckley home. Nock had been editor of *American Magazine* and then *The Nation* before becoming coeditor of the original *Freeman*. His best-known book was *Memoirs of a Superfluous Man*, in which he expressed an almost mystical belief in a "Remnant" of elite writers and thinkers who would one day build a new and free society on the ruins of the modern welfare state. There is a significant difference between Nock's Remnant and Ayn Rand's über-capitalist vision in *Atlas Shrugged*—Nock borrows from the Bible, Rand from Nietzsche.

Buckley admired Nock's passionate antistatism, his radical rhetoric, and his willingness to stick by his ideas regardless of whether they were out of step with the times. He always meant to do a book on Nock, he later admitted, saying, "He has always fascinated me."

After attending Oxford on a Rhodes scholarship, Kendall began teaching at Yale in 1947 and immediately plunged into controversy, roundly criticizing the idea of the "open society" and the notion that all questions are open questions. He argued that all polities, including democracies, have an orthodoxy they have a right to defend against anyone who would fundamentally change it. Kendall supported legislation outlawing the Communist Party, whose goals violated the political orthodoxy necessary for America's survival.

Enrolling in Kendall's political science seminar, Buckley became a political disciple and personal friend of the "wild Yale don." Kendall taught the young Buckley to read political theory with the close attention to the text that the political philosopher Leo Strauss advocated. Buckley later said, "I attribute whatever political and philosophical insights I have to his tutelage and his friendship." He was struck by Kendall's Nock-like metaphor that the conservative forces were strung out in isolated outposts over a wide front. Buckley would later conceive *National Review* as a fortress behind whose walls conservatives could collect their strength and prepare to attack the enemy—the Establishment.

When he began assembling the editorial staff for *National Review*, Buckley was eager to enroll the former communist agent and spy Whittaker Chambers, author of the acclaimed autobiography *Witness*. He made several trips to Chambers's Maryland farm in the hope of bringing him on board his new magazine. Buckley and Chambers became friends, but Chambers nevertheless said no. At least one biographer has suggested that Chambers thought Buckley and his colleagues were too ideological; he preferred the "Beaconsfield position," a more pragmatic approach to politics. "That is what conservatives must decide," Chambers wrote Buckley, "how much to give in order to survive at all; how much to give in order not to give up the basic principles."

In the beginning of *National Review*, Buckley was more the idealist, but in time and under the influence of a fourth thinker and close colleague, James Burnham, he would become more of a realist. Burnham was strongly anticommunist yet a disciple of realpolitik in domestic politics, qualities Buckley sought in a senior editor. Burnham, too, had been thinking about the need for a weekly magazine on the right that dealt with the issues of the day, and he quickly accepted Buckley's offer to join his magazine.

Kendall, Chambers, and Burnham all agreed that communism was the overriding challenge confronting America. Chambers's linking of liberalism and communism helped to justify Buckley's ready condemnation of the left. Burnham would make the same point in his book *Suicide of the West*, asserting that for a liberal there is no enemy to the left.

These four great intellectual influences on Buckley were different in many ways, especially in temperament, but their similarities were telling. All were highly educated—two of them had studied at Oxford—and all were men of faith. Most important, they were united in their opposition to the liberal zeitgeist. Buckley learned and borrowed freely from all of them.

Almost everything Bill Buckley did was political. The most obvious was the founding of *National Review*, which he saw from the beginning as not merely a magazine but also the voice and the conscience of a movement. He had specific goals in mind: keep the Republican Party, the primary political vehicle of conservatives, tilted to the right; eliminate any and all extremists from the movement; flay and fleece the liberals at every opportunity; and push hard for a policy of victory over communism in the Cold War.

Did the movement need a youth arm? Well, invite a hundred of the brightest young conservatives to your home to start a national youth organization. Voilà—Young Americans for Freedom.

Was the Republican Party of New York, the most populous state in the union, too liberal? Sit down with Daniel Mahoney, Kieran O'Doherty, and other activists and found a conservative alternative, the Conservative Party of New York, without which, for example, James L. Buckley would not have been elected to the U.S. Senate in 1970.

Did conservatives need a psychological boost after the 1964 drubbing of presidential candidate Barry Goldwater? Was there a real danger of New York congressman John Lindsay, the golden boy of the liberal establishment, becoming president one day? Would his chances be reduced if he were seriously challenged in New York's mayoral race? Yes, yes, and yes. Therefore, announce that you are a candidate and participate in a series of debates to reveal Lindsay to be more brass than gold.

In truth, Bill Buckley was almost all political all the time. Whether meeting with Richard Nixon, counseling Ronald Reagan, supporting and then criticizing the Iraq War, endorsing the transfer of the Panama Canal to Panama, welcoming neoconservatives, or ejecting John Birchers, he defended his vision of ordered liberty and saw it as his mission to guide American conservatism into becoming a major political force.

Given his wealth and social standing, Buckley could have been the playboy of the Western world, but he chose instead to be the Saint Paul of the conservative movement.

POWERHOUSE

Ed Feulner was a thirty-year-old congressional staffer when he and Paul Weyrich, two years younger and also a Hill aide, came up with the idea for a conservative think tank that would provide timely, reliable, concise research to members of Congress and their staffs to use in deciding the best possible public policies. It sounds simple, even obvious, but no one in the think-tank world had committed to such an approach before. The American Enterprise Institute studiously avoided trying to influence the outcome of a debate, sending its studies to Congress after a vote had been taken. Brookings specialized in books and long monographs that busy congressmen and their staffs rarely had the time to read.

In the early 1970s, Feulner and Weyrich were fighting in the trenches of Capitol Hill against an overwhelmingly liberal force. They knew what they needed—solid but digestible research that pointed out the weakness of the liberal position and the strength of the conservative view on issues from federal spending to national defense. And they needed it *before* their congressmen voted.

As obvious an idea as it was, three years passed before Joseph Coors donated $250,000 and enabled the founding of a small think tank of twelve employees, one mimeograph machine, and two dogs. When I interviewed Coors, I asked why he had gambled $250,000 on an untested organization led by two young, unknown congressional aides? Because, he answered, they had a business plan and because they wanted to make a difference right away.

Four years later, the Heritage Foundation was a modest-sized think tank still relegated to the Washington fringe, conducting its research in relative obscurity. Then there arrived as its new president and CEO the man who had thought of it in the first place—Ed Feulner. Over the next four decades Feulner built Heritage into a Washington powerhouse.

Here was a story I wanted to tell, and I did so in *Leading the Way: The Story of Ed Feulner and the Heritage Foundation* (2013).

Ed was an action intellectual who believed in the power of ideas but understood they would remain powerless unless transformed into relevant policies and programs through marketing and publicity. He was an astute manager with an MBA from Wharton who believed in leadership by consensus. He looked to those around him, especially longtime COO Phil Truluck, to pilot the ship when he was on the road visiting world leaders and raising funds. He was a committed conservative who understood that Heritage and the conservative movement should grow and prosper together. He was a prodigious fundraiser because he always talked about the mission first and money second. He was energetic, decisive, able to get quickly to the heart of an issue or problem. He had certain rules for success:

- Don't let the urgent overwhelm the important.
- Never assume the competition or the enemy is standing still.
- There are no permanent victories or defeats in Washington.
- People are policy. Without the best people in place, even the best ideas don't matter.

He was an incurable optimist whose sign-off on his correspondence was (and is), "Onward!"

He was a gambler who in early 1980 approved the research and in-house publication of *Mandate for Leadership: Policy Management in a Conservative Administration*, a thousand-page volume containing more than two thousand recommendations to move an administration in a conservative direction. The Reagan administration adopted some two-thirds of the recommendations in part or in whole over the next eight years.

Under Ed's leadership, Heritage supported High Frontier, an early version of Reagan's SDI (Strategic Defense Initiative). It wrote a major part of the historic welfare reform act of 1996, which transformed welfare into workfare for the first time. It played a major role in school choice, leading to the charter school movement and stricter teacher guidelines. It produced a study on homeland security in advance of the 9/11 terrorist attacks that George W. Bush's administration largely adopted.

Despite these undoubted successes, Feulner was forced to concede that it was no longer enough to present the most persuasive policy paper to a congressman or senator and expect him to vote the right way. Politics trumped principle time after time. In the permanent campaign world of Washington, something more tangible than logic and reason was required. Recalling Reagan's words that "if you can't make them see the light, make them feel the heat," Feulner and his senior managers decided that Heritage should raise the temperature. The vehicle was Heritage Action for America, a 501(c)(4) lobbying organization.

When Ed Feulner stepped down in 2013 after thirty-seven years as president, Heritage was a $90-million-a-year enterprise with three hundred employees and four buildings. It was routinely described as the most influential conservative think tank in Washington and arguably the world.

Over the next four years and under its new CEO, former senator Jim DeMint of South Carolina—one of the most principled and respected conservatives in the Senate—it encountered unexpected difficulty in integrating the research and lobbying operations of the two organizations. Critics said Heritage was becoming too "political." By mutual consent, Senator DeMint and Heritage parted ways, and Ed Feulner returned to pick up the reins until a new president could be selected.

OFF TO COMMUNIST CHINA

In addition to letting me write about eminent conservatives, Heritage sometimes dispatched me to a college campus or a grassroots group to talk about American conservatism. Sometimes the foundation sent me far away. Which is why in November 2003, I—along with Heritage's China expert, John Tkacik—found myself in Beijing. I was a little uneasy. I was, after all, not only a fellow at the right-wing "running dog" capitalist Heritage Foundation but also chairman of the Victims of Communism Memorial Foundation and the last secretary of the Committee of One Million (Against the Admission of Communist China to the United Nations).

I had been invited by the Chinese Association for International Understanding—run by the international liaison department of the Chinese Communist Party's Central Committee—to lecture on the origins of modern American conservatism. But what if I were too free-market or too anticommunist in my remarks? Only half-jokingly, I asked my Heritage colleagues as well as my students at Catholic University to be prepared to launch a rescue operation if I disappeared into the *laogai* (forced labor camps).

But in fact the audiences at People's University in Beijing and Fudan University in Shanghai were studiously polite and eager to learn all they could about American conservatism, although I discovered they already knew an astonishing amount. They asked questions like: "Is U.S. conservatism Lockean or Burkean in its origins?" and "Are Vice President Cheney and Defense Secretary Rumsfeld traditional or neoconservatives?" When I presented a copy of my book *The Conservative Revolution* to our host at a welcoming dinner, he thanked me, adding casually that he had already read it. I wondered: was he trying to flatter me or had he in fact read it?

One scholar asked me why I had left out Newt Gingrich in my lecture—wasn't the 1994 election a critical event in the development of

At the Great Wall of China

the conservative movement? Yes it was, I admitted, and apologized for
not mentioning it. Another asked me for my opinion of the importance
of Bill (not Irving) Kristol. I spent considerable time disabusing my hosts
of their erroneous idea that Cheney and Rumsfeld were neoconservatives.
It was clear, from their questions, they believed neocons and "imperialists"
like Paul Wolfowitz were determining U.S. foreign policy and therefore
U.S.-China policy. They brought up Taiwan every time—it was a question
of Chinese sovereignty, they explained. Taiwan was Chinese territory.

They nodded their heads when I characterized the Great Leap
Forward and the Cultural Revolution as colossal mistakes by Mao but
remained motionless when I brought up Tiananmen Square. I stressed
that U.S.-China relations could be advanced only if they were based on a
mutual respect for the truth—and that included the truth that hundreds
and possibly thousands of pro-democracy students had been killed in
Tiananmen Square in June 1989. There was no nodding of heads.

In Shanghai, the director of the Center for American Studies at
Fudan University talked about a "love and hate" relationship that existed
between China and America. He said that America still had too much of
a Cold War mentality. The United States, he suggested, should learn how

to accommodate to a "rising China" (a revealing phrase given the "rising sun" of Japan in the pre–World War II period). There must be more contacts between the two countries, he said, to correct misperceptions. He quoted Mao, who said in 1956 that he saw a day, however distant, when the Chinese people and the American people would be friends. Out of politeness, I did not point out that it was difficult to be friendly with a nation whose founder initiated policies responsible for the deaths of as many as sixty million of its citizens.

Like many visitors, I was impressed by the hundreds of giant cranes and soaring skyscrapers in Beijing and especially in Shanghai, by the all-day traffic jams equaling those of Los Angeles and Washington, by the reported annual income of China's urban population at around $5,000 to $10,000 for a family of three. That put about 250 million people on the road to the "middle class." You could see, and John Tkacik concurred, that China was in a hurry to become an economic powerhouse.

And yet, while the Forbidden City—the former residence of the Chinese emperors—was no longer closed to visitors, many things in the People's Republic of China were not open to discussion, such as:

- *The millions who died under Mao Zedong's rule.* Mao was revered as the Long March leader who defeated the Nationalists and united the country, but his role as the instigator of the misnamed Great Leap Forward and the Cultural Revolution was rarely mentioned.

- *Deng Xiaoping's central role in the Tiananmen Square massacre.* Deng was lauded as the wise author of China's economic liberalization and ensuing prosperity. Unacknowledged was his order to the People's Liberation Army (PLA) to snuff out the pro-democracy demonstrations in Tiananmen Square. Crushed beneath the PLA onslaught was the symbol of the demonstrators' dreams—the thirty-two-foot-high gleaming white Goddess of Democracy (the icon at the center of our Victims of Communism Memorial).

- *Forced labor camps.* Despite the personal testimony of dissidents Wei Jingsheng, Harry Wu, and other former prisoners, Chinese officials routinely denied the existence of the *laogai*, a national network of an estimated one thousand forced labor camps in which millions of prisoners produced goods that were then sold to the West. Wu and others have estimated that several million prisoners died in the *laogai*.

While in China, I learned of "Stainless Steel Mouse," a twenty-two-year-old Chinese student put in prison because she expressed herself too freely on the Internet. Chinese authorities preferred to talk about China's first astronaut, Yang Liwei. But which was the truer symbol of the new China the communist regime was trying to build—the student or the astronaut?

A prominent Chinese academic insisted that political pluralism was "not far away"—there had been voting in the villages and county elections would soon follow. But I knew that the Communist Party picked all the candidates. The professor quoted a popular slogan in southern China— "Big Society, Little Government." But Tkacik reminded me that the skyscrapers piercing the sky over Beijing and Shanghai were joint ventures with Chinese government agencies, including the PLA and state corporations, with the government always retaining a majority interest.

One Sunday morning in Beijing, I went to Mass along with my young female escort officer. The church, really a cathedral, was packed with worshippers for the 11 A.M. service, which included a superb choir, a booming organ, lots of incense, and long lines of recipients of the Eucharist. Impressed, I asked how many Catholic churches there were in Beijing (then a city of 14.5 million). Two others, she replied proudly, although they were not so large. I politely refrained from pointing out that this left the great majority of Chinese Catholics without a parish church or priest.

My visit to mainland China was the culmination of a long-held desire inspired by Dr. Judd, who often remarked that the Chinese were the strongest people he had ever known and were destined for greatness if they had a government that truly represented their best interests. But what governed China in 2003 was the Communist Party, whose primary interest was retaining its political power. That remains the party's central objective to this day.

As I stood in the middle of a tranquil Tiananmen Square one crisp morning and watched the kites flying overhead and hawkers selling gloves and caps and regarded the giant portrait of Mao overlooking the square, I thought to myself: it is as though Mao never died and the Goddess of Democracy never existed.

31

"DEAR BILL"

I met Bill Buckley in September 1960, at the founding of Young
Americans for Freedom at his family's home. Our correspondence
began soon after—and lasted nearly fifty years.

As was his practice, Bill conscientiously answered every one of my
letters even when they did not warrant it. He had been taught that anyone who wrote him deserved a response, even if only a sentence of two.

BILL'S EPISTLES

I sent one of my first letters to Bill Buckley in early 1964, after I had been
appointed director of information of the Goldwater for President Committee. I knew that Bill favored Goldwater and would do what he could
to help his campaign.

On February 28, I wrote Bill asking him to help us approach conservative "authors" for their endorsement. His reply shocked me:

> Dear Lee:
>
> I put in an enormous amount of time on exactly the subject
> you raise, and after several sessions with Russell Kirk and Ernest
> van den Haag and Frank Meyer, at the last of which Bob Schuch-
> man [YAF's first chairman] was also there, wrote an extensive

memorandum on the kind of project you now bring up. I sent it to Jay Hall, who turned it over to Goldwater, who turned it over to Mr. [Ed] McCabe (whom I have never met). I offered, in connection with that memorandum, to do anything I could to help develop the idea. It is my opinion, for what it is worth, that the project will be much more difficult to assemble now than it would have been when I wrote in December. I would however still be glad, along the lines of that memorandum, to do what I can, provided it is still possible to hold together the nucleus we then put together. I suggest the easiest way to proceed is for you to get hold of a copy of that memorandum from Goldwater's office and then let me have your views on it. O.K.?

Yours cordially,
Bill

I was nonplussed. I had never heard of any such memorandum or meetings or offers to help from the man who had almost invented the movement that the senator needed to get nominated and elected. I made calls. I talked to people. Eventually I learned that Buckley's offer—cosigned by Russell Kirk, who had written speeches for Goldwater, and Brent Bozell, close collaborator on the senator's manifesto, *The Conscience of a Conservative*—had been rejected by Bill Baroody, our de facto campaign chairman. Baroody had the ear of the king and was not going to share it with anyone, especially "ultra-conservatives" like Buckley, Kirk, and Bozell.

I was so embarrassed that I never responded to Bill's generous offer to help us even after our initial rebuff. In a memoir, Goldwater admitted that he had erred badly in banning Buckley and the others and blamed it on Baroody. Goldwater lamented that he learned too late what had happened to take any corrective action. It was one more blunder in a campaign that our treasurer, Bill Middendorf, later described as a "glorious disaster," an all-too-accurate phrase.

In February 1965, following our defeat, I was still at the Republican National Committee but knew I would soon be leaving. I wrote Bill about a column in which he had deplored the absence of a conservative Catholic journal. "It seems to me," I wrote, "that with such writers as yourself, Brent Bozell and Garry Wills [such a] publication is a very real possibility. I would be happy to contribute such talents as I have." He wrote back:

Dear Lee:

Thanks a lot for your note. I am dictating this from Switzerland, hence the brevity of the reply. If the project gets off the ground, I'll promise to let you know.

Yours cordially,

Bill

Shortly thereafter, the project did leave the ground, piloted by Brent Bozell, who named the magazine *Triumph* and hired as one of his first employees Anne Stevens Edwards. Anne would come home to our apartment on Van Ness Street in Northwest Washington with stories about Brent's determination to publish a "true" Catholic magazine, his reaching out to conservative religious and laity, his nonstop phone calls to old comrades and new friends, all fueled by endless cups of coffee and dollops of bourbon. When she became pregnant with our first daughter, Elizabeth, Anne reluctantly gave her notice, hopeful that Brent would be successful but concerned by his work habits. Did he ever sleep? she wondered. She was saddened but not surprised to learn later that Brent suffered from bipolar disorder. As the historian Patrick Allitt has written, *Triumph* had a short but meaningful life from 1965 to 1975, publishing articles by the likes of Dartmouth professor Jeffrey Hart, historian John Lukacs, and political philosopher Thomas Molnar and influencing the faith of conservatives like the founding president of Christendom College, Warren Carroll.

In late September 1965—in the middle of his mayoral campaign—I sent Bill a copy of Terry Catchpole's and my little book, *Behind the Civil Rights Mask*, calling it "provocative" and "excellent ammunition" at cocktail parties. In view of his star performance in the New York City mayoral race, I asked Buckley, only half-kidding, whether he was "willing to run in 1968 for either President or Vice President."

Dear Lee:

I am delighted by your book. It has all kinds of fascinating information. I'll look for an opportunity to plug it.... I only lately heard that it was on account of your special kindness that I was surrounded by friends when I spoke at the National Press Club. You are a thoughtful friend, and I most certainly will rely on you when I run for President! I may even rely on you when I don't run for President.

My affectionate greetings to your wife, mother and father.

Yours cordially,
Bill

In early 1974, I invited Bill to deliver the featured address at the concluding banquet of the annual meeting of the World Anti-Communist
League in Washington. I figured he would not be able to resist addressing the most celebrated group of anticommunist fighters in the world.

Dear Lee:
       Very well, I shall be there. I have asked Mrs. Babcock to waive
the fee, but I shall bill you the expenses. However, if there are foundation funds or contributions that exceed the cost of the conference,
I shall expect you to make a contribution of some sort to NATIONAL
REVIEW. Okay?
       Yours cordially,
       Bill

In February 1975, I wrote Bill about the launch of *Conservative Digest*,
which I told him would present in digest form the best of conservative
writing and thinking across the subject spectrum—politics, health, education, economics, the fine arts, and the news media. I explained that I
had had the idea of such a monthly magazine for more than a decade but
could never interest an investor until I mentioned the magazine to Richard Viguerie. Richard agreed to pay the bills and serve as president and
publisher while I would be editor. "I hope," I concluded, "that you will
allow us, from time to time, to reprint articles from *National Review*."
       Bill's reply was guarded, in keeping with a handwritten note to Bill
Rusher in the upper right-hand corner of my letter that I saw only later
when going through Bill's papers. He wrote, "I think this calls for a very
careful response."

Dear Lee:
       Thanks for your note. I will want to look at it before making any
firm commitment, for the obvious reasons. My best to you and Dick
Viguerie. With warm regards,
       As ever,
       Bill

In November 1976, I wrote Bill after he spoke at our Washington
conference "The United States and China After Mao," held just two

months after Mao's death. Bill spoke at the luncheon, following remarks by Sol Chaikin, president of the International Ladies' Garment Workers' Union. What better way to demonstrate the nonpartisan nature of anti-communism than to present the fiery union leader and the conservative movement leader side by side?

In my letter I thanked Bill, saying I thought his arguments against de-recognizing the Republic of China while recognizing the People's Republic of China eloquent and persuasive. Bill was not so sure.

Dear Lee:

Thanks for your terribly kind note. Especially appreciated under the circumstances as I was rather tired from the trip to Hawaii and didn't feel I had performed as fluently as I should have. It is a remarkable tribute to your powers of organization that you got together such a large group so soon after the election, and with such interesting people. Thanks so much for your kind remarks about AIRBORNE [Bill's latest book] which I hugely appreciate. With warm regards to you both,

As ever,
Bill

Anne and I both attended *National Review*'s twenty-fifth anniversary dinner in New York City in November 1980, but it was Anne who wrote the better thank-you to Bill, which I include along with Bill's gracious reply:

Dear Bill:

Since I usually have to rationalize trips away from children, home and office for my middle-class Irish-Italian, traditional-libertarian-stop-ERA feminist conscience, I thank *National Review* for having birthdays.

And I thank you for all the years of being you. The Anniversary Dinner was lovely. I feel as though I've been a month in Europe and have come home refreshed instead of exhausted. First a smashing election and then a celebration with you and so many friends, it must be a peek at heaven!

With congratulations and affection, I remain
Cordially,
Anne

Dear Anne

I know it violates protocol—you should never thank anybody for a thank-you letter, but I wanted you to know how much yours meant to me.

Affectionately.

Bill

In August 1986, I wrote Bill a long letter about my decision to withdraw from public relations and become a full-time teacher and writer. I asked for his help in making the transition. Here are my letter and his reply, sent two weeks later:

Dear Bill:

Five years ago, I decided to gradually withdraw from public relations and begin a new career in the field of teaching and writing. Since then, I have received my PhD in World Politics from The Catholic University of America, founded a program on political journalism at Georgetown University, edited *Conservative Digest* for two years, served as a Fellow at Harvard's Institute of Politics, and am now writing a monthly column on national politics for the *Boston Globe*.

But I have learned that old stereotypes die hard, and I am still thought of by many of our mutual friends as a PR man. They keep asking me if I would do this or that publicity job, and I keep explaining that I am no longer in the PR business but would be happy to do some writing, editing, or lecturing for them.

So here I am coming to you, who published my very first article way back in February 1958, and asking, Is there anything I can do for *National Review*? As you know, I am a good editor and can still put words, sentences and even paragraphs together, as the enclosed *Globe* columns show. I don't know who is writing Cato [an inside Washington column], or if there is a need to supplement John McLaughlin's contributions [then *NR*'s Washington editor]. I am open and amenable to almost anything.

If I sound a little anxious, I am. But I am also determined to stay on the course I set five years ago, convinced that it is the right one for me.

With deep appreciation for your help and counsel through the years, I remain

Sincerely,

Lee

Dear Lee:

There are no openings for regular work at *NR*, so that at this point all I am in a position to do is tell you that we are open to any freelance contributions that strike your fancy and ours. I wonder whether you did the correct thing, given the terrific need the conservative movement has for gentlemanly, honest, and profound PR work. So much stuff is being produced, of resonant value, which goes so unadvertised as to be virtually ignored.... Think about that.... With warm regards,

As ever,

Bill

I did think about it, but stuck to my decision, no longer obliged to worry about rent, payroll, unemployment compensation, health insurance, and satisfying clients who rarely said "well done" even when I was able to gain front-page coverage for them.

In November 1990, following Joseph Sobran's generous review of my Judd book in *National Review* and my several suggestions about a possible *Firing Line* segment about Dr. Judd, Bill responded in a characteristically thoughtful way.

Dear Lee:

How wonderfully generous of you to write as you did. It occurs to me that you and Anne have been working in the same vineyard for very nearly as long as I have, and deserve the congratulations owing to you. I trust the book on Walter is doing well. It was admirable of you to undertake it especially since people when they reach a certain age slip from public notice. You have done a great service not only professional, but personal.

With warm regards,

Bill

In December 1992, I spent two days at the Sterling Library at Yale, going through Bill Buckley's papers "in search of Barry Goldwater," whose biography I had begun working on. I reported to Bill that I had "found some very helpful material" and then asked him to contrast and compare Goldwater and Ronald Reagan—"in what way are they most alike? Most different?"

Bill's response was succinct.

Dear Lee:

Am glad you had a rewarding time at New Haven. The two are very different men, and Reagan is a better strategic political planner than Barry Goldwater. I look forward enormously to your evaluations of them.

With warm regards,
Bill

In September 1993, Bill received an award in the name of someone whom he admired above almost all others—Walter Judd. He came to Washington to accept the first Walter Judd Freedom Award from the Center for International Relations. Always generous in his thank-yous, Bill was extravagant on this occasion.

Dear Lee:

It is always a pity when a forced leave taking of the kind I had yesterday leaves you with insufficient time appropriately to thank your hosts. On the other hand if I had an hour to do so, it could not have been appropriate. The words you used would have humbled Lorenzo the Magnificent. I appreciated them in proportion as I am unworthy of them, which suggests the magnitude of my indebtedness to you. And if you will permit me, it gave me a special thrill that the Edwards Clan was so fully involved in the venture. Your enchanting daughter [Elizabeth], meeting me at the airport and briefing me so fully about every subject that interested me; and dear Anne, ghosting for the venerable Walter, and otherwise superintending an affair so well-run that the host even got a glass of wine! Thank you my friend. I am, as for so long, in your debt.

As ever,
Bill

APPRECIATIONS

I had long wanted to write about Bill Buckley's Catholic faith, and in February 1995, *Crisis* magazine published my profile under the title "Catholic Maverick," which was provocative but misleading. Bill was a faithful Catholic in love with Christ who said the Rosary every day. When a *Playboy* magazine interviewer asked whether "most dogmas, theological as well as ideological, do not crumble sooner or later," Bill replied firmly,

"Most, but not all." When the interviewer pressed him—"How can you be so sure?"—back came the ringing words "I know that my Redeemer liveth."

It was on the issue of contraception that Bill most openly opposed the Magisterium of the Church. Following the publication of the papal encyclical *Humanae Vitae* (1968), he said that the anticontraception dogma grew out of an "anti-Manichaean argument" that "fleshly pursuits were unhealthy." Two decades later, when I interviewed him, he said that the Church had to decide between contraception and abortion (which he firmly opposed), because if it continued to insist that "contraception violates the moral law," it would weaken its proper and needed moral arguments against abortion.

When I asked Bill whether he had read Dr. Janet Smith's powerful book *Humanae Vitae: A Generation Later* or was familiar with her case against contraception and for natural family planning, he admitted he had not. I promised to send him a copy. Two years later, when he published *Nearer, My God: An Autobiography of Faith*, he quoted extensively from Smith's book and said, "My own incomplete understanding of the natural law balks at the central affirmation of *Humanae Vitae*, even as I'd of course counsel dutiful compliance with it." The shift in Bill's position attests yet again to the power of a book.

I ended my profile by writing that Bill Buckley was fiercely loyal to the institutions that had nurtured him—Church, family, and country. Notwithstanding "the quiet triumph of secularism in the past thirty years," he was ever ready for battle and declared with Chesterton that "the men signed of the Cross of Christ go gaily in the dark." He was, in the words of his friend and fellow conservative Father Richard John Neuhaus, "a Catholic with all flags unfurled pursuing his vocation."

In receipt of the *Crisis* profile, Bill wrote:

Dear Lee:

Just saw your fine and generous piece. I will reserve tickets for my beatification!… Re Goldwater [I had suggested a *Firing Line* based on my forthcoming biography of the senator], will talk to [my producer] Warren Steibel. We would need an anti-Goldwater right-winger who would attack him for his current positions. Nominations?

Warmest,

Bill

In late 1995, I did a Goldwater program on *Firing Line* contra Barry Lynn, the seasoned head of Americans United for Separation of Church and State, and held my own, although I was as nervous as a kid on his first day at school, afraid that WFB would use a word with which I was not familiar. I need not have worried—Bill scaled down his vocabulary when he saw how nervous I was.

By early January 1997, I had finished *The Power of Ideas*, my history of the Heritage Foundation, and I invited Bill to write a brief preface about Heritage's role in advancing the conservative movement over the past twenty-five years. Searching for analogies, I said, "I know you get many requests, Bill, but it seems to me that a Preface by Bill Buckley to the Heritage history is a perfect fit—like J. S. Bach and W. Landowska." I knew, of course, about Bill's passion for Bach and that the famed harpsichordist (Bill played the same instrument) lived in Stamford, Connecticut, not far from Bill.

> Dear Lee:
>   Okay. I come back from Switzerland on the 17th of March. If you will have the book ready in some sort of shape by then I'll read it and gladly oblige.
>   With warm regards,
>   Bill

His five-hundred-word preface was all that Heritage and Ed Feulner could wish, underscoring Ed's leadership, the Reagan administration's dependence on Heritage research, the remarkable growth of the foundation from a Tinkertoy engine into a mighty dynamo, "the dominant think tank in the country." He concluded: "We breathe more securely in the knowledge that high ideals, and right reason, are maintaining their eternal equilibrium in the awful tumult of an age that struggles so very hard to suppress American idealism. The power of ideas, indeed."

I had been thinking about writing a political history of the conservative movement for years, and once I started writing, it did not take me long to finish a good first draft. In the spring of 1998, pressed by my editor to secure an endorsement from a bestselling author, I wrote Bill once again. I enclosed the galley proofs of *The Conservative Revolution* and asked for a blurb—"a sentence or two." That was not unreasonable, but I gave him a deadline of just two weeks, which was.

One week later, Bill replied:

Dear Lee:

You want a brief blurb:

Here is the history of the conservative movement—by a conservative. The author is literate, comprehensive, acute. His book is an extraordinary accomplishment: readable, exhaustive, revealing. An indispensable addition to the political shelf.

Now, let me say that I absolutely marvel at what you have accomplished. How DO you do it? Even the help of Anne does not account for it. It seems to me yesterday that you completed your Heritage book. Trollope would not have performed at that speed. And how you took in, and classified, and used such broad material....

You truly are a heroic figure.

My heartiest congratulations.

Bill

We all love to be appreciated, but "heroic" was over the top. I responded, thanking Bill for the "blurb"—what a demeaning word for something so helpful to the potential buyer of a book—and for including me in *National Review*'s forthcoming Barry Goldwater issue (the senator died May 29, 1998). I pointed out that my piece would come some forty years after my first appearance in the magazine, "again thanks to you."

"WOULD THERE BE THE EARTH WITHOUT THE SUN?"

In the late 1990s, as I continued to seek financial support for the Victims of Communism Memorial Foundation, it occurred to me that our bipartisan cause would be helped if I were a member of the prestigious Council on Foreign Relations and could talk to fellow members about the foundation's objective of informing people about communism's victims and crimes.

Through Heritage and the Philadelphia Society, I had come to know neoconservative-turned-conservative Midge Decter, and she agreed to nominate me for membership. I then asked WFB to second my nomination, which he did with the following:

Dear Sirs/Ladies:

I write to second the nomination of Lee Edwards, by Midge Decter.

I've known Lee Edwards about forty years. He wrote a piece for *National Review* while serving in Germany just after the Korean War. I have seen him frequently over the last forty years and continue to marvel at his industry. He has been primarily concerned with the development of the conservative movement in America and has written definitive books on the subject, including a biography of Ronald Reagan, another one of Walter Judd, and of Barry Goldwater. He has also edited a book on Pope John Paul and has two books in the making.

In manner he is gentle, soft-spoken, and very bright. He has earned his doctorate and has energetically participated in the cultural and journalistic life of Washington, D.C., and in foreign countries. All of this is detailed in his c.v.

I am honored to have the privilege of seconding his nomination.
Yours faithfully,
WFB

Not even the reputation of Midge Decter and the rhetoric of William F. Buckley Jr. could convince the Council on Foreign Relations' Committee on Admissions, and my application for membership was politely rejected. No reason was given, but I like to think it was because I was not always "soft-spoken" in my anticommunism.

As president of the Philadelphia Society on its fortieth anniversary, I was tasked with persuading Buckley, a founder of the society in 1964 along with Milton Friedman, to deliver the keynote address at our national meeting in Chicago. To my delight, Bill agreed to join us, waiving his fee and asking only that we cover his expenses and provide a good white wine in advance of his remarks.

I had the privilege and the challenge of introducing Bill. I asked myself: is it possible to say something new about someone who had been introduced thousands of times? I resolved not to use the usual clichés—a "renaissance man," "rapier wit," "tireless advocate," etc. I waited for inspiration until one morning, while shaving, it came out of nowhere: why not introduce him using the titles of his books?

And so on the evening of April 30, 2004, I began:

Is it possible to say anything about Bill Buckley that has not been said before? Well, Did You Ever See a Dream Walking? Or Airborne? Racing Through Paradise? At Cruising Speed—or perhaps on Overdrive?

Then you've had a glimpse, however fleeting, of our keynote speaker.

He's a polymathical man: Saving the Queen, Searching for Anti-Semitism, Rumbling Left and Right, Unmaking a Mayor, Tempting Malachey, Inveighing as he goes.

He's a 24/7 man: with Elvis in the Morning, at Execution Eve, On the Firing Line for more than quarter of a century.

He's fond of High Jinx and Stained Glass, and ready for Marco Polo If You Can...imagine it.

He's a faithful man, often found with A Hymnal, murmuring Nearer, My God.

He's a Redhunter with a Jeweler's Eye, on the lookout for McCarthy and His Enemies.

Spytime is his kind of time, filled with strange and mysterious passwords like See You Later, Alligator and Mongoose, RIP.

He's a conscientious man, proposing Four Reforms, revealing what the Governor Listeth, keeping a United Nations Journal, expressing Gratitude to Our Country.

He's perpetually plotting—a Last Stand for Tucker, a first fall for Blackford Oakes, une histoire pour Henry Tod, all, alas, Brothers No More.

He's a restless man, sometimes in Nuremberg, sometimes on an Atlantic High, sometimes waiting for a Windfall or the Fall of the Berlin Wall.

Yes, he's come a long way from God and Man at Yale, but ever Up from Liberalism.

Reflecting that Happy Days Were Here Again, our speaker asked the quintessential existential question, Who's on First?

One thing is for certain: he's always Getting It Right, for the Right Reason, and with the Right Word.

How important is Bill Buckley to the modern American conservative movement? Let me borrow from [Polish dissident leader] Lech Wałęsa, who was once asked how crucial the Voice of America and other American media were to the existence of Solidarity. Wałęsa replied, and I say the same thing about Bill and American conservatism:

Would there be the earth without the sun?

Ladies and gentlemen, fellow conservatives, please welcome the incandescent William F. Buckley Jr.

Notwithstanding my kind words about him, Bill said he was still going to speak kindly of me. "I keep wondering," he said, "when Lee Edwards will receive the critical attention he has earned with his continuing work as historian of our movement." He called my most recent book, a history of the Intercollegiate Studies Institute, "wise, penetrating, and readable." He described my historical essay about the Philadelphia Society, published in the program, as "a remarkable feat of research and organization."

Having made me bow my head and blush, just a little, he proceeded in his prepared remarks to salute the essential contributions of Barry Goldwater, Ed Feulner, and Don Lipsett, among others, to the conservative movement. He highly praised Albert Jay Nock, an early libertarian influence on him, for his emphasis on the importance of an intellectual Remnant like the Philadelphia Society.

Bill rejected Nock's innate pessimism, however. "We are devoted here to the proposition," he said, "that what we do and say and write *does* matter, does have effect." It can be held "with utmost seriousness," Bill said, that the work of the society, especially the annual meetings, "is proof of our substantiality. I have been with you from the beginning, and my investment of one hundred dollars in our society [used to open a bank account], I insist... has surely yielded a historic harvest. I am in your debt and so is the Republic."

In July 2004, I sent Bill a copy of my *Human Events* review of his latest book, *Miles Gone By: A Literary Autobiography*, which was a selection of previously published writings that presented a narrative survey of him at work and play. The personally chosen pieces, I wrote, revealed what mattered most to William F. Buckley Jr.—family and home, sailing and skiing. He counted *National Review*, at the center of American conservatism for nearly fifty years, as his most significant political achievement.

He was particularly proud of one subscriber, Ronald Reagan, who would emerge, he wrote, "as the principal political figure of the second half of the twentieth century." Reagan's most significant achievement, wrote Bill, reflecting the anticommunist passion that had driven him all his life, was the president's characterization of the Soviet Union as "an evil empire," setting in motion the forces that led in less than a decade to the dissolution of that empire.

I wrote in my review that publication of *Miles Gone By*, in Bill's seventy-ninth year, afforded conservatives an opportunity to thank the author "for demonstrating that it is possible to remain true to one's principles and faith and to make a difference in the world, in fact, to change the world."

In my cover letter, I said, "I am very aware that time is marching on for all of us. But I remember Dr. Judd saying when he was about 87 that he really had to cut back on all he was doing. And he did—when he died at 95."

In May 2005, as was my custom, I sent Buckley a copy of my short biography of Ed Meese, which elicited the following response:

> Dear Lee:
>
> I have read your book on Ed Meese. It is exemplary. We learn everything there is to know about Ed as a public man, and not a little about him as a private man. The book is wonderfully readable, and touches down on important points in recent history, and critical people in that history. It leaves certain questions slightly unsettled, but then so does history. My deepest congratulations.
>
> Always with high regard,
>
> Bill

I had inspected Bill's papers at Yale for my Goldwater biography as well as my history of the conservative movement, but I wanted to visit them again for a long-contemplated project, *Three Who Made a Movement*, a tripartite biography of Russell Kirk, Bill Buckley, and Barry Goldwater. I was an admirer of Bertram Wolfe's classic study *Three Who Made a Revolution* (that is, Lenin, Trotsky, and Stalin) and planned to show how the three American conservatives, sometimes in concert, sometimes independently, shaped the conservative movement in its founding years from 1948 through 1964. Aware that Sam Tanenhaus was writing Buckley's authorized biography, I assured Bill in my January 2007 letter that I would be careful not to invade Tanenhaus's turf. Bill replied, playfully:

> Dear Lee:
>
> You will make me nervous, since I am to be a biographical subject of your next book. I shall promise not to misbehave any time between 1948 and 1964.
>
> Thanks for your continuing help on Goldwater.
>
> Warmest ever,
>
> Bill

He was writing a short memoir about his times with the senator—
Flying High—and contacted me a few times about such details as "Did
he wear spurs?" My recollection: "No." Six months later, although suffering badly from emphysema and other ailments, Bill took the train
from Stamford to join us in Washington for the June 12 dedication of
the Victims of Communism Memorial and to receive the 2007 Truman-
Reagan Medal of Freedom, in the company of old friends Joe Lieberman
and Jack Kemp.

It was, so far as I have been able to determine, his last public address.

With William F. Buckley Jr., circa 1974

32

———

THE MAKING OF
A MEMORIAL

The year 1989 has rightly been called the "Year of Miracles," for it was within the span of only twelve months that communism—which had built the largest prison in history behind an iron curtain—collapsed, almost without a shot being fired. As president of the Victims of Communism Memorial Foundation (VOC), I watched events in Eastern and Central Europe unfold with mixed jubilation and trepidation. This was the year we had been waiting for, a year that a few wise men had predicted would happen: President Reagan had told the British Parliament in 1982 that Marxism-Leninism was headed for the ash heap of history. Zbigniew Brzezinski, an early member of VOC's National Advisory Board, had predicted that Marxism-Leninism was doomed to fail because it was "an alien doctrine...imposed by an imperial power culturally repugnant to the peoples of Eastern Europe." Ambassador Lev Dobriansky, VOC's chairman and a lifelong student of Soviet communism, said bluntly, "The Russians are not ten feet tall" and the key to bringing down the evil empire was the "captive nations" inside the Soviet Union and Eastern and Central Europe.

The miraculous year began with Erich Honecker, East Germany's communist boss, boasting that the Berlin Wall would stand for at least another hundred years. In February, Václav Havel was jailed in Prague for participating in human rights protests. Roundtable talks began in Poland between leaders of the outlawed Solidarity union and the communist government, although the communists had insisted that Solidarity was "a spent force." In March, seventy thousand people demonstrated in Budapest on the anniversary of the 1848 revolution, demanding a withdrawal of Soviet troops and free elections—just as they did in the 1956 revolution.

In April, Solidarity and the communist Polish government agreed to the first open elections since World War II and to restore Solidarity's legal status. In May, the Hungarian communist government started to dismantle the Iron Curtain along its border with Austria. Havel was released from jail after serving only half his sentence.

In June, Solidarity won an overwhelming victory over communist opponents in the Soviet bloc's first free elections in forty years. Imre Nagy, who had led the 1956 Hungarian uprising against Soviet domination, was given a hero's burial in Budapest.

In July, Soviet leader Mikhail Gorbachev reminded the Council of Europe meeting in Strasbourg, France, that he rejected the Brezhnev Doctrine, saying, "Any interference in domestic affairs and any attempts to restrict the sovereignty of states, both friends and allies or any others, are inadmissible."

In August, negotiations between Solidarity and the communists resulted in the selection of Poland's first noncommunist prime minister—a Solidarity member—since the early postwar years.

In September, an East German exodus began when Hungary opened its borders with Austria for more than thirteen thousand Germans. Another seventeen thousand East German citizens fled via West German embassies in Warsaw and Prague. The communist leadership and the anticommunist opposition in Hungary agreed to institute a multiparty political system.

In October, hundreds of thousands began demonstrating every Monday evening in East Germany, leading to the forced resignation of communist party boss Erich Honecker. In November, a tidal wave of East Germans poured across the border when travel restrictions were lifted and the Berlin Wall came down.

Bulgaria's chief communist stepped down after thirty-five years of rule as fifty thousand people gathered in Sofia demanding reforms. Millions of Czechs and Slovaks walked off their jobs and onto the streets, and the communist government in Czechoslovakia collapsed.

In December, free elections in Bulgaria were promised, and mass demonstrations took place in the Romanian cities of Timişoara and Bucharest. The year ended with the execution of Romanian despot

Nicolae Ceaușescu and the election of Václav Havel as the president of Czechoslovakia's first noncommunist government since the communist coup of February 1948.

TIANANMEN SQUARE

Things were far different in the People's Republic of China. In the spring of 1989, thousands of students, workers, and ordinary citizens began gathering in Tiananmen Square in Beijing calling for an open dialogue with the communist government and urging political reforms like open elections. As the number of demonstrators in the square exceeded one million and similar demonstrations began occurring in other major cities, the communist government's fear of a countrywide rebellion escalated. Deng Xiaoping imposed martial law, but that did not affect the martial spirit of the youthful demonstrators, who were now calling for democracy.

Early in the morning of June 4, 1989, while East Europeans were drawing closer to their goal of a free and democratic region, Deng ordered troops and tanks to sweep clean Tiananmen Square and tear down the thirty-two-foot Goddess of Democracy statue. Hundreds and perhaps thousands of mostly Chinese students were killed. Many were jailed as "counterrevolutionaries" and for conspiring to overthrow the government. The brutality of the Chinese communist regime, loyal to Mao's dictum "Political power grows out of the barrel of a gun," shocked many in the West who had been excitedly describing the events in Tiananmen Square as "the week that changed the world."

As well as I thought I knew him, I was not prepared for Walter Judd's reaction. I was in the audience when he told a group of student leaders that the massacre was "one of the most encouraging things that's happened in China" in a long time. Some of the audience (including me) gasped at his words. It was "encouraging," he calmly explained, because "it proves that communism . . . has failed" to satisfy the wishes and wants of the Chinese people. The Chinese communists have "exposed themselves until even the blindest can see that they are barbarians; they're not true Chinese."

He predicted there would be other rebellions in China, and that they too would probably be crushed for a while longer. Nevertheless, he felt that an end to communism's control was in sight. "I've said all along that I hope this awful [tyranny] can be brought to an end by the close of this

century. I think it may even be sooner." He added, "Tyrants have almost
always looked invincible until the last five minutes and then all of a sudden they fall apart."

Three months later, the Berlin Wall came tumbling down, setting
off a delirium of celebration not only in Germany and Eastern Europe
but around the world. I, too, celebrated and shed tears, thinking of those
East Germans who had tried and failed to escape their communist captors. I sat entranced on Christmas Day as Leonard Bernstein and the
Berlin Philharmonic—in the shadow of the Brandenburg Gate—gave a
passionate performance of Beethoven's Choral Symphony in which the
concluding "Ode to Joy" became an ode to "*freiheit*"—freedom. Next, I
thought to myself, "*svoboda*" in Moscow.

GENESIS

One Sunday afternoon in early January 1990, Anne and I and our elder
daughter, Elizabeth, home from her graduate studies in international
relations at the University of Virginia, were talking politics over brunch
following Mass. Two months earlier, I said to Anne and Elizabeth, there
had been dancing in the streets and champagne toasts on top of the Berlin
Wall. Yet few people wanted to discuss why communism had collapsed—
or examine its unparalleled murderous record. A general amnesia, even
in the former communist countries, seemed to be spreading throughout
the free world.

Suddenly, Anne said, "You know what we need? We need a memorial
to the victims of communism!"

"Terrific idea!" I said and wrote down on a paper napkin, "Memorial
to victims of communism" and stuck the napkin in my pocket. I resolved to
call Lev Dobriansky, responsible for the 1964 building of a monument to
the nineteenth-century Ukrainian poet and patriot Taras Shevchenko in
the heart of Washington's Embassy Row. Lev and I had worked together
since the early 1970s to promote National Captive Nations Week each
July—our 1976 rally at the Democratic National Convention in New
York City had been one of our most successful events. He would be familiar with the process of building a Washington memorial.

As I reflected on what would be necessary for such an undertaking—
obtaining congressional support, organizing and publicizing a parent organization, selecting a design, raising funds, enlisting experts on
communism—it struck me that my life had been a preparation for such

a venture. I had worked in Congress, I knew every reputable anticommunist in the country and some not so reputable, I had started a half dozen not-for-profit organizations, I had put my clients on the covers of national newspapers and magazines, I had raised millions of dollars, and I knew the importance of staying focused on a goal. It would be a historic project—the first memorial in the world to *all* the victims of communism, more than 100 million of them in some forty nations.

Lev enthusiastically endorsed the idea, and we drew up a plan of action for what he called the "Great Adventure." The first step was a congressional resolution authorizing an international memorial to the victims of communism. I drafted the resolution, drawing on the language of the Shevchenko resolution. We were explicit about the central responsibility of the Soviet Union for the deaths of millions of victims:

(1) Since 1917, the rulers of empires and international communism led by Vladimir I. Lenin and Mao Tse-tung have been responsible for the deaths of over 100,000,000 victims in an unprecedented imperial communist holocaust through conquests, revolutions, civil wars, purges, wars by proxy, and other violent means;

(2) The imperialist regimes of international communism have brutally suppressed the human rights, national independence, religious liberty, intellectual freedom, and cultural life of the peoples of over 40 captive nations;

(3) There is a danger that the heroic sacrifices of the victims of communism may be forgotten as international communism and its imperial bases continue to collapse and crumble; and

(4) The sacrifices of these victims should be permanently memorialized so that never again will nations and peoples allow so evil a tyranny to terrorize the world.

Lev began talking to his contacts on Capitol Hill to discover who was interested in sponsoring the resolution in the House and the Senate. Congressman Jerry Solomon (R-NY), a ranking member of the House Ways and Means Committee, was the first sponsor of the memorial resolution, introducing it in 1990. Over the next three years, prominent Democrats as well as Republicans signed on as sponsors, including Senators Jesse Helms (R-NC), Claiborne Pell (D-RI) (chairman of the Senate Foreign Relations Committee), and Joe Lieberman (D-CT), and Representatives Dana Rohrabacher (R-CA), Tom Lantos (D-CA), Ileana Ros-Lehtinen (R-FL), Lee Hamilton (D-IN) (chairman of the

House Foreign Affairs Committee), and Robert Torricelli (D-NJ). Two congressional staffers were especially helpful to us: former Marine Paul Behrends, in the office of Representative Rohrabacher, and Anne Smith, a staff member of the Senate Foreign Relations Committee under the patronage of Senator Helms.

Although a number of congressmen signed on as cosponsors of our resolution, we did not muster sufficient support for legislative action, including hearings. In December 1993 Providence intervened. President Bill Clinton and Russian president Boris Yeltsin scheduled a summit meeting in late December. Seeking to advance U.S.-Russian relations after the Cold War, Clinton submitted to the solidly Democratic Congress on very short notice the "Friendship 'R-Us" Act, which established a new economic and cultural foundation between the two former adversaries.

Congressional leaders sought unanimous approval of the bipartisan measure, expecting no opposition. But Behrends and Smith saw an opportunity and persuaded their bosses to seize it. Rohrabacher in the House and Helms in the Senate both objected to unanimous consent. Anxious to pass the act and with time running out, House Speaker Tom Foley and Senate Majority Leader George Mitchell asked the naysayers what might change their mind. Back came the reply: attaching to the Friendship Act a resolution authorizing the design and construction of a Washington memorial to the victims of communism.

In short order, the Victims of Communism Memorial resolution was vetted by the National Security Council, the State Department, and other government agencies. Rohrabacher and Helms withdrew their objections. Following pro forma debate in the House and the Senate, Congress unanimously passed Public Law 103-199, authorizing the Victims of Communism Memorial, and President Clinton signed the law on December 17, 1993. The other signatories were House Speaker Tom Foley and Senate president pro tempore Robert Byrd (D-WV). A lineup of Helms, Rohrabacher, Clinton, Foley, and Byrd was bipartisanship writ large.

Section (b) of the law states: "The National Captive Nations Committee, Inc. (NCNC) is authorized to construct, maintain, and operate in the District of Columbia an appropriate international memorial to honor victims of communism." It further states that the NCNC is encouraged to create "an independent entity" to construct and maintain the memorial and that this entity should include as "active participants . . . all groups that have suffered under communism." That "independent entity" was to be the Victims of Communism Memorial Foundation.

A providential pattern had been established with the passage of Public Law 103-199. Time and again, when VOC confronted a seemingly insurmountable obstacle—legislative, bureaucratic, or financial—something or someone miraculously intervened. In this case, two of the staunchest anticommunists in Congress used a summit meeting between a liberal Democratic president and a former member of the Soviet politburo to advance the Great Adventure.

We had congressional authorization and a provisional grant of federal land for the memorial. But Public Law 103-199 stated that "no federal funds" could be spent on the "establishment" of the memorial. The organizers—that is, Lev and I and others—would have to obtain nongovernmental support from U.S. individuals, foundations, and corporations. Fortunately, the law did not prohibit us from seeking funds overseas from governments or other entities.

GETTING STARTED

Lev and I came to an agreement regarding incorporation, the officers, and the initial board of directors. Lev would be chairman and I would be president and CEO. He nominated ethnic representatives with whom he had worked for years. I proposed people who were anticommunist to the core and of means. Attorney David Rivkin, who was a former Georgetown University student of Lev's, and his associate Lee Casey turned out to be marvelously helpful, obtaining VOC's tax-exempt status and serving as our pro bono legal counsel for the next decade and a half. Lev and I had frequent phone conversations and I consulted him on major decisions. We agreed that the end goal should be a memorial museum and not just a monument.

As a brand-new organization, we needed well-known experts on communism to give us standing. We invited the three leading authorities in America to join our national advisory board—Robert Conquest of the Hoover Institution, author of the definitive work *The Great Terror*; Harvard historian Richard Pipes, who had served on the staff of the National Security Council under President Reagan; and Zbigniew Brzezinski, national security adviser to President Carter. All agreed to serve, forming an impressive anticommunist troika.

We also needed prominent people for our International Advisory Council. With the help of Paula Dobriansky, Lev's well-connected daughter, and others, we lined up Elena Bonner, widow of the famed

Russian dissident and Nobel laureate Andrei Sakharov; former Polish president Lech Wałęsa, a Solidarity founder and Nobel laureate; former Czech president Václav Havel, leader of the Prague Spring; former Lithuanian head of state Vytautas Landsbergis; former Hungarian president Árpád Göncz; and Armando Valladares, a courageous Cuban dissident whom Fidel Castro had imprisoned for twenty years for alleged counterrevolutionary activity.

Asked to explain the importance of the monument, Conquest replied: "It will be a warning as well as a memorial. It will be a warning to anybody that totalitarian rule produces deadly results." Asked by a skeptical reporter why he had endorsed a victims of communism memorial, Brzezinski said, "This Museum is needed because too many people are too eager to forget that Communism caused many more deaths than even Nazism."

In the spring of 1995, Lev and I met for the first time with John Parsons, a senior official of the National Park Service, which oversees all memorials and monuments in Washington and the country. Parsons gave us a memorandum titled "Steps for Establishing a Memorial in the Nation's Capital." There were twenty-four separate steps to be negotiated, from legislation, site selection, and design approval to fundraising and construction. Step #24 reads: "Memorial is dedicated and transferred to NPS (National Park Service) or GSA (General Services Administration) for management with accompanying as-built operation, maintenance, and preservation plans." But it was made clear to us that VOC, not the NPS or GSA, would be responsible for operation, maintenance, and preservation. As we prepared to leave his office, Parsons said quietly, "It's going to take longer than you think."

A MEMORIAL MUSEUM

From the beginning, we thought in terms not only of a memorial but also of a museum, along the lines of the U.S. Holocaust Memorial Museum, located just off the national mall and within view of the Washington Monument. Knowing the Holocaust Memorial Museum had raised $164 million in private funds, we set a goal of $100 million for our memorial museum—$100 million for the 100 million people who had died under communism through executions, deliberate famines, forced labor camps, relocation, and other violent means. Half of the $100 million would be for our building, the other half for continuing operations and an endowment. We did not want to build a memorial museum and not have the funds to operate it.

The $100 million goal seemed reasonable and justifiable, but we soon learned how naive we were. We kept waiting for wealthy patrons from former communist countries to come walking through the door with large checks in their hands. But no one ever did—until twenty years later.

We were trying to conduct a national capital campaign with no seed money, no donor base, and no paid staff. By the spring of 1999, five years later, we had raised less than a million dollars. I had failed to persuade major fundraisers like Steve Winchell, Bruce Eberle, and Richard Viguerie to accept VOC as a client. They were sympathetic to the cause but skeptical about the public's response. One commented to me, "Your timing is not good. Most of the wealthy anticommunists have passed away." Our single largest donor in the early years was the investment guru Sir John Templeton, who gave us $10,000 because Lev had befriended him while serving as U.S. ambassador to the Bahamas, where Templeton lived.

Most of my friends kept telling me that we were engaged in an impossible task: Anticommunism was yesterday. China wasn't communist—look at all those skyscrapers in Beijing and Shanghai. Even hawks like John McCain were saying let bygones be bygones and visiting Vietnam. We should drop the economic sanctions on Cuba—what good had they done? More than once between 1994 and 1999 I almost gave up. I drafted a letter of resignation that I kept in my desk. Fundraising was not something I enjoyed, but fundraising was what needed to be done. I didn't quit for two reasons: (1) Lev Dobriansky argued that we couldn't let the captive nations and peoples down and that we should be patient—the right patron would come walking through our door one day; and (2) I couldn't forget the Hungarian uprising and the pledge I had made. Even so, it was clear that what we were doing wasn't working.

Our first step was to raise our profile. We initiated an annual ceremony to award the Truman-Reagan Medal of Freedom to a deserving individual or organization that had demonstrated lifelong opposition to communism and other forms of tyranny and public support of freedom and democracy. We named the medal after the president when the Cold War started (liberal Democrat Harry Truman) and the president when the Cold War effectively ended (conservative Republican Ronald Reagan). I have been criticized by some conservative anticommunists for using Truman's name (the former president said in a 1956 TV interview, for example, that he did not think Alger Hiss was a communist spy). But Truman's central role in fashioning the policy of containment, which blocked Soviet attempts to dominate Western Europe in the postwar period, is undeniable. The Truman-Reagan Medal of Freedom honored the principle of bipartisanship that has guided the VOC from the beginning.

The first recipients of the Truman-Reagan Medal of Freedom in 1999 were Elena Bonner, Andrei Sakharov's widow; AFL-CIO president Lane Kirkland, who died of cancer just months before our ceremony; Vytautas Landsbergis, former head of state of Lithuania; and Bulgarian diplomat Philip Dimitrov. Since then, the VOC has awarded the Medal of Freedom to more than fifty champions of freedom, including Václav Havel, Lech Wałęsa, Pope John Paul II, Senator Joe Lieberman, William F. Buckley Jr., Michael Novak, Senator Jesse Helms, Soviet dissident Vladimir Bukovsky, Hungarian prime minister Viktor Orbán, Solidarity activist Anna Walentynowicz, Czech victim of communism Milada Horáková, Heritage Foundation president Ed Feulner, Chinese pro-democracy activist Wei Jingsheng, Vietnamese dissident Đoàn Viết Hoạt, South Korean general Paik Sun-yup, Cuban dissident Guillermo Fariñas Hernández, and Soviet dissident Alexander Podrabinek.

Our second step was to stop depending on volunteers and hire professionals to administer the affairs of the foundation. Robert Schadler, who had extensive knowledge of international relations through his government and nongovernment service, was our first executive director. Bob set up our first office and expanded the donor base. Bill Tucker and Anne Meesman of Tucker & Associates were retained to administer the annual Truman-Reagan Medal of Freedom awards, usually held at a foreign embassy. Everybody agreed that the food and particularly the vodka at the Polish embassy were outstanding.

Providence again visited us. In 2003, following a national search, Jay Katzen, a former foreign service officer and a highly regarded member of the Virginia state legislature, became the VOC's first full-time president. After almost a decade, Lev stepped down as chairman, becoming chairman emeritus, and I succeeded him as chairman. I like to think that Jay Katzen and I made a pretty good team.

Energetic and experienced, Katzen drew up a fundraising plan, began visiting potential individual donors and organizations, and worked closely with the board as we shifted from building a memorial museum to a three-step objective: (1) building a memorial on Capitol Hill; (2) launching online exhibits about communism; and (3) raising the funds for an international museum on communism in downtown Washington or near the National Mall.

After showing little enthusiasm for our vision of a $100 million museum, the National Park Service said it would be pleased to work with us on a memorial. Donors reacted favorably to our $1 million fundraising goal. Ethnic communities, led by the Vietnamese American community in Northern Virginia followed by the Latvians, Lithuanians, and Estonians, stepped up their participation. With Bill Tucker's guidance, in 2003 we invited President George W. Bush to be our honorary chairman. Tim Goeglein in the White House brought the invitation to the attention of his boss, Karl Rove. Sitting presidents rarely serve on nongovernmental boards, but to our delight, President Bush said yes. That prepared the way for his agreeing to speak at the dedication of the memorial.

AFTERSHOCKS

All the while, we felt the aftershocks of the collapse of the evil empire. In the early 1990s, Russian president Boris Yeltsin opened up the Soviet archives to Western researchers, like our friend and colleague Herbert Romerstein, who proved once and for all that Whittaker Chambers had been telling the truth that Alger Hiss had been a Soviet spy. But after two years, the archives were again closed.

Funds for Perm, the one Gulag camp in the former Soviet Union that had turned into a museum, dried up. The only memorial to Stalin's victims, the historian Martin Malia wrote, is a stone from the Arctic prison camp of Solovki placed in a corner of Lubyanka Square, where the KGB's former headquarters stands. Lenin's statue still dominates many city squares, and "his mummy reposes honorably in its [Red Square] mausoleum."

In the mid-1990s, the unpredictable Yeltsin confounded his critics by narrowly defeating the communists in a hotly contested presidential election and steering Russia toward the West, most visibly by his acceptance of Poland, Hungary, and the Czech Republic as new members of NATO. As the historian William Roger Louis wrote, "Without Yeltsin's acquiescence NATO . . . would have taken a different direction."

Tired and suffering from a variety of ailments, probably accentuated by his heavy drinking, Yeltsin decided to step down as president and personally selected as his successor a Yeltsin loyalist and former KGB colonel, Vladimir Putin. On May 7, 2000, Putin was inaugurated and vowed to "preserve and develop democracy," while inviting as a guest Vladimir Kryuchkov, the former KGB director who had orchestrated the unsuccessful 1991 coup that Yeltsin had almost single-handedly defeated. In the years to come, President Putin would provide abundant proof that authoritarian rule had returned to Russia and enable VOC to argue that our mission to tell the truth about communism and its legacy in countries like Russia was more timely than ever.

Throughout Eastern Europe, few ex-communist officials were tried or punished. Many began new and lucrative careers in politics or business. In the 2000s, however, an anticommunist conservative reaction set in, exemplified by the election of Viktor Orbán as prime minister of Hungary and Andrzej Duda as president of Poland.

In China, Deng Xiaoping's economic reforms had their impact, creating a sizable Chinese middle class and a coterie of millionaires, most of them party members and high-ranking military officers. Economic growth averaged about 10 percent annually during the 1990s but dipped the following decade. KFC restaurants and Starbucks coffeehouses sprang up by the hundreds and then the thousands. Amway annually did more than a billion dollars' worth of business. But China was still neither a free nor an open society. The crime of counterrevolution remained on the books. Most trials took place in camera. The death penalty was widely used, and thousands were executed every year, many of them publicly. There were at least 100,000 political prisoners in the *laogai*. Harsh persecution of Tibetans and Muslims in Western China continued apace.

Where a communist regime still prevails, the French historian Stéphane Courtois wrote, the rulers have either covered up their actions, as in China and Cuba, or continued to promote terror as a means of control, as in North Korea. Regarding the last, *The Black Book of Communism* estimated in 1997 that there had been "more than 3 million victims in a country of 23 million inhabitants that has lived under Communism for 50 years." On the other side of the world, in Cuba, more than 100,000 Cubans were in a camp, prison, or open-regime site between 1959 and the late 1990s. Between 15,000 and 17,000 people were shot, some personally killed by Fidel Castro's favored executioner, Che Guevara. With Cuba and its communist regime struggling following the end of Soviet aid in the billions of dollars annually, Castro said in 1994 that he "would rather die than abandon the revolution." The Cuban people were not consulted and continued to suffer. Castro finally died in 2016, but liberalization did not follow, with the number of arbitrary arrests of dissidents soaring to nearly 10,000 that year.

TOWARD A MEMORIAL

VOC continued to track communism's offenses against human rights and liberties even as it addressed the critical question of memorial design. We solicited the opinions of our national advisory board, our international council, ethnic communities, donors, academics, and friends. The suggestions included a replica of the Berlin Wall; a Gulag barracks; a killing field of Cambodia complete with skulls; an escape boat used by Vietnamese and Cubans; a broken or otherwise defaced statue of Stalin, Lenin, or Mao; a cell in the infamous Lubyanka prison; a watchtower; and barbed wire, lots of barbed wire.

Two icons led the list: the Brandenburg Gate and the Goddess of Democracy statue in Tiananmen Square. After months of discussion and debate, the board of directors unanimously selected the democracy statue as the core of our memorial because (1) it calls to mind the Tiananmen Square massacre and the continuing communist oppression in the world's most populous country; (2) it is based on the Statue of Liberty in New York Harbor, reflecting man's indomitable desire to be free; and (3) it has become a global symbol of freedom and democracy, with replicas in France, the United Kingdom, Nigeria, Taiwan, Canada, and San Francisco's Chinatown.

We did not conduct a national design competition as had been done with the Vietnam War Veterans Memorial and other Washington monuments. The National Park Service advised that such a competition would be time-consuming and expensive. Carl Gershman, president of the National Endowment for Democracy and a member of our national advisory board, recommended Thomas Marsh as a sculptor and designer. A noted California artist, Marsh had already made a bronze replica of the Goddess of Democracy for San Francisco's Chinese community, working closely with Chinese students, several of whom had been in Tiananmen Square in June 1989.

I contacted Marsh, who before I finished explaining our plans agreed to create a special bronze replica for us and to waive his fee (which would have been in the six figures). He explained that he had vowed not to profit from anything he did in connection with Tiananmen Square. Politically conservative and a recent Catholic convert, Thomas became a good friend and a valued member of the VOC team.

We then received most unwelcome news: Jay Katzen reluctantly tendered his resignation as president. His contributions had been significant and long lasting: we committed ourselves to building a memorial, setting aside the idea of a museum for the time being; he raised more than $200,000 for the memorial; he helped us find Hartman-Cox, a premier Washington architectural firm, to oversee design and construction. Hartman-Cox assigned us a top associate, Mary Kay Lanzillotta. Petite and unflappable, Mary Kay had guided many other clients through the twenty-four-step maze of building a Washington monument. VOC was more than a client to Mary Kay, who had done postgraduate study in Moscow and understood the importance of our memorial. As a budgetary measure, we decided not to seek another president but to have me assume the unpaid position of chairman and CEO.

NEIGHBORHOOD NEGOTIATIONS

Even Mary Kay could not help when the members of Advisory Neighborhood Commission (ANC) 6C—a small but influential city agency—voiced strong opposition to our memorial's being erected on a small plot of land a half block from the Supreme Court. At an open hearing, aroused citizens protested that they used the space for sunbathing, Frisbee throwing, and walking their dogs. They argued that the memorial was bound to increase foot and vehicular traffic and would destroy the small-town atmosphere of the neighborhood. Despite the support of other homeowners who lived on or near the square, ANC 6C voted against the memorial, although it did pass a resolution endorsing the construction of a Victims of Communism Memorial on Capitol Hill. That turned out to be an important concession.

Following the rejection, I contacted Glenn DeMarr of the National Park Service, who said, "Let's go for a drive." We drove around Capitol Hill looking for sites until we stopped at a triangle of land at the intersection of Massachusetts Avenue NW, New Jersey Avenue NW, and G Street NW, two blocks from Union Station, four blocks from the U.S. Capitol, and across the street from the Georgetown Law School. The third-of-an-acre site was within the purview of the same ANC 6C that had already turned us down, but the new site—which DeMarr said was available—was surrounded by office buildings rather than private residences or apartments. No one had used the area for any purpose, human or canine, for years. It had been a victory garden during World War II.

We learned that the key person for approval was Lawrence Thomas, a veteran commission member whose jurisdiction included the proposed site. He was recovering from illness in a nearby nursing facility and had not attended an ANC meeting in some time. Mary Kay and I decided to visit Thomas.

One Sunday afternoon, we spent two and a half hours standing and talking with the sixty-nine-year-old African American, who had walked with Martin Luther King Jr. and was a political ally of former Washington mayor Marion Barry. We answered dozens of questions: "How will this benefit my constituents?" "How long will it take?" "Will construction tie up traffic?" Finally, Thomas looked up from his wheelchair and said, "Well, I want you to know one thing—I don't like communism." Why hadn't he said that an hour earlier? I asked myself, trying to ease my aching legs.

Thomas agreed to introduce a resolution in favor of the memorial at the next ANC 6C meeting the following Tuesday evening. Two days later, Glenn, Mary Kay, her colleague Gail Douglass, and I were anxiously waiting for Thomas's arrival. At ten minutes past seven, when the meeting was supposed to start, he had not appeared, and I could see the commission getting ready to begin the meeting. And then we heard the clanking sound of a wheelchair and Thomas came rolling down the aisle, taking his place at the end of the table amid warm greetings from his fellow commissioners. He said loudly, "Let's get this show on the road. I have a resolution to introduce."

The vote was unanimous for our memorial. Over the next twelve months, the National Capital Planning Commission approved the site, and the Commission on Fine Arts approved the design—despite protests to the State Department and the National Park Service by the Chinese communist ambassador. "This memorial will hurt U.S.-China relations," he said to a State official, who responded that the memorial was a private and not a governmental project. The official suggested that the ambassador direct his objections to the VOC. He never did.

33

THE FINAL STEP

Ll that remained was to raise the necessary funds. But that was no small task. A National Park Service official had originally estimated that the memorial—without the bubbling fountain and the dramatic lighting we had considered and rejected because of cost—could be built for an estimated $500,000, including construction, architectural and design fees, and other expenses. If $500,000 sounds low, it is, and was possible only because the federal government had donated the land and sculptor Thomas Marsh, God bless him, had waived his fee.

By early 2005, VOC had raised only half the necessary amount, a little more than $250,000. Karl Altau of the Joint Baltic American National Committee, Randal Teague of the Fund for American Studies, Anhthu Lu of the Northern Virginia Vietnamese Community, and other foundation board members began an aggressive fundraising campaign among friends and colleagues. We hired Mari Patterson Rusch as a fundraising consultant. Rusch, along with Alexandra Preate and Michael Tew of CapitalHQ, organized a reception and dinner honoring Lech Wałęsa in New York City. We netted more than $50,000, because Wałęsa was a star attraction and because of the special generosity of Catherine Windels at Pfizer. A targeted direct-mail campaign produced a list of more than a thousand contributors who gave from $5 all the way up to $10,000.

We sent proposals to corporations Lockheed Martin and Phillips International and foundations like Heritage, the Fund for American

Studies, Young America's Foundation, Earhart, and the Shelby Cullom Davis Foundation. Pew Charitable Trusts was the leading foundation, with a grant of $50,000, which surprised many conservatives. I had met Rebecca Rimel, the president of the trusts, at the unveiling of a J. Howard Pew statue at Grove City College. I was there because I had written *Freedom's College*, the history of the college. Rimel was there because Pew had been a leading benefactor of the college for decades. When I described the Victims of Communism Memorial, Rebecca responded that Mr. Pew would have certainly supported the memorial and invited me to submit a proposal.

We adhered to a bare-bones operations budget, made possible by dozens of volunteers, such as Teri Ruddy and Marie Ciliberti, and a host of interns, including Tony Nunes, Melinda Haring, Kenneth Cribb, and the tireless Caitlin Carroll. I and all the other board members served without compensation.

But as fast as funds were raised and deposited in our account, the price of the memorial kept climbing—from $500,000 to $600,000, $750,000, $900,000, almost double what had been first calculated. Reasons for the increase included inflation; the rising cost of bronze, stone, and other materials; and fees for an environmental survey ($22,000) and to Hartman-Cox (about $150,000 in all), which was leading us through the many steps required for a Washington memorial. It turned out that several steps had substeps. And the National Park Service stipulated that *all* the money had to be deposited in the bank before it would issue a construction permit.

In early 2006, we set a new (and we hoped final) goal: $950,000, which included the construction cost of the memorial plaza, the molding and casting of the democracy statue, architectural and other fees, a $50,000 contingency, a wayside sign (required), and a 10 percent fee of the construction costs (about $70,000) to be paid to the National Park Service. The service required the last fee to cover any extraordinary damage caused by earthquake or deliberate vandalism. The National Park Service fee did not cover maintenance of the memorial, which was the sole responsibility of the Victims of Communism Memorial Foundation in perpetuity. Because of this last obligation and at Lev's suggestion, we opened a special bank account and deposited an initial sum of $20,000.

By mid-2006, some twelve years since our incorporation, we had in the bank more than $850,000 thanks to the continuing help of Ed Feulner of the Heritage Foundation, Tom Phillips of Phillips International, Randal Teague and Roger Ream of the Fund for American

Studies, Catherine Windels of Pfizer, Ron Robinson of Young America's Foundation, Jon Utley of the Freda Utley Foundation, Abby Moffat and Diana Davis Spencer of the Shelby Cullom Davis Foundation, Rebecca Rimel of Pew Charitable Trusts, Ingrid Gregg and David Kennedy of Earhart, Jack Snyder and Barbara Reinicke of Lockheed Martin, Charles Hoeflich, Andreas Traks, George Strake, the Conrad Hilton Foundation, the Sarah Scaife Foundation, Richard and Helen DeVos, and others. Phillips International was the number-one corporation, with gifts totaling $75,000.

We also benefited from the governmental and private-sector support of the Republic of China, totaling some $75,000, as well as the Czech Republic, Estonia, Latvia, Lithuania, Georgia, Bulgaria, the Slovak Republic, and Poland. Hungary, which would make a most generous gift several years later for a museum, contributed $5,000 for our memorial. We set a ceiling of $75,000 for gifts from any one source. Some parties wanted to give more, but I insisted that no individual, company, or government could give more than 10 percent of the cost of the memorial. This preempted any charge of favoritism.

But we were still short $75,000. Where to go? We had contacted just about every anticommunist source I could think of. Then I remembered that a year earlier we had submitted a proposal for a $25,000 grant to the Knights of Columbus, the largest Catholic lay organization in America and stoutly opposed to communism, the implacable enemy of the Church since the Bolshevik Revolution. We had never received a response. The Grand Knight of the Knights was Carl Anderson, who had been the chief of staff for Senator Jesse Helms, a cosponsor of our enabling legislation. Why not, I thought, ask the senator, who had received a Truman-Reagan Medal of Freedom, to intervene with his former aide on our behalf?

I drafted a letter and tried to reach the now retired senator, only to discover that because of age and poor health, he had moved into a nursing home. But the senator's daughter offered to show him the proposed letter on her next visit. Shortly thereafter, she reported that her father had approved and signed the letter. She said it might well be his last "official" communication. Two weeks later, we received a cordial letter from Grand Knight Anderson along with a $25,000 Knights of Columbus check. We had again benefited from an unusual combination of forces—in this case, the personal relationship between a Southern Baptist senator and a Roman Catholic lay leader.

Several promising foundation proposals were pending, but we were anxious to deposit the final $50,000 before inflation and other factors drove the cost of the memorial any higher. We decided to seek a bank loan. One of the people whom I approached as a guarantor of the note was Alfred Regnery, then publisher of the *American Spectator* and a VOC board member. "Don't bother with the bank," Al said. "I'll loan the money." With Al Regnery's $50,000 in hand, we notified the National Park Service that we had raised the funds needed to build the memorial.

On September 8, 2006, the National Park Service issued a permit to the Victims of Communism Memorial Foundation for the construction of a memorial at U.S. Reservation 77B at the intersection of Massachusetts Avenue NW, New Jersey Avenue NW, and G Street NW, in accordance with Public Law 103-199, Section 905, enacted December 17, 1993. A donation of $68,213, equal to 10 percent of the estimated cost of construction (excluding architectural and artists' fees), was paid to the National Park Foundation for "the perpetual maintenance and preservation of the Victims of Communism Memorial." Notwithstanding that language, all parties understood that the foundation and not the Park Service was responsible for the upkeep of the memorial.

Hartman-Cox had already talked to the Forrester Construction Company of Maryland, one of the area's top construction companies, about serving as general contractor, and to the Lorton Contracting Company to do the stonework. Contracts were signed and commitments were made to finish the memorial by June 12, 2007, the twentieth anniversary of President Reagan's memorable "Mr. Gorbachev, tear down this Wall!" speech at the Brandenburg Gate.

34

DEDICATION DAY

Experts have told me that no memorial has been built in a shorter period of time—just nine months—than the Victims of Communism Memorial. And we maintained the highest professional standards all the way. You can see it for yourself the next time you visit Washington, D.C.—we're two blocks from Union Station at the corner of Massachusetts Avenue NW and New Jersey Avenue NW, across from the Georgetown University Law Center.

Our groundbreaking took place on September 27, 2006. Undersecretary of State Paula Dobriansky was the featured speaker. Unfortunately, Lev was too sick to join us and to hear his daughter salute the victims of communism, whose sacrifice, she said, will be remembered with the memorial, which "will stand after we no longer do." The other speakers were Representative Dana Rohrabacher, an original congressional sponsor of the memorial, and Joseph Lawler of the National Park Service. "Washington is a city of memorials and monuments to great events and great leaders," I said to the VIP audience, which included the ambassadors from Poland, the Czech Republic, Hungary, Latvia, Lithuania, Estonia, and the Republic of China (Taiwan). "We are proud that our memorial, dedicated to the more than 100 million victims of communism, will join this distinguished list."

In early February 2007, I traveled with Gail Douglass of Hartman-Cox, Keith Kern of Forrester Construction, and Manuel Seara of Lorton Contracting to Cold Spring, Minnesota, to visit the Cold Spring Granite Company. "Frozen Spring" was more like it. Wearing hard hats and woolen long johns, we inspected and approved the stone to be used for the memorial plaza and the statue base. We toured the sprawling facilities of Cold Spring, the largest granite company in the world, which ships some fifty trucks of stone each week to its customers.

In late April, sculptor Thomas Marsh and I visited the Nordhammer Foundry in Northern California, reluctantly bypassing some promising vineyards. Owner Rolf Kriken, a sculptor himself, explained the months-long process of sculpting, molding, casting, baking, and pouring that produces a bronze statue—a process invented in China some four thousand years ago. How appropriate, I thought. We were joined by Steve Krochman, another California sculptor, who had made the mold for the democracy statue, which was shipped across the country, arriving in Washington in late May.

D-DAY

A week before the dedication, Tim Goeglein at the White House told me that it looked promising for President Bush to come, but all we could say publicly was that the president had been "invited." My Positive Mental Attitude kicked in, and I said confidently, "He's coming."

I remember how excited I was when I received the confirming call from the White House just three days before D-Day (Dedication Day). "This is an outside event, correct?" the aide asked. When I said yes, she said, "Well, be prepared. It's going to be expensive." While I knew there were extra costs when hosting a president, I didn't realize all that was involved until we met with the Secret Service and a White House consultant on public events at the memorial site. The consultant—actually a charming fellow—quietly read the required items:

- A sturdy ten-foot-by-ten-foot platform with an escape hatch and chute in case the president had literally to drop out of sight in an emergency: $25,000
- A large, reinforced, three-sided tent into which the presidential limousine would pull: $5,000
- Banners, shrubs, and other foliage that would serve as a backdrop and shield the president from any potential shooter behind him: $5,000

- Extra police to handle traffic as well as a platoon of security guards to handle a crowd of about a thousand: $10,000

We had budgeted $50,000 in case the president did come, but after the Secret Service was through, the amount jumped to almost $75,000. It was worth every dollar.

After his fine remarks at the dedication ceremony, President Bush stepped down from the platform and "walked the line," shaking the hands of people in the first row. One person standing there was Joseph Wu, the director of Taiwan's trade and cultural office in Washington, D.C., and its unofficial ambassador to the United States. It was the first time since Jimmy Carter had derecognized the Republic of China in 1978 that an American president and a Taiwanese diplomat had met face-to-face. The picture of the two officials shaking hands appeared on the front pages and on the evening newscasts of every Taiwanese outlet the next day, as well as in many other foreign media. We had deliberately placed Ambassador Wu in the middle of the front row, hoping for just such a close encounter of a diplomatic kind.

Other speakers at the dedication ceremony included Congressmen Tom Lantos and Dana Rohrabacher. The only survivor of the Holocaust to serve in Congress and now chairman of the House Foreign Affairs Committee, Lantos had been a cosponsor of our congressional resolution and an early member of our National Advisory Board. In his keynote address, delivered as usual without a text or any notes, Tom said that "everyone who has tasted communism, from Albania to Estonia, knows that without the United States this existential struggle would have been lost." He compared what he called "distorted Islamic fascism" with godless communism and predicted that NATO would be revitalized "as the military arm of the civilized world and see to it that no Nazism, no communism, no Ahmadinejad-ism will prevail on this planet." It was the last public speech that Lantos, as eloquent a speaker as anyone in Washington, would make, as he succumbed to cancer early the following year.

I first met Rohrabacher in the 1960s at one of Ed Butler's Square Power conferences and stayed in touch with him when he was a speechwriter for President Reagan. Dana was known for his passionate defense of human rights and fierce anticommunism. That June morning he noted that throughout the Cold War, political and intellectual elites opposed a firm American stand against communism. Echoing Tom Lantos, Dana said that now that the Soviet Union was no more, the same voices had taken to denouncing a strong American stand against radical Islam.

In the audience were two victims of communism from Vietnam—Dan Ho and Henry Tran. Ho served in the Army of South Vietnam in the 1970s and was imprisoned by the communists for seven years. He left Vietnam after his release and came to the United States in 1990. As he took his seat, he looked at the Goddess of Democracy statue and said, "This is like me. She escaped tyranny like I did." Tran was a ranger in the South Vietnamese Army who spent six and a half years in a communist prison. "Life is not long, and I spent it in war and jail," Tran said, "but I am enjoying my life now in my second country, America."

A highlight of the morning ceremony was the laying of the first wreath by Joseph Sergei and Catherine Raisa Spalding, our daughter Elizabeth's adopted children, whom she and her husband, Matthew, had brought back from a Moscow orphanage.

Following the dedication, most of us walked one block to a reception in the Hall of States of the National Guard Association, where we were served hors d'oeuvres, cold drinks, and ninety-second remarks by ambassadors and ethnic leaders. At 2 P.M., we moved to the other side of Union Station and the Allison Auditorium of the Heritage Foundation for a roundtable discussion, "The Victims and Crimes of Communism."

Our panelists knew about communism from personal experience and lifelong study. They were Richard Pipes of Harvard; Paul Hollander of the University of Massachusetts at Amherst; Alan Kors of the University of Pennsylvania; Harry Wu, who spent nineteen years in the Chinese *laogai*; Pedro Fuentes Cid, jailed by Fidel Castro for questioning the Cuban "revolution"; political leader Tunne Kelam of Estonia; Dr. Michael Szporer, an expert on Poland and the Solidarity movement; and dissident leader Tran Tu Tranh of Vietnam.

They all had worthwhile things to say, but I was struck by Alan Kors's criticism of higher education. He said that academia had "failed to put the massive crimes of communism in their proper context." Pointing to the widespread public ignorance about communism, Alan cited "the lack of intellectual diversity" in higher education as a central cause. Because universities failed "to hire pluralistically in history and political science," he concluded, "we're not going to get enlightenment about the victims of communism from the American professoriate. It will have to come from civil society."

It will have to come from institutions like the Victims of Communism Memorial Foundation, I said to myself. I had already been thinking about VOC's next steps after the dedication of the memorial, including virtual exhibits and a high school curriculum on communism. Kors's comments about academe, an indictment really, made me all the more determined to move ahead with our plans.

That evening, at our gala awards dinner at the downtown Marriott Hotel, we celebrated the dedication, awarded the Truman-Reagan Medal of Freedom to Bill Buckley and the late Democratic senator Henry M. (Scoop) Jackson, and were inspired by the words of Elena Bonner, widow of Nobel laureate Andrei Sakharov. Through her daughter-translator, Elena told stories of the terror under Stalin—"a world swarming with the eyes and ears of informers," in the words of one dissident—and the isolation that she and her husband were condemned to by the neo-Stalinist Brezhnev.

You would not have known that Bill Buckley was ill and had taken the train from Stamford, Connecticut, over the protests of his son, Christopher, who asked his father, with considerable exasperation, why he was traveling all those miles to receive one more award, of which he already had a trunkful. What Christopher did not understand was that the award and the occasion marked a milestone in Bill's lifelong battle against communism. He wanted to be present with fellow anticommunists like Joe Lieberman and Jack Kemp when they celebrated the dedication of a memorial to the millions of victims he had prayed for all his life. That the president of the United States had accepted the memorial on behalf of the American people made the evening all the more memorable for Bill, who remarked to me how pleased he was that I was being recognized.

THE LORD'S DAY

I began my dinner remarks by quoting Psalm 118: "This is the day that the Lord has made; let us rejoice and be glad in it." I reassured everyone I was not going to give a sermon—"I wouldn't dare after the invocation by Bishop Tokes," who had precipitated the people's revolt against the Romanian dictator Ceaușescu in December 1989—but I did want to say that "we would not be here tonight without the Lord's intervention on more than one occasion over the last sixteen years." I saluted Lawrence Thomas, the veteran civil rights leader who had marched with Martin Luther King Jr. and who supported our memorial at a critical D.C. neighborhood meeting. I mentioned how Senator Jesse Helms, a staunch Southern Baptist, had persuaded the equally staunch Roman Catholic Knights of Columbus to contribute $25,000 when our fundraising had stalled.

I thanked those who had made the memorial possible, starting with Anne, "my partner, editor, and senior counselor," who had first suggested the idea of a memorial to the victims of communism in January 1990; cofounder Lev Dobriansky, unable to join us because of illness; Ed Priola, who had come on board as a volunteer only two weeks earlier but had quickly become my right and left hand; and sculptor-designer Thomas Marsh.

"Our Jewish brothers and sisters understand what is at stake," I said. "They understand that history must not be forgotten lest it be repeated. They keep reminding the world of the Holocaust, crying, 'Never again!'" I said, "We cannot, we must not, we will not forget those who died and are still dying under communism. Never again must nations and peoples permit so evil a tyranny to terrorize the world."

In his remarks, Bill Buckley talked about a German film, *The Lives of Others*, which he called the "best film" he had ever seen, an opinion shared in part by the Academy of Motion Picture Arts and Sciences, which presented *The Lives of Others* with an Oscar for the Best Foreign Language Film of 2005. It tells the story of a veteran East German Stasi agent who via electronic devices listens to the conversations of a young playwright and his girlfriend as they become increasingly critical of the communist regime. Instead of reporting them, the agent finds himself agreeing with their criticism and protects them, a testament, Bill said, to the ability of the spirit of freedom to "corrupt" a seemingly incorruptible communist.

We made sure Bill had white wine and sat between Joe Lieberman and Jack Kemp. He was in high spirits surrounded by those who believed as he did that communism was the most deadly scourge of the twentieth century. Forty-eight hours later, Bill was in the hospital being treated for a serious infection, complicated by his emphysema. His brief remarks at our dinner, lasting no more than ten minutes, were the last public talk of a sixty-year career of public speaking. I believe he was determined that his last speech would be about something that had motivated him all his life.

THE POWER OF STUBBORNNESS

The dedication of the Victims of Communism Memorial drew national and even international attention. The *New York Sun* devoted an editorial to the president's address, quoting Bush that it was important to recall the lessons of the communist era "because the evil and hatred that inspired the death of tens of millions of people in the twentieth century is still at work in the world." Syndicated columnist Cal Thomas described the memorial as "a reminder of man's capacity to do evil" and added that he wished there were a similar structure to the "leftist academics, clergy and journalists who enabled communism to survive by writing and speaking lies about its true nature."

In fact, VOC has given an honored place to Paul Hollander, whose *Political Pilgrims* is a classic study of duped Western intellectuals. Such dupes include Sidney and Beatrice Webb, Jean-Paul Sartre, and Lincoln Steffens, who famously said after visiting the Soviet Union, "I have seen the future, and it works." In pursuit of Utopia, they could not bring themselves to look at the monstrous reality of the Holodomor, the Great Terror, the Gulag, the Cultural Revolution, the *laogai*, and the killing fields of Cambodia.

"The timing of the dedication [of the memorial] could not have been more appropriate," wrote Heritage Foundation fellow Helle Dale, "as Russia settles on a more and more revanchist course of confrontation." Noting that it took seventeen years to build the memorial, Dale wrote that "even when you have a good idea and a good cause, determination and dedication are indispensable."

I would add that stubbornness helps. Several of my friends told me, reluctantly of course, that a memorial to the victims of communism in Washington, D.C., the citadel of political correctness, was not possible. Their skepticism made me all the more resolute.

The *Washington Times* named me its "Noble" of the week, explaining that few people have the determination to stick with a project for seventeen years. "Mr. Edwards is one of those people, and he saw his dream realized on Tuesday with the unveiling of the Victims of Communism Memorial on Capitol Hill." But it was not "my" dream or my memorial. It belongs to the more than 100 million men, women, and children who have died under the yoke of communism.

Confirmation of the need for our memorial came from the head of the Russian Communist Party and the Chinese Communist Foreign Ministry. Gennady Zyuganov said that the dedication of the memorial was "nothing else but an ill-conceived propaganda attempt to distract the attention of the world public from the atrocities of American imperialism in general and of the current U.S. administration in particular." The atrocities, according to Zyuganov, included "CIA secret prisons in Eastern Europe" and the "American concentration camp in Guantánamo." He attacked President Bush for referring to the "alleged crimes" of the Soviet Union, which Zyuganov described as an example of "true democracy."

Communist China's Foreign Ministry denounced the memorial and President Bush's remarks as "Cold War thinking" and an "attempt to defame China." A spokesman said that "we resent and oppose the U.S. acts and have lodged strong representations with the U.S. side. The U.S. should stop interfering in the internal affairs of other countries." But how could we not "interfere" with China's one-child policy, complete with abortions and forced sterilizations, and not speak up for the many thousands of Chinese political prisoners in the *laogai*?

When both the Chinese communists and the Russian communists denounce you, you know you're doing the right thing.

We were praised for our initiative by leading conservative organizations in America as well as by foreign governments. Over the next several years, on behalf of the Victims of Communism Memorial Foundation, I received the Charles Hoeflich Lifetime Achievement Award from the Intercollegiate Studies Institute, the Walter Judd Freedom Award from the Fund for American Studies, the John Ashbrook Award from the Ashbrook Center, the Reed Larson Award from Accuracy in Media, and a Legend of YAF award from Young America's Foundation. Abroad, I was honored with the Order of Merit from the Republic of Hungary, the Friendship Medal of Diplomacy from the Republic of China (Taiwan), the Millennium Star of Lithuania, and the Cross of Terra Mariana from Estonia.

ONLINE EXHIBITS

Two years later, in June 2009, we launched our online exhibits, devoted to presenting the ideology, the history, and (most important) the legacy of communism. People from around the world could learn the story of communism from Marx to Mao and beyond. They visited our site by the tens of thousands from more than 150 nations.

They explored exhibits about the nations that have suffered the most under communism, led by the Soviet Union and China and including Cambodia, North Korea, Vietnam, Cuba, and the nations of Eastern and Central Europe and the Baltics. They inspected our multimedia Timeline of Communism, which used film, photographs, newspapers, radio, and television to trace communism from Lenin and the Bolshevik Revolution to the present. They "walked" through our Gallery of Heroes, which featured Truman, Reagan, Havel, Wałęsa, Pope John Paul II, and others who have led the fight against communism. They also visited our Hall of Infamy with its portraits of Lenin, Stalin, Mao, Castro, Pol Pot, Kim Il-sung, and other communist tyrants. They read essays by Robert Conquest on the Great Terror and Richard Pipes on the origins of communism.

We added a separate "wing" that allowed you to visit the Gulag in Siberia—complete with armed guards, watchtowers, searchlights, and barking dogs—and to step inside a snow-covered barracks with its wooden beds, minuscule heating stove, and tiny slop bucket. I await the day when some entrepreneur will produce a video game that challenges you to escape the Gulag despite the guards and the dogs and the freezing temperatures of a Siberian winter.

Two men were most responsible for our online exhibits—Ed Priola, VOC's director of public affairs, and filmmaker Marcus Kolga, head of Liefa Communications, based in Toronto. Ed joined us in May 2007 as a volunteer one month before the dedication of the memorial and quickly became indispensable to the foundation and me. He knew how to work with ethnic Americans and foreign nationals, having carried out assignments for the Center for International Private Enterprise in Afghanistan, Albania, and Romania. He was a detail person, having served as an advance man for the Reagan and the Bush presidential campaigns. He liked big challenges, such as preparing for President Bush's outdoor address and finding the best organization to produce our virtual museum.

As VOC's director of public affairs, Ed talked to more than two dozen firms before inviting seven vendors to submit formal proposals. The clear choice was Liefa Communications because of (1) its ability to find and collect outstanding archival and graphic images of communism; (2) its willingness to operate within our budget; and (3) its president, Marcus Kolga, an award-winning filmmaker and the grandson of an Estonian dissident who had been sent to the Gulag. Because of his grandfather's experience, Marcus understood the evils of communism and welcomed the opportunity to create online exhibits about them.

We held the official launch at the handsome Northwest D.C. residence of Adrian Vierita, the Romanian ambassador to the United States, who called our site an important initiative that should "put to flight the doubts that some people have about the nature of communist regimes." He said that the online nature of our exhibits was "a natural consequence of the communications revolution that brought down communism in Eastern Europe." Marcus used the latest technology to allow live Internet streaming of the ceremony and to bypass communist blocking.

The global nature of our exhibits was underscored by a message from the New York City representative of the Dalai Lama and a video from Dr. Maria Schmidt of the Terror House museum in Budapest.

As with our memorial, communists took notice of our site. "Home of the Revolutionary Left," one of the world's largest online communist forums, spent a lot of time discussing our launch. Some Marxists labeled our exhibits "terrible" or "pathetic." One admitted grudgingly that it was "not a bad effort." Another Marxist feared that students might use the site as a "reference for [school] projects." Where did they get the money for such a well-designed and attractive site? several wondered.

Despite the left's suspicions, we did not receive one dollar from the U.S. government. We went to private citizens of all backgrounds and nationalities who understood the critical need to educate people, especially young people, about communism and the blessings of liberty.

TEACHING THE RISING GENERATION

That led us to our next major undertaking—*Communism: Its Ideology, Its History, and Its Legacy*, a curriculum on communism for high school students. The key participants were Dr. Paul Kengor, the bestselling historian and expert on communism at Grove City College, and Claire McCaffrey Griffin, an educational consultant with more than thirty years of experience in civic education, who made certain that our curriculum met the highest teaching standards. Claire, Paul, and I cowrote the text.

It took us more than a year and a half to produce our nine-lesson plan because we vetted every lesson with an eighteen-person review board of public, private, and homeschooling teachers. The lessons cover Marx, Lenin, Stalin, Mao, Kim Il-sung, the Berlin Wall, Vietnam, Cuba, and Eastern Europe and the fall of communism. Each lesson contains a background essay, student-centered activities, assessment options, and a C3 section, "Communism's Contemporary Connection." (If you're curious to see it and perhaps use it in your school, go to victimsofcommunism.org.) The curriculum is being used in dozens of schools and awaiting approval by several boards of education.

In the lesson "Karl Marx and His Legacy," the student is given a handout with quotations from Marx, George Washington, and Martin Luther King Jr. and asked to match the quote with the individual. The quotations are taken from *The Communist Manifesto*, Washington's Farewell Address, and Dr. King's "I Have a Dream" speech. Once the student has matched five or six quotes, he is asked to volunteer his answers and explain his reasoning. The student is then shown the correct answers and asked the following questions:

- Are you surprised by any of the correct IDs, and if so, why?
- Do you see any themes in the quotes? [Suggested answers: liberty, freedom, religion, property, violence]
- How would you compare and contrast the views of Marx, Washington, and King on these topics?

The kinds of students we have in mind for our curriculum are at Washington University in St. Louis, where they built a mock Soviet prison to mark the twentieth anniversary of the fall of the Berlin Wall. The display was a four-sided wooden structure with fake barbed wire on top and Soviet propaganda posters on its sides. Students dressed as prisoners stood inside the mock Gulag, some of them with fake blood on their prison clothing. Others were dressed as Soviet soldiers who patrolled around the structure. But university officials demanded removal of the exhibit, which they said was "unsafe." The students responded that the university action was censorship but declined to appeal the decision out of respect for the administration. Clearly, there is much work to be done.

THE GETMAN COLLECTION

Ukrainian artist Nikolai Getman was just another victim of communism consigned to the Gulag, but he was released in 1953 with Stalin's death and spent the next forty years painting a history of life and death in the Gulag. His haunting paintings have been compared to Aleksandr Solzhenitsyn's classic work *The Gulag Archipelago*. Getman painted in secret—even concealing what he was doing from his wife—lest the KGB discover his work, destroy it, and send him back to the Gulag. He explained that he created the images to serve as a reminder of "communism's cruel inhumanity," which he hoped would never be forgotten. Through the generosity of the Jamestown Foundation (especially Jim Kimsey) and the Heritage Foundation, VOC has been given this unique collection.

I met Nikolai, who was wearing a turtleneck sweater and had a trimmed white beard, in 1997, when his collection was displayed in the Russell Senate Office Building in Washington, D.C., for a couple of weeks. He was delighted that his collection was beyond the grasp of the KGB. At a Smithsonian reception, the historian Robert Conquest said that the Getman paintings portrayed a system in which "death was caused by unbearable toil, by cold and starvation, by unheard of degradation and humiliation, by a life that could not have been endured by any other animal."

Another important VOC initiative is our Witness videos, which present the personal stories of those who lived under communism. VOC has interviewed dozens of people, including Daniel Magay, who won a gold medal for Hungary at the 1956 Olympics but decided he could no longer live a privileged life under communism; American Jon Utley, born in Moscow, who traveled to Siberia to learn that his father had been executed in a Gulag camp in the 1930s on trumped-up charges; Anhthu Lu, who fled Vietnam with her father in a small boat that barely survived stormy seas and pirates; and physician Nal Oum, one of the few Cambodian intellectuals to escape the killing fields of the Khmer Rouge. Ukrainian academic Myroslav Marynovych, who spent more than a decade in the Gulag and who received the 2014 Truman-Reagan Medal of Freedom, recounted how the communists had warned him, "If you are not with us, you are against us." Marynovych replied, "Okay, I will be against you."

In February 2015, VOC launched *Dissident*, an online voice for news and commentary on communism with early contributions by Catholic biographer George Weigel; Russian historian Richard Pipes; Elizabeth Spalding and me about our new book, *A Brief History of the Cold War*; Matias Ilivitzky on the troubling new friendly relationship between Greece and Russia; and Cuban dissident Guillermo Fariñas Hernández, recipient of the 2015 Truman-Reagan Medal of Freedom, on the greatly increased (yes, increased) communist surveillance since the opening of diplomatic relations between Cuba and the United States.

VOC executive director Marion Smith traveled to Hong Kong in the fall of 2014 and brought back a troubling report on the stepped-up surveillance of Chinese dissidents by the communist authorities. As a result, VOC announced it would sponsor a China Forum to examine U.S.-China relations in three key areas: human rights and political development, trade and economics, and foreign policy and security. The first China Forum, held in November 2015, brought together some fifty Chinese dissident leaders, the largest such gathering in America since the Tiananmen Square massacre in 1989. They resolved to keep meeting and planning and organizing to bring about a free and democratic China.

A VOW

The explanation for this blitzkrieg of activities—and the above is by no means complete—is simple. Twenty-five years after the fall of the Berlin Wall followed by the dissolution of the Soviet Union, communist regimes still rule China and Cuba as well as Vietnam, North Korea, and Laos. The legacy of communism is all too evident in Russia in the person of Vladimir Putin, a neo-Leninist eager to expand Russia's sphere of influence and a ready practitioner of the dark arts of the KGB—as the murders or suspicious deaths of exiled businessman Boris Berezovsky, Russian journalist and Putin critic Anna Politkovskaya, American journalist and *Forbes* editor Paul Klebnikov, and ex-KGB officer Alexander Litvinenko prove. The need for someone to tell the truth is urgent, and VOC has emerged as the primary disseminator of information about communism in all its guises. VOC will not rest until *all* captive nations and peoples are free and independent.

Our vow—my vow—was reinforced by the passing of Robert Conquest, the dean of Russian historians, in August 2015 at the age of ninety-eight. No one—not Aleksandr Solzhenitsyn or George Orwell or Stéphane Courtois and the other authors of *The Black Book of Communism*—was a more compelling and convincing chronicler of communist crimes and victims than Conquest. His most famous work is *The Great Terror: Stalin's Purge of the Thirties*, published in 1968 at the time of the Prague Spring and based mainly on unofficial sources. Conquest estimates that in 1937–38, seven million people were arrested, one million were executed, and about two million died in labor camps (the Gulag). Dismissed as gross exaggerations at the time by leftists, the figures were later corroborated by Soviet historians and opened Soviet archives. In a 1991 edition of *The Great Terror*, Conquest wrote that the official records "show things to be rather worse than I originally suggested."

In 1994, he was among the very first historians to join VOC's national advisory board. In 2001, I asked Bob to give us a few words about our work. Here is what he wrote me: "It is important for all of us to keep our memories of these dreadful events fresh. It is not only that we mourn the victims. We must also, for their sake and our own, keep before us a major historical truth—and one that was for long denied or distorted the world over. The lessons must be learnt, and the Victims of Communism Memorial Foundation will serve as a constant education."

Indeed we shall.

35

CHIMERA?

I was delighted at the record number of embassies (twenty-four) that attended the eighth anniversary of the memorial's dedication in 2015; at the eloquence and courage of our Truman-Reagan Medal of Freedom honorees, Alexander Podrabinek of Russia and Guillermo Fari-ñas Hernández of Cuba; at the enthusiasm and efficiency of our young staff; and at the success and the potential of the China Forum. Still, I could not forget what Anne and I had dreamed of from the beginning—to build a museum on communism in the heart of Washington. For lack of money, more specifically seed money, the dream remained that until Providence again came calling.

I knew of Viktor Orbán because in 2001 the young prime minister of Hungary had visited the White House and told President George W. Bush that the capital of the United States needed a museum on communism to educate future generations about the history of the Cold War, the nature of communism, and its long-lasting effect on countries around the world. I expressed VOC's deep gratitude to the prime minister, and in 2002 we awarded Orbán the Truman-Reagan Medal of Freedom. In June 1989, while still a student, he had electrified a crowd of 100,000 Hungarians gathered in Hero Square in Budapest by calling for an end to communism. He subsequently organized the Fidesz Party and led it to victory in 1998. Fidesz lost in the 2002 parliamentary elections to the Socialists.

Seven years later, I was in Budapest participating in a panel discussion of "Europe After Communism" with Orbán as a fellow panelist. He exuded confidence, as the polls showed that if the Hungarian elections were held then, Fidesz would easily defeat the Socialists, and Viktor Orbán would again be prime minister. Following the panel, I met with the PM-to-be. He wasted little time, saying (in English) that if he was elected, Hungary would make a significant donation to help make the goal of an international museum on communism a reality. As I recall, he mentioned the figure of $1 million.

I was stunned. I had received no hint of what Viktor wanted to talk about. Here at long last was the money we needed to begin realizing our long-held dream. I stammered my thanks and promised we would be prudent in our use of the gift. He smiled, shook my hand, and was gone, leaving me to begin praying for a Fidesz victory.

My prayers were helped by the Socialists, who governed so poorly for eight years that in 2010 Fidesz won a two-thirds majority in the elections. Orbán was a man of his word. There followed nearly two years of negotiations over the terms of the grant, the rationalization of U.S. and Hungarian regulations and laws regarding grants, the requirement of regular progress reports, and the division of the grant into an initial gift of $200,000 followed by a second tranche of $800,000.

Essential to the signing of the ten-page single-spaced agreement was Marion Smith, whom I had met at Heritage and had spotted as a strong candidate for executive director of VOC. As the founder and president of the youth-oriented Common Sense Society, active in much of Europe, Marion knew all the players in Hungary, in part because of Hungarian-born Anna, his strikingly beautiful future wife. By reason of his education in international relations and his stellar Heritage research on U.S. foreign policy, he was knowledgeable about the Cold War and communism. He was smart, articulate, a committed anticommunist, familiar with fundraising, and just twenty-eight. The VOC board unanimously approved my recommendation to hire Marion Smith as our executive director and CEO, effective February 2014.

With the Hungarian grant, VOC was able, for the first time in our twenty-year history, to open a real office—at 300 New Jersey Avenue NW, two blocks from the memorial—and hire staff. Marion transformed the Victims of Communism Memorial Foundation into the go-to organization for information about communism. With a generous gift from Hungarian-born Thomas Peterffy, founder of Interactive Brokers, VOC initiated in 2016 an advertising campaign at major U.S. airports—

and Times Square in New York City—that exposed collectivism and promoted free enterprise. We also began planning seriously for 2017, the hundredth anniversary of the Bolshevik Revolution.

Everything we do is calculated to get us closer to the day when we can break ground for an international museum on communism, which will be located as close to the Mall as the National Park Service and Congress will allow. I have no doubt that day will come because of the dark legacy of communism reflected in the authoritarian actions of Russia and the communist regimes of China, Cuba, North Korea, Vietnam, and Laos, the neo-Marxist teachings in many of our high schools and universities, the resolute spirit of the millions of ethnic Americans from captive nations past and present, and the Americans whose fathers, sons, uncles, and friends died in Korea, Vietnam, and a hundred other outposts opposing communism during the Cold War.

There will be an international museum on communism because I believe with all my heart and soul that God did not bring us all this way only to leave us when we are within sight of our goal.

36

TRUMPED

In 1964, I had an insider's view of a rancorous, mendacious presidential campaign. The media declared Senator Barry Goldwater "psychologically unfit" to be president, and Democrats said his campaign left them hearing the sound of Nazi boots in the streets.

Fifty-two years later, I watched the 2016 presidential campaign unfold as a no-holds-barred mud-wrestling match. Hillary Clinton and Donald Trump surrogates—and sometimes the candidates themselves—hurled scurrilous charges. Convinced that a President Trump would turn America into an isolated far-right dictatorship, the mass media disseminated every imaginable story and rumor about him. Following Trump's narrow win in the Electoral College (and Clinton's narrow victory in the popular vote), outraged protesters took to the streets and to college campuses chanting, "Not Our President!"

The 2016 election was not easy on the right either. Trump's nomination and campaign were controversial within the Republican Party, to put it mildly. Certain factions of the party did not back his candidacy—indeed, at least a dozen sitting Republican senators and twenty-five Republican House members said they would not vote for him—and some who opposed Trump saw at least as much danger as promise in his election.

If Trump's nomination as the Republican presidential candidate was improbable, his election as our forty-fifth president had seemed impossible. The polls were wrong, the pundits were wrong, and the establishment was wrong. But the people wanted change, radical change, and that is what Trump promised them.

There are secondary reasons why Trump won, ranging from Clinton's robotic performance to his use of Twitter and other social media. But I believe the primary reason for his success is that Trump tapped into a constituency that has been at the center of the Republican Party and the conservative movement for six decades—Middle America.

It has had different names over the years—the Forgotten Majority, the Silent Majority, the Moral Majority, the Tea Party. But beginning with Senator Robert Taft in 1952 and extending through the 2016 election, Americans of a grassroots, populist inclination have often voted for Republicans and have done so as much because of what those Republicans stood against as what they stood for. Taft, Goldwater, Ronald Reagan, and Newt Gingrich in their different ways rejected the claims of the nation's elites to rule. Those Republicans who didn't, like George H. W. Bush and Mitt Romney, often fared far worse.

And so in 2016, grassroots voters rejected every one of the establishment Republican candidates and nominated an ex-Democrat billionaire outsider who promised he would change the direction of the country and make America great again. It was achingly simplistic, but it was what millions of anxious, fed-up Americans (and by no means all of them white) wanted to hear. Clinton's contemptuous description of Trump supporters as a "basket of deplorables" seems to have driven these voters more firmly into the Republican's camp.

In the wake of Trump's victory, and with majorities in the House and Senate, the Republican Party faced a decision about how it would govern. The party has always comprised distinct factions with their own interests, often united by a common enemy as much as a common cause. And each now had its own vision of how to move forward. Some paleoconservatives, who declared that post-Reagan conservatism was dead, thought the election should point back to a pre–World War II isolationism. Some establishment Republicans hoped they could now have their way and wondered whether they might jettison those embarrassing Trumpsters who got them there. And some middle-of-the-road conservatives were willing to work with President Trump for the simplest of reasons—nearly sixty-three million Americans voted for him.

Other conservatives felt stymied and had difficulty seeing a way forward because they had not seen in Trump the principles they wanted the right to stand for. But in their confusion, they mistakenly conflated the conservative movement and the Republican Party.

A MOVEMENT AND A PARTY

The conservative movement and the Republican Party are two *different* institutions—different in structure and in objective. The modern conservative movement is an intellectual movement founded some sixty years ago on ideas drawn from American history and articulated in the Declaration of Independence and the Constitution. Its founders include intellectuals like F. A. Hayek, Russell Kirk, and William F. Buckley Jr. The Republican Party is a 160-year-old political party dedicated to winning elections—often, but not always, based on ideals of limited government and free enterprise. Its heroes are Abraham Lincoln, Calvin Coolidge, and Ronald Reagan.

The fates of the intellectual movement and the political party are not inextricably tied together, although the movement has used the GOP as its principal political instrument since 1964. One may prosper without the other, as the GOP did in the 1950s, when the movement barely existed. Both enjoyed success in the 1980s under Reagan. The Republican establishment lost touch with the people during the Bush and then the Obama years, while the movement extended its influence at the state and local levels through the Tea Party and state debates about right-to-work laws and school choice.

Regardless of what liberals and some on the right predict about the movement, conservatives should not despair or look for real estate in Canada. Conservatism has been down before. The movement seemed on the edge of extinction after the crushing Goldwater defeat in 1964. It was deemed at a political dead end in 1976 after Reagan's failure to capture the Republican presidential nomination. It was consigned to the political periphery after Bill Clinton's "Third Way" victory in 1992. The Obama victories of 2008 and 2012 were interpreted by the liberal establishment as a definitive repudiation of conservative ideas.

But each time, like the fabled phoenix, the conservative movement has risen with renewed strength and determination, scoring decisive political victories with the election of President Reagan in 1980; the Republican capture of the House of Representatives in 1994 after a gap of forty years; the success of the populist Tea Party in 2010; and the political tsunami in 2014 that produced Republican majorities in the U.S. Senate and the House, as well as thirty-one states with Republican governors, twenty-three of which also enjoyed Republican-dominated state legislatures.

And all this success occurred only on the political side of conservatism. Conservatism also enjoys a widespread intellectual presence.

The past five decades have seen conservative ideas thrive, from Nobel laureates in economics, to the wide circulation of prominent conservative columnists and the *Wall Street Journal* editorial page, to bestselling books, to popular and prolific magazines and websites like *National Review*. There are influential programs at colleges and universities throughout the country, such as those run by the Intercollegiate Studies Institute and the Federalist Society. The conservative movement is also fortunate to be well funded by generous foundations and individuals committed to the cause, and well endowed with brilliant academics and writers to spread the word.

Conservatism is, by its nature, rooted in the values and traditions that have always made America great. And the movement has long found a home and common cause with the Republican Party, in part because of their mutual rejection of socialism and leftism, which have rarely been represented as forthrightly as they were in the 2016 election. But more important, conservatives have aligned themselves with the Republican Party in their commitment to our founding principles of life, liberty, and the pursuit of happiness.

By reason of their political, intellectual, and cultural power—and the movement's direct link with the American Revolution and the roots of Western civilization—conservatives are best positioned to confront the problems and divisions revealed by the 2016 election, and it is conservatives who will shape our institutions to address them. Indeed, conservatives have every reason to be optimistic that their movement will continue to influence the Republican Party and the future of the country. To consider how they might do that, consider why conservatism has had such staying power in modern America.

THE ROOTS OF RESURGENCE

What is the source of conservatism's rejuvenating power? Generous foundation gifts? Skilled grassroots organization? Luck? Is it explained by the pendulum theory of politics, wherein the balance of political power swings left for a generation, then right, then left again, forever? Has Providence responded to the fervent prayers of evangelical pastors and congregations? Or does the power of American conservatism lie in something at the very heart of the republic—first principles proclaimed by our Founders and developed from our history and Western civilization stretching back more than two thousand years?

In his book *We Still Hold These Truths*, Matthew Spalding presents ten core principles that define our national creed and common purpose:

> *Liberty* is the grand, overarching theme of our nation's history; *equality, natural rights*, and the *consent of the governed* are the foundational principles that set the compass of our politics; *religious liberty* and *private property* follow from these, shaping the parameters of our nation's day-to-day life; the *rule of law* and a *constitutionalism* of limited government define the architecture that undergirds our liberty; all of these principles culminate in *self-government*, in the political sense of republican governance and the moral sense of governing ourselves; and lastly, *independence* encompasses the meaning of America's principles in the world.

These principles have guided and inspired four groups that have shaped the modern conservative movement and built a foundation that can withstand even major political quakes. First came the philosophers, the men of ideas and imagination like Hayek and Kirk. Next came the popularizers, the men of interpretation like Bill Buckley and George Will, who translated the often arcane ideas of the philosophers into a common idiom. Then the politicians, the men of action like Barry Goldwater and Ronald Reagan, drew on the conservative ideas discussed in the media and the marketplace for their political campaigns and legislative proposals. All three groups were financed by a fourth group—the philanthropists, the men of means and vision like Henry Salvatori, Joseph Coors, and Richard Scaife, who provided the money for groundbreaking books, new magazines, and often-controversial political proposals.

Although sometimes at odds over tactics, these individuals hung together in good times and bad. Indeed, it was because they often stepped up in response to the bad times that their project proved enduring. Just when the left seemed most deeply entrenched, in the late 1940s, as the whole world seemed to be turning toward state power and it was easy to assume that President Harry Truman would carry forward Franklin Roosevelt's progressive New Deal, a willingness to resist arose in key places.

The left's enthusiasm for a "democratic" socialism characterized by various creative forms of government ownership alarmed intellectuals on the right. Prominent among them was the Austrian economist F. A. Hayek, who in April 1947 organized a meeting of thirty-nine free-market economists, historians, political scientists, philosophers, and journalists in Mont Pelerin, Switzerland. According to the historian R.M. Hartwell, Hayek's idea was to establish "a kind of international academy of political philosophy" with the aim of "regenerating the ideas of classical liberalism and in order to refute socialism." Ever the optimist (unlike Joseph Schumpeter, who wrote of the inevitable coming of socialism), Hayek believed that the global shift toward socialism could be challenged and reversed. He emphasized the role of intellectuals "in historically shaping political and economic opinions."

The founding of the Mont Pelerin Society was an important first step in the long march of modern American conservatism as it evolved from an intellectual movement into a political movement and finally into a governing movement. An initial guidebook for that march was Hayek's *The Road to Serfdom*, which became one of the most talked about political books of the post–World War II era. *Reader's Digest* placed *Serfdom* at the front of the magazine—the first time a book had ever been so featured—and the Book-of-the-Month Club distributed more than 600,000 copies of the *Digest* edition.

Among the many who read the *Reader's Digest* version of *The Road to Serfdom* were two World War II veterans—Ronald Reagan, a film actor eager to resume his career but soon to be plunged into Hollywood politics, and Barry Goldwater, a Phoenix businessman looking for a new challenge, perhaps in local politics. Both Reagan, a liberal Democrat at the time, and Goldwater, a conservative Republican, responded enthusiastically to Hayek's emphasis on the indispensability of the individual.

In 1953, three years after the liberal critic Lionel Trilling insisted that conservatism expressed itself only in "irritable mental gestures which seek to resemble ideas" and that "liberalism is not only the dominant but even the sole intellectual tradition" in America, the young political philosopher Russell Kirk published his rejoinder, *The Conservative Mind*. At first, liberals dismissed the book, saying condescendingly that the title was an oxymoron, but they were forced to reverse themselves when they read Kirk's powerful, impassioned work. *The Conservative Mind* is a 450-page overview of Anglo-American conservative thinking from the late eighteenth century until the mid-twentieth century, as well as a scathing indictment of every liberal nostrum, from human perfectibility to economic egalitarianism. It demonstrates convincingly that America had had a conservative tradition since the founding, formed by such politicians and writers as Edmund Burke, John Adams, Nathaniel Hawthorne, Daniel Webster, John Calhoun, Abraham Lincoln, Orestes Brownson, George Santayana, and T.S. Eliot.

With one book, Russell Kirk made conservatism intellectually acceptable. Until *The Conservative Mind*, conservatives called themselves everything from individualists to Jeffersonians to traditionalists. After *The Conservative Mind*, remarked one young man of the right, "We are all conservatives now."

These two books by Kirk and Hayek, along with Whittaker Chambers's *Witness* and Richard Weaver's *Ideas Have Consequences*, formed something like the early conservative canon—representing the traditional, libertarian, and anticommunist strains of conservatism.

But conservative ideas had not yet taken hold in the minds of most Americans or their political leaders. Conservative victories, wrote Buckley, were "uncoordinated and inconclusive" because the philosophy of freedom was not being expounded systematically in the universities and in the media. Buckley founded *National Review* in 1955 to combat the liberals, compensate for "conservative weakness" in the academy, and "focus the energies" of the movement. The prospectus for this new conservative magazine declared that it was possible to "rout intellectually" the jaded liberal status quo with the "vigor of true convictions"—a synthesis of the libertarian, traditional, and anticommunist wings of American conservatism.

If *National Review* had not been founded, wrote the historian George Nash, "there would probably have been no cohesive intellectual force on the right in the 1960s and 1970s." Nash does not go far enough: the launching of *National Review* was a deliberate political act that shaped the modern American conservative movement in the post–World War II era.

One other important task had to be accomplished before the conservative movement could operate effectively in the political realm: it had to be as philosophically united as possible. Traditionalists and libertarians had been snapping at one another in the pages of *National Review* and elsewhere. One conservative—Frank Meyer—was convinced that beneath the differences lay a consensus of principle. Through articles, books, and countless midnight telephone calls, Meyer communicated his synthesis of the differing strains of conservatism, which came to be called "fusionism."

The core principle of fusionism is that "the freedom of the person [is] the central and primary end of political society." To Meyer, man was a rational autonomous individual, and freedom was "the essence of his being," indispensable to his pursuit of virtue. The state had only three functions—national defense, the preservation of domestic order, and the administration of justice between citizens.

Yet, Meyer insisted, modern American conservatism was not classical liberalism, which had been weakened by utilitarianism and secularism. Conservatives sought to save the Christian understanding of "the nature and destiny of man." To do that, they had to absorb the best of both main branches of the conservative mainstream—traditionalist and libertarian. Meyer insisted he was not creating anything new but articulating an already-existing conservative consensus—"the consensus forged so brilliantly by the Founding Fathers in 1789."

Meyer argued that religious and traditional precepts were needed to undergird freedom, which could not exist on the relativist-materialistic premises of modern thought. Liberty was linked to American religion because it was the source of ethical choice and was "a unique by-product of Western faith." Practically speaking, said M. Stanton Evans, Meyer was arguing that "the conservative movement was a movement," not a jumble of factions. And as a movement it could go forth "to smite the liberal-left behemoth."

And it would, as Barry Goldwater paved the way politically for Ronald Reagan, who became a transformational president at home and abroad. Although Reagan was not able to roll back government, he led the way in restoring Americans' confidence in themselves and in America, sparking an unprecedented period of economic prosperity and ending the Cold War at the bargaining table and not on the battlefield.

Ever since, conservatives have sought another Ronald Reagan with his fusionist philosophy to carry out the objectives of a more limited constitutional government, an untrammeled free market, and a restoration of Judeo-Christian values in our society. They have become increasingly frustrated by their failure to find another Reagan, their frustration compounded by the unwillingness or the inability of Republican leadership in Washington to reduce the size and scope of our Leviathan government.

In the 1980s, the external threat of communism and the calming presence of Reagan persuaded most conservatives to sublimate their differences for the greater good. But with the collapse of Soviet communism and the departure of President Reagan, disagreements among the varying kinds of conservatism came to the surface with more intensity.

Perhaps above all, the basic questions of the role of government became a point of contention. Some libertarian conservatives, like Ron Paul, began to argue that government is *always* the problem. That contradicted Ronald Reagan, who in his first inaugural address specified that "*in this present crisis*, government is not the solution to our problem; government is the problem [emphasis added]." He was a limited-government conservative, not a no-government one. But antagonism to government in all its forms spread, affecting everything from voter turnout to respect for the Congress and the presidency.

Through the 2000s conservative divisions grew—over the role and size of government, over America's role in the world, and over the state of the culture.

TWENTY-FIRST-CENTURY CONSERVATISM

What, then, is the state of the American conservative movement today? Any successful political movement must first have a relevant philosophy. It is a given that conservatives of all stripes honor the Constitution and its established system of checks and balances. They agree that government should be limited, individuals should be free and responsible in their freedom, and there can be no lasting liberty without virtue, public and private.

These are not just conservative ideas but American ones that have their roots in the founding of the republic. But they are in many respects under assault. Gallup reported in January 2016 that, while conservatives continued to outnumber both moderates and liberals in the United States, as they had since 2009, their thirteen-point edge over liberals—37 percent to 24 percent—was the smallest margin since Gallup started routinely asking the question in 1992.

More than ever before, the American people seem to be accepting of more government, not less—of having their personal security ensured from birth to death by a Washington bureaucracy. Gallup reports that two-thirds of Americans do not want any cuts in Social Security or Medicare. And Donald Trump won the Republican Party nomination pledging to avoid such cuts.

The conservative movement has divided on how best to respond to this shift in public attitudes. One of the more sophisticated responses to emerge in recent years is that of the "reform conservatives"—sometimes dubbed "reformicons"—led by *New York Times* columnist Ross Douthat, *National Review* executive editor Reihan Salam, *National Review* senior editor Ramesh Ponnuru, and their most systematic thinker, Ethics and Public Policy Center fellow Yuval Levin. Writing in the venerable journal *Modern Age* in 2015, Levin said that reform conservatism seeks to "transform American government along conservative lines, into a government that works to sustain and expand the space between the individual and the state; to strengthen the family, civil society, and the market economy and make their benefits accessible to more Americans; to help the poor not with an empty promise of material equality but with a fervent commitment to upward mobility; and to strengthen the middle class by lifting needless burdens off the shoulders of parents and workers."

The reform-conservative agenda includes lower taxes, Social Security reform, the replacement of Obamacare, and opposition to farm subsidies. These are not new ideas. Several of them, like calling for an end to farm subsidies, can be found in Goldwater's 1960 manifesto, *The Conscience of a Conservative*. But in seeking to make government less intrusive, they also seek to make it more functional, rather than merely smaller.

Their ideas sparked lively debate within the conservative movement. In February 2015, for instance, the libertarian Shikha Dalmia expressed puzzlement that conservatives "have ended up with a mix of old and new liberal ideas that thoroughly scale back the right's long-running commitment to free markets and limited government."

But before the 2016 presidential primaries, the prospects for political unity on the right seemed reasonably strong. Where social conservatives rejected acquiescence to America's secular turn, reformicons like Levin and Ponnuru asserted that they were as socially conservative as any evangelical. One reformicon, Pascal-Emmanuel Gobry, put it simply in 2013: "There is simply no path to victory for a socially liberal Republican Party." Even the Tea Partiers and reformicons could find common ground: as Ponnuru wrote, conservatism "should be home to everyone who takes seriously the task of strengthening the constitutional structure of a limited accountable government that serves rather than masters civil society."

And then came Donald Trump.

"THERE IS NO SUCH THING AS A LOST CAUSE"

The implications of Trump's success—his extraordinary takeover of the Republican Party and his dramatic general-election victory—for the future of conservatism remain difficult to discern. Trump clearly spoke for the kinds of disaffected Americans who have long supplied a ready audience for conservative ideas and candidates. But he also pushed aside key tenets of the conservative approach to governing, including some that unify essentially all the various factions of the conservative movement.

Some conservatives are inclined to see the 2016 election as a triumph for the Republican Party that may not be so triumphal for conservatism. But 2016 presented an opportunity for conservatism.

The fact is that conservatism is stronger, not weaker, than the GOP. Whatever the future of the Republican Party, the conservative movement will prevail for the very reasons that have underlain its endurance and strength for six decades.

I have been a player in and a historian of the conservative movement for some six decades. What has sustained conservatives is not their legions or their organizational skill or their use of the media or their fundraising prowess or even their persuasive leaders. It is the power of their ideas—linked by the priceless principle of ordered liberty—and the application of those ideas to the problems of the day. The conservative agenda has the best solutions to the problems that led so many Americans to vote for the radical change that Trump promised. It is up to conservatives to convince their fellow Republicans to pursue the right path.

This should give conservatives confidence. There will be challenges in the years to come, but conservatives are well positioned to overcome them and thrive. And ultimately, they are better positioned than their political adversaries to unite the country and to strengthen it.

So it has always been that conservative values are most needed in times of crisis and doubt and anger and even fear: when there is a need for prudence, not rashness; for custom, not the impulse of the moment; for a transcendent faith, not a fatal conceit; for reform, not revolution. As we seek solutions to problems that seem unsolvable, we should recall the wisdom of the poet T. S. Eliot, who reminded us that there are no lost causes because there are no gained causes. There is only the unceasing struggle to preserve life, liberty, and the pursuit of happiness for ourselves and those we love.

37

CODA

Looking back over the years, I ask myself inevitably: what difference have I made?

Well, I have written numerous books that will help future Americans understand better the conservatives of the late twentieth century and early twenty-first century and their consequential role in American politics. And let me say that I could not have done all the research, interviewing, travel, writing, and rewriting without the generous support of the Heritage Foundation. For the past twenty years, as the Distinguished Fellow in Conservative Thought with the B. Kenneth Simon Center for Principles and Politics at Heritage, I have had the best think-tank job in Washington.

Starting with my first biography of Ronald Reagan five decades ago and in all my writing since, I have sought to describe what conservatives hope to achieve:

- A government limited by the Constitution and with common sense as a guide
- Policy makers who acknowledge with Michael Novak that "as human lungs need air, so does liberty need virtue"
- People in every walk of life who take responsibility for themselves and their families

- A strong national defense, because peace is made secure only through strength
- Collaboration between Wall Street and Main Street to preserve free enterprise, the economic system that produces more prosperity and freedom than any other

While a Positive Mental Attitude (PMA) is the secular idea that sustains me in the daily battles, the Trinity is the spiritual reality that has enabled me to manage the adversaries, skeptics, and "friends" who dismissed the idea of a memorial to the victims of communism as a chimera. I never gave up (well, almost never) because I know we do not live in a forsaken world.

It has been more than a quarter century since the fall of the Berlin Wall and the collapse of the Soviet empire, an event that Václav Havel called as important a historical event as the fall of the Roman Empire. But the exhilaration of those happy days has given way, in many places, to feelings of disappointment and discouragement. It is clear that we are not at the end of history.

China is ruled by a totalitarian Communist Party of almost ninety million members. North Korea builds hydrogen bombs and the missiles to aim them at targets near and far. Vietnam routinely jails those who advocate free speech and assembly. Laos languishes under Marxist-Leninist-Maoist thought. Cuba arrests thousands of dissidents in the wake of a new U.S.-Cuban relationship. Russians yearn for a return to empire and applaud their leaders' attempts to influence the outcome of a U.S. presidential election. Poland and the Baltics wonder whether they are next. The KGB Bar in New York City does a booming business, and Che Guevara is still lionized on many of our campuses.

Is tyranny winning and freedom losing?

If we take a second look at the world, however, we see something quite different. China's vaunted economic machine is slowing down. More North Koreans, like the young human rights activist Yeonmi Park, are risking their lives to defect. Communist Cuba has opened a Pandora's Box with its diplomatic agreement with the United States, letting loose the irrepressible spirit of freedom. The Baltic states and Poland and other countries in Eastern and Central Europe are joining hands and forces in the face of Russian economic, political, and military aggression. The Victims of Communism Memorial Foundation and other institutions, using both the old and the new media, are disseminating more and more of the truth about the other holocaust—communism.

History teaches us that crises produce leaders, unleash creativity, unify former opponents, and bring a swift end to tyrants. That is what happened with the sudden fall of the Berlin Wall and the ensuing dissolution of the Soviet Union.

ENDINGS

How, then, to end this memoir? I turn to my favorite president. In late 1981, I called Mike Deaver at the White House to ask whether I might present a copy of my newest biography to President Reagan (the one with the cover that blared, "Complete Through the Assassination Attempt"). Mike said he thought it was possible.

In early December, I made my way through the security gate and into the West Wing of the White House. I was escorted into the Oval Office (surprisingly small), where the president greeted me with a wide smile and a firm handshake. I was struck by his evident good health and youthful appearance. He had always looked at least a decade younger than his actual age, but it seemed to me that he was growing younger, not older, in the presidency.

"Mr. President," I said, "here is a copy of my latest biography of you. As you may recall, I wrote your first political biography way back in 1967."

"Well, thank you, Lee, that's very thoughtful of you."

As we stood there chatting and the photographer snapped away, I saw the president glancing down at the cover with its bold, black-on-yellow banner, "Complete Through the Assassination Attempt."

Finally, the president looked up and, with that irresistible smile spreading across his face, said, "Well, Lee, I'm sorry I messed up your ending."

I burst out laughing. How typical of Reagan to make light of his near-death experience. I have never faced death, but I have tried not to take disappointments or defeats or myself too seriously. I have been inspired by Chesterton to go gaily in the dark, holding high the Cross of Christ. After I met with President Reagan, I renewed my resolution to keep writing and speaking and teaching about conservatism and to keep telling the truth about communism, knowing that in the end the truth will make, and keep, us free.

Acknowledgments

A memoir is a look back. For me, it has meant writing about my favorite things—politics and politicians, freedom and tyranny, the City of Man and the City of God. I realize now how providential were a host of people, including Bill Buckley, who published my first article in *National Review*; Denny Kitchel, who gambled by making me director of information of the Goldwater for President Committee; Marvin Liebman, whose move from New York City to London left the Committee of One Million (Against the Admission of Communist China to the United Nations) without a secretary, a post I did my best to fill; Donald Goodyear, whose years-long embezzlement led me to close down Lee Edwards & Associates and seek a PhD and a new career; Hugh Newton, who asked me to write the history of the Heritage Foundation, which led to my becoming the foundation's Distinguished Fellow in Conservative Thought; my always-there wife, Anne, who responded, after I moaned that people were forgetting about the bloody crimes and numberless victims of communism, "We need a memorial to the victims of communism."

I am indebted to ISI Books editor Jed Donahue and then–ISI president Chris Long, who said the Intercollegiate Studies Institute would be delighted to publish my memoir after I had been turned down by several other publishers. Jed's professional touch improved the manuscript significantly. I am grateful to the interns and research assistants like Isabel Nelson, Leslie Grimard, and Josiah Lippincott for their help. I thank research specialist Ron Savich, who dug deep into my papers at the Hoover Archives, uncovering things I had forgotten or misplaced, like my private diary of the Goldwater campaign.

I am grateful to Ed Feulner, Heritage's once and once again president, who has given me the freedom and the encouragement to write some twenty books about one of the most extraordinary political developments of the past seventy years—the modern American conservative movement.

I thank God for my family—beginning with Anne, for more than fifty years of common sense and patience with my many vagaries; for daughters Elizabeth and Catherine and sons-in-law Matthew and Michael for their love and inspiration; and for our eleven grandchildren—eight boys and three girls!—for the joy they bestow. How blessed can one man be?

Index

Coast Guard, 215
Colby, William, 109, 218
Cold Spring Granite Company, 325
Cold War, the, 13, 18, 30–31, 82, 84, 93, 168,
  210, 212, 215, 227, 236, 239, 253, 259, 265,
  275, 279, 282, 286, 310, 313, 326, 331, 335,
  337–39, 347; peaceful end of, 173, 227, 279
  (*see also* Berlin Wall: fall of the)
Coleman, J. D. (Stets), 106
Colette (French novelist), 12
Collapse of Communism, The (Edwards), 272–73
Collins, John, 138
Colorado, 192, 194
Colson, Charles, 161
Columbia Lighthouse for the Blind, 179
Columbia River, 64
Columbia University, 210, 272
Columbus, Ohio, 119, 162
Columbus Dispatch, 55
Comiskey Park, 5
Commission on Fine Arts, 319
Committee Against Summit Entanglements
  (CASE), 17
Committee for a Free China, 167, 213, 218, 220,
  263
Committee for a Free Congress, 193. *See also* Free
  Congress Foundation
Committee for Fairness to the Presidency,
  185–86
Committee for Responsible Youth Politics, 182
Committee for the New Majority, 197
Committee for the Survival of a Free Congress,
  193
Committee of One Million, 90, 157, 164–65,
  167–69, 263, 285
Committee on Conservative Alternatives
  (COCA), 197
Committee on the Present Danger, 211
Committees of Correspondence, 23
Common Cause, 193
Common Sense Society, 338
communism: collapse of communism in Europe,
  173, 272–74, 279, 305–7; spread throughout
  the world in the 1970s, 209–10, 212. *See also*
  China: Communist China; Soviet Union;
  anticommunism
Communism: Its Ideology, Its History, and Its Legacy
  (curriculum), 333
Communist Manifesto, The (Marx), 333
Compton, Ann, 253
Concord, NH, 55, 57
Concord Monitor, 55

conflict managers, 172–73
Congregationalists, 265
Congressional Record, 81
Congressional Research Service (CRS), 16
Connally, John, 42, 180, 252
Connecticut, 19, 137, 139, 298, 328
Connor, Eugene "Bull," 36
Conquest, Robert, 1, 119, 214, 272, 311–12, 332,
  335–36
Conrad Hilton Foundation, the, 332
Conscience of a Conservative, The (Goldwater), 19,
  31, 41, 50, 64, 103, 131, 230, 236, 290, 349;
  anticommunism arguments in, 31–32
conservatism: beginning of the conservative
  movement, 15–25; black conservative movement, 179–80; constituency at the center
  of the, 341; divisions in the conservative
  movement, 341, 343, 347–50; indispensable
  institutions of, 275–76; major strains of conservatism in 1960, 21–22; neoconservatives
  (*see* neoconservatives); paleoconservatives
  (*see* paleoconservatives); reform conservatives (*see* reform conservatives); and the
  Republican party, 341–43; roots of resur-
  gence, 343–48; traditional conservatives,
  20–21, 195–96, 201; twenty-first century
  conservatism, 348–49
Conservative Caucus, 193–95
Conservative Digest, 3, 155, 158, 189–91, 201,
  203, 206–8, 240, 251–52, 255, 292, 294
Conservative Establishment, 25
*Conservative Intellectual Movement in America
  Since 1945, The* (Nash), 276
Conservative Mind, The (Kirk), 33, 345–46
Conservative Party of New York, 282
Conservative Party of the United Kingdom, 115,
  210
Conservative Political Action Conference
  (CPAC), 193, 197, 250
Conservative Revolution, The (Edwards), 231,
  271–72, 285, 298
Constitution, the, 65, 68, 80, 99, 105, 112, 142,
  157, 227, 277, 342, 348–49, 351; and origi-
  nal intention, 276–78
Constitution Hall, 138–42
containment, policy of, 164, 236, 314
contraception, 297
Contract with America, 16, 22, 231–32
Conversation at Gettysburg (TV program), 107,
  123
Coolidge, Calvin, 342
Cooper, Chester L, 109